Fragments of Culture

Fragments of Culture

The Everyday of
Modern Turkey

Edited by
Deniz Kandiyoti
&
Ayşe Saktanber

I.B.Tauris & Co *Publishers*
LONDON · NEW YORK

Published in 2002 by I.B.Tauris & Co Ltd
6 Salem Road, London W2 4BU
175 Fifth Avenue, New York NY 10010
www.ibtauris.com

ISBN 1 86064 427 9

A full CIP record for this book is available from the British Library

Typeset in Baskerville by Dexter Haven Associates, London
Printed and bound in Great Britain by MPG Books Ltd, Bodmin

Contents

Acknowledgements

This book has its origins in numerous encounters, fortuitous meetings and heated exchanges among a group of scholars working in and on Turkey who felt that conventional social scientific investigations often failed to 'get under the skin' of current social transformations. We also felt that a sustained reflection on the case of Turkey could contribute to broader debates on post-coloniality, post-modernity and globalisation. This growing sense found a more concrete focus during Ayşe Saktanber's visit to the University of London in 1996, made possible by a Higher Education Link Project between the Gender and Women's Studies Programme at the Middle East Technical University and the School of Oriental and African Studies, sponsored by the British Council. The idea of editing a volume featuring new scholarship on Turkey was followed up by a two-day workshop at the Middle East Technical University in Ankara on 20 and 21 March 1998, enabling contributors to dialogue with one another in an intimate setting.

We owe thanks to numerous individuals and institutions who contributed to this project, both during its long gestation period and its final realisation. We wish to thank the British Council for its logistical support and the Middle East Technical University for its generous hospitality. The voluntary input of Aslı Özataş-Baykal and Deniz Artun to the organisation of the workshop was invaluable and greatly appreciated. Credit is due to our contributors, who were able to stay with this project through the ups and downs of their personal lives, which were unusually eventful. Hakan Yılmaz, whose work on popular music would have enriched this collection, had to withdraw at a late stage of the project. We would like to acknowledge his contribution to the work of the group. We would also like to thank Martin Stokes, who agreed to contribute an Afterword within a tight time-frame. Finally, our thanks are due to Philippa Brewster for her patience and support, as well as her excellent editorial advice.

Deniz Kandiyoti, London
Ayşe Saktanber, Ankara

Editors' Note

As this volume was being prepared for publication, Turkey found itself in the grip of the deepest financial crisis in its republican history. Alarming rates of business failure, soaring unemployment and declining living standards presage a painful period of economic and political instability, compounded by a profound legitimacy crisis for the political establishment. In retrospect, one of the contributions of this volume may be to offer a multifaceted chronicle of a defining moment in modern Turkish history – that of post-1980s liberalisation, which set in motion processes of social transformation that reconfigured the cultural, economic and political landscape of the country. Whatever the outcomes of the current crisis, we believe that the analytical perspectives presented in the pages that follow will be of enduring value, and assist us in coming to grips with the turbulent times ahead.

Deniz Kandiyoti, London
Ayşe Saktanber, Ankara

Introduction:
Reading the Fragments[1]

Deniz Kandiyoti

...as the modern public expands, it shatters into a multitude of fragments, speaking incommensurable private languages; the idea of modernity, conceived in numerous fragmentary ways ... loses its capacity to organise and give meaning to people's lives.

Berman, 1982, p.17

In some neighbourhoods residents wait in line to buy bread that is a few pennies cheaper; in others all the glitzy displays of wealth can be found. Luxury sedans proliferate while homeless children become more visible on the streets. There are sections of the city where a photographer could frame a crowd scene and pretend it to be from Kabul; others could stand in for any modern neighbourhood from a European city.

Keyder, 1999, p.195

Whether we endorse Berman's gloomy prognosis or not, Keyder's description of the city of Istanbul vividly speaks of a process of social fragmentation and differentiation in Turkey that has yet to be fully captured by social scientific paradigms. This state of affairs is not of merely local relevance but reflects a broader crisis of representation following the demise of grand narratives of social change grounded in different variants of modernisation theory and political economy. The turn to theorising various states bearing the prefix 'post' (post-modernism, post-industrialism and post-Fordism) has made the crisis especially acute in parts of the world that do not participate in these processes in equal or comparable ways.[2] The global reach of 'modernist' paradigms may have dissolved into localised debates with a strong regional flavour.[3] In Turkey, this has resulted in a disabling lag between academic writing and the concerns expressed locally through debates in the press, television or general commentary about what we might call the 'quotidian'. Cutting-edge commentary has increasingly become the province of newspaper columns, popular Turkish-language texts[4] and journalistic accounts[5] that reflect upon the cultural and political mood of the post-1980s.

1

The antecedents of this apparent disjuncture are worth reflecting upon. For a long time, conventional social scientific analysis in Turkey has been strongly state and institution-centric, focusing on policies and institutions as if these were acting upon a seemingly inert society.[6] Rarely have the study of patterns of social stratification and of culture remained further apart. At a time when the sociology of Western societies was theorising the connections between the production of styles and tastes and the reproduction of class and status, and while students of sub-cultures were explicitly referring to the dynamics of hegemony and resistance, scholars of Turkey, and of the Middle East more generally, were utilising the blunt tools of modernisation theory. This resulted in attempts to fit myriad complex and contradictory cultural phenomena into the conceptual straitjacket of 'tradition' and 'modernity'. Kasaba (1997, p.23), in his incisive critique of modernisation theorists' streamlined version of Ottoman/Turkish history, points out that the messiness and complexity of social transformation was overlooked to portray modernisation as 'a disciplined and unambiguous process'. The combined effects of modernisation and Marxist theories in the formative years of Turkish social science often translated into powerful statements of teleology. The inevitable transformation of society from traditional, rural and less developed to modern, urban, industrialised and more developed, or alternatively, from feudal to capitalist, meant that the complexities on the ground could either be dismissed or treated as transient forms,[7] often absolving social scientists from engaging in serious cultural analysis.

Paradoxically, the very success of critiques of modernisation and the turn to post-colonial theory may have unwittingly skewed our field of vision by privileging the themes of Islam versus the West in studies of the Middle East. Post-colonial scholarship itself flourished in the midst of the crisis of representation referred to above. Indeed, despite their apparent divergence, the 'modernist' paradigms (whether of Marxist or liberal bourgeois extraction) rested upon certain shared assumptions: a faith in the efficacy of scientific rationality, a particular conception of progress, a vision of emancipation based on the liberal concept of the autonomous individual, in short, the shared legacy of Enlightenment ideas. It is this very set of shared assumptions that became the target of attack by post-structuralist critics, from whom many students of post-coloniality derived inspiration.[8] Central to this attack was the notion that the universalist claims of grand narratives of emancipation foundered on the exclusion from subjecthood of the non-West, the non-white and women. Critics of modernity treated it as a powerful discursive construct whose dark underside became manifest in the practices of racism, colonialism and sexism. Foucault's writings on the nature of modern orders and on the mechanisms of surveillance and disciplinary power deployed through modern institutions had a defining influence on post-colonial scholarship, despite the fact that they took France and Northern Europe as their primary object. This influence was largely mediated through Edward Said's *Orientalism* (1978), widely considered one of the founding texts of post-colonial studies.[9] Said combined the central insights of Foucault about the mutual relations of knowledge and power with Gramsci's notion of hegemony to argue that Western power enabled the production of knowledge about other cultures which, in turn, became an instrument of further Western domination. One of the major contributions of post-colonial scholarship was to draw attention to the formative influence of colonial encounters in the shaping of national cultures and nation-states. Even in countries such as Ottoman Turkey and Iran, that did not experience direct colonial rule, European hegemony and the perceived 'backwardness' of their respective societies created a terrain for ideological contest in which notions of 'catching up', imitation of the West, cultural corruption and authenticity continued to have a purchase on political discourse.[10] The projects of modernisation evidenced in post-colonial nationalisms (Chatterjee, 1986, 1993), modernist currents for women's emancipation (Abu-Lughod, 1998) and the later 'developmentalisms' of post-independence states (Mitchell, 2000) were all subjected to renewed scrutiny in the light of a critical rethinking of modernity.

Post-colonial scholarship undoubtedly introduced a more imaginative language with which to talk about cultural production, dismantling binaries such as East/West, traditional/modern and indigenous/foreign to analyse, instead, the processes of cultural hybridisation that characterise alternative modernities.[11] But the colonial encounter, however loosely defined, remained at the centre of most analyses with an implicit centre–periphery model of power and the dissemination of knowledge. This often made local cultural forms appear as necessarily reactive, making more self-referential analyses of political and cultural processes difficult to achieve. Moreover, Hall (1996) introduced a note of caution in his otherwise complimentary assessment of post-colonial studies by noting a growing divergence between two halves of the current debate on late modernity – the post-colonial and the analysis of new developments in global capitalism. He attributed this state of affairs to the fact that post-colonial scholarship has been most fully developed by scholars in the humanities who were unwilling or unable to address contemporary transformations in global capitalism and the rejection of reductive forms of economism which have, in some instances, gone as far as dispensing with political economy altogether. Nonetheless, post-colonial criticism, in conjunction with post-structuralism, from which it partly derives its inspiration, firmly inscribed critiques of modernity as a political project and of nationalist developmentalism into the canon of the social sciences.

In Turkey, this critique took the specific form of questioning the Kemalist legacy and the nation-building project of the early republican period. Among works in this genre, Bozdoğan and Kasaba's (1997) *Rethinking Modernity and National Identity in Turkey* steers a difficult and nuanced course, trying to establish distance from 'both the self-righteous authoritarianism of Kemalist nationalism and the anti-individual and anti-modern authoritarianism of certain aspects of Islamist politics' (p.7). A distaste for extreme forms of cultural relativism which, wittingly or otherwise, sanction the worst excesses of cultural conservatism and an unwillingness to deny the potentially liberating effects of modernity unites its contributors. There are also repeated expressions of the sense of anachronism attaching to state-led, top-down versions of modernisation at a point in time when 'globalising trends and high technologies of the market' are finding their way into Turkey. Bozdoğan and Kasaba assert that 'as these global trends ensnarl the country with all their energy and unruliness, official modernisation, with its singularity, austerity and paternalism, appears woefully inadequate both as a source of inspiration and as a mechanism of control in economics, politics and cultural production' (p.5). Indeed, the relationships between sovereignty, state power and territoriality are now being redefined in ways that are more complex and uncertain than at the epoch in which the modern nation-state was being established, and the repercussions are being felt in Turkey as elsewhere.

It is not surprising that the turn to globalisation as a central analytic category has produced more sustained attention to changes in the consumption of material products and the circulation of people, technologies, images and ideas (mainly, though not exclusively, through the media), creating increasingly intricate and unpredictable linkages.[12] The binaries of 'global' and 'local' now displace 'modern' and 'traditional', substituting a spatial metaphor and hierarchy for the temporal hierarchy implicit in modernisation theory. Although there is no consensus on either the nature or the effects of globalisation,[13] the global system is depicted by some as consisting of 'nodes', such as 'world cities', that act as nerve centres of complex international transactions, with different localities positioned in expanding concentric circles of increasing marginality.[14] This, Öncü and Weyland (1997) argue, 'creates an image of the world that is empty beyond global cities, a borderless space which can be reordered, integrated, neglected or put to use according to the demands of globally articulated capital flows' (p.6). They suggest that globalisation entails processes of 'localisation' the dynamics of which cannot be reduced to the logic of global flows, since these find expression in the struggles over resources and meanings of different contending social groups. Keyder's (1999) powerful account of the city of Istanbul reflects a similar logic. He argues that the unevenness in the pace of globalisation feeds a cultural conflict revolving around the definition of locality and identity, between the globalisers and the localisers, a conflict fuelled by widely discrepant access to the material benefits of globalisation. The incorporation of a small segment of the population into the opportunity structures offered by the new economic dynamics, with the attendant proliferation of products and services catering to their expensive lifestyles, at a time when middle-class incomes are being eroded, social services are deteriorating and new waves of impoverished migrants are arriving in the city, creates a volatile mix. Whether the arena of cultural contest currently pitting secularists against Islamists in Turkey can be fully explained with recourse to 'positive appropriations of globalisation' versus reactive positions of different stripes remains a matter for debate. What must retain our attention, however, is an unambiguous recognition of the mutual interpenetration of the arenas of the market, culture and politics. Indeed, as Navaro-Yashin asserts in this volume (Chapter 10) the categories of 'culture' and 'economy' have been the subject of unproductive reifications, over-looking their mutual embeddedness and leading to a facile mapping of culture onto the 'local', casting the 'global' as somehow exogenous.

I also argued elsewhere (1997) that the polemical perspectives adopted by both apologists for Turkish modernisation, and its critics, have been especially deficient in interrogating the notion of the 'modern' itself, and charting its local specificities. This has meant that studies of the ways in which codes of class and status were produced, reproduced and politicised as competing cultural styles, preferences and orientations have been largely absent from sociological and anthropological accounts of Turkey.[15] The transformations brought about by the political economy of the post-1980s, precipitating both a greater fragmentation of social identities and an increasing complexity in their public articulation, makes this absence even more glaring, stimulating public intellectuals and the media to fill the intellectual gap. Indeed, the mutual 'culturalisation' of politics and 'politicisation' of culture can only be interpreted through a serious engagement with emerging arenas of subcultural expression and cultural production. It is to this urgent and complex task that the contributors to this volume address themselves.[16]

The volume is structured around three major themes. Part I deals with changing patterns of social differentiation and stratification, and the ways in which these are mediated through habitat, consumption, cross-class encounters and educational practices. Part II examines cultural production and the politics of culture through analyses of language, folklore, film, satirical humour and the symbolism of Islamist political mobilisation. Part III addresses itself to the issue of shifting social identities both in Turkey and diasporic communities in Europe.

New axes of social differentiation

There is an established tradition of reflection about socioeconomic transformation in Turkey. Themes such as the penetration of capitalism into rural areas, rural-to-urban migration and changing urban stratification have received sustained attention. So have shifts in state policies from the single-party regime of 1923–50, the transition to multi-party democracy after the 1950s and the politics of economic liberalisation and privatisation since the 1980s, with their attendant effects on elite formation and social stratification. It is perhaps surprising, in this context, that studies going beyond indicators of socioeconomic status and income distribution to probe deeply into lifestyles and cultural preferences have been relatively rare. It may be the joint legacy of both a society that, in demographic terms, remained predominantly rural until relatively recently and of modernisation theory, which privileged the rural/urban split (as a proxy for 'tradition' and 'modernity'), that has led to the relative neglect of urban stratification (as distinct from urban form and settlement). The study of the so-called 'middle classes' was, until recently, not an area of particular academic priority. However, one of the effects of liberalisation policies in Turkey, as elsewhere, was to set in motion a process of unprecedented fragmentation and polarisation within the middle classes, leaving the salaried and especially public sector employees increasingly badly off, while some employees of multinational firms and other members of the private business, corporate and financial sectors were able to secure world-class incomes. The expressions of these new differences are writ large everywhere, from the housing patterns of the more affluent to an explosion of avenues for new and more sophisticated forms of consumption. This has prompted a renewed interest in understanding the economic and cultural underpinnings of new forms of middle-class identity.

In Chapter 1, Sencer Ayata focuses on community and culture in the new middle-class suburban areas of Ankara, where higher disposable incomes boost the demand for bigger houses and private motor vehicles. The growth of *sites* (from the French, *cité*, and pronounced in the same way), suburban housing estates that involve a mix of high- and low-rise apartment blocks, terraces, semi-detached and detached houses as well as luxury villas, has been remarkable over the last decade, and they have become an ubiquitous feature of the Turkish urban landscape. Among Istanbul upper and middle classes, Öncü (1997) notes that this new suburbanisation has led to the creation of an image of the 'ideal home' – mediated by images of high-tech Western-style consumerism as a marker of middle-class status. Aksoy and Robins (1994), meanwhile, suggest that the 'escape' of the rich into homogenous settlements could have deleterious consequences for civic life.

The inhabitants of the *site* studied by Ayata appear to revel in the homogenous, single-class nature of their community, their sense of order and civility, and most of all in what they are able to exclude: 'city life and its vulgar mix of lower classes, the new rich and the Islamists'. The *site* is also a strongly gendered space dominated by women in the daytime, where women's important role in the management of family consumption gives them a special role in the production and display of the insignia of middle-class status – usually through home decoration and the display of household goods. To the extent that impressing others derives not only from wealth but also from styles of consumption, as Bourdieu (1984) asserts in his study of distinction, women emerge as key players in the competition over status. Another consequence of *site* life is an increase in the autonomy and domestic seclusion of the family as a result of increased physical and social distance from relatives and friends in the city, freeing them from community control. Here Ayata makes distinctions which are crucial to comprehending the life-world of this stratum. He notes that suburbans distinguish between three kinds of social control: 'The urban masses are believed to have little self-restraint, to be guided often by their instincts and emotions, high-tempered, ill-mannered, and therefore insufficiently civilised. The second group constitute the strongly communitarian, who under the pressure of external sources of authority tend to behave uniformly. Reference here is mainly to the Islamists, who are believed to lack both self-autonomy and the capacity for rational critical thinking. The truly civilised are regarded as those who have developed individualities, those who can think and act autonomously, who have powerful mechanisms of internal control, people with self-restraint who know how to behave in public.' (p.38)

This phenomenology of social control may have unexpected ramifications. It becomes highlighted, for instance, in the behaviour of a particular *site* whose hitherto atomised and apolitical residents got together to collect money and erected a bust of Atatürk in the main square when the Islamist Refah Party won the municipal elections in Istanbul in 1994.[17] This symbolic gesture may have been more an act of exorcism than an engagement with real politics. It does, however, raise the issue of the deeper and more complex sources of perceived threat for the secular middle classes and the intricate interplay between lifestyle choices perceived as mutually antithetical.

The practices of 'othering' involved in delineating the boundaries that separate different social categories in Turkey have rarely been the subject of social scientific investigation. In Chapter 2, Özyeğin highlights the role of cross-class encounters between the *kapıcı* ('doorkeeper' or 'janitor') and their families with apartment residents in the maintenance of the latter's middle-class status. Instead of residing in the *gecekondu* ('squatter') districts, where most rural-to-urban migrants live, the *kapıcı* lives cheek-by-jowl with his middle-class employers, creating an arena of interaction where projections of stigma and pollution are deployed to keep these dangerously close 'outsiders within' in their place. Özyeğin suggests that social distancing from the doorkeeper families is a typical practice in the self-definition of the identity of the middle classes. As middle-class women allocate more of their time to activities such as the close supervision of children's homework in preparation for competitive school entrance exam-inations, driving them to ballet, piano and foreign-language classes, or allocating personal time to private gyms, diet centres and other beautification activities, they are able to pass on the toils of bodily domestic labour to their maids. Özyeğin sensitively describes the tense, antagonistic intimacy that unites and divides maids and madams in Turkey and provides examples of what she calls 'class work' – the mending of what employers perceive as class wounds and dealing with a sense of guilt which is shrewdly manipulated by their domestic workers. The polarity between modernity and tradition is clearly unable to accommodate the complexity of the cultural practices of these groups, although it is used as the means of the self-conscious articulation of their differences.

There is little doubt that class cultures in Turkey are increasingly being shaped and redefined through the medium of consumption. Although we may concur with Miller (1995) that the movement of consumption to centre-stage is part of a global phenomenon, the specific meanings with which different consumption habits and styles are invested, and the way these define social identities, can only be captured through detailed ethnographies. This holds true in Turkey not only for middle-class *site* residents in Istanbul (Öncü, 1997) or Ankara (Ayata, Chapter 1), but also applies to Islamists whose fashion industry is examined in detail by Navaro-Yashin (Chapter 10) and German Turks' consumption preferences, perceptively analysed by Çağlar (Chapter 13).

Since the liberalisation policies of the 1980s, there has been a proliferation of new shopping venues, ranging from exclusive boutiques featuring *haute couture* brand names at the upper end of the market to hypermarkets and large shopping malls catering to a wider clientele. The internationalisation of retail trade and services (with high-street brands such as Benetton rubbing shoulders with fast-food chains like McDonald's) has left an undeniable imprint on the larger urban centres. These developments have given rise to numerous contradictory out-comes. As Navaro-Yashin illustrates in Chapter 10, shopping malls were received in Turkey through the prism of a polarised politics of culture between secularists and Islamists. The heated debates in the Turkish press suggest that both Islamists and secularists used this 'new consumerism' as an item of their public discourse. While some sections of the Islamist press offered nostalgic invocations of the traditional bazaar, whose rhythms were punctuated by those of daily prayer, in contrast to the ostentation of Western-style consumerism, sections of the secularist press hailed shopping malls as a development of the future. Public discourse notwithstanding, Islamist apparel retail chains are availing themselves of all the trappings of modern marketing (including advertisements and floor shows), while Kocatepe Mosque in Ankara, sensitively analysed by Meeker (1997), stands over three floors of shopping space with boutiques featuring most of the same goods as the malls, flanked by a multi-storey car park. In economic and sociological terms, constituencies that are divided by their public rhetoric may be united by a world of commodities in which they occupy slightly different market 'niches', which are themselves diversified by cleavages of wealth and rank.

Another noteworthy development is the marked 'feminisation' of the shopping experience in Turkey, since both shoppers and sales assistants are predominantly female. The figure of the housewife as the 'global dictator' of world consumption, invoked by Miller (1995), attains a new and rather more momentous significance in the Turkish context. As Durakbaşa and Cindoğlu explain in Chapter 3, this 'feminisation' has taken place through a series of significant historical shifts, moving from the exclusively masculine world of the traditional market (*charshi* or bazaar) to the creation of modern department stores (Bonmarché), catering for the needs of the modernised wealthy classes at the turn of the century, and, finally, the rise of mass consumption after the 1960s. Unlike Western societies, in which shopping constitutes a natural extension of women's domestic and housekeeping tasks, in most Muslim societies the market remained a strongly gendered space from which women were habitually excluded. However, with the advent of mass consumption, and of shopping malls in particular, women consumers came into their own in numerous new ways. Unlike the street, the mall is a 'closed' public place where bright lighting, hygienic interiors and closed-circuit cameras provide a 'monitored' space which is considered safe. This provides a 'legitimate' use of urban space, where women can carry out their tasks as housewives – whose roles now include shopping – while they enjoy a measure of leisure glancing at the displays and sampling the varied cuisines on offer, from Mexican tacos to döner kebab. Among the middle classes, as Ayata shows in Chapter 1, it is women's role to transmute income and wealth into taste and status, a role which invests them with a recognised area of expertise and a new source of domestic power. However, some of the residual ambiguity of women's status in the new public realm of shopping is evidenced by the low status of female shop assistants, who, despite attempts to 'professionalise' sales services, may be subject to harassment and humiliation. That this sometimes happens at the hands of women shoppers themselves hints at the discrepancies of class that are being enacted through encounters at the counter.

An area of public consumption that has undergone significant transformation since the 1970s is that of education, with far-reaching implications for patterns of elite recruitment and social mobility. The Law of Unification of Education, passed in 1924 after the establishment of the republic, put all educational establishments under the authority of the Ministry of Education, providing universal secular education, transmitted through a uniform national curriculum. Public mass education became the major engine for the formation and recruitment of cadres in republican Turkey. It was a democratic force that propelled large numbers of people from rural and provincial backgrounds into the ranks of the professional middle classes and the state bureaucracy. However, over time a multitude of factors acted to fragment, limit and diversify educational provision, creating unprecedented discrepancies in opportunities for social mobility. The increasing demographic pressure of the younger age groups, the decrease in public funding for education and the increasing privatisation of educational provision all contributed to a steady process of 'educational deregulation'.

Access to higher education in Turkey, which until relatively recently was exclusively public, is secured through a centralised and highly competitive university entrance examination. Access to good quality secondary education establishments, especially to those well positioned in the league tables of university entrance exams, has become a critical resource for the achievement of social mobility and the reproduction of class. The deficiencies of the overcrowded public education system are increasingly being palliated by private 'crammer' colleges coaching students for entrance exams at considerable cost. Education is neither free nor exclusively secular, especially since the proliferation of İmam-Hatip lycées after the 1970s (Akşit, 1991), vocational schools for the training of religious personnel, which reinvented themselves as secondary education establishments with curricula in the full range of subjects taught in secular lycées, providing an alternative route of access to higher education. Technical and administrative cadres, originating from Imam-Hatip backgrounds, with higher education diplomas in a wide variety of subjects increasingly joined the ranks of recruits to jobs in governmental and para-statal organisations.[18] The mix of educational provision grew even more complex with the proliferation of new private schools alongside the more established private foreign language lycées and new elite publicly funded high schools in parallel to open-access public education of declining quality.

The diversification of educational provision not only created different routes of access to coveted university places and jobs but, as Ayata and Acar clearly demonstrate in Chapter 4, produced alternative educational cultures inculcating a different sense of gender and personhood in their students. Their study, based on a comparison of three types of schools in Ankara – an Imam-Hatip lycée, a prestigious private lycée and a public school – clearly shows that these establishments not only prepare very different social trajectories for their students but also reproduce different class and gender orientations.

The contributions to Part I illustrate, each in their different way, how codes of gender, styles of consumption and cultural preferences are implicated in the production of an increasingly complex process of social stratification in Turkey. The topography of signs, symbols and meanings which serve to signal and articulate different lifestyle options and cultural orientations form part of a broader repertoire of symbolic resources which deserve detailed examination in their own right.

The politics of culture and the culture of politics

A feature of Turkish modernisation that is routinely invoked by all commentators concerns the extent to which the Kemalist reforms represented a comprehensive onslaught on practically every aspect of Ottoman social life: from the alphabet and the vocabulary used, to men's headgear, women's attire and the comportment of the sexes in public life. These policies were, in part, reliant upon imaginings of the nation centred around a new notion of 'Turkishness' that broke away from the fetters of an Ottoman past, now considered decadent and retrograde. The 'laicisation' of Ottoman/Turkish history was achieved by establishing its links to Central Asiatic origins and presenting it as one more link in the chain of ancient Anatolian civilisations, rather than one more glorious chapter in the history of Islam. The cultural policies of early republicanism underscored the Western orientation of the ruling elite; state-controlled radio broadcast Western classical music and stylised versions of folk tunes, monuments and buildings reflected a high modernist aesthetic, and mixed-sex youth paraded in shorts and uniforms during national celebrations in the context of a resolutely secular school system.

Some authors, such as Aksoy and Robins (1997), go as far as invoking the duality of an 'official' culture versus a 'real' one to highlight the levels of alienation which republican cultural engineering elicited among the common people. They treat items of popular culture, such as low-brow commercial films or popular music (in particular the genre of *arabesk*, sensitively analysed by Stokes, 1992) as so many eruptions of the marginal and the repressed into the realm of cultural expression. A reified conception of 'real' culture thus authorises explanations of changing genres with reference to 'the return of the repressed', whereby suppressed cultural forms, whether these be the unbridled emotionalism of the popular classes or Islamic forms of expression, can re-emerge once the censorship of a monolithic centre is weakened or challenged. This 'frozen mammoth' approach to cultural production, to use a Freudian metaphor, overlooks a much more complex dynamic which the chapters in Part II attempt to elucidate.

Chapter 5, by Mardin, and Chapter 6, by Öztürkmen, deal with two areas which can be considered primary sites for the articulation of national identity: those of language and folklore. Mardin shows the extent to which the categories of 'real' culture (or culture of the people) and 'official' culture (Ottoman high culture, in this case) may themselves be deployed as ideological constructs mobilised in the service of a specific political project. He offers a critical historical perspective on the language reforms which, starting from the nineteenth century, attempted to create a Turkish literature in the vernacular, closer to the language of the 'people'. Mardin suggests that it is the continuity between Ottoman and Turkish – rather than their much vaunted difference – that made the transition at all possible. He also shows that successive layers of vernacularisation had already taken place before the republic, but that the last step – the adoption of the Latin alphabet – achieved the double target of delinking from Arabic, and hence Islamic culture, and the creation of a national self – a bifurcation the effects of which are still unresolved. After the 1960s, the two positions in the language debate – the proponents of New Turkish (*Yeni Türkçe*) versus those of Ottoman Turkish – were appropriated and politicised by the political left and right to such an extent that vocabulary could serve as a signal of political orientation (much in the way that accents may betray class or regional origins).

Another arena in which national belonging is enacted and displayed is that of folklore dance performances, which have become a ritualised and routine component of Turkish public life, from school graduation ceremonies to political rallies. In Chapter 6, Öztürkmen contextualises folk dance as a genre within the cultural history of modern Turkey. The popularity and increasing commercialisation of this medium meant that local genres of dance did not survive intact, but melded and merged into one another, with more popular forms gaining ground and others being forgotten.[19] The canonised folk dance repertoire in urban Turkey acquired a uniform character and became standardised as a totally new cultural form which could only have come into existence in the cultural milieu of the nation-state. The folk dance experience that arose after the 1970s was 'national' by its nature, Öztürkman suggests, in contrast to the earlier folk dance genres which were imagined as 'national'. Most importantly, her work also illustrates how the evolving 'natural history' of genres and their changing appropriation by different social groups through time makes distinctions between the 'official' and the 'popular' somewhat spurious.

In Chapter 7, Seçil Büker discusses the extent to which Turkish film has been reflective of public tastes and changing audiences. She treats stardom in Turkey as a social phenomenon acting as a barometer of shifting moods and ideologies. She sets up parallels between the 'modern' identity imposed by the early ideals of republicanism, crystallised in the blonde Greta Garbo look-alike Cahide Sonku, and the phenomenon of rising capitalism and the new icon it gave birth to, Türkan Şoray. The populist nostalgia that displaced earlier elitist leanings was reflected in Turkish film production, especially in the comedies of the 1960s. Films enacted familiar social dramas (country bumpkin comes to town, pure girl led astray, unscrupulous *noveau riche*) that audiences could readily relate to. Türkan Şoray came to epitomise the beloved of the people, the dark girl, whom the new urbanites – who had become a substantial part of the viewing public – could identify with and take to their hearts.

When it comes to social commentary, however, graphic humour and the art of caricature has a much longer pedigree of social satire than any other genre, going back to Ottoman times (Akman, 1998). Öncü (1999) develops a cogent argument to the effect that satirical humour has always been a vehicle for the negotiation of changing cultural boundaries in Turkey – between the Europeanised elites of the metropolis and the more modest middle classes at the turn of the century, and between the provincialism and uncouth manners of the new rich from Anatolia (depicted through the character of the *hacıağa*) and the civility of Istanbulites in the early republican era. Since the 1980s, she suggests that the cultural battle lines have shifted yet again, this time to vulgarity and over-consumption among the lower urban strata. In Chapter 8, Öncü offers an incisive reading of a particular genre of graphic humour, so-called *maganda* cartoons, in which the *maganda* portrays a particular style of lumpen and unsocialised masculinity. *Maganda* humour, Öncü suggests, is the product of a new generation of youth in the process of discovering the cultural codes of sexual permissiveness at a time when sexuality has become a form of public spectacle displayed every-where in the media. It is about debunking and ridiculing the conventional emblems of masculine power (such as physical strength and sexual drive), depicted through the offensive and ridiculous figure of the *maganda*. For all its apparent novelty, however, this form of humour feeds into an ongoing urban narrative and is part of the boundary work necessary to maintain social distinctions that may threaten to become blurred unless they are actively maintained through practices of inclusion and exclusion.

The delineation of new boundaries and forms of cultural expression have been central to discussions of identity politics in Turkey, and to analyses of emerging Islamist identities (Göle, 1996; Saktanber, 1994; Toprak, 1994). In Chapter 9, White examines the contradictory impulses running through the seemingly unified symbolic repertoire of the Islamist Virtue Party. These impulses crystallise around the erasure of class and status cleavages in the party, the party's attempt to situate itself as the party of the poor and disadvantaged, while at the same time attempting to reclassify Islamic symbols as elite cultural markers. There are also contradictions between female Virtue activists' bid to carve out new areas of autonomy for themselves within the traditional expectations of their community and male cadres who express a desire to reinforce traditional female roles and enhance their own autonomy by, for instance, supporting polygamy, illegal under Turkish law.

White's description of a Virtue Party rally highlights both elements drawn from a common repertoire of national politics (flags and folk dances) and the distinctive features of Islamist politics (sex segregation of the audience and Islamic dress). In her discussion of Islamic youth in Chapter 11, Saktanber similarly points to areas both of continuity with Turkish youth subcultures, especially those on the left, and of distinctiveness centring around codes of modesty.

Modesty codes may themselves be laden with multiple meanings. White comments on a video clip at the opening of the rally portraying affluent lifestyles at a reception held by a political party of the centre-right, showing elegant guests, women in low-cut dresses and wine flowing freely, counterpoised with the misery of children with close-shaven heads picking their way through garbage. The populist message conveyed is of the alienation of the secularist ruling classes from the people, and Virtue's authentic claim to represent their concerns. The modestly covered, 'classless' women at the rally provide a severe visual reprimand to the affluent women in low-cut dresses. On the other hand, *tesettür* (or Islamic 'covering') is also deployed as an elite marker that distinguishes *engagé* women from their 'traditional' counterparts among the popular classes. In other words, the *nouveau* Islamist elite also introduces and circulates new markers of distinction and cultural legitimacy. White challenges the spurious distinction made between political Islam and identity politics, demonstrating instead the intimate links between cultural identity, socioeconomic class and politics in the everyday context of political action.

The contributions to Part II show how existing symbolic repertoires, which have evolved through the long and troubled history of Turkish modernisation, are both drawn upon and utilised, making the meanings articulated in different genres intelligible to a wide Turkish public, and reinvented and put to new uses as the changing social scene brings new strata and identities to the fore. This repertoire is further expanded and enriched by global images of what it means to be 'modern', up-and-coming, Muslim, sophisticated or young. The arena of popular culture cannot be captured solely with reference to the presumed tensions between hegemonic and subaltern identities, but, as Saktanber clearly demonstrates in Chapter 11 in her treatment of 'Muslim' cinema, pop music and writing, must be sought in the interplay and intersection of parallel worlds of meaning and cultural production. In this context, the search for a 'real' culture inevitably reveals itself to be an exercise in establishing political legitimacy – a move that may easily acquire authoritarian overtones, by selectively proscribing certain cultural styles and preferences as undesirable or inauthentic.[20]

Shifting identities at home and abroad

The relatively brief history of republican Turkey has been marked by fundamental shifts in the configuration of society: from a multi-ethnic entity centred on cosmo-politan Istanbul to a more uniformly Turkish/Muslim polity with its capital in Ankara; from a predominantly rural country with a narrow state elite to a capitalist society with diversified, competing elites, teeming urban centres and a sizeable European diaspora. The demographic phenomena involved, such as population growth, rates of urbanisation or emigration, have been attentively documented. These may successfully convey the sheer scale of mobility of the Turkish population, but often fall short of capturing the full complexity of the unfolding social landscape.

The discussion of social identities offered in Part III is necessarily partial and does not presume to offer a panoramic view of Turkish society.[21] It does, how-ever, highlight by means of a range of examples how the ideologies of the market and the state, the circulation of commodities and symbols interact and coalesce in the constitution of new identities.

Chapter 10 by Navaro-Yashin and Chapter 11 by Saktanber examine different facets of new Islamist identities. Navaro-Yashin situates the politics of identity between secularists and Islamists within the context of a consumer market for goods, and draws attention to the close links between consumer culture and the politics of identity in Turkey. She analyses the market for 'veiling apparel' led by fashion companies such as Tekbir, and for secularist paraphernalia, like the Atatürk lapel button and badges, that have become extremely popular since the mid-1980s. It is particularly interesting to note the extent to which 'secular identity' became self-consciously produced by fashion companies as a reaction to the development of an Islamist clothing market. What were previously marketed as unmarked, 'standard' modern clothes acquired new meanings, with some secularist fashion houses acting as the standard-bearers of Atatürk's dress reforms. Both Islamists and secularists started wearing and displaying the respective insignia of their political allegiances. However, far from representing antithetical values, Navaro-Yashin claims that despite variations within secularist and Islamist modes of consumeristic practice, commodification is a shared domain rather than one that divides them. She uses a *tesettür* fashion show, complete with catwalk and glamorous models, as a metaphor for some of the central contradictions that create

internal divisions within Islamist constituencies and that also make the rise of
modern shopping malls, discussed in Chapter 3, a matter for moral, evaluative
judgements.

In Chapter 11, Saktanber examines the characteristics of an emerging youth
culture in the context of Islamist political subcultures in Turkey. This new Islamic
youth shares many common features of youth culture generally in its search for an
alternative way of life. Moreover, its claims to distinctiveness are based not only on
the religious orientation of its members but on the popular culture they are
attempting to create. Following Fiske (1994), Saktanber suggests that this popular
culture cannot be described only in terms of consumption, the buying and selling
of commodities, but also involves an active process of generating and circulating
different meanings and pleasures within the social system. In an attempt to
capture the contours of this emerging popular culture, she analyses the codes and
conventions in the writings of Muslim intellectuals, the new genre of Islamic cinema
and 'green pop' (*Yeşil Pop*) as examples of a parallel stream of cultural production,
and thus shows how an Islamic popular cultural 'taste' comes into being as intermingled with the codes of religious faith.

Articulations of Islamic identity in Turkey, coalescing around gendered
codes of Islamic modesty, are taking place against a background of increasing
visibility of alternative and deviant identities. In Chapter 12, Kandiyoti offers an
ethnography of male-to-female transsexuals in Istanbul who inhabit a world
of entertainers and prostitutes. Although the visible presence of transsexuals in
urban space is an ostensibly global phenomenon, as is their international circulation in search of jobs and surgery, Turkish transsexuals come up against the
administrative–legal apparatuses of the state in their search for a new identity and
the pink card[22] that confers on it official confirmation. What motivated the choice
of this seemingly marginal subject was precisely the possibility of capturing this
nexus of interactions between the ideologies of gender, state and market in
Turkey as they play themselves out in the lives and bodies of the so-called *travesti*.
That the area of gender is laden with multiple symbolic, emotional and political
meanings is amply illustrated in all the contributions to this volume. However, the
transgression implied by transsexualism opens up new vistas on the operations of
gender in Turkey, denied to us by the more routine observation of heterosexual
transactions. The interactions of the *travestis* with state apparatuses at critical
junctures of their lives, when applying for new identity cards, trying to avoid
military service or being handled by police, communicate powerful messages of
their stigmatisation as a deviant minority. On the other hand, the images of fast
living, glamour and consumption that they project, as well as the market networks
in which they circulate, from chic boutiques to society surgeons, encapsulate the
mainstream of the post-1980s, with its emphasis on material success and making
it fast (*köşeyi dönmek*) to an uncomfortable degree. The discomfort they elicit is
therefore multifaceted, and tells us as much about the malaise of Turkish society
as about their own troubled existence.

No account of social identities could be complete without a recognition of
the diasporic dimension of Turkish existence. Since the 1960s there has been
an outflow of Turkish labour migrants to Northwestern Europe, with Germany

taking the lion's share (about 2.3 million Turks, accounting for 30 percent of the foreigners in the country). Turkish migrants have not only become a stake in the multiculturalist policies of the countries that host them and fuelled debates on the limits of democratic citizenship in Europe, but have also remained tied to their country of origin in multiple ways, some hoping to reinsert themselves in Turkish society through eventual return. They often own apartments and houses in Turkey, which they use infrequently but lavish great care upon, invest in a variety of businesses, and participate in expatriate politics. However, the strategies of first- and subsequent-generation migrants denote not only different modes of insertion into the host society but also very different understandings of self and culture. The fact that Germany was represented by a German Turkish group at a recent Eurovision song contest and that young German Turkish writers and film-makers are finding a new voice suggests that they have entered the arena of cultural production in their own right.

Chapter 13 by Çağlar and Chapter 14 by Yalçın-Heckmann offer comple-mentary perspectives on the strategies of identity management of different generations of migrants. Çağlar offers an analysis of the ways in which goods and consumption practices become an arena for the social positioning struggles of German Turks both in Germany and in Turkey. She takes as her point of departure the fact that the decoration and organisation principles of their homes in Germany and Turkey are strikingly different from one another. The same object – a coffee table – elicits totally different criteria of choice in the two contexts. Çağlar relates these preferences to the contrast between the 'introvert' living-rooms in Germany, which show little concern with display and fashion and more with biographical continuity through objects from Turkey, to the 'extrovert' Turkish ones, in which the display of conspicuous wealth encourages the choice of matched furniture sets and the appearance of a busy display room. She suggests that regardless of their economic standing a severe deficit of symbolic capital thwarts German Turks' aspirations to mobility in Germany. Their aspirations to middle-class status may be equally thwarted in Turkey, where their status as *Almancıs* carries negative connotations. The returning migrants try to detach their living-room decoration from the negative symbolism of an *Almancı* lifestyle by means of a particular array of furniture in their homes, through which they try to assert and emulate a middle-class lifestyle. These patterns, which characterise the tastes of first-generation migrants, find little favour among the second generation, which signals its social distance from the parental generation by developing an aversion to the goods and styles that go into the making of an *Almancı* identity. Consumption items function not just as items of desire but also objects of active dislike and avoidance in the process of crafting new identities.

Yalçın-Heckmann discusses how the identities of second and third-generation Turkish migrants are defined and negotiated through representations in the German media. The labels attached to Turks have changed significantly over time. From being named 'guest workers' (*Gastarbeiter*), with its connotations of temporary residence, they have now achieved the ambivalent status 'foreign/Turkish co-citizens', with the appellation 'German Turk' gaining wide currency for the second generation. Yalçın-Heckmann argues that the hyphenated identities of German

Turks are loaded with ambivalence. She shows how the tactical usage and management of these identities by second-generation migrants creates greater room
for manoeuvre and the ability to resist the cultural categories of the dominant
culture. Hyphenated identities also imply a critical positioning vis-à-vis the parental
generation. German Turks may adopt diverse strategies of identity management
– either by occupying subcultural niches within Germany or seeking social mobility
in Turkey. Their attempts at appropriating and shaping their representations in
the German media opens up new spaces of creative contest.

     Whether at home or abroad, social identities are not there to be merely
lived, but are the object of redefinition, display, manipulation and contest.
Gaining access to arenas in which these cultural contests may be played out – such
as markets for the circulation of commodities, or the media in which images are
circulated – forms an intrinsic part of the politics of identity.

Conclusion: not so much a paradigm as a way of seeing

What, the reader may wonder, is achieved by offering what may appear a collection
of vignettes on Turkish society, beyond illustrating the restlessness and ephemer-
al nature of social and cultural forms that theorists of post-modernity make so
much of? Is this not another clear-cut illustration of successive social scientific
paradigms chasing after an ever-changing, elusive reality?

     We would like to believe that it is about something more. It is also about
realising the emancipatory potential of post-colonial theory by authorising scholars
to look at their societies 'close-up', even if these do not happen to be in the post-
industrial West. This potential risks being aborted by an approach that keeps
its gaze fixed on a hegemonic West and engages in increasingly sophisticated
restatements of the reciprocal entanglements of East and West, to the detriment
of a more vigorous engagement with evolving local cultural forms. Having
'provincialised' the West itself and removed it from its pedestal as the representative of a universal standpoint, it is almost as if we are still struggling to fill the
theoretical gap. Some speak of a de-centred universe, others of a global system
still structured by growing disparities in power, and yet others retreat into forms
of cultural relativism celebrating all forms of assumed 'indigeneity'. What
remains constant, however, is the frequently derivative nature of the production
of knowledge about non-Western societies inserted into broader scenarios –
whether these be colonisation, modernisation or globalisation – as bit players
in a global drama. Not for them the narcissistic self-indulgences of Western
cultural analysis, that takes as its object the finer points of this or that subculture
or some emerging genre. The parallax effect that makes crowds in Cairo
and Istanbul look rather similar, one veiled woman much like another, is still
firmly in place. The 'local' gaze loses its radical potential when it apprehends
its object only through the lenses of a distant spectator. This volume invites and
compels the reader to do otherwise; it forces attention to the minutiae of daily
life, which, from home decoration to cheap magazines, reveal the intricate
weave of society. It also speaks of the determination of a group of scholars to

refuse the cardboard cut-outs that may be held out to them as models of their society, and to settle for nothing less than painstaking, and frequently painful, cultural analysis.

Notes on Introduction

1   An earlier version of this chapter was presented at the Campagna-Kerven lecture on Modern Turkey, Boston University, 28 April 1999. I would like to thank the sponsors and organisers of the event and the commentators in the audience.

2   In his discussion of post-modernism and the discipline of anthropology, Richard Fardon (1992, p.34) remarks that 'Postmodernism is largely preoccupied with the life-styles of an indeterminate proportion of about a quarter of the world's population'. Whether we concur with his judgement or not, it is hard to deny that post-modern writing may have an introverted quality that speaks to the concerns of the post-industrial West, while the non-West has to make do with the label 'post-colonial'.

3   Writings on the Middle East have been dominated by analyses of the ascendancy of Islamist tendencies and movements, narrowing some of the common ground that, say, world systems theory had opened up with other regions such as Latin America or Africa. Similar guiding 'thematics' may be discerned for other regions (such as poverty and structural adjustment in Africa or democratic and market transition in the former Soviet Bloc), with globalisation serving as an overarching category that still awaits full theoretical elaboration.

4   Gürbilek (1992) or Kozanoğlu (1995) are good examples of this genre.

5   Kelsey (1996).

6   I am not suggesting, in any way, that a focus on the state is no longer relevant. On the contrary, the changes which state apparatuses have undergone since the 1980s are worth analysing in their own right. I am merely noting a tendency in earlier writings to ignore the agency of non-state, non-elite social actors. This may not be too surprising if we consider that the trope of the Middle East as a timeless 'village' society threatened by looming forces of social change exhibited remarkable staying-power over time (Gilsenan, 1990). If, following Keyder (1997), we also concede that 'modernisation-from-above' was what characterised the early republican project, it is understandable that the agency of the modernising elites should be privileged, with 'society' acting as a silent and amorphous partner.

7   Here I have in mind the lengthy debates inspired by structural Marxism concerning the resilience and/or functionality vis-à-vis expanding capitalism of pre-capitalist forms in rural or artisanal production. In Turkey, these debates generated a substantial literature on the role of petty commodity production in both rural and urban areas. For all their undoubted merit, these debates rarely got 'under the skin' of the phenomena they studied because of a seemingly unbridgeable chasm between political economy and micro-sociology. A notable exception may be found in the pioneering work of Kıray, which combined sensitivity to new cultural forms with analyses of the broader thrust of social

transformation. Many of the themes in this volume, such as attention to patterns of stratification and consumption and material culture, were central to her ground-breaking work.

8   Moore-Gilbert (1997) points to the divide between post-colonial criticism, which has much earlier antecedents in the writings of those involved in anti-colonial struggles, and post-colonial theory, which distinguishes itself from the other by the incorporation of methodological paradigms derived from contemporary European cultural theories into discussions of colonial systems of representation and cultural production. These latter clearly bear the imprint of post-structuralist influences.

9   The term 'post-Orientalism' refers to the turning-point represented by Said's *Orientalism*, and to the new generation of studies following its publication. Here I prefer to use the term post-coloniality, which has a broader referent.

10   The ways in which Jalal Al-Ahmad's notion of *garbzadeghi* ('westoxication') was employed by Ali Shariati and other ideologues of the Islamic Revolution in Iran are well known. In Turkey, these debates are even broader and more diffuse, with historical antecedents in the ideological currents of the Second Constitutional Period (1908–19).

11   For a cautionary note, however, on how the concept of hybridity may end up reinscribing the essences it was meant to transcend, see Çağlar (1997).

12   Appadurai (1990) attempted to capture the nature of global flows with reference to different spheres of circulation that he labelled 'ethnoscapes', 'mediascapes', 'technoscapes', 'finanscapes' and 'ideoscapes'.

13   Held et al. (1999), for instance, distinguish between the hyperglobalist, sceptical and transformationalist theses, whose views on both the scope and implications of globalisation differ significantly.

14   This emphasis is particularly apparent in the works of Castells (1989) and Sassen (1991).

15   This is not meant to indicate an absence of sophisticated commentary on social change in Turkey. See, for instance, Kıray (1991) and Beller-Hann and Hann (2001). An analysis of the more specific question of the ways in which culture has been politicised may be found in the work of Saktanber (forthcoming) on the building of an Islamic 'quotidian' by a group of people in Ankara referring to themselves as conscious (*şuurlu*) Muslims.

16   This volume makes no claims to comprehensiveness, but reflects the research interests of the contributors. Large areas of great significance, such as the construction of ethnic and sub-national identities, the role of the mass media, television in particular, and the realm of civic associations are not included, but clearly deserve detailed attention. See, for instance, Eickelman and Anderson (eds) (1999).

17   Personal communication by a resident of the *site* in question.

18   This is why the reform of the educational system in 1998, raising compulsory primary education to eight years and abolishing middle schools (grades 6 to 8) produced such an outcry among Islamists. The effect of the reform was to produce a steep decline in enrolments to Imam-Hatip institutions, which are no longer competitive as a conduit to university education.

19 A similar argument is made by Stokes (1991) with respect to folk music and the transformations it underwent through the policies of TRT (Turkish Radio and Television).

20 This is one of the reasons why it may be claimed that the defenders and critics of Turkish modernisation may, at times, come to represent two sides of the same discursive coin; the behaviours condemned as obscurantist and backward by the former may be recuperated as 'authentic' by the latter, casting the West and its fellow-travellers as alien and corrupt. In either case, the stigmatisation of 'internal others' serves as an instrument of enforced conformism and anti-individualism. Recognising this as a powerful strand that runs deep in Turkish society constitutes one of the more painful tasks of social criticism.

21 In particular, a discussion of ethnic identities, such as the Alevi and the Kurds, constitutes a significant omission. Studies of ethnic identities as subcultural identities are still relatively scarce, undoubtedly because of the high degree of politicisation of such identities.

22 All Turkish citizens are provided with colour-coded identity cards – blue for men and pink for women – crucial to all 'official' transactions, from obtaining a passport to marriage and military service.

References

Abu-Lughod, L. (ed.) (1998), *Remaking Women: Feminism and Modernity in the Middle East*, Princeton University Press, Princeton, NJ

Akman, A. (1998), 'From Cultural Schizophrenia to Modernist Binarism: Cartoons and Identities in Turkey (1930–1975)', in F.M. Göçek (ed.), *Political Cartoons: Cultural Representation in the Middle East*, Marcus Wiener Publishers, Princeton, NJ

Akşit, B. (1991), 'Islamic Education in Turkey: Medrese Reform in Late Ottoman Times and İmam-Hatip Schools in the Republic', in R. Tapper (ed.), *Islam in Modern Turkey: Religion, Politics and Literature in a Secular State*, I.B. Tauris, London

Aksoy, A. and K. Robins (1994), 'Istanbul Between Civilisation and Discontent', in *New Perspectives on Turkey*, no 10, pp.57–74

– (1997), 'Peripheral Vision: Cultural Industries and Cultural Identities in Turkey', *Paragraph*, vol. 20, no 1, pp.75–99

Appadurai, A. (1990), 'Disjuncture and Difference in the Global Cultural Economy', *Public Culture*, vol. 2, no 2, pp.1–24

Beller-Hann, I. and C. Hann (2001), *Turkish Region: State, Market and Social Identities on the East Black Sea Coast*, James Curry, Oxford

Berman, M. (1982), *All That Is Solid Melts Into Air: The Experience of Modernity*, Verso, London

Bourdieu, P. (1984), *Distinction: A Social Critique of the Judgement of Taste*, Routledge, London

Çağlar, A. (1997), 'Hyphenated Identities and the Limits of "Culture"', in T. Modood and P. Werbner (eds), *The Limits of Multiculturalism in the New Europe*, Zed Books, London

Castells, M. (1989), *The Information City: Information Technology, Economic Restructuring and the Urban–Regional Process*, Blackwell, Oxford

Bozdoğan, S. and R. Kasaba (eds) (1997), *Rethinking Modernity and National Identity in Turkey*, University of Washington Press, Seattle, WA, and London

Chatterjee, P. (1986), *Nationalist Thought and the Colonial World*, Zed Books, London
— (1993) *The Nation and its Fragments: Colonial and Post-Colonial Histories*, Princeton
    University Press, Princeton, NJ
Eickelman, D.F. and J.W. Anderson (eds) (1999), *New Media in the Muslim World: The
    Emerging Public Sphere*, University of Indiana Press, Bloomington and Indianapolis, IN
Fardon, R. (1992), 'Postmodern Anthropology? Or, an Anthropology of
    Postmodernity?' in J. Doherty, E. Graham, and M. Malek, (eds) *Postmodernism
    and the Social Sciences*, Macmillan, London
Fiske, J. (1994), *Understanding Popular Culture*, Routledge, London and New York
Gilsenan, M. (1990), 'Very Like a Camel: The Appearance of an Anthropologists's
    Middle East', in R. Fardon (ed.), *Localising Strategies: Regional Traditions of
    Ethnographic Writing*, Scottish Academic Press Ltd, Edinburgh
Göle, N. (1996), *The Forbidden Modern: Civilisation and Veiling*, The University of
    Michigan Press, Ann Arbor, MI
Gürbilek, Nurdan (1992), *Vitrinde Yaşamak* (*Living in the Shop Window*), Metis, Istanbul
Held, D., A. Mc Grew, D. Goldblatt, and J. Perraton, (1999), *Global Transformations:
    Politics, Economics and Culture*, Polity Press, Oxford
Kandiyoti, D. (1997), 'Gendering the Modern: On Missing Dimensions in the Study of
    Turkish Modernity', in S. Bozdoğan and R. Kasaba (eds), *Rethinking Modernity and
    National Identity in Turkey*, University of Washington Press, Seattle, WA, and London
Kasaba, R. (1997), 'Kemalist Certainties and Modern Ambiguities', in S. Bozdoğan
    and R. Kasaba (eds), *Rethinking Modernity and National Identity in Turkey*,
    University of Washington Press, Seattle, WA, and London
Keyder, Ç. (1997), 'Whither the Project of Modernity? Turkey in the 1990s', in S.
    Bozdoğan and R. Kasaba (eds), *Rethinking Modernity and National Identity in
    Turkey*, University of Washington Press, Seattle, WA, and London
— (ed.) (1999), *Istanbul: Between the Global and the Local*, Rowman & Littlefield
    Publishers, Lanham and Oxford
Kelsey, T. (1996), *Dervish: The Invention of Modern Turkey*, Hamish Hamilton, London
Kıray, M. (ed.) (1991), *Structural Change in Turkish Society*, Indiana University Turkish
    Studies Series, Bloomington, IN
Kozanoğlu, C. (1995), *Pop Çağı Ateşi* (*The Fire of the Pop Age*), İletişim, Istanbul
Meeker, M.E. (1997), 'Once There Was, Once There Wasn't: National Monuments
    and Interpersonal Exchange', in S. Bozdoğan and R. Kasaba (eds), *Rethinking
    Modernity and National Identity in Turkey*, University of Washington Press, Seattle,
    WA, and London
Miller, D. (1995), 'Consumption as the Vanguard of History', in D. Miller (ed.)
    Acknowledging Consumption, Routledge, London
Mitchell, T. (ed.) (2000), *Questions of Modernity*, University of Minnesota Press,
    Minneapolis, MN
Moore-Gilbert, B. (1997), *Postcolonial Theory: Contexts, Practices and Politics*, Verso, London
Öncü, A. and P. Weyland (eds) (1997), *Space, Culture and Power: New Identities in
    Globalising Cities*, Zed Books, London
Öncü, A. (1997), 'The Myth of the "Ideal Home" Travels Across Cultural Borders to
    Istanbul', in A. Öncü, and P. Weyland, (eds), *Space, Culture and Power: New
    Identities in Globalising Cities*, Zed Books, London

— (1999), 'Istanbulites and Others: The Cultural Cosmology of Being Middle Class in the Era of Globalism', in Ç. Keyder (ed.) *Istanbul: Between the Global and the Local*, Rowman & Littlefield Publishers, Lanham and Oxford

Saktanber, Ayşe (forthcoming), *Living Islam: Women, Religion and Politicisation of Culture in Turkey*, I.B. Tauris, London

— (1994), 'Becoming the "Other" as a Muslim in Turkey: Turkish Women vs Islamist Women', *New Perspectives on Turkey*, no 11 (Fall), pp.99–134.

Sassen, S. (1991), *The Global City: New York, London, Tokyo*, Princeton University Press, Princeton, NJ

Stokes, M. (1992), *The Arabesk Debate: Music and Musicians in Modern Turkey*, Clarendon Press, Oxford

— (1993), 'Hazelnuts and Lutes: Perceptions of Change in a Black Sea Valley', in P. Stirling (ed.), *Culture and Economy: Changes in Turkish Villages*, The Eothen Press, Huntingdon

Toprak, B. (1994), 'Women and Fundamentalism: The Case of Turkey', in V.M. Moghadam (ed.), *Identity Politics and Women*, Westview Press, Boulder, CO

I

NEW AXES OF SOCIAL

DIFFERENTIATION

1

The New Middle Class and the Joys of Suburbia

Sencer Ayata

In the last decade or two, cities in the developing world have tended to become more heterogenous, stratified and fragmented. Work, accommodation and recreation are increasingly separated, so that each is located in different parts of the city, while residential segregation gathers pace as architecturally and socially distinct neighbourhoods are formed. The emerging residential fragments tend to vary significantly in terms of physical environment, types of housing and security of tenure. The majority of people continue to live in areas where tenure is insecure, building is not authorised, and utilities and municipal services are inadequate. In such low-income residential areas, communality is limited to the immediate neighbourhood, communitarian organisations based on primordial and religious identities (such as associations based on place of origin) shape everyday life, and relations with the political authorities are largely mediated through patron-client ties. At the other extreme are the middle and upper classes, who live in well-equipped, isolated and socially homogeneous neighbourhoods. Affluent middle-class families are increasingly moving to the outskirts of the city, to the suburbs, where they can effectively differentiate themselves from, and avoid interaction with, people from the lower classes, and where they can exercise strong rules of exclusion and inclusion. Cities are thus divided into a number of localities in which imagined differences between classes and cultures are established as social and spatial boundaries. In the fragmented city, encounters between different groups are increasingly marked by tension, suspicion and discrimination, and the promise of incorporation tends to wane as groups emphasise their irreconcilable differences (Caldeira, 1996).

Few studies attempt to examine the new axes of social and cultural differentiation in Turkish urban spaces. In the case of Istanbul, Aksoy and Robins (1994, 1995) underline the culturally fragmenting and conflict-generating aspects of the globalisation process, and the tendency on the part of the rich to escape from urban tension and conflict to isolated homogeneous settlements, a development which, according to the authors, has lethal consequences for civic life and public intercourse. Öncü (1997) points to the search for a clean social environment among Istanbul's middle and upper classes in what she calls the 'ideal home', a symbol, by and large, of middle-class identity and status. The new suburban villages claim to bring together country life and new urban facilities in order to promote new lifestyles.

This chapter focuses on community and culture in the new middle-class suburban areas of Ankara. The new suburban spaces and middle-class culture are examined in terms of the subjective experiences of individuals and families, emergent practices and activities, and changing power relations. Middle-class perceptions of the new middle-class milieu involve a powerful desire for escape from pollution, street life and social heterogeneity, as well as an emphasis on family intimacy and rule-bound society and order. The major public activity in the suburb is shopping, and middle-class identity is forged mainly through consumption. Suburban life is also gendered, and women play a leading role in displaying family wealth to outsiders, through both their homemaking and their consumption practices, which determine the relative standing of their families. The chapter also points to the problems that work-centred men experience in relating to the more feminine realms of home life and consumption. The closing section focuses on processes of personal individuation, both in the use of household space and the lack of communal control over private life. Finally, it describes the growing emphasis on the body as a focal point of identity, and how the proliferation of body maintenance activities relates to middle-class aspirations for a 'healthy', i.e. pollution and crime-free, environment.

The data used in this study comes from two different sources. The first involves 116 interviews conducted in one of the new suburban districts of Ankara in 1993; 38 interviews were with women, 36 with men, in addition to 42 household surveys seeking general information about the family and the housing situation. The ethnographic material, however, comes mainly from fieldwork carried out in 1998 in Koru Sitesi, located in the same district, where 26 families were interviewed in depth.

The new axes of class and spatial differentiation in Ankara

The population of Ankara, a bare 25,000 when it was declared the capital of the new Turkish republic in 1923, and still only several hundred thousand at the end of the Second World War, had reached three million by 1997. Until the 1990s, the city had a dual pattern of housing. The poor rural-to-urban migrants typically lived in the *gecekondu* (squatter) areas on the outskirts of the city, in dwellings usually built by themselves on what was often illegally occupied public land. The other development, one that imprinted itself strongly on almost all Turkish cities, including Ankara, was the vast expansion of middle-class residential areas of apartment blocks in central parts. The flat ownership system underlying this particular pattern of housing was developed as a response to severe housing shortages resulting from high land prices, insufficient infrastructural investment, and people's limited purchasing power. The system has achieved co-operation between landowners, building contractors and private purchasers. The convergence of interests between these three parties has effectively pre-empted the need for large-scale investment in housing: on the one hand, the building contractor avoids having to invest in land by offering a fixed share of the planned development to the landowner, and on the other, uses money paid in advance from purchasers as capital (Balamir, 1996).

In the 1980s and 1990s, Ankara became a more complex, segmented and fragmented city. The previous dual structure was significantly altered as the middle classes increasingly moved to the outskirts, and the growth of apartment housing outstripped the spread of *gecekondu* settlements. Lower-middle and middle-class residential areas are now found both in the city centre and the outskirts, and in the latter the *gecekondu* has lost ground to the new middle-class suburbs.

The spread of the city like a grease stain, the overcrowding of its centre, the growing heterogeneity of its population, excessive increases in land prices, and the gradual invasion of housing areas by business, led local authorities and city planners to open the city's western corridor to new construction. The linear development of the city along this axis was very much based on government efforts to provide cheap land for housing. Large plots of public land, well-equipped with infrastructure, were given either to co-operatives or to large-scale developers, and both state and private banks contributed significantly to the financing of new housing there (Tekeli, 1996; Türel, 1996). As construction gained pace in the 1990s, a vast area of suburban housing of nearly 300,000 units was created. The government, the building societies and either co-operatives or large-scale private developers were the main players in this new system of housing provision.

The new housing area is divided by vast tracts of largely empty public land, and lies between a northwestern belt of lower-middle-class apartment housing and a southwestern belt of middle- and upper-class residential areas made up of a mix of high and low-rise apartment blocks, terraces, semi-detached and detached houses, and luxury villas. The individual housing complexes, whether built by private developers or co-operatives, are bounded and compact units, called *sites*, each having a name of its own and a separate administration responsible for maintaining, planning and developing the whole *site* environment – roads, parking lots, sporting facilities, green spaces and, in the case of the more affluent ones, tennis courts, swimming pools, shopping areas, schools and convention centres. This pattern is increasingly becoming the norm in the new Turkish urban landscape.

The image of the city

The inhabitants of the *site* see Ankara as a more organised city than others in Turkey, stressing that despite the many difficulties and inconveniences the city provides better access to services and opportunities. Although they refer lovingly to certain parts and aspects of the city, their evaluation is on the whole essentially negative. Middle-class people tend not to retreat from the kinds of trait that Wirth

(1957) described in his celebrated essay 'Urbanism as a Way of Life', the super-ficial, utilitarian, segmental, secondary nature of urban social relations. On the contrary, they want to see more anonymous relations in the city. Furthermore, those interviewed in the *site* mention that they find the kind of diversity and heterogeneity in European and American cities highly stimulating, entertaining and pleasant. In the case of Ankara, and indeed Istanbul too, what they dislike is the unstable, unpredictable and impermanent nature of social relations, which they tend to associate with the 'uncivilised' masses.

The *site* people first complain about the various physical problems involved in living in an extremely dense and crowded urban environment: these would include the inadequacy of the infrastructure, excessive noise, traffic congestion and aggression, air pollution, and the breathless and exhausting pace of urban life. While some seem concerned about the encroachment of business and new money into residential areas, others are excessively disturbed by the vivid images of poverty, class polarisation, and increasing cultural divergence in the city. The hulking concrete blocks built with an apparent lack of any aesthetic concern, the mess on the streets, and the relative lack of entertainment and cultural facilities are other sources of complaint.

The suburban middle classes tend to distinguish themselves sharply from the city crowd, whom they see as utterly provincial, vulgar and uncivilised. Not only is the man in the street deemed totally unpredictable, but also not to know how to live with others, how to behave in public, or how to participate in civic society. The urban masses also include politically reviled characters such as the Islamist woman wearing the 'turban' and the extreme nationalist with his long unkempt moustache. 'Inferior' manners, such as hanging towels on the balcony, leaving shoes on the doorstep, and going outdoors in pyjamas are also vehemently despised. Most significant, however, is the fear of aggression: street behaviour is always coloured with the danger of fierce argument and violent attack, even in cases of minor confrontation and dispute. Emotionally laden situations – in which one may lose one's temper – are the most feared, since they create the risk of behaving like 'the man in the street', with the accompanying loss of status.

Middle-class people are particularly sensitive about the disturbances and intrusions commonly experienced in crowded places: the sense of being engulfed by a mass of people with unshaven faces, unbrushed teeth, unpleasant body odours and loud voices is seen as a smothering of the soul, for the very reason that an individual cannot distance or separate himself/herself from others. Hence the powerful desire on the part of the new middle class for class segregation as a way of eliminating contact with the vulgar multitude.

Far more important, however, is the perception of city life as one of total chaos and unordered diversity. The emphasis on order is an important feature of the middle-class mentality, and stems mainly from formal education and comparison with Western cities, either based on personal experience or the mass media. Similarly, middle-class people find a striking contrast between the disorderly city and the orderly home and office environment.

Many things in the city are seen as disorderly: the potholes in the streets, garbage left on the pavements, irregular parking and beggars on every corner.

The residential areas in the inner city are engulfed by shops, business and the street crowd. Disorder is immanent everywhere in the wide mix of city uses, functions, people and places. In Ankara, one place strongly disliked by many is the Sıhhiye Bridge area situated on the main boulevard connecting the traditional and modern business centres, Ulus and Kızılay. This highly transient habitat is the focus of many different kinds of activity: it is a working-class transport hub densely crowded with buses, minibuses and commuter trains, a retail shopping area characterised by the cacophonous blend of street vendors' cries and Arab music – which appals the elites – from the cassette shops; nearby, the three main city hospitals are daily visited by thousands of people with diverse backgrounds; there is a university campus and a number of schools, office and residential blocks, and finally Ankara's Palace of Justice.

At work and at home, the middle classes place great emphasis on categorisation, differentiation, demarcation and separation in order to draw boundaries between functions, activities, people, places and time. A bank manager compares city disorder with the orderly life in his workplace, where work and leisure, workplace and home, customers and staff, specialists and areas of specialisation, papers and currencies, and sections of office space are carefully demarcated. The emphasis on differentiation between objects and thought patterns parallels efforts to differentiate social conditions. The middle-class obsession with order and the desire to maintain class distinction are closely entwined, for distinction can be maintained only where there is order, where everything is in the right place.

The city, by contrast, projects the image of a jungle: a densely populated place of immense variety, constant struggle and great disorder, where contact with strangers can be dangerous and where one risks mixing with undesirables. The partitioning of the city is one way of avoiding urban disorder, and thereby finding solace, peace and comfort in the socially and functionally separated social space of the suburb. In this highly organised environment, street life, with its vulgar masses, confusion and turbulence is effectively shut out. Order is maintained, and thus disorder and pollution – two closely inter-related phenomena, according to Douglas (1979) – are effectively eliminated.

One other comment on the strong middle-class aversion to urban life in Ankara is revealing. As a city, Ankara has a scarcity of both natural and historical attractions. This extremely new and modern city had a homogeneous elite community and culture until the 1970s, and it was this aspect of the city that its predominantly bureaucratic middle class enjoyed. The city, however, has lost its charm in the eyes of its middle-class inhabitants, both the old bureaucratic and the new managerial and entrepreneurial types, as it has grown in size, complexity and heterogeneity.

The *site*, class and community

The *site*, and indeed the whole southwestern sprawl in Ankara, is a highly homogeneous and segregated single-class residential area. Work and industry, as well as lower-income residences, are decisively excluded. Some exceptions are the four university campuses, a few government buildings and the new shopping malls (discussed in Chapters 3 and 10). The latter, however, tend to consolidate the isolation of the middle classes by making them less dependent on the city.

In style, the *site*, and indeed the whole middle-class southwestern suburban area, is a peculiar mixture of traditional Turkish apartment housing and the more separated residences redolent of the middle-class and some of the more popular working-class suburbs of American and European cities (Clark, 1996). The Koru Sitesi, for instance, contains 1600 dwellings, of which 1300 are blocks of flats while the remaining are terraced houses, semi-detached houses and detached villas. Compared with their Western counterparts, the suburban areas in Turkey have fewer green spaces and much smaller private gardens. Nevertheless, the housing density is lower in the suburb than in the city. The *site* has regular streets, a well-shaped, polished and monitored environment, and provides punctual and efficient services for its inhabitants. Unlike those in many Turkish villages and towns, the neighbourhood environment in the *site* is clean and tidy. *Site* administration thus puts an end to the popular criticism that Turks care for their homes but not their neighbourhood.

The well-known argument put forward by Gans (1962), that the behaviour and personality patterns ascribed to the suburb are in reality those of age and class is also relevant in this particular context. Indeed, the majority of the *site* inhabitants are of middle age, and both very young and elderly couples are significantly absent. On the other hand, in the 1980s and 1990s the middle class – not only its bureaucratic and military, but also its recently expanding professional, managerial and entrepreneurial components – has become a sizable element of the urban population. The expansion of this class in Ankara can be seen as the outcome both of the growth of the civil service and of a managerial and entrepreneurial middle class. The middle class can be distinguished not only in terms of wealth and property but also through its distinctive consumption patterns and lifestyles. In the Turkish context, a wide section of the middle class tends to distinguish itself from other classes through culturalised lifestyle choices; this involves a strong emphasis on secular values and a secular group identity defined in opposition to the Islamist middle classes that lead their segregated existence in other parts of the city.

Suburban society is highly gendered too. Although gender role differentiation is not overt, there exists a marked tendency to associate home and the domestic field primarily with women. In the new suburban areas, two-thirds of the married women are university graduates, and nearly half of them work outside the home. Furthermore, especially during the day, women are more visible in the neighbourhood. In the self-definition of the suburb, gender thus appears as important as class.

In *site* life, an emphasis on civility is an element of cultural homogeneity and a marker of middle-class identity. The inhabitants of the *site*, among whom cultural cleavages are claimed to be almost negligible, are defined by mutual self-respect and respect for other people's privacy. Although not shared by everyone, the perception of the *site* population as a community of select and civilised people finds wide approval. The community is also defined by what it excludes: city life and its vulgar mix of the lower classes, the new rich and the Islamists.

The suburb is both a home and family-centred place, and suburban life is based on a sharp spatial division of home and work: it is, by and large, a public place whose centre is a private one. The reduced size of the family and the insulation of its nuclear variant are the two prominent characteristics of the suburb. For instance, in the southwestern belt of Ankara the average family size is only 3.4 members. The nuclear family seeks to increase the distance between itself and the wider kinship group. Inner-city apartment housing also promotes the privacy of the nuclear family, but it is largely in the suburb that the trend towards its separation from work, street life and the kinship and neighbourhood community has become so decisive. Although the majority continue to socialise mainly with acquaintances from the city, the general tendency is one of a weakening of social relations due to the increased physical distance (İpek,1998). For instance, all *site* residents mention that 'dropping in' has been completely replaced with pre-arranged visits since they moved to the *site*.

The elderly and full-time housewives in particular develop strong friendship networks based on the extensive cultural homogeneity in the area. Hence, women establish networks among themselves to organise a wide range of activities such as tennis, walks, bicycle rides, cinema-going, bridge parties and mutual home visits. Children too are an important source of sociability, and a major focus of leisure activity, for full-time mothers, who talk while watching their children play, and together take them to ballet, ice-skating, basketball and gymnastics. Although clubs – frequently mentioned as one of the major features of suburban life, together with the garden and the family (Chambers, 1997) – are largely absent, the *site* differs from apartment housing in its organisation of a wide range of community-based activities: festivals and carnivals on special days, and the arranging of tickets and transport to go to the opera, concerts and theatre.

The gender order

Men's lives and worlds often contain more duality than women's, as they move back and forth between the male-dominated work and city life and the more private, domestic and feminine world of home. Suburban life reinforces and sharpens such differences. How men relate to the feminine gendered suburban spaces of private life is therefore an important question (Cross, 1997).

Although both men and women have a clear preference for suburban life, men are fond of the home environment for specific reasons. It is regarded as a shelter that protects the family against the dangers of street life, a source of moral solace in a corrupt world, and a place where one seeks refuge from the pressures of everyday life at work and and in the city. It is enjoyed for its comfort and peace: here one can relax physically and mentally, and be at ease with oneself, or, as some men formulate it, be one's 'real self', as opposed to the other-oriented self of public life. Men also seem to enjoy their own success through the home. The house itself, as well as the household goods it contains, are generally associated with men's professional success. A middle-aged computer engineer expressed this in the following words; 'I like looking around at home, at the furniture, at the tiles, at their beautiful and orderly patterning, and enjoying the fact that the whole thing is my own creation'.

Most middle-class men are highly work-centred, 'workaholic' as some women tend to describe it. Men emphasise that their workplace, the office, though not necessarily its wider environment in the city, is as clean and orderly as home. Wives, including many who work themselves, but the housewives in particular, see work fundamentally as the men's domain. Men are believed to extend work deliberately, finding excuses to go to work on their days off or stay late in the evenings. One woman thus described work as her husband's 'mistress', implying a seductive relationship between the two. Excessive absorption in work is more common among middle-aged entrepreneurs, professionals, managers and high-level bureaucrats than among the young and the old, as well as among those disaffected with their current work.

The escape to work takes place in the cultural matrix of a highly competitive society in which men are expected to demonstrate their personal merits, abilities and talents through success in the world of work. In Turkish society in general, and particularly among the middle classes, home ownership, good education for the children, and hence family status, largely depend on a person's achievement in work. Men seek and derive both personal satisfaction and fulfilment from work. The urge to work also involves a desire to escape from the overwhelmingly feminine world of home and the feminine-gendered suburban environment. This was expressed clearly by a small businessman:

> Home is the women's sphere. Work is mine. I always prefer it there at work. The workplace is exclusively mine, and I don't share it with anybody. It is not that I do not like home but I am always tempted by work. There is nothing in my office reminiscent of or that can be associated with home. I simply adore my work.

Masculine domesticity involves various negotiations, compromises and conflicts with women in the private life of the home. Men clearly tend to see home and various activities associated with it as predominantly the women's sphere. One major exception is house maintenance: men show wide interest in carpentry and various kinds of do-it-yourself activities. With the growth of suburban housing, the number of shops selling do-it-yourself tools and equipment has increased rapidly. Women report that at weekends their husbands go around the whole day with tools in their hands, looking for something to fix. A middle-aged villa owner gives a vivid description of this relationship between masculinity and house maintenance:

> Anything that has to do with water, pipes, bulbs, gas, fuel, garage, basement, that is with the physical management of the house, is naturally a man's job. I feel a secret but deep pride in the upkeep of the house. A detached house is masculine, in the way an apartment flat is not. I maintain the sub-structure of the house while my wife beautifies its superstructure.

The display of masculine domesticity can be more of a problem in flats. One extreme case was that of a woman complaining about her husband: 'He either goes around the house the whole day with a screwdriver in his hand, or he watches football, or enjoys being with his eight hamsters, which live smack in the middle of the living-room'. The wife who saw this situation as a form of masculine intrusion into the domestic sphere seemed highly reluctant to describe home as a sacred haven to which one escapes from the disorder of the city.

Men usually come home late and tired. The majority say that they do not contribute to household chores, at least not on a regular basis. Their participation in housework may include tasks like preparing salad and fruit juice, cooking Sunday breakfast, and making a barbecue, especially when guests are invited. Both the younger and the more elderly men are more likely to take an active interest in household chores, while the workaholics tend to neglect these most. Thanks to increased family prosperity, almost every household can afford domestic help, ranging from maids who come only once or twice a week to those living in.

In the living-room, there is usually a man's corner, in which the man reads papers, dozes and watches television, mainly news and sports, usually holding the remote control in his hands. Among suburban middle-class families one of the most outstanding aspects of masculine domesticity is football: for some at least, football is the most important source of excitement in life and the main subject of conversation among friends. To please their husbands, and to make them feel that home is enjoyable, wives not only tolerate football but even pretend that they too are interested in it. One typically suburban form of entertainment that both men and women do enjoy together is going to the cinema, as evidenced by the opening of a rash of suburban cinemas.

In particular, the elderly and those who find their work alienating emphasise the virtues of domesticity and privacy, showing a marked interest in feminine-gendered activities. A woman architect describes the orientation of her sixty-year-old husband:

> My husband is indeed a very different kind of person. He virtually cuts himself off from the outside world. Home for him is a temple. Whenever I ask he simply refuses the idea of going out, saying, 'Is there really any place to go?' Even when I make him go out, he prefers to sit in the car, which he thinks is homely. His favourites are watching TV and food shopping. Whenever he turns off the TV, you hear him saying, 'OK, I'll go and make some dessert'.

The shift from strongly masculine to feminine roles and activities usually comes with old age. Once devotion to work wanes, those middle-class men who have neither wide access to networks within modern patterns of association nor to the traditional community of neighbours and relatives suddenly find themselves in a vacuum with nowhere to turn other than home.

The secular middle classes reject both the traditional understanding of the inequality of the sexes and the more recent Islamist view that emphasises spiritual equality while rejecting social equality. Therefore, the discourse on sexual equality is an important constituent of secular middle-class identity, defined in opposition to both the traditional and the Islamist. They disagree, in principle at least, with the ideology of domesticity that confines women to the home while establishing work and the public as male spheres (Hall, 1990). Furthermore, the highly prevalent middle-class discourse about companionship in marriage emphasises that men should be equally responsible and active in the management of household affairs.

Despite all this, gender roles are far from symmetrical: they are divided, though in more subtle ways, as men's and women's domains. Home is thus established as the women's sphere in that women are more often at home, it has greater emotional significance for them, and the domestic space is more feminised. Men tend to see home predominantly as the women's sphere of influence and action. In addition to being wives and mothers, women are seen as homemakers and managers of the house, in charge of provisioning, decoration and the management of family 'appearances'. This gives women a central role in the management of family consumption.

There is an intricate relationship between women's taste and men's success: the income earned by the husband or family is transformed into family prestige by means of women's skills in homemaking, and the display of household goods. As men devote themselves to earning more, women, either entirely on their husbands' behalf, or with money they themselves have or earn, concentrate on consumption and creating a homely and tasteful environment in the house. Thus, as the income of the household and the share of family income going towards housing costs increase, the whole sphere of ever-expanding and diversifying household consumption tends to be established primarily as that of the women. This is indeed a novelty in a society where rural and first-generation migrant women in cities have minimal contact with the market, and where the vast majority of urban women have a say over consumption only in those areas seen as the extension of their practical household skills, areas such as shopping for food, children's clothing and items like garments, bedsheets and towels.

Among the suburban middle classes, patina is ostensibly absent: even those who claim a good family background tend to have inherited only a few pieces of china and jewellery or some pictures from parents and grandparents. Where there are few visual signs of age in household objects, the acquisition of middle-class trappings is open to all, and new money can make easy inroads into what seem established middle-class habits and environments. In such a context, the aestheticisation of everyday life in dress, grooming, cars and house decoration gains great importance.

Consumption is an extensive and complex activity involving not only purchasing but also the conception of desire for objects, searching and window shopping, as well as the display, maintenance and repair of objects. In many of these phases of consumption, suburban women are more active than men. With the advent of consumer culture, the proliferation of shopping malls, the increasing range of goods and the scale of their display, women became more visible in the typical consumption environments, spending more time on the consumption activity itself. Although men in some middle-class families are also involved extensively in consumption, especially in the suburban context, consumption and feminine identity tend to fuse in new forms and situations.

One such novelty is the suburbanisation of consumption and the increased feminisation of the new suburban shopping spaces. For instance, women form both the majority of customers and sales staff in the shopping malls and department stores. As the latter provide regular free bus services from a number of points, women have easy access to suburban malls, where they enjoy more freedom in predominantly female company. In such places, women can wander and window-shop for longer without being disturbed by masculine gazes, as they probably would be in the city. They can thus stroll freely for hours developing a 'female gaze'. This enables women to examine prices, contents and possible uses of goods in detail. Traditionally, however, women were extremely restricted in their behaviour in public; mothers, for instance, used to tell their daughters to walk straight and not to look around when they were out on their own. Therefore the mall represents a significant loosening of the strictures on women in public spaces.

In the growing consumer economy, goods not only increase in number and variety, but they become more subtle and complex, making consumer choice primarily a matter of personal taste. As domestic aesthetic becomes an important determinant of social status, proper consumption depends more and more on a knowledge of goods and ways of using them. For women, television, friends and, even more so, magazines are the basic sources of such information and instruction. Suburban women exhibit great interest in fashion and decoration magazines that tell the reader how to consume in a manner appropriate to class and other relevant status categories. Women thus report that one of their favourite private joys is having coffee in the kitchen while looking at those magazines that help them to dream about and desire new goods, and envisage their arrangement in the house. The magazines are highly instrumental in developing new tastes and lifestyles.

The house is not just a place where one escapes from the world, but is also an opening onto it. Since the entertaining of friends at coffee mornings, women's gatherings, bridge sessions, dinner and weekend parties takes place at home, the house is always on display. Although husbands and grown-up children do take an active interest in house decoration, women spend more time and energy and assume greater responsibility in managing household consumption. Meanwhile, in middle-class houses, both in the suburb and the city, not only the parlour (*salon*), as was the case in the past, but the whole house, both as a place of beauty and physical welfare, has become an object of consumption and is on display. The kitchen, for instance, is more open to visitors as, especially in the case of villas, guests are invited there directly. Their increased visibility makes families put more money, care and attention into them. Women's appropriation of home decoration and display are illustrated by the following remarks:

> Everyone in the family shows some interest in the decoration of the house but I am the most influential person in the family. The demand from the children for increased participation in decision-making has increased as they have grown older. Nevertheless, I treat everyone else only as my assistants.

> Home management for me is both work and housework. My husband asks my opinion even if he wants to buy a needle for the house.

> My husband sees the house as my domain. Unless we talk he will not buy.

Men, on the other hand, are more concerned about economic costs, accepting their wives' superiority in matters of taste:

> My wife makes the choices. My contribution ... well I'm rather quick in decision-making. She spends lots of time sorting out the alternatives and when we go out together we come to a decision in a minute or two. I never interfere with regard to type and colour. I have full trust in her very fine taste.

> Well, I wouldn't say that I was totally excluded. Maybe, I too made some contributions to decoration. Yet, I rarely feel like buying something for the house. What do I buy? I buy pictures, I buy shoe polish and I buy do-it-yourself equipment. When I feel like buying something, though very rarely, I ask my wife's opinion. You see, I am not as good as her in these things. First, she has more time. Furthermore, she has a good talent for matching things, that is, she can visualise the right object for another object in the house, something I cannot do.

Women are regarded as more educated in aesthetics, which covers cleanliness and order but even more so the matching of the right colour, form and style, that is the art of bringing the right things together. Corrigan (1997, pp.105, 106) distinguishes between two different kinds of matching. In the first type, unity derives from the aesthetic characteristics of the set itself, in the second from the consumer who imposes her own standards of unity on objects. Hence, in the second case, the items are picked here and there, often reflecting the personal history of the consumer. This projection of oneself onto home decoration is more highly valued among those sections of the suburban middle classes that claim better taste. Here the household furniture reflects women's biography, personal history and identity. Conversely, matching in the sense of buying a set – though not necessarily with objects like cutlery – is seen as rather vulgar. For instance, a living-room dominated by a settee and four armchairs of the same colour and design is associated with new money, the Islamist middle class, and the lower-middle classes, all of whom are seen as poorly endowed with cultural capital. The new rich, especially, are despised for hiring professionals to decorate their houses.

Attitudes to shopping differ among middle-class women of different consumption and status categories. Those claiming higher levels of cultural capital tend to distinguish sharply between utilitarian shopping and that which involves an awareness of style, and has a symbolic dimension to it. They try to distinguish themselves from those who entertain themselves in supermarkets, as can be inferred from these statements by *site* women:

> ... with the coming of a nearby food supermarket, this place has become a site of weekend attraction for people of every kind, and the charm of the whole area has been ruined; I want to tell these people that this place belongs to me, and that they should go where they belong.

Another woman described her next-door neighbours in the following words:

> Their furniture is Beymen (a leading clothing and furniture company) style. Such people move to a new house with just their suitcases. They totally abandon their previous neighbours and neighbourhood. These people keep talking about the same expensive shops, the same expensive restaurants, and the same expensive holiday resorts. Their houses are arranged by professional decorators. These climbers finally confirm their upward social mobility by bringing a dog into the house.

As such statements indicate, women play a dual role in social class differentiation. By establishing a tasteful and well-ordered house, they affirm the middle-class status of their family and distinguish themselves from those classes below. They also play a prominent role in determining a specific status category for their family within the middle class itself, that is within the hierarchy of taste, as Bourdieu (1984) uses the term. A general interest in style, in presentation, and in appearance is very important for the middle class as a way of indicating identity and status. To the extent that impressing others derives not only from wealth but also consumption, women tend to be the key actors in competition over status.

The suburban trend towards increased domesticity, privacy and feminisation of the home does not result in the increasing seclusion, passivity and conformity of the women in society and the marginalisation of their roles in the family. The dominance of female consumer choice and women's superior position in the hierarchy of taste over men produces two important outcomes. First, the prestige of homemaking skills rises and, secondly, this leads to the empowerment of women in both the family and society as the hierarchy of taste becomes as important as the hierarchy of wealth. Taste, the art of appropriate consumption and impressing others, is not, for women, only a means for personal fulfilment but also a significant asset that helps them to promote and reinforce their power in society.

Male culture lays greater emphasis on hard work, the struggle for power, and the pursuit of pecuniary success. In modern society, however, self-expression resulting from awareness of feelings and exposure to varied experiences in life is revealed mainly through the subjectively comprehended experience of consumption (Corrigan, 1997). Among middle-class suburban families, the expression of unique aspects of the personality through consumption and lifestyle is typically identified with women. Referring to Bourdieu's (1984) well-known work on distinction we can conclude that in the suburb, as the 'masculine' involves a leaning towards the accumulation of economic capital and political power, the expressive feminine is oriented towards the concentration of cultural capital.

Individual and community

The *site* is conceived as a community of equal, but unique and autonomous, individuals. The generalisable aspects are those that distinguish the middle classes from others, and the unique codes and styles are what separate them as individuals, families and status categories.

In the *site*, both the autonomy and the domestic seclusion of the family increase as a result of increased physical and social distance from relatives and friends in the city. Also, a street-level community which involves constant watching of individuals, fault-finding and malicious gossip hardly exists. Individuals are more distant and reserved, and everyone is expected to mind his or her own business. In the suburb, conventions and proprieties are less rigid, and they are less imposed on individuals. Consequently, there is less community control in *site* life. Such individuating and emancipating aspects of suburbia in the Turkish context contrasts with the description of the suburb in the Western literature as a place of standardisation, monotony and conformity (Mumford, 1961).

Suburban people tend to distinguish between three kinds of social control. The urban masses are believed to have little self-restraint, to be guided often by their instincts and emotions, high-tempered, ill-mannered, and therefore insufficiently civilised. The second group constitutes the strongly communitarian, who under the pressure of external sources of authority tend to behave uniformly. Reference here is mainly to the Islamists, who are believed to lack both self-autonomy and the capacity for rational critical thinking. The truly civilised are regarded as those who have developed individualities, those who can think and act autonomously, who have powerful mechanisms of internal control, people with self-restraint who know how to behave in public. Such people are sensitive about their physical appearance, enjoy the many entertainments of modern life, and are relatively more relaxed in their behaviour; in short, they are very much characterised by what Featherstone (1996, p.45) calls controlled 'de-control of emotions'. People who fall into this pattern wear sports clothes, actively seek the varied pleasures of modern life – holiday resorts, cinema, high culture, food and drink – and, most important of all, do not exclude women from domestic and public entertainment.

The retreat to home and family is closely associated with increasing loyalty and the intensification of social and emotional ties within the family. Marriage for love and companionship, and increased care and sensitivity about children are also salient aspects of suburban family life. The desire for domestic seclusion is a part of the process through which the middle classes search for unity and order by separating themselves from other groups and activities.

The increased privacy in middle-class family life promotes personal individuation, and the suburb tends to reinforce this process for reasons to do with both the use of space and time. In the suburb, as houses become larger, families get smaller in size, the major effect of which is the increase of individual living and private space. Rooms designated for special functions, for example the study and the bedroom, give the individual more potential to be alone; thus, in the *site*, children often have not only their own bedrooms but also their own bathrooms. Thanks to increased purchasing power, the children have personal belongings, like wardrobes or dressing tables, as well as radios, television and music sets, and computers in their own rooms. The individualisation of consumption at this particular level makes individual family members free to choose entertainment according to their personal tastes.

Suburban life also promotes and consolidates the increase of private time. The sharp separation of home from work, street life and the city, the insulation of the nuclear family, and the increased amenities in the neighbourhood enable individuals to enjoy larger blocks of personal free time. For instance, planning the weekend and filling it with a multitude of private activities, such as gardening, bicycle riding or simply having a walk is easier in the suburb. On the other hand, since individuals have different working hours and tend to use their free time for different purposes, private time and family time do not always coincide. The family meets only temporarily as the children watch television, play computer games, listen to music and study in their rooms, the women devote most of their time to housework, homemaking, fine cooking, body care, feminine networks and shopping, and the men watch football, read newspapers, or simply sit and contemplate. Thus, as an outcome of the increased privatisation of space and time in the suburb, personal life is separated from family life so that the life of the individual becomes divided between three different spheres: work life, family life and personal life.

Family control over its individual members tends to relax as parents become less authoritarian and are less demanding of their children. At home, children are less supervised, they are allowed to go out on their own at night provided they remain in the *site*, and on a number of important issues their views are taken into account. The individual often takes precedence over the family.

In the suburban context, the expression of the self and individuality to the outside world is most manifest through dress and clothing. Dress is an important indicator of social status, a way of expressing the self and of displaying the body. Although dress reveals similarity and union with one's major reference group, it also reflects the need for differentiation, the desire to emphasise dissimilarity, and to feature individual uniqueness or specific status characteristics.

In ceremonial work – that is effort directed towards making symbolic arrangements – as well as in everyday life, the emphasis is on tailoring, with a tendency to avoid long and loose clothes that signify both the traditional as well as the Islamist dress codes. Clothes are expected to suggest, if not totally reveal, the form of the body. On the other hand, there exists an equally powerful tendency among the adult population to avoid eye-catching and tight-fitting clothes. The *site* people also want to show that they are in tune with fashion but not slaves to it; those dressed completely from the leading fashion shops are despised as fashion victims – the 'Beymen type' once again. Especially, the women show the utmost care in revealing their personal tastes through their accessories and outfits. Finally, in everyday dress, the emphasis is on flexible codes and relaxed styles. As rules of dress become less rigid, people outside the home tend to prefer casual dress or sports apparel on the streets.

Despite over-riding similarities, there are also subtle codes that reveal status. The more affluent families living in houses and larger flats not only look more elegant and chic, even when working in the garden, but they try to emphasise their distinctiveness by wearing the more expensive designer jeans, shorts, sports-wear and so on. For such people, reading dress to infer taste and status is always an important occupation.

The appearance of the body itself is also an important aspect of individual identity, and is reflected through an emphasis on body maintenance and health – various hygiene practices, healthy diets and the heavy use of cosmetics, beauty aids and grooming. What symbolises this orientation in the house is gleaming kitchens and bathrooms and, in the *site*, sporting activities and facilities.

The *site* people are at pains to stress the differences in body care between the suburb and the city, remarking on the contrast between the healthy and disciplined physical appearance of the suburban people and the loose, dirty and weary appearance of the urban crowd. The good-looking body, increasingly a marker of middle-class identity, is a source of pride and moral superiority, whereas its opposite in the city represents moral laxity. The city people are often described as worn-out, with signs of wear-and-tear on their bodies, the marks of pollution, disease and early ageing. Thus they are identified with ill-health, the wear-and-tear of age, and threats to the body from within. The city and its crowd thus symbolise the very opposite of youth, health and life. In this last respect, the suburb and suburban life are seen as bulwarks against that which the *site* people fear most: old age, illness and death.

Conclusion

The recent expansion of the urban middle class in Turkey is an outcome of steady economic growth and the increased globalisation of the economy in the last decade. A new layer in Turkish society has emerged as the middle class proliferated to include in its ranks an ever-increasing range of professional, managerial and entrepreneurial elements in addition to the bureaucratic component that used to be so pronounced in Ankara, as the capital city. The new middle classes, through their access to either high educational qualifications, expertise or capital, benefit from increased wealth and disposable income. This above all tends to boost the demand for bigger houses and private motor vehicles, the major factors behind the rapid expansion of suburban settlements.

The new middle class, noted for its powerful desire for order and predictability, is also the major custodian of the values of rationality, individual autonomy, secularism, the rule of law, environmental concern and globalism. Economic growth and rising middle-class living standards engender both higher levels of consumption and a search for a new way of life that implies consuming with style and taste.

The suburbanisation process that gained new momentum in the 1990s is by and large an extension of middle-class mentality, practices and culture. The notion of a suburb first entails a powerful tendency towards class segregation, the flight to a homogeneous and isolated neighbourhood, involving a decisive separation from both the lower classes, viewed with contempt, and the turmoil of street life. The juxtaposition of two separate but closely inter-related processes needs special emphasis here: the increase in the wealth and prosperity of the middle and upper classes at a time when inequalities in income distribution in the country has tended to grow rapidly, and the deepening of cultural cleavages between the affluent and the masses as the former increasingly emphasise Western standards in quality of life. Thus, from the other end of the spectrum, a recent study (Erman,1998) on the problematic issue of the 'integration' of rural migrants in the cities contends that

> ... as long as rural migrants are placed asymmetrically in the urban society... as long as they feel economically exploited or socially excluded and denied social recognition as equal, as long as they cluster in *gecekondu* settlements, then the categories of rural and urban will not disappear; they will exist as a means of migrants positioning themselves against the urban elites.

Secondly, the emphasis on order implies the vision of a community of like-minded individuals with uniform rules that govern neighbourhood conduct, by and large a plea for a lawful society. Thirdly, against the social heterogeneity of the city, marked by intense competition, social division and cultural fragmentation, the suburb invokes a search for unity of experience in the isolation of home and family. Fourthly, the suburban home and life are primarily feminine-gendered social spaces where women gain a new status through claiming superior taste through the consumption by which middle-class families forge their distinctive identities. Marks of distinction are manifested in the details of dress, cars and house decoration as expressions of personal and familial taste and identity. In this particular respect, consumption is the major dynamic in suburbia. Finally, on the part of the individual, the suburb involves an emphasis on self-definition and autonomy that involves progressive dissociation from intimate relations with strangers and from the claims of larger groups.

The suburb is a refuge in which one escapes the threatening elements of city life (Fishman, 1996), and tends towards excluding the 'other', but does so as Mumford (1961) points out, by exaggerating the difference between the inside and the outside. The middle-class withdrawal to the suburb can be seen as a decisive and uncompromising break with the outside, the other and its own past, but also as a form of retaliation against wider society through the creation of an alternative mentality, social organisation and lifestyle to emulate.

Acknowledgement

I owe deep gratitude to Umut Beşpınar, fourth year student in the Department of Sociology at the Middle East Technical University, for her invaluable contributions to the fieldwork carried out in Koru Sitesi.

References

Aksoy, Asu and Kevin Robins (1994), 'Istanbul between Civilisation and Discontent', *New Perspectives on Turkey*, no 10 (Spring), pp.57–74
– (1995), 'Ezilen İstanbul'un Dönüşü', *İstanbul*, no 14
Balamir, Murat (1996), 'Making Cities of Apartment Blocks', in Yıldız Sey (ed.) *Housing and Settlement in Anatolia: A Historical Perspective*, Türkiye Ekonomik ve Toplumsal Tarih Vakfı, Habitat II Sergisi Kitabı, İstanbul
Bourdieu, Pierre (1984) *Distinction: A Social Critique of the Judgement of Taste*, Routledge, London
Caldeira, P.R. Teresa (1996), 'Building up walls: the new pattern of spatial segregation in Sao Paulo', *International Social Science Journal*, 147, March
Chambers, Deborah (1997), 'A Stake in the Country: Women's Experiences of Suburban Development', in Roger Silverstone (ed.), *Visions of Suburbia*, Routledge, New York, NY
Clark, David (1996), *Urban World/Global City*, Routledge, London
Corrigan, Peter (1997), *The Sociology of Consumption*, Sage, Cambridge
Cross, Gary (1997), 'The Suburban Weekend: Perspectives on a Vanishing Twentieth-Century Dream', in Roger Silverstone (ed.), *Visions of Suburbia*, Routledge, New York, NY

Douglas, Mary (1979), *Purity and Danger*, Routledge & Kegan Paul, London

Erman, Tahire (1998), 'Becoming "urban" or remaining "rural": the views of Turkish rural-to-urban migrants on the "integration" question', *International Journal of Middle East Studies*, vol. 30, no 4

Featherstone, Mike (1996), *Consumer Culture and Postmodernism*, Sage, London

Fishman, Robert (1996), 'Bourgeois utopias: visions of suburbia', in Susan Feinstein and Scott Campbell (eds), *Urban Theory*, Blackwell, Oxford

Gans, Herbert (1962), 'Urbanism and Suburbanism as Ways of Life', in Arnold M. Rose (ed.), *Human Behaviour and Social Processes: An Interactionist Approach*, Houghton Mifflin, Boston, MA

Hall, Catherine (1990), 'The Sweet Delights of Home', in Michelle Perrot (ed.) *A History of Private Life IV*, The Belknap Press of Harvard University Press, Cambridge

Mumford, Lewis (1961), *The City in History*, Harcourt, New York, NY

İpek, Melek (1998), 'Uydu Kentler', *Yaşam*, no 7

Öncü, Ayşe (1997), 'The myth of the "ideal home": travels across cultural borders in Istanbul', in Ayşe Öncü and Petra Weyland (eds), *Space, Power and Culture*, Zed, London

Tekeli, İlhan (1996), *Türkiye'de Yaşamda ve Yazında Konut Sorununun Gelişimi*, T.C. Başbakanlık Toplu Konut İdaresi Başkanlığı, Konut Araştırmaları Dizisi, no 2, Ankara

Türel, Ali (1996), 'Ankara'da Ruhsatlı Konut Sorunu', in Tansı Şenyapılı and Ali Türel (eds), *Ankara'da Gecekondu Oluşum Süreci ve Ruhsatlı Konut Sunumu*, Batıbirlik Yayınları, no 1, Ankara

Wirth, Louis (1957), 'Urbanism as a Way of Life', in Paul K. Hatt and Albert Reiss (eds), *Cities and Society*, Free Press, New York, NY

2

The Doorkeeper, the Maid and the Tenant: Troubling Encounters in the Turkish Urban Landscape

Gül Özyeğin

Introduction

Expressions are abundant in the recent literature of deep conceptual discomfort with the distinction between the 'modern' and 'traditional' as a major framework for studying economic and social transformations in 'industrialising' societies, and particularly in examining emerging modalites of life and identity.[1] It has been argued that this polarity not only precludes consideration of important sources of difference, complexity and diverse meanings of modernity, but also fails to recognise the changing face of modernity. Students of Turkish modernisation have also started seriously to interrogate the project of modernity in Turkey, and have called for the distinction between the modern and traditional to be used not as an organising assumption but rather as a topic for intense investigation (Bozdoğan and Kasaba, 1997; Kandiyoti, 1997). These scholars seek to study 'the specificities of the "modern" in the Turkish context' (Kandiyoti 1997, p.113). How is modernity variously understood and experienced? What aspects of elite-driven notions of modernity are accepted, reworked or changed by so-called 'traditional' segments of society, in which domains of life and how? How is the tension between the modern and traditional expressed concretely in the daily organisation of the lives and conduct of those said to be caught between these forces?

These questions have only recently made an impact on the discourses and research agendas of social scientists. It is no accident that the development of feminist theory – with its insistence on gender constructions as fundamental aspects of social order and cultural change – on the one hand, and the demise of 'modernising' and developmentalist projects on the other, have placed these questions on the agenda. These are significant questions largely ignored by the dominant paradigms of Marxist and modernisation thought, which focus on changes in judicial, economic, political and institutional spheres, but fail to explore the cultural consequences of these transformations. These two perspectives also fail to recognise the various unequal and contradictory forms of modernity, and the 'life worlds' (Mardin, 1997) of those people whose subjectivities and social lives were to be transformed by the project. Kandiyoti (1997, p.129), for instance, notes that 'the assumed inexorable march of society from traditional, rural, and less developed to modern, urban, industrialised, and more developed, or, alternatively, from feudal to capitalist, meant that complexities on the ground could be dismissed as "transitional" forms'.

Now, an increasing number of scholars take a pluralist stance, accepting that fragmentation and multiple combinations of forces of modernity and tradition are indispensable in considering Turkish social order at the end of the century. They call for more intense studies of new identities and modalities of life arising from modernisation.[2] To this end, Migdal (1997, 253–4) recently suggested that 'the effects of the modernity project can be found not in examination of elites and their institutions exclusively, nor in a focus solely on the poor or marginal groups of society, but on those physical and social spaces where the two intersect'. He draws our attention to the significance of interactive processes: 'The challenge is to illuminate their [those formerly excluded groups] encounter with the modernity project – the changes in them that this encounter produced and their surprising ability to transform the project itself'.

In the pages to follow, I offer a 'critical tale'[3] of a group of rural migrants and the encounters they have with urban classes through their work and services as maids and doorkeepers. Apartment buildings and middle-class homes constitute a physical and social space of cross-class intersection and interaction. The principal actors of this critical tale are those rural migrants in Turkish society with the most deeply rooted sense of their own distinctiveness and displacement, by virtue of their living at the physical and cultural margins of the middle classes that they serve. The case of doorkeepers and maids provides a critical context for a close examination of the gendered cultural aspects of the stratification system and cross-class relations, because of the intimate connection between this group and urban classes, and their geographical distance from established squatter settlement communities, where most rural migrants live.

I look at the hierarchically interconnected worlds of doorkeepers, maids and tenants,[4] and alternative meanings of urban living from the perspective of those 'marginal' to it yet simultaneously 'central' to the creation and maintenance of a middle-class cultural existence and identity. By focusing on the self- narratives of containment that emerge from their experiences in the 'workplace', of living with a well-established stigma of servitude, the chapter addresses the question of consciousness of class inequality and how migrants, with a past identity as peasants, imagine, understand and practice what they perceive as modernity and tradition. I argue that in the process they invent new forms of cultural difference in the Turkish urban landscape which do not fit neatly into the polarising categories of 'modern' and 'traditional'. My analysis here is based on data obtained through a survey of 103 wives of doorkeepers, in-depth interviews and participant observation. I also take into account the perspectives of middle-class women who employ maids, drawing upon data collected through focus-group interviews with 18 employers. Although my focus is on the doorkeepers and their wives, who also work as domestic workers, I build a comparative framework by incorporating material from squatter settlements, in order to sort out the relationship between class and gender.

My aim is to make the following three inter-related arguments. First, I wish to move the debate about the opposition between tradition and modernity some steps further, to suggest that these forces exercise a special potency in people's lives, as an organiser of experience and consciousness, especially in the encounters with the urban middle classes, and the dominant constructions of gender and class inequality. I agree with those who argue that modernity and tradition, as categories of analysis, often fail us as we attempt to understand the complexities of cultural change. However, the centrality of this opposition in the constitution of the subjectivities of those at the margins of modernity should not be ignored. This raises questions about how we might simultaneously abandon this opposition yet preserve it in analysis.

Second, following in the footsteps of those who have suggested that we study the meaning of the modern, I propose a similar interrogation: we should also explore the specifics and diverse meanings of tradition, the conditions in which traditional practices are sheltered, nurtured or reconfigured, and the meanings attributed to tradition by those thought of as its bearers. I examine these questions here with particular reference to the relationship between tradition and locality. I follow Thompson (1996) in arguing that traditional practices are not only temporally defined, but are spatially specific and spatially defined. What I seek to emphasise is the significance of space and locality in the assertion or reassertion of traditional practices with regard to gender and authority relations. The experiences of doorkeepers and maids illuminate alternately inhibiting and enabling aspects of location, and how tradition is maintained in practice.

Third, I want to uncover and emphasise the centrality of male power and traditional notions of patriarchy to the configuration of gender and class dynamics, particularly in the ordering of relationships between middle-class women and domestic workers. More specifically, I will demonstrate that patriarchal control over migrant women's labour makes their labour expensive and scarce. In other words, traditional patriarchal prerogatives limit middle-class women's access to cheap, readily available domestic wage labour. I go on to illustrate how both groups of women strategically use their understandings of domination and the patriarchal construction of women's identity in the management of their relationships. By forging an intimate link between men of peasant origin and elite women through the case of domestic service in Turkey, I demonstrate the power of structurally weak actors in cross-class relations.

The culture of exclusion: 'outsiders within'

Located in the heartland of Anatolia, Ankara has had only a brief history as an urban centre, despite a rich past dating back to the Hittite period. Ankara, a provincial town of 20,000 inhabitants, was designated the capital of the Turkish republic by Atatürk in 1923 in the hope of modernising Turkey's less-developed regions and decentralising its Istanbul-focused economy. The government initiated extensive programmes to create a capital city that would symbolise the modernisation of Turkey, with planned housing, large boulevards, cultural centres, opera houses, parks and public services (Bozdoğan, 1997; Tekeli, 1984). Dubbed Turkey's most planned city, Ankara has grown faster than any other major city in Turkey, housing about two-and-a-half million people by 1985. Ankara experienced one of the highest rates of urban population growth in Turkey between 1950 and 1970, with an influx of migrants from the country's rural areas. As a result, Ankara now has a higher percentage of squatter settlements than does any other Turkish urban centre. An astonishing 72.4 percent of the total city population in 1980 were squatter-settlement dwellers (Keleş and Daniels, 1985, p.165). Sharp socio-economic hierarchies are clearly reflected in the city's geography: the lowest income groups are concentrated in the belts of squatter settlements surrounding the city's planned core, modern Ankara. It is here, in Ankara's modern core, that the more affluent sectors of the population reside in the very same apartment buildings that house, though floors below, doorkeeper families.[5]

Unlike the majority of the migrants in cities, doorkeeper families live and work in middle- and upper-class areas, the husband employed as *kapıcı* ('door-keeper'[6] or 'janitor' in Turkish), the wife as domestic worker. The doorkeeper's main duties include operating the central-heating system, caring for the maintenance of the apartment block (keeping the building and grounds clean), taking out the residents' daily rubbish, buying and distributing fresh bread[7] twice a day, grocery shopping for residents, providing building security, collecting monthly main-tenance fees from tenants, and disposing of refuse from coal-burning furnaces. Duties may also include walking tenants' dogs, tending gardens or taking tenants' children to school. The doorkeeper deals with strangers (for example salespeople and beggars), and protects the building and the tenants from potentially disturbing and threatening elements. In short, his job is to provide order by policing the door, ensuring its sanctity and preventing its violation. Wives of doorkeepers constitute a prime pool from which middle-class tenants recruit waged domestic labour. Because of this, wives of doorkeepers rarely navigate in the wider domestic labour market (they very seldom leave the apartment block and its vicinity, especially unaccompanied), but have a virtual monopoly over domestic service.[8]

The rise of the doorkeeper and his family as a significant figure in the Turkish urban landscape occurred during the early 1960s with the passing of a law[9] that urged replacement of single-family homes with apartment buildings in order to house a growing middle-class population. This new collective housing created an occupational niche initially filled by the first generation of migrant men and subsequently nurtured as a source of work as more and more peasants came to the city.

The creation of middle-class housing in the city's rapid growth was a response to the expansion of the urban middle classes, but was also significant in restructuring the boundaries between the private and public spheres along class lines. The growth of the middle classes promoted the incorporation of rural migrants/peasants into middle-class domestic spheres, creating a powerful common physical and symbolic space for encounters between urban and rural classes. While these rural migrants became an increasingly indispensable part of middle-class existence, the middle class came to define itself in contradistinction to the peasants. Indeed, the contact between these groups gave rise to intensified forms of boundary-defining activity. The emergence of this occupational role for migrant men also helped to consolidate the definition of the housewife role for middle-class women, who performed tasks of homemaking, nurturing and sociability within the confines of the domestic arena. This arrangement generated a gender division of labour that implicitly limited opportunities for housewives to act and interact in the streets, shops and markets of the public sphere. If not originally designed to exercise patriarchal power over women, these structural reconfigurations have often perpetuated it. Doorkeepers who stood between housewives and the street not only saved the women from the mundane chores of purchasing and daily provisioning but also 'protected' them from the outside world and encounters with strangers, all the while reinforcing spatial gender boundaries. In fact, doorkeepers significantly figured in the routines of women's everyday lives. The intimacy between these urban middle-class women and peasant men was strange. The doorkeeper was the only man, except their husbands, who saw these women in every mood and state. The doorkeeper saw them early in the morning, when they were still in their robes with tangled hair, and when they were dressed up to go out. The doorkeeper knew what they cooked every day, who visited them, with whom they visited, whose husbands came home drunk, and who failed to pay the electricity bill. He fixed their leaky plumbing and helped them move heavy furniture. He kept an eye on children playing outside. As a collectively shared servant and handyman, he freed these women's husbands from their already limited domestic responsibilities while protecting these women from 'the defiling, sordid elements of life', to recall Davidoff's phrase (1974:412). Their position also gave these women a sense of power over men, albeit of a different class.

Through their cheap labour, doorkeepers create an orderly and comfortable existence for middle- and upper-class urban populations in Turkey. This occupation creates a meeting place for urban/modern and 'modernising' populations by situating doorkeeper households in an 'outsiders within' position in urban space, literally symbolised by the location of their quarters in the dark basement apartments. Despite their sharing the same gate, roof and neighbourhood, doorkeeper families and building tenants understand each other in the classical terms of upstairs and downstairs.

Doorkeeper families are not haphazardly scattered throughout middle- and upper-class areas, but have formed and maintained communities based on kin and place (town or village) of origin. This clustering through reconstitution of regional communities in the midst of the middle- and upper-middle-class urban space is also clearly reflected in my survey: 83 percent of the wives of doorkeepers interviewed, for instance, reside near male relatives and/or fellow migrants from the same town origin also working as doorkeepers in the immediate neighbourhood. As doorkeeping became an occupational enclave for many migrant men from rural areas, their wives became the mainstay of the domestic labour force in these neighbourhoods. Unlike their sisters who settled on the margins of urban space and became full-time housewives, doorkeeper wives began to work in the homes of tenants. Such employment gave husbands control over their wives' experience of waged work and choice of employers. These women now hold a virtual monopoly over the domestic service industry: only 14 percent of the door-keeper wives from the sample – who were randomly selected for interview – reported having never been a domestic worker.

Doorkeeper families share many features with the larger squatter-settlement community,[10] including patterns of migration and class origin, but a collective, occupation-based identity sets them apart from migrants in squatter settlements, who are occupationally heterogenous. Although they establish and maintain communities among themselves, doorkeeper households are physically isolated from other migrants in squatter settlements. Their locality generates distinctive grammars of life for these people, who otherwise share a past identity as peasants with the migrants of the squatter settlements. Locality structures the totality of migrants' lives in terms of their social relations: housing conditions, different lev-els of family privacy, the kinds of schools their children attend, and generally their relationship with modernity and urbanness. In other words, this division speaks more directly to the ways in which 'migrantness' is lived out. If we use the metaphor of 'outsider' to define the marginalised position of the migrant in urban space, then the doorkeepers could be called 'outsiders within',[11] a description of the deeper experience of marginality that arises from their being more within. Squatter-settlement migrants, on the other hand, could be called 'outsiders', a term that captures their community-based collective experience of relative distance from the within. It is this 'outsiders within' status of doorkeeper families and their claim to an equal use of urban space that challenge the existing divisions in the city and cause 'pollution', causing middle-class employers to look for ways to avoid contact.

The doorkeeper always lives with his family, in the dingy basement flat of the building in which he works, a job benefit that offers little in the way of professional pride. Housing conditions not only preclude any sense of shared space with tenants, but also constitute an important element in the formation of stigma and contempt from the middle-class occupants. Many of the apartment blocks visited for this study, new or old, confined doorkeepers to damp underground chambers with little light and less ventilation. The majority (70 percent) consist of only two rooms with a half kitchen, and often no adequate bathing facilities.[12] Doorkeepers and their wives complain that 'we are stuffed in under the ground,' and 'our children do not see the face of the sun'. In other words, a contemptible existence is emphasised by the spatial juxtaposition of tenants and doorkeepers.[13]

Although the spatial layout of doorkeeper dwellings, like squatter-settlement houses, display some variety, all share the same unsettling qualities. The distribution of rooms gives no sense of enclosure to inhabitants. A typical doorkeeper apartment, for instance, has huge exposed pipes passing through the living-room. In some apartments, going from one room to another means stepping around the building's boiler, from which coal dust or refuse are carried. Windows are typical of those found in basements, being too small and placed too high to admit light. Such housing conditions create and perpetuate a sense of discomfort and alienation, a home often described by its occupants as a prison.

Doorkeepers' feelings of confinement and displacement are mirrored by the contempt in which they are held by building residents. The stigma permeates the doorkeeper's life, extending to both job and family. I argue that this stigma results from the dangerously close day-to-day proximity of the doorkeeper to the middle-class residents whom he and his family serve. Following Douglas (1989), I argue that stigma symbolically serves to prevent the pollution seen to result from the doorkeeper's occupation of the physical and cultural margins of middle-class dwellings. He not only has low status (as do members of other low-status occupations), but he is also treated as having power that challenges the ordering of class and status-based inequalities as well as urban–rural divisions within the Turkish city, for margins are the most dangerous point in any social structure. The middle class keeps these dangerously close outsiders within, in their place, by acts of contempt. Stigma, by structuring the interactions among members of each class, serves to affirm the social distance felt to be undermined by the physical proximity and lack of ritualised social contacts, especially among children.

Contempt, as seen in the following accounts of doorkeepers' wives, is typically expressed in terms of the doorkeepers' children, especially with regard to their isolation and alleged uncleanliness:

> You are home-bound; you can't leave home for a visit for your enjoyment. You are like a prisoner. They see you as a dog on their doorstep, we are beneath them/they hold us in low esteem. They say we don't know how to eat food (meal-time behaviour); they say our homes smell.

> The main problem is with children. As they grow up they become unhappy, they start asking why we are doorkeepers.

> They belittle, humiliate doorkeepers' children. They look at doorkeepers as unclean, they are all villagers. They treat us with contempt.

> They despise you. We are considered unclean and ill-bred/ill-mannered. They see us as different, they don't want to associate with us.

> They despise doorkeepers. They warn their children, 'Don't play with door-keepers' kids, they would contaminate you with microbes'... We're humans too, only our appearance does not fit with theirs.

> Regardless of how well you dress and groom your kids, they are still identified as the doorkeeper's kids. They still don't play with our kids.

> It's the name of doorkeeper that is bad. We are looked down, treated as inferiors. We are conceived as evil, unclean people ... that is the worst part.

Such testimonies voice the doorkeeper families' profound sense of being stigmatised. Perceived poor hygiene becomes the symbol and symptom of a deeper character structure, a sign of an essentially contemptible existence. Accusations of uncleanliness go beyond aesthetics, and suggest an evaluation of moral character – of both the doorkeeper and his family. This criticism is especially hurtful to wives for, as women, they are held responsible for family hygiene.

Looked at from a Douglasian perspective, stigma is attached to those persons and groups that reside at the margins of society, thereby functioning to define those margins. Douglas says witches, novices and unborn children, for example, are threatening, because they have no official place in the patterning of society. Marginal persons, those whose status is ambiguous or weakly defined, are dangerous because the margins are the most vulnerable point in any social structure; there- fore, in policing the margins the 'centre' strengthens itself. Viewed from this perspective, doorkeeper families are marginals – outsiders within – in the city, for they belong in neither the apartment block (in the same sense as tenants do) nor in the squatter settlements. They are seen as carriers of pollution and disorder.

Even when relegated to the bottom of the class hierarchy and made a sub- ordinate group in cultural and economic terms, doorkeeper families are still to be feared and avoided because of the symbolic threat of close contact with them. Urban classes are concerned with the confusion caused by the blurring of their boundaries. This concern with the maintenance of boundaries and fear of pollution seems greater among members of the middle class whose concern with status distinctions stems from a particular class insecurity, what Ehrenreich calls 'fear of falling'. Social distancing from the doorkeeper families is, in this sense, a typical practice in the self-definition of middle-class identity.[14] But under what conditions are boundaries perceived to be threatened? The location of doorkeepers' homes at the bottom of the apartment building and their positions as order-takers do not seem to satisfy middle-class tenants' need to demarcate social boundaries. I argue that social boundaries are perceived to be undermined when they are, in practice, permeable, in situations where a great deal of mixing is going on, in this case through children. In this way the possibility of mixing is made a reality, not only through the proximity of living quarters but also through the doorkeeper families' claim for a fair share of the opportunities that the city promises.

The threat of mixing that may be caused by the doorkeeper and his wife is handled by established rituals. Social contacts of a highly ritualised type occur between doorkeeper families and tenants, in order to assert and reassert class and status differences, in the form of an asymmetrical participation in the systems of exchange. For instance, the giving of unreciprocated gifts by the tenants places doorkeeper families in a supplicant position. During religious holidays, when social visits are exchanged between relatives, friends, neighbours and acquaintances, doorkeepers visit the tenants but their visits are not reciprocated. This practice is part of established cultural norms which allow superiors (in age and status) not to reciprocate without appearing to be acting unfairly.

In the case of children, however, there are either no routinised forms of exclusion or they are more difficult actually to implement. Hence the threat established by the unregulated mixing of the doorkeepers' children with the middle-class children of the neighbourhood. They attend school together, share desks, play at the same playground, hang out at the same neighbourhood corner, get hair cuts at the same barber, ride in the same school bus and walk the same routes to school.[15] This mixing of children, which may even lead to cross-class romantic attachments, is a function of the structural conditions of the doorkeepers' work.

Tenants respond to this perceived 'pollution' by creating elaborate symbolic means for segregating doorkeeper families.[16] Uncleanliness, odour, demeanour and manners constitute the terms of a symbolic distancing vocabulary, provided by the stigmatised group's actual involvement in 'dirty' work,[17] their unhygienic housing conditions, and their peasant background.

Sheltering tradition

The structure of doorkeeping both confirms and denies continuity with past tradition. The apartment building constitutes a spatial zone where tradition can persist: it acts as a container of traditional action, along with important social transformation in terms of gender roles. In this section, I will discuss the complex ways in which the organisation of doorkeeping inhibits possibilities for 'becoming modern' and reimposes traditional forms of class and gender servility upon these migrants.

The migration of peasant women often results in their 'housewifeisation' (Şenyapılı, 1981; Ayata and Ayata, 1996). Women, especially married women, in migrant communities are not allowed to work outside the home. Squatter settlements would seem to offer an abundant domestic labour pool, yet few squatter women seek employment as domestic workers.[18] Patriarchal opposition to women's paid work, rooted in deep-seated anxieties about perceived threats to women's sexual purity, modesty and men's honour, drastically limit the sorts of work women can perform and the contexts in which they can work. What I want to emphasise here is the importance of the doorkeeper connection in rendering employment in domestic service an acceptable form of work for migrant women. In other words, domestic service, which is organised via the doorkeeper connection, minimises the disruption to traditional controls over women's work.

The following summary represents a somewhat homogenised account of women's position in agricultural production in Turkey, which has become more diverse since the 1950s with the increased mechanisation and commodification of production. From this account, we can begin to see a pattern of continuity, and understand why employment in domestic service organised through doorkeeper connections is thought acceptable, and not constituting a threat.

Studies of rural women in agricultural production systems offer similar descriptions of the organisation of production and women's place in these systems (Sirman, 1988; Berik, 1987; Kandiyoti, 1990). From these studies, several important features relevant to my discussion here may be summed up as follows: women's multitude of economic activities – whether in the form of agricultural production, small-scale manufacturing or husbandry – have been founded on a household-based economy organised under a patriarchal structure of authority. Although female labour is central to the production process in this predominantly family-based peasant economy, this production system is mainly characterised by the absence of autonomous female economic activity and independent female earnings. Women are central actors in forming and maintaining kinship and intra-household relationships upon which production operations rest, but they have no independent access to the market and depend on men's representation. Furthermore, when women are employed as waged labourers (seasonal workers to pick cotton, olives or fruit) or in small-scale manufacturing, for example carpet weaving, their wages are negotiated by and paid to the head of the household, and as a result women control no cash.

Employment in modern sectors of the labour market is characterised as impersonal, rational and legalistic, with centralised control and fixed work routines, as well as other regulations, and this is believed to limit the control of the husband. There is not only limited flexibility in such systems to incorporate the husband's involvement effectively, but also the labour in the workplace takes the wife out of the home and necessitates interaction with the non-kin and unrelated men who are fellow workers, employers or clients within contexts free from the social controls characteristic of rural-based work. Any labour relation that excludes the husband as a principal party – either as an active organiser, supervisor or representative of labour – removes his protection and control over his wife, potentially undermining a husband's expected role.

The institution of doorkeeping, however, spatially unites the supply and demand of domestic labour and thus ensures the continued presence of the protective paternalistic gaze. In effect, women can undertake paid domestic labour without leaving the home or the oversight of their husbands. Employment in domestic service, especially in the prevalent form of multi-family work, provides conditions under which husbands can maintain traditional forms of control over women's work and their wives' work-related conduct. For instance, the husband acts as an organiser of his wife's labour: he can easily afford to choose or veto those she works for.[19] She does not navigate in the wider domestic labour market. In fact, she never transgresses the socio-geographic boundaries of her neighbourhood: she very seldom leaves the apartment block and its vicinity to work; the relations between employer and worker are frequently grounded in personal ties; and the payment of the domestic worker's wages may even go to the husband.

This patriarchal dynamic is central to understanding the present operation of waged domestic labour as an occupational domain, as well as generating particular configurations of gender and class dynamics in Turkey. Restrictions on rural migrant women's labour make domestic labour comparatively scarce and expensive, unlike in the domestic labour markets of other industrialising countries, where domestic service is primarily performed by young, single women who migrate alone to urban centres and constitute a large supply of cheap labour (Jelin, 1977; Chaney and Castro, 1989; Kuznesof, 1989; Duarte, 1989). The abundant supply of labour sustains live-in domestic service and inhibits the development of more contractual employer–employee relationships. By controlling women's labour, Turkish patriarchy has helped to modernise domestic service. Prohibitions on female independence, mobility and wage earning have made for a limited and expensive labour supply and rendered live-in domestic help impractical. Instead, domestic labour is performed as day-work for multiple employers and organised on a more contractual basis than domestic work in other developing countries. Tradition here engenders modern forms of labour relations. It is also ironic that the elite women's access to what might have been a cheap and readily available labour supply is being circumscribed by this patriarchal structure.

Tradition is also maintained in another way. Imprecise boundaries between work and home ultimately involve all household members in the labour experience of the doorkeeper. In other words, the doorkeeping institution, despite its formalisation as a service occupation, does not allow the doorkeeper to become an individualised wage labourer. On the contrary, it reconstitutes the migrant family as a labouring unit whose male head directs its combined labour processes. In the process, doorkeepers' wives partially retain their former unpaid family worker status, and attain a new independent earner identity as domestic workers. It is a labour system based on the exploitation of family labour that both builds on and reinforces the gender- and age-based hierarchical relations within the family. As one woman remarked ironically, 'You become the daughter-in-law of all the residents/tenants of the apartment house,' expressing a perceived reconstitution of her role as a hard-working bride at the service of her status superiors in the domestic hierarchy of the patrilocal extended households of her early marital years in the village.

Yet the same institution, by tying the husband to the home, generates some changes in the traditional gender division of labour, especially with regard to childcare. In the streets of middle- and upper-class Ankara, when most men are away at offices playing the role of distant breadwinner fathers, it is not unusual to see other men strolling at an easy pace, holding a toddler's hand. These men are doorkeepers whose wives are out working, and are also thought to constitute the most traditional segment of men in Turkish society. Inside the home, do the same men also change nappies, feed small children, cook and wash the dishes afterwards?

The majority of domestic workers with young children are able to work full-time (5–7 days a week) due to their husbands availability to meet the demands of young children. Doorkeeper husbands contribute significantly to childcare – 60.6 percent of these men are involved in taking care of infants. To what extent does the doorkeeper husband's home-centred occupation create the possibility of overcoming some of the constraints of gender norms in family work? While this objective condition appears to have affected the gender division of labour in the area of childcare, there is no sign of a fundamental change in other areas of household work. There is considerable evidence to suggest that the doorkeepers, as well as their working wives, amply compensate for such apparent deviations in the area of childcare by performing their appropriate gender roles 'backstage'. Answers to questions such as 'who gives the children lunch', 'who cooks the lunch' and 'who does the dishes' provide us with some hints of what the doorkeeper fathers actually do in the home, when they engage in childcare, and whether their daytime child-care activities expand to include some of the surrounding household work, typically done by mothers. Husbands feed the children, but their contribution to the lunch primarily consists of heating up the food that their wives have prepared the night before and putting the dishes in the sink, thus leaving much of the routine care of household work to wives.

While the 'home-bound' nature of the occupation of doorkeeper produces an 'objective' condition for a redistribution of household and childcare work, this objective condition does not work to break the strong link between doing household work and gender-role identity.[20] In fact, I argue that this link becomes even stronger in this case because the doorkeeper's very occupational role is prone to generate a gender anxiety, which is easily and typically managed by avoidance of 'female' chores. Within the normative structure of the patriarchal gender order, the private (inside) is associated with the feminine and the public (outside) is associated with the masculine. 'A husband's place is not in the home', as Oakley parodically puts it (Oakley, 1974, p.153). These spaces not only symbolise gender roles but also serve to reinforce them. Manliness is performed, cultivated through activities, work roles and social practices that take place in the extra-domestic realm. Those men who spend a great deal of time within the home are considered less masculine (one of the domestic workers expressed the idle and captive condition of her husband by saying, 'Look [pointing out her husband], he sits around the house all day, like a woman'), while women who frequently inhabit external space risk social disapproval for their trespassing in male realms. The doorkeeper's locus of work and his occupational role do not conform to socially defined notions of the masculine: he is placed in an position in which he must function as non-assertive, subordinate, dependent, on call, attentive to the needs of his social superiors. He must learn the social skills necessary to cope with subordinate status. These characteristics are traditionally associated with the female role in Turkish society. Everyday conversations and observations reveal that both doorkeepers and their wives are acutely sensitive to how they are perceived, especially by their fellow migrants, the squatter-settlement dwellers. They often talk about how their fellow migrants are critical of their servitude and feminisation, how they ridicule doorkeepers by making fun of the bread-basket in which he carries bread to distribute to the tenants and the deferential behaviour of the servant to his social superiors.[21] Also, wives of ex-doorkeepers, who are in a position to express the intensity of the degradation they had experienced, cited the unbearability of servitude as the reason why their husbands had switched jobs. They said that their husbands could not bear to be doorkeepers.

In addition to avoiding feminine household chores, doorkeepers have ample structural opportunity to reinscribe their masculinity in a range of strategic ways: a preference for the unused title of 'licensed heating-system operator' in place of 'doorkeeper' suggests an attempt to achieve a dissociation from the negative (servile and feminine) associations of the occupation and to masculinise it. Doorkeepers overly frequent male-only spaces of sociability, such as coffee houses, and play cards in the service of their masculinity. As explained above, they leave the most feminine janitorial tasks to their wives. The overwhelming majority of women are the main source of household income, but these husbands exert substantial control over the handling of household money, which they control and manage, while wives rarely deal with money after handing over their wages. His home-bound and shopping-centred occupation creates a potent mechanism that affects and directs the internal structure of the household economy, con-straining women's control over their own earnings.

(Re)making polarised identities: maids and madams

In Turkey, as elsewhere, waged domestic labour takes place at an important junction of gender and class inequality. Waged domestic labour is central to the processes of both the reproduction of class and the traditional gender division of labour. It constitutes a strategically useful arrangement for middle- and upper-class women to escape domestic work, and it provides a crucial strategy for women employers to avoid confronting the traditional gender division of labour within the household. Thus, it has been argued that one class of woman escapes some of the constraints of gender stratification by using the labour of women most severely limited by class, race and ethnicity-based inequalities (Rollins, 1985; Glenn, 1986; Romero, 1992). Women who buy other women's labour are criticised for not contesting the patriarchal gender division of labour, and thus perpetuating it (Hartmann, 1981).

In addition to allowing middle-class women's better participation in the public sphere by taking the burden of the second shift, domestic service creates a new class of women who perform the heaviest, most repetitive aspects of housework. Gregson and Lowe (1994, p.110) describe this process:

> ...household cleaning in middle-class households is no longer just a gender-segregated task...it is also being constructed as an occupation for working-class women. The corollary of this position is that in certain middle-class households cleaning is no longer being seen as a suitable use of middle-class women's time-space.

What is crucial about this process is that waged domestic labour plays a pivotal role in the creation of polarised middle-class and working-class versions of femininity.

Nevertheless, these generalisations miss the lived realities of workplace interrelations. Before focusing the discussion on the relationship between domestic workers and employers, it is first necessary to review broadly the changing structure of Turkish society that promotes the emergence of these polarised feminine identities, and domestic workers' diverse and often ambivalent responses to being cast as menial labourers, and their resistance to complete proletarianisation. These work to undermine some of the polarising tendencies.

The social transformations initiated with the transition from state-controlled capitalism to a privatised and liberalised market economy since the early 1980s have restructured women's relations to the home in ways that have altered their traditional ties to domesticity. The structural transformations most relevant to an examination of the relations between middle-class women and domestic workers include the development of the modern public sphere, the rise of new consumption forms, and changes in the education system (Özbay, 1995). This is not to say that old sources of identity, including mothering and housekeeping, have given way to radically new ones.[22] Attention to these changes is necessary to understand the divide between public and private, and the changing roles women play in the articulation of class distinctions and social mobility.

By the mid-1980s, the liberalised market economy, with its expansion of advertising, mass communications, consumer credit and commercial leisure, had cultivated an important change in Turkish urban classes' relationship to consumption, both quantitatively and qualitatively. Changes in consumption are dramatically altering the way in which middle-class women now use their labour and time. The emergence of new consumption sites – such as malls, mega-markets, shopping centres and department stores, which combine leisure and entertainment and shopping – represents an important example of how an expanding global market economy is changing women's activities outside the home while recasting definitions of female sociability. The immense increase in packaged foods available in Turkey, for instance, has led to a corresponding decrease in the amount of time women spend in the kitchen.[23] Women's activities increasingly take place outside the domestic sphere, marking the end of women's relative socio-spatial exclusion from urban public life.

Another equally important transformation taking place in modern Turkish society is the growing privatisation of education at all levels, with enduring effects on class stratification and middle-class social mobility. Fierce competition for entrance to the best schools demands parents' close attention to their children's curricular and extra-curricular activities (ballet and piano lessons, foreign-language and art classes). Parental oversight of education now includes identifying and securing a private tutor and/or finding the best prep schools, and has become a primary preoccupation for both housewives and their working counterparts.[24] All these activities take women away from home, expand the public sphere in which they perform motherhood, and put them into new relations of sociability and competition with their peers. It should be stressed here that these new roles entail new definitions of good, successful motherhood, while strengthening women's identity as autonomous actors in the public arena. Özbay (1995, p.109–10) summarises this point:

> The fact that women acquire identity through the family is more clearly defined with the expansion of capitalism. As women shoulder additional responsibilities connected with the social status of the family in 1980s Turkey, they appear to take over from men the capacity to act as family representative ... As women identify their social status with that of the family, the rise or fall in status of any member of the family confers new status on them, and gives the impression of social mobility. They consequently direct their activities toward increasing the status of the family, especially that of its male members.

There is another trend, however, which is potentially at odds with women's family-bound class identification: women engage in a very individualised process of self-construction in their focus on bodily health and beauty. The focus for women's consumption is no longer limited to family and class. A growing emphasis on cosmetics and beauty products, reinforced by the proliferation of magazines, advice literature and advertising, has increasingly changed the terms of the cultural constitution of female identity. The proliferation of private gyms (*jimnastik salonları*) and diet centres that cater mainly to women, especially housewives, also marks an increasing body-centredness. It signals the emergence of a new feminine self, more 'individualised', set apart from other family members. Middle-class women's investments in this domain are made possible, in large part, by the availability of domestic workers, who save them from physical labour. Moreover, these new cultural practices of femininity also play a key role in accentuating differences in appearance between 'traditional' women (domestic workers) and 'modern' women. Domestic workers, who are deprived of the means of participating in this individualised body-focused culture, do not, however, remain unaffected by it. As I will illustrate, middle-class women's investment in modern feminine identities powerfully affects their daily relationships. It is with such contexts in mind that we must view the emergence of new modes of femininity and new ways in which gender and class are articulated through domestic service. These changes speak to the rapid socioeconomic reconfiguration of Turkey and, in turn, the varied responses of individual actors to these changes.

First I would like to explore further the role played by waged domestic service in the construction of contrasting class-based femininities, by looking at the mode of employment in domestic service, an analysis of which reveals that the transformation of peasant women into 'working-class' women is by no means uncomplicated or complete. Although the unique arrangement of supply and demand structures facilitates a process of proletarianisation, domestic workers place themselves right between the two extreme, undesirable, ends of a continuum: traditional maids and proletarianised house cleaners. The majority of domestic workers in my study (91 percent) have multiple employers; only a small number of workers is tied to a single employer. Workers with multiple employers, however, are not a homogeneous group. I analysed the mode of employment of domestic workers by identifying more elaborate employment patterns. The configuration of three variables – number of works days worked per week, total number of employers, and number of repeated visits to the same employer in a week – showed that domestic workers are distributed along a continuum between 'specialists', who sell their labour for rigidly defined tasks, mostly heavy cleaning, and 'generalists' (traditional maids), who sell their labour time for loosely defined tasks. The majority of domestic workers are situated toward the 'specialist' end, among specialist positions the most objectively advantageous being that of multiple weekly visits to the same employer: it involves shorter hours, a lower work volume, better task variety and a greater chance of patronage[25] benefits. In contrast, complete specialisation, labouring in a different home every day, returning to the same workplace infrequently, brings greater control over the labour process, but involves performing the most dirty and physically exhausting labour repeatedly. This level of proletarianisation in domestic service confers a menial identity to workers, and fosters an image of physically strong and resilient women – reminiscent of their definition as peasant women. In different ways, domestic workers do not wish to embrace this peasant-like proletarianised imagery, while also equally rejecting a servant imagery associated with being tied to a single employer.

Needless to say, domestic workers' preferences among different modes of employment also have significant implications for different groups of middle-class women. By situating themselves right between the two undesirable extremes, they choose those employers who can afford their labour most frequently. This means that women in the lower echelons of the middle classes continue to make 'undesirable' employers, and remain in a position of competition with their upper-middle-class sisters.

Intimate weapons of the weak

Domestic workers' class subordination is grounded in a tense relationship between two women who are at once allies ('sisters') and antagonists. With a few exceptions historical and cross-cultural discussions of the relationship between employers and domestic workers assume that employers define both the identity of domestic workers and the nature of the relationship.[26] In these accounts, the woman employer is seen as an actor, but her domestic worker is conceptualised as a subordinated subject. In rare cases, she is described as a 'resisting' subordinate who deliberately brackets off her degraded work-related identity from her social life (Dill, 1988; Cock, 1980). These dominant analytical approaches view power as linked to relations involving domination and subordination between the two women as top-down and merely repressive. They begin with a rather simplified ('common-sense') notion of power as oppression, the exercise of which engenders and shapes resistance on the part of the oppressed. Because of the structural inequalities dictating the capacities of the domestic worker and of the employer to exercise control in their interaction, the employer is often assumed to be the active agent, possessing effective means of eliciting compliance with her commands. As Hansen (1989, p.11) notes, 'the difference results from the participants' unequal power, which enables the employer to issue commands more often than the servant can choose not to obey'. One need not deny this overall imbalance to argue that it fails fully to explain the complex interpersonal processes by which relations of work and class are produced. Against these views, I argue that this relationship must be examined within a framework that views domestic workers as active subjects who are nevertheless operating within a culturally and economically constituted structural inequality. I also argue that this negotiation is often not a question of 'resisting' a dominant mistress. The intimate relationship between the worker and the employer is one that is constructed reciprocally. The management of the relationship is a product of their interaction, and this interaction takes place against a highly structured background of community, patriarchy and the experience of gender identity and social class.

This perspective allows us to reveal the ways in which domestic workers are actors attempting to pursue their own interests rather than passive objects of their employer's power strategies. In order to realise or pursue their respective self-interests, which are often defined in opposition to each other (as sellers and buyers of labour), domestic workers and women employers engage in kinds of social interaction that involve acts of manipulation, compliance, manoeuvring and mutual accommodation. It is crucial, therefore, to understand the ways in which the self-interests of employers and workers are expressed, negotiated and contested between two women in the home workplace. What kinds of symbols and idioms are created, invoked and manipulated in the pursuit of self-interest? What kinds of skills and resources do the actors employ in the production of work relations as they conduct their mundane interactions? These are the questions I will attempt to answer in the following discussion.

The interactions between employers and the workers are organised and practiced as ways of dealing with potential conflicts and anxieties arising from the nature of domestic service. The structural sources of tension and conflict are many: how are the roles of employer and employee defined in the private sphere? How are perceived conflicts arising from the blatant disparity between the material conditions of life (registered in clothing, furniture etc) foreseen and managed?

How are the more universal conflicts that arise from this visible class relationship (buyer and seller of labour) managed in the context of the household? These problems are resolved by a few typical strategies. I call such strategies 'work' to register the fact that there is more work entailed by domestic service than cleaning and other contracted tasks. The term 'work' also underscores the fact that the interaction between these two categories of women is not limited to supervision of work by a non-working supervisor. Work strategies are practised by both the employer and the domestic worker. They can be conceptualised as strategies of management of the situation through the presentation of an image of oneself in the expectation of training the other party into a certain behavioural interaction (Goffmann, 1959). As we will see, when these strategies are successful the job gets done better, and potential identity problems are avoided or resolved. However, the very strategies of managing domestic service are prone to create their own tensions for the participants.

The rules and norms of domestic service are structured by the values and practices associated with family life, in which the home, as opposed to the work-place, is an arena for personal and private relationships. Thus, 'family' is the metaphor through which the labour relations are lived. Defining the workplace in the terms of the private sphere makes it difficult to demarcate the roles of 'employer' and 'employee'. This is exacerbated in cases where housewives are employers, and find themselves shifting uneasily between their two roles. There is no language in which the actors can articulate conflicts of interests or conceptualise their relations as purely relations of buyers and sellers of labour. The periodic appearance of a stranger is naturalised through the use of a familial or kinship idiom. Intimacy starts with form of address, when the employer, regardless of her age, becomes *abla* ('older sister') and the domestic worker automatically becomes *kardeş* ('younger sister') and is addressed by her first name.

Both workers and employers perceive the creation of intimacy as very important. For domestic workers, receiving good treatment is not just limited to the desire to 'be treated as a person' and 'not to be looked down on'. Good treatment includes 'social closeness' (*yakın olmak*) and connectedness, a realisation of the older sister/younger sister metaphor in practice. Intimacy also ensures domestic workers better patronage benefits. On the other hand, a desirable degree of 'intimacy' guarantees better work results for the employer, who gets work done as prescribed, gets tasks done that were not originally negotiated as part of the job description, and gets emergency help during holidays and other special occasions when she wants to change the schedule on short notice at the expense of the worker's other employers. On the part of the domestic worker, intimacy ensures better patronage benefits.

As we will see, this worker–employer intimacy is always strategic. By 'strategic', I want to suggest that such intimacy is a means of pursuing opposed interests rather than emotional relations. Intimacy is generally defined as substantial empathy for one another's joys, concerns and problems. It requires that two actors share more-or-less similar values and that they have sufficient common experiences to be able to understand each other's perspectives. Thus, by definition, intimacy entails some denial of difference. In domestic service it functions as a strategic device for covering up and making manageable some of the differences in status and class structuring the relationship.

Although domestic workers and their employers otherwise belong to radically different worlds, they draw upon their common, gender-based qualities as wives and mothers, and skills (as culturally recognised intimacy makers), and utilise patriarchal gender beliefs in their interaction as they negotiate the terms and conditions of the work arrangement. They utilise those aspects of women's experience that reflect their shared accommodation of the power of husbands. As I noted before, it is exclusively a woman's job to find, screen, recruit and manage a domestic worker. However, husbands, as the embodiment of patriarchal power, are invisible yet important actors in domestic work relations. While the two women do not necessarily share the same understanding of the patriarchal norm of female subordination, and experience them differently in various spheres of their lives, both parties allow, if not actively seek, mediation of supposedly shared patriarchal assumptions about women's subordinate position in the family and status in society in their interaction. This shared understanding and vocabulary, while playing an important role in reducing the sense of difference between the two groups of women and creating a sense of intimacy and even solidarity, nevertheless reinforces patriarchal definitions of women's identity. For example, when the domestic workers want to set a particular schedule (leaving early or coming late), or when they want to quit, they routinely invoke their husband's authority. This may or may not be an excuse, because husbands do have control over their work conditions. The point of exaggerating or making up the excuse of a husband's prohibition is to challenge or negotiate work arrangements. In so doing, however, they inevitably tie themselves more closely to their status as social inferiors vis-à-vis their men. Autonomy at work is thus gained at the price of naturalising patriarchal control by re-affirming it as an instrument of negotiation.

Employers may use the same tactic. They introduce their husbands into the relationship to avoid a prompt pay raise ('I can't ask him now; he's crabby these days ... let's wait until next month'), to get more work done, to get unscheduled help, to set extra visits during holiday periods, to set certain restrictions over the kinds of amenities the domestic worker is allowed to use (telephone etc), and to excuse themselves from helping out.

The structures underlying these episodes perhaps represent a more general set of mechanisms whereby subordinates invoke their own subordinate status while appearing to assert their discontent with their superiors. Both women refer to an immediately appreciated, pre-established and unquestionable pecking order in exchanges that can be summarised as follows: I would like to do what you ask (because we have a 'close relationship', 'we are sisters'), but this man, who regrettably has the ultimate say in my doings, does not let me. The employer women and the domestic workers collectively presume and invoke hierarchial circumstances in which both legitimately present themselves as lacking ultimate authority and being subject to the same type of patriarchal control.

Husbands are not, however, only 'symbolically' introduced. In some cases, patriarchal control has a more direct presence in the relationship. Some domestic workers' husbands actually oversee their wives' work arrangements and appropriate their income. Against such husbands, the employer and the worker consider themselves natural allies, trying to reduce the possibility of the appropriation of the worker's earnings. Employers sometimes do this by keeping a portion of the workers' wages in a savings account or by buying gold and keeping it for them. Sometimes, they pay extra money unbeknownst to the worker's husband. It is important to note that such extras are not regarded as a bonus, but part of the legitimate pay.

How are class inequalities between domestic workers and employers perceived and dealt with in their daily interactions? Domestic workers have direct knowledge and experience of their employer's social lives and consumption patterns. Employers believe, rightly, that domestic workers are well placed to observe the enormous difference between their own and their employer's lifestyles. They think that the domestic worker's observation of this disparity gives rise to class envy – by creating material and emotional resentment. In response, employers perform what I call 'class' work, the mending of what they perceive as 'injuries of class' (Sennett and Cobb, 1972). Feelings of 'class guilt' are, to a large degree, shrewdly elicited and sustained by domestic workers. A series of examples concerning the consumption of meat, which is an important cultural class marker, imbued with religious and folk significance, illustrates how this 'class work' is performed.

An employer reported the following incident. One day she had *börek* ('pie') with ground beef for lunch, and her worker made an appreciative remark. The employer offered her the recipe and told her how easy it is to make. Her worker responded by saying, 'I couldn't make it because we can't buy meat'. The employer woman encouraged her to use spinach or lentils instead of meat. Since the employer believed that domestic workers can only learn by example, two weeks later, despite her personal dislike of spinach, made a *börek* with spinach to show her maid how it could be as delicious without meat.

Another employer described a practice which she said she uses frequently. While she eats leftover food, she cooks a fresh meal, preferably with meat or chicken, for the worker to show that she's being treated well. The purpose of doing this, she explained, is also to show that 'we also eat left-overs'. Another employer said that after repeatedly hearing her domestic worker complain that she couldn't buy meat for her children, the employer told her, 'Look at us, we all have high cholesterol, meat is not good for your health'.

Employers believe that such strategies make their workers' lives more pleas- ant, reduce the contradictions that they believe their workers experience, and help make them content with their lives. This sentiment, often expressed among housewife employers, indicates that the domestic workers are quite successful in eliciting class guilt. One employer described how she sees the domestic workers' situation: 'They are caught between two worlds. They can't be in either of them.' Employers feel it is their responsibility to bridge this gap, or at least the perception of it. Employers thus perform valuable class work by teaching the poor to live within their wages, restricting the scope of their demands (or complaints) and narrowing their aspirations. One question here is whether this work is really meant to benefit the worker or to protect the employer. These tactics primarily seem to benefit employers, by reducing the intensity of what they perceive as the emotional exploitation inflicted by the workers. When domestic workers say, 'I can't buy meat for my children,' 'School has started, but my kid goes in shoes with holes,' or 'This meal is delicious but my children are eating bread and cheese now,' employers might be right to think that they are being emotionally manipulated.

The existence of friendship networks among employers also creates the means for manipulating their charitable behaviour. An important tactic utilised by domestic workers is to create competition among employers by pitting one against the other by talking about the favours bestowed by another employer: 'Employer X bought my children this and that; big sister Y contributed toward our house payment'.

I was present in a conversation in which one domestic worker told another that she took off one of her six golden bracelets before she went to work, because she planned to ask for an advance. That sixth bracelet was brand new, and she thought that her 'older sister' might notice the addition and be reluctant to give her the money. She takes the favours not as one who is dependent on her mistress's whimsical benevolence, but more like a savvy worker who elicits the favour by strategically managing the way she is perceived by her employer.

The following account by an employer is typical:

> She was working here yesterday. I called her around noon to tell her that there were a variety of fruits in the refrigerator, such as apples and plums that she should help herself to. She said, 'I have already eaten, Older Sister; I ate the cherries in the fridge'. She had eaten a full bowl containing about a kilogram of cherries. You know how expensive cherries are at this time of the year... they are about 7.000TL a kilogram (the equivalent of one third of a domestic worker's daily salary). She can't afford it herself. Even we can barely afford it. She is inconsiderate. They envy us; they are doing all this on purpose.
>
> She emptied a bottle of my expensive night cream, even though I provide vaseline for her hands. I also realised that she was using my perfume instead of the lemon-cologne I had offered her. I told her that is not a perfume, but a cleanser I use to take off my make-up [to avoid her using the expensive stuff]. She said, 'Oh, I thought it was cologne'.

Through these discourses and behaviours the domestic workers articulate and inflict class guilt. Employers 'do' their class work to cope with the guilt. Housewife employers experience this work as 'benevolence', or as a response to 'emotional exploitation', because they interact with the worker directly. Working employers, however, being away from home, are not subject to emotional exploitation. Instead, the domestic workers tend to get what they want by direct action rather than by cajoling the employer to 'give' it. Hence, housewife employers are burdened by guilt and blame themselves, while working women place the blame on the domestic worker.

Domestic workers' experience of class inequality on a daily, sustained basis nurtures attitudes among them that result in an affirmation of traditional feminine roles. Numerous times during my interviews and conversations with domestic workers they portrayed and judged middle-class employers by recounting episodes that demonstrate their own acute awareness of class injustice and the implications of the income gap between classes. Their narratives repeatedly illustrate ways in which their employers miserably failed to 'do' their gender appropriately. In domestic workers' accounts, employers' class privilege is conflated with a failure to perform properly the responsibilities of their gender as women. The following fragments from interviews with different domestic workers illustrate this articulation of class inequality with gender:

> I know how much she [the employer] spends on a bottle of nail polish: it's worth my daily salary.

> Well ... I don't know if you can call this woman [the employer] a woman. Can you call her a woman if she cannot wash her own underwear, and lets a stranger, like me, do it for her?

> They [employers] are so lazy. The other day, one of them was going away. She made me prepare her suitcase. She cannot even pack.

> They are so lax with their children ... they don't teach their kids the value of money. They buy expensive stuff for the kids and the kids abuse them. She [the employer] bought an expensive pair of trainers for her son the other day, and the next day the kid comes home with a torn trainer. She says nothing, doesn't punish the kid. The sneaker gets thrown away without a word.

> She [the employer] does not even cook a simple lunch; she orders kebabs. You know how costly they are ... sometimes more than what she pays me for a day's work.

Although domestic workers emulate the styles and tastes of middle-class women in their daily child-rearing and homemaking practices, it would be too simplistic to say that their self-definitions as women are entirely modelled on their urban middle-class employers. On the contrary, articulations of class inequality through the criticism of gender enables them to define their own identities against urban/middle-class femininity, and in the process they re-affirm the value of traditional femininity and their own moral superiority as women and mothers.

The contrived nature of the behaviour designed to over-rule the genuine differences and the unequal nature of the domestic service arrangement is best revealed when employers talk with the outside observer (although the researcher, as a middle-class woman, is also an 'insider') about their true, unbridgeable distance from their domestic workers. They believe that they are functioning as positive modernising agents for their domestic workers. The workers are expected to learn good housekeeping and modern values from them. However, when a domestic worker's emulations take the form of assertions of independence from her husband, or when she buys pretty houseware or luxury gadgets, it is perceived as transgressive. They are supposed to behave and consume within their means and 'know their place'. The employers firmly believe that the domestic workers are ultimately not like them, and should not pretend that they are, or aspire to be so. The pretention of a shared womanhood among the women of different classes is hence confined to the sphere of intimacy that the work relation requires.

It might seem plausible to conclude that both groups of women are victims of a patriarchal gender order that implicates both classes of women. Yet, if they are victims of this system of domination, they are not passive victims, because women do not simply accept patriarchy, or fight against it. Instead, they selectively utilise and negotiate patriarchal gender beliefs among themselves in numerous, less visible and rather equivocal ways in their day-to-day interactions with each other. Through such experiences, and from different positions within a patriarchal gender order, employers and domestic workers construct a language to discuss and negotiate the labour process and reconcile the diverse experiences of their lives. They connect to one another and seek to assert difference in their simultaneous efforts both to reinforce and alleviate the consequences of class inequalities and differences in class cultures.

Conclusion

This chapter, in a broader context, is concerned with women and men who have uprooted themselves from their original peasant communities to find better lives for themselves in urban centres, and with the close encounters that they have with urban classes through their work and services as maids and doorkeepers. The experiences of doorkeepers and maids capture some of the dimensions of cross-class relations and raise questions about the everyday lives and subjectivities of people situated in the new social arenas accompanying the rapid social trans-formations that have occurred in Turkey.

In the classificatory systems of the social sciences, these people are placed in a position of liminality, and are understood as if in transition or in the process of moving from one fixed status to another, and are therefore studied from the perspective of integration and assimilation into modern, urbanised structures and institutions of life. In a sense, the doorkeepers and their wives embody this idea of liminality in its fullest sense, especially in the way in which they are situated in the social landscape of Ankara. They are quite literally liminal, since a doorkeeper signifies being neither inside nor outside, but at the threshold. 'Door' symbolically captures the essence of the doorkeeper's condition. He stands in a marginal position, for he belongs entirely neither to the apart-ment block (as the tenants do) nor to the squatter settlements inhabited by their fellow migrants.

The layers of experience that are created by this encounter make apartment blocks special types of places with different meanings for their inhabitants: door-keepers and tenants. The meaning of living and working in such a space of liminality for doorkeepers and their families mean that this is a place of sub-servience, containment, incarceration and a painful stigmatisation, but also autonomy, merging with urban classes and distinct from other traditional migrants. Their very indefinability, their ability to blur class lines, invests them with powers that challenge the ordering of classes and peasant–urban divisions within the city.

I have argued that the polarity between modernity and tradition, the urban and the rural, is unable to accommodate the complexity of the cultural practices of doorkeeper families, situated within middle-class domestic life, and central to the very creation and maintenance of a middle-class cultural existence and identity. This urban middle-class existence, perhaps ironically, supports and depends on the continuation of traditional forms of conduct and authority relations among these new urbanities.

The experiences of doorkeepers and maids, who live and work in middle-class domestic environments where many of the constitutive elements and relationships of modern domestic life are generated, and where sensibilities, habits and mentalities associated with modern identities are disclosed, embody the complex interaction between the traditional and the modern. It is simplistic to suggest the existence of an unmediated transfer of values and practices, or an uncritical appropriation, as a result of this encounter. Yet I do not mean that doorkeepers and their families never emulate middle-class styles and tastes. They do try to acquire the commoditised markers of urban status and modern style within the context of their limited access to the desired goods. Almost every migrant household I visited had a set of cups and saucers for 'Nescafé', which was rarely drunk but signifies urban sophistication. They bake chocolate cakes rather than plain ones, because plain cakes have a rural, unprestigious identity. Cubed sugar, rather than the less expensive loose variety, signifies urban, modern refinement, and is prized accordingly. They display sensibilities of modern parenthood: it is imperative that they, as parents – like their urban, educated counterparts – should accompany their children to the university entrance examination and wait outside for the duration of the exam, because this type of psychological support is important to their children's success. These are just a few examples of categorical investment in modernity. Like commodities and cultural practices, identities and characters are understood and judged in terms of the traditional–modern opposition. Women attribute men's prohibition of them working, as well as other restrictions on physical mobility and social activity, to their husband's peasant backwardness, inability to overcome the constraints of tradition, and failure to modernise. In these women's discourse, there is no generalised or universal 'men' or 'husbands'. They refer instead to 'our men' and 'our husbands', conceptualised in opposition to imagined modern men. The terms in which they evaluate male behaviour and conduct when discussing the division of labour at home, marital love or wife-beating reflect this symbolic opposition of peasant and modern masculinity.

Thus, the real importance of this encounter lies elsewhere: it entails development of a particular self-reflexivity in which the conduct and feelings of the self are continuously assessed for their modernity and urbanness. It is a mode of being that involves a continuous monitoring of one's own conduct, feelings, behaviour and action in relation to the distinction between the modern and the traditional. Seemingly trivial aspects of everyday life are invested with this anxiety. They reinscribe the binary opposition even as they change its very form.

Exploring the specifics of tradition and modernity – how they are deployed pragmatically and as ideological values – allows us to understand how the negotiated response generated by this encounter deliberately offers visions, experiences and social practices that are neither modern nor traditional, leaving the significance of this distinction undisturbed. The centrality of this dualism in people's understanding poses a serious challenge to theoretical attempts to abandon the opposition. Failure to acknowledge the tradition–modernity binary in interpretation or analysis risks misconstruction of the terms most central to the self-understanding and world-view of its subjects.

Notes on Chapter 2

1   For some theoretical and empirically-grounded discussions, see Mary Beth Mills (1997), Ong (1988), Thompson (1996), Luke (1996), Adam (1996), Abu-Lughod (1998).

2   Lila Abu-Lughod suggests that the most powerful way of dismantling binary oppositions between modernity and tradition, the West and the East, is '... to fearlessly examine the processes of entanglement' (1998, p.16). The essays in *Remaking Women* she edited offer rich explorations of the ways in which various projects of modernity in the Middle East were fashioned in complex encounters between the colonising Europe and the colonised Middle East. Their examination of the local cultural dynamics show the complex ways in which ideas and practices considered 'modern', 'European' and progressive were selectively utilised and renegotiated.

3   A term coined by John Van Maanen to define a type of ethnographic analysis that is 'strategically situated to shed light on larger social, political, symbolic or economic issues' (Van Maanen, 1988, p.127).

4   I use the term 'tenant' in this article for the sake of convenience. With this term I refer to middle- and upper-middle-class residents of an apartment block, regardless of their real status as owners or tenants, to whom a doorkeeper provides services. The gender of the 'tenant' is female in a double sense: first, women are the chief clients of doorkeepers, from whom the doorkeeper takes 'orders'; and second, they are the employers of doorkeepers' wives as domestic workers.

5   The average family income of the highest income group residing at the core was six-and-a-half times that of the lowest income groups living in squatter settlements (Türel, 1987, p.164).

6   The closest approximation for this job title in the North American context is 'janitor' or 'super', or 'concierge' in France, though neither fully describes the Turkish doorkeepers' work and occupational identity. For a study of janitors in the US context during the 1950s, see Ray Gold (1952).

7   Bread is the main component of diet in Turkey.

8   Only 23 percent of domestic workers – 24 cases out of 103 – have no in-house employers. These domestic workers work for employers in surrounding neighbourhoods.

9   Known as the 'Flat Law' (Keleş, 1985; Çulpan, 1979).

10   It is well documented that migrant families in Turkey tend to establish neighbourhoods in squatter settlement areas which are highly homogeneous in terms of family kin, village and town of origin (Duben, 1982). Sencer Ayata (1988) explores the meanings given to living in an apartment block among a group of Ankara residents who recently moved to there from squatter settlements. His

analysis reveals that these two types of accommodation are defined in opposition to each other by these 'new' tenants; while the squatter settlement embodies negative values attached to the rural and traditional, the apartment block represents modernity and modern values. From the perspective of the doorkeeper families I studied, apartment block residency is inextricably linked with occupation, and therefore the meaning of being a resident there is quite different, especially since the definition of 'tenant' includes having access to a building doorkeeper.

11   I am borrowing this notion from Collins (1991), who uses it to describe the marginal status of black intellectuals in academic settings. She argues that by making creative use of their marginality, these 'outsiders within' produce distinctive knowledge.

12   About 18 percent live in apartments with single room; 11 percent live in apartments that have more than two rooms. The average household size is 4.3.

13   The sample of the doorkeeper group was drawn equally from middle- and upper-middle class districts of Ankara. I was expecting that serving these two different classes would create different housing conditions and thus a hierarchy within doorkeepers. Surprisingly, there was no correspondence between the level of luxury of apartment blocks in which doorkeepers work and the conditions and size of apartments they are given in the basement of the same buildings. Sub-standard housing conditions are the norm rather than exception, regardless of the class location of the building.

14   Here I assume that the middle class, especially those of more recent provincial origin, maintains much greater control, or is more concerned, than the upper class over the informal contact between their children and those of doorkeeper families, for the reasons mentioned above. Another reason for relative upper-class lack of concern is the fact that the daily lives of upper-class children rarely cross with those of doorkeeper children. For instance, upper-class children are more likely to go to private schools, and possess sub-cultural markers that the doorkeeper children cannot afford. Although I do not have distributional data to make this generalisation, the inference seems warranted by comments such as, 'The ones who treat us as their inferiors are the ignorant ones,' and, 'We get this kind of treatment only from those who do not know their place'. Another interpretation is equally plausible: perhaps the wife of the doorkeeper receives the same kind of treatment from upper-class tenants, but feels more embittered and resentful toward middle-class tenants, since the income–status difference between them is less pronounced, and therefore that middle-class tenants have less right to treat them as social inferiors. Yet, when controlled for variables such as middle- versus upper-class neighbourhoods and the length of the service, no significant differences emerged between those who expressed experience of stigmatisation and those who did not. This further suggests the pervasiveness of the stigma attached to doorkeeper families. Also, see Ayata and Ayata (1996, p.125) who argue that the desire not to 'mix' is stronger among the middle classes who achieved this status only recently.

15   I think we can also talk about a sense of future-oriented fear of 'mixing' from the perspective of the middle classes. It is worth noting that compared with other migrant families who live in squatter settlements, children of doorkeeper families

are more likely to achieve inter-generational mobility. Doorkeepers' children
have higher educational attainment and lower drop-out rates than children of
squatter-settlement families in my sample.

16   See Davidoff (1974 and 1976) for a thorough analysis of the operation of a whole
symbolic system based on the divisions between dirt and cleanliness through
which distinctions based on class and gender were elaborated throughout the
nineteenth century in England.

17   During my study in 1990, the city-wide conversion of the heating systems of
apartment-buildings in Ankara (a city notorious for high air pollution) to natural
gas was taking place. By eliminating the dirtiest tasks from the doorkeeper's
role, this technological change will have shifted the occupation's focus towards
more personal services. But I think it is unlikely that this conversion would
produce any drastic changes in the way in which doorkeeper families are seen as
carriers of pollution as long as it remains a residentially based occupation and
doorkeeper families are uneasily incorporated into middle-class environments.
Another important consideration for possible future changes in the structure
of doorkeeping is the intensification of suburbanisation since early 1990s.
Suburbanisation in Turkey is taking forms that are quite dissimilar to the process in
the US. In Ankara, for instance, the suburbs are comprised of high-rise apartment
buildings, single-family homes with fences and backyards, and upper-class villa-
type developments. Some of them contain doorkeeper quarters and incorporate
a doorkeeper and his family. Others have been designed to avoid the need for
a doorkeeper by the inclusion of garbage chutes and the use of professional
uniformed cleaners, gardeners and uniformed guards to keep out undesirable,
polluting elements. New suburbanites in Ayata's study (this volume) explain
their relocation to the suburbs as a desire to be with their own kind. This quest
to create homogeneous communities, they explain, derive from their frustration
with 'social pollution', 'crowdedness' and 'mixing of classes' that have permeated
the city neighbourhoods, streets and public places.

18   About half of the domestic workers in my squatter-settlement sample had taken
up employment in domestic service when their husbands had been employed as
doorkeepers. In addition, a recent representative survey (Çınar, 1991) conducted
among subcontracted female homeworkers in the squatter settlement neighbourhoods of Istanbul found that the majority of respondents (40 percent) cited
employment in domestic service as being not only the most desired job but also
the most feasible (45 percent). Yet it was found that the main reason for not working
outside the home is the withholding of the husband's permission (55 percent).

19   The organisation of domestic service with multiple employers means greater
flexibility in the choosing suitable employers, and the effect of losing an employer
deemed undesirable by the husband is financially inconsequential in the long run.

20   Conceiving of gender as an ongoing task poses the question of what is produced
through household work and childcare (Berk, 1985; West and Zimmerman,
1987). Berk writes, 'At least metaphorically, the division of household labour
facilitates two production processes: the production of goods and services and
what we might call the production of gender. Simultaneously, household members
"do" gender, as they "do" housework and childcare' (Berk, 1985, p.199).

21   On the other hand, the doorkeepers criticise the squatter group for letting their
     children grow up in a disorderly environment with bad influences.
22   For instance, only 16.2 percent of the urban female population in metropolitan
     areas was employed in 1994 (State Institute of Statistics, 1995, p.12).
23   *Mantı* (dumplings with meat filling), a traditional dish requiring a good half-
     day's work and a lot of socialising among female relatives to prepare, are now
     sold in the take-out section ready for cooking.
24   All these developments mark the end of traditional attitudes of middle-class parents
     to the schooling of children embodied in a Turkish saying, 'the flesh belongs to
     you, the bones to me' (*eti senin kemiği benim*), which expresses the complete trust
     placed in teachers as the representative of the paternalistic Turkish state in
     moulding, disciplining, and creating productive citizens of the Turkish republic.
25   The concept of patronage appropriately characterises certain significant aspects
     of the interaction between the employer and the domestic worker. In about one
     third of the cases, relations with employers entailed some degree of patronage.
     It varied by the kinds of benefit (or favours) received, and could include help in
     placing family members and significant others in urban jobs, interest-free loans
     in the form of advances, aid in children's education, and the gifting of discarded
     or brand new items. For an extensive discussion of this issue, see Ozyegin (1996).
26   For exceptions, see Hansen (1989) and Lasser (1987).

References

Abu-Lughod, Lila (ed.) (1998), *Remaking Women: Feminism and Modernity in the Middle
     East*, Princeton University Press, Princeton, NJ
Adam, Barbara (1996), 'Detraditionalization and the Certainty of Uncertain Futures',
     in Paul Heelas, Scott Lash and Paul Morris (eds), *Detraditionalization: Critical
     Reflections on Authority and Identity*, Blackwell, MA
Ayata, Ayşe (1989), 'Gecekondularda Kimlik Sorunu, Dayanışma Örüntüleri
     ve Hemşehrilik', Turkiye II, Sosyal Bilimler Kongresine Sunulan Tebliğ,
     ODTÜ, Ankara
Ayata, Sencer (1988), 'Toplumsal Çevre Olarak Gecekondu ve Apartman,' *Toplum ve
     Bilim*, 42, Summer
Ayata, Sencer and Ayşe Ayata (1996), 'Konut, Komşuluk ve Kent Kültürü' ('Housing,
     neighbourliness and urban culture'), *Housing Research Series* 10, Ankara: T.C.
     Prime Ministry, Housing Development Administration
Berk, Sarah Fenstermaker (1985), *The Gender Factory*, Plenum Press, New York, NY
Berik, Günseli (1987), *Women Carpet Weavers in Turkey: Patterns of Employment, Earnings
     and Status*, International Labour Office, Geneva
Bozdoğan, Sibel and Reşat Kasaba (1997), 'Introduction', in Sibel Bozdoğan and
     Reşat Kasaba (eds), *Rethinking Modernity and National Identity in Turkey*, University
     of Washington Press, Seattle, WA
Bozdoğan, Sibel (1997), 'The predicament of modernism in Turkish architectural
     culture: an overview', in Sibel Bozdoğan and Reşat Kasaba (eds), *Rethinking
     Modernity and National Identity in Turkey*, University of Washington Press, Seattle, WA

Chaney, Elsa M. and Mary Garcia Castro (eds) (1989), *Muchachas No More*, Temple University Press, Philadelphia, PA

Çınar, Mine (1991), *Labor Opportunities for Adult Females and Home-Working Women in İstanbul, Turkey*, the G.E. von Grunebaum Center for Near Eastern Studies, University of California, Los Angeles, CA, Working Paper no 2

Cock, Jacklyn (1980), *Maids and Madams: A Study in the Politics of Exploitation*, Raven Press, Johannesburg

Colen, Shellee (1986), '"With respect and feelings": voices of West Indian child care and domestic workers in New York city', in Johnetta Cole (ed.), *All American Women: Lines That Divide, Ties That Bind*, Free Press, New York, NY

Collins, Patricia Hill (1991), 'Learning from the outsider within: the sociological significance of black feminist thought', in Mary Fonow and Judith A. Cook (eds), *Beyond Methodology*, Indiana University Press, Bloomington and Indianapolis, IN

Çulpan, Oya (1979), 'Kent Yaşamında Bir İşlev Türü: Kapıcılık' ('A type of function in urban life: caretaking'), unpublished associate professorship thesis, T.C. Hacettepe Universitesi, Sosyal ve Idari İlimler Fakültesi, Ankara

Davidoff, Leonore (1974), 'Mastered for life: servant and wife in Victorian and Edwardian England', *Journal of Social History* 7, no 4, p.406–28

– (1976), 'The Rationalization of Housework', in Barker and Allen (eds), *Dependence and Exploitation in Work and Marriage*, Longman, London

Dill, Thornton B. (1988), 'Making your job good to yourself: domestic service and the construction of personal dignity', in Ann Bookman and Sandra Morgen (eds), *The Politics of Empowerment*, Temple University Press, Philadelphia, PA

Douglas, Mary (1989), *Purity and Danger: An Analysis of the Concepts of Pollution and Taboo*, Ark Paperbacks, London and New York

Duarte, Isis (1989), 'A question for the feminist movement: household workers in the Dominican Republic', in Elsa Chaney and Mary Castro (eds), *Muchachas No More*, Temple University Press, Philadelphia, PA

Duben, Alan (1982), 'The significance of family and kinship in urban Turkey', in Çiğdem Kağıtçıbaşı (ed.), *Sex Roles, Family and Community in Turkey*, Indiana University Press, Bloomington, IN

Ehrenreich, Barbara (1989), *Fear of Falling: The Inner Life of the Middle Class*, Pantheon Books, New York, NY

Fenstermaker, Sarah, Candace West and Don H. Zimmerman (1991), 'Gender inequality: new conceptual terrain', in Rae Lesser Blumberg (ed.), *Gender, Family, and Economy: The Triple Overlap*, Sage, Newbury Park

Glenn, Nakano Evelyn (1986), *Issei, Nissei, Warbride: Three Generations of Japanese American Women in Domestic Service*, Temple University Press, Philadelphia, PA

Goffman, Erwing (1959), *The Presentation of Self in Everyday Life*, Doubleday Anchor Books, New York, NY

– (1963), *Stigma: Notes on the Management of Spoiled Identity*, Prentice-Hall, Englewood Cliffs

Gold, Ray (1952), 'Janitors vs tenants: a status-income dilemma', *American Journal of Sociology* LVII, pp.487–93

Gregson, Nicky and Michelle Lowe (1994), *Servicing the Middle Classes*, Routledge, New York, NY

Hansen, Karen Tranberg (1989), *Distant Companions*, Cornell University Press, Ithaca, NY, and London

Hartmann, Heidi (1981), 'The family as the locus of gender, class, and political struggle: the example of housework', *Signs* 6, no 3

Hochschild, Arlie R. (1983), *The Managed Heart*, University of California Press, Berkeley, CA

Jelin, Elizabeth (1977). 'Migration and labor force participation in Latin American women: the domestic servants in the cities', *Signs* 3, no 1, 129–41

Kandiyoti, Deniz (1997), 'Gendering the modern: on missing dimensions in the study of Turkish modernity', in Sibel Bozdoğan and Reşat Kasaba (eds), *Rethinking Modernity and National Identity in Turkey*, University of Washington Press, Seattle, WA

— (1990), 'Rural transformation in Turkey and its implications for women's status', in Ferhunde Özbay (ed.), *Women, Family and Social Change in Turkey*, Unesco

Katzman, David (1978), *Seven Days a Week: Women and Domestic Service in Industrializing America*, Oxford University Press, New York, NY

Keleş, Ruşen and Michael N. Danielson (1985), *The Politics of Rapid Urbanization*, HM, New York, NY

Kuznesof, Elizabeth (1989), 'A history of domestic service in Spanish America, 1492–1980', in Elsa M. Chaney and Mary Garcia Castro (eds), *Muchachas No More*, Temple University Press, Philadelphia, PA

Lasser, Carol (1987), 'The domestic balance of power: relations between mistress and maid in nineteenth-century New England', *Labor History* 28, pp.5–22

Luke, Timothy W. (1996), 'Identity, meaning and globalization: detraditionalization in postmodern space-time compression', in Paul Heelas, Scott Lash and Paul Morris (eds), *Detraditionalization*, Blackwell, MA

Maanen Van, John (1988), *Tales of the Field: On Writing Ethnography*, University of Chicago Press, Chicago, IL

Mardin, Şerif (1997), 'Projects as methodology: some thoughts on modern Turkish social science', in Sibel Bozdoğan and Reşat Kasaba (eds), *Rethinking Modernity and National Identity in Turkey*, University of Washington Press, Seattle, WA

Migdal, Joel S. (1997), 'Finding the meeting ground of fact and fiction: some reflections on Turkish modernization', in Sibel Bozdoğan and Reşat Kasaba (eds), *Rethinking Modernity and National Identity in Turkey*, University of Washington Press, Seattle, WA

Mills, Mary B. (1997), 'Contesting the margins of modernity: women, migration, and Consumption in Thailand', *American Ethnologists* 24, no 1, pp.37–61

Oakley, Ann (1974), *The Sociology of Housework*, Pantheon Books, New York, NY

Ong, Aihwa (1988), 'Colonialism and modernity: feminist representations of women in non-Western societies', *Inscriptions* 3, no 4

Özbay, Ferhunde (1995), 'Changes in women's occupation inside and outside the home,' in Şirin Tekeli (ed.), *Women in Modern Turkish Society*, Zed Books, London

Özyeğin, Gül (1996), 'Verwandtschaftsnetzwerke, Patronage und Klassenschuld Das Verhaltnis von Hausangestellten und ihren Arbeitgeberinnen in der Turkei', ('Kin networks, patronage and class guilt: employer-employee relationships in domestic service in Turkey), *Frauen In Der Einen Wel* 2, pp.9–28

Rollins, Judith (1985), *Between Women: Domestics and Their Employers*, Temple University Press, Philadelphia, PA

Romero, Mary (1992), *Maid in the USA*, Routledge, New York, NY, and London

Ruiz, Vicki L. (1987), 'By the day or week: Mexicana domestic workers in El Paso', in Carol Groneman and Mary B. Norton (eds), *To Toil the Livelong Day*, Cornell University Press, Ithaca, NY

Sanjek, Roger and Colen Shellee (eds) (1990), *At Work in Homes: Household Workers in World Perspective*, American Ethnological Society Monograph Series no 3

Sennett Richard and Jonathon Cobb (1972), *The Hidden Injuries of Class*, Knopf, New York, NY

Scott, James (1985), *Weapons of the Weak: Everyday Forms of Peasant Resistance*, Yale University Press, New Haven, CT

Şenyapılı, Tansı (1981), 'A new component in metropolitan areas: gecekondu women', in Nermin Abadan Unat (ed.), *Women in Turkish Society*, E.J. Brill, Leiden

— (1982), 'Economic change and the gecekondu family', in Çiğdem Kağıtçıbaşı (ed.), *Sex Roles, Family and Community in Turkey*, Indiana University Turkish Studies, IN

Sirman, Nüket (1988), 'Peasants and family farms: the position of households in cotton production in a village of Western Turkey', unpublished PhD thesis, University of London

— (1995), 'Friend and foe? Forging alliances with other women in a village of Western Turkey', in Şirin Tekeli (ed.), *Women in Modern Turkish Society*, Zed, London

State Institute of Statistics (1995), *Women in Statistics: Turkey 1985*, Unicef, Turkey

Tekeli, İlhan (1984), 'Ankara'nin Başkentlik Kararının Ülkesel Mekan Organizasyonu ve Toplumsal Yapıya Etkileri Bakımından Genel bir Değerlendirmesi', *Tarih İçinde Ankara*, Mimarlik Fakültesi, ODTÜ, Ankara

Thompson, John B. (1996), 'Tradition and self in a mediated world', in Paul Heelas, Scott Lash and Paul Morris (eds), *Detraditionalization*, Blackwell, MA

Türel, Ali (1987), 'Ankara Kent Formunda Konut Alanlarının Gelir Gruplarına Göre Farklılaşması', in ODTÜ Şehir ve Bölge Planlama Bölümü Çalışma Grubu, *Ankara 1985'den 2015'e*, Ajans Iletim, Ankara

West, Candace and Don H. Zimmerman (1987), 'Doing gender', *Gender and Society* 1, no 2, pp.125–51

3

Encounters at the Counter: Gender and the Shopping Experience

Ayşe Durakbaşa and Dilek Cindoğlu

This chapter traces the feminisation of shopping in parallel with the rapid pro-liferation of shopping malls in Turkey since the 1980s. The masculine world of the traditional bazaar *(charshi)* has been gradually transformed with the emergence of the high-street department store since turn-of-the-century Ottoman modernisation. New shopping districts and promenades developed in the main cities of Turkey, especially after the 1960s, and shopping visits and window shopping became part of mainly middle-class housewives' routines. Gradually women's control over the household budget and consumption has increased in urban centres, because of the changing roles and tasks related to children and homemaking. One main focus is the inter-relationship between the change in the homemaking activities of women of the new middle classes and the rise of malls. We also describe how shoppers from different class backgrounds benefit from a web of shopping venues, ranging from the neighbourhood grocer, to open marketplaces, to malls and hypermarkets.

The malls and entertainment centres that have become centres of urban life and culture recently mark the development and accentuation of a distinctive taste among the upper classes and an increased socialisation in urban culture, especially among the youth of the lower classes.

The social atmosphere in these malls reflects both the fluidity of a post-modern consumption culture and the structural inequalities of class and gender. We describe the various dramas enacted between shoppers, shop assistants and shop managers, parallel with the changes in the organisation of the shop as a social setting. Hence the last section of the chapter looks at the work conditions of sales personnel as important actors in the shopping scene vis-à-vis shoppers.

The rise of malls in urban Turkey

In the 1980s, the process of economic liberalisation in Turkey led to a shift in pre-vious policies of protectionist import substitution to a new development strategy based on the promotion of domestic export industries, and the encouragement of foreign investment. This has led Turkey to open up to the world socio-culturally as well as economically. Alongside these changes there has been a shift from scarcity to abundance in goods and services.

In the last decade, big cities witnessed the emergence of new malls and superstores, such as Ataköy Galleria (Istanbul, in 1988), Atakule (Ankara, in 1989), Karum (Ankara, in 1991), Metro (Ankara, in 1990), Kipa (Izmir, in 1994), Carrefour (Istanbul, in 1993), Carrousel (Istanbul, in 1995), Akmerkez (Istanbul, in 1995), Outlet Centre (Izmit, in 1997), Bauhaus (Istanbul, in 1996). These are ultra-modern buildings developed either in the heart of upper-middle-class neighbourhoods or on the outskirts of the city, which can be only reached by car. In both cases, these multi-storey constructions are welcoming yet intimidating to visitors, not only with expensive shops but also with luxurious interiors. The shining spotless marble floors contrast with the habitually dusty and muddy streets of Turkey. Most of the time these malls have food courts occupied by Western food chains, such as McDonalds and Burger King, along with Turkish döner kebab or sweet shops, where visitors can enjoy familiar food in a non-familiar setting.

An overview of the increasing activity of international retailers in Turkey, starting from the late 1980s, suggests that Turkey became a desirable target for multinationals as a result of the new development strategy and its positive effects on the growth rate and per-capita income. Between 1985 and 1993, GNP per capita increased in real terms at an average annual rate of 3 percent. Turkey's demographic characteristics also made it favourable, especially for international food retailers. According to the latest census, Turkey has a population of more than 62 million, with an annual population increase rate of 2.2 percent. The population is young, especially compared with the ageing population in Europe (more than 60 percent of the population being below thirty years of age) (Tokatli and Boyaci, 1997, p.104). There is a high rate of urbanisation and an increasing concentration of the population in the main cities, such as Istanbul, Ankara, Izmir, Adana and Bursa.[1] On the other hand, income distribution is skewed, giving some segments of the population great purchasing power. The richest 20 percent of the population takes more than half of the GNP, and is concentrated in the major cities.[2]

In 1990, 74.26 percent of Istanbul inhabitants, 70 percent of Ankara inhabitants and 60 percent of Izmir inhabitants had a stable income, whereas the proportion is 38.4 percent in Turkey as a whole. So there is a large group with considerable purchasing power who constitute the clientele of the new shopping sites (Sönmez,1996, pp.126–7). Thirty of Turkey's 52 hypermarkets are concentrated in Istanbul, and it is estimated that they cover 25 percent of the retail trade in Turkey and 50 percent of retail trade in Istanbul. The market is still unsaturated, and many foreign and domestic companies are planning to enter it (Sönmez, 1997). Visible material affluence exists alongside high population growth, rapid urbanisation, high inflation, unemployment, unequal income distribution and huge disparities between urban and rural life. Figures show that consumption has increased tremendously.[3]

In a cross-cultural study of materialism carried out by Ger and Belk (1990), it has been argued that individual-oriented materialism can go together with collectivist cultural orientation. Ger suggests that this explains especially the behaviour of Turkish female shoppers (p.189): 'If materialism is linked to enhancing the material well being of, and consumption for a unit, that unit may be a single individual in some cultures, several individuals (close friends and family members) in other cultures' (p.190). There is a noticeable shift in consumption culture towards the materialistic, enhanced by incentives such as credit cards[4] and the onslaught of images in advertising, as well as change in the consumption patterns of urban households, with women of all classes becoming more involved in handling the family budget. Women of all classes use a variety of outlets for shopping, especially for the needs of the family, and develop new skills to benefit from what each has to offer. The shopping scene is rich, with the outlet and its practices differing according to the type of goods sold, and with wide variety in outlet design and in the drama of the act of buying and selling.

From the *charshi* to the mall

The first observation about shopping in Turkey is the influence of a sex-segregated culture on shopping practices. The *charshi* – an element of the architectural planning of Ottoman town centres, composed of small shops directed by guild associations – is predominantly a male domain in which sellers and buyers are mostly men. The entry of women into this public domain as shoppers is a relatively recent phenomenon, and has been monitored by the family and the community quite closely. Women, as buyers, had very limited access to *charshi*, and would mostly have been accompanied by men, children or servants. The remnants of this practice are still prevalent in the provincial towns where the market continues to be a male-dominated space. Itinerant peddlers sometimes brought goods to the doorsteps of women customers. The *bohçacı*, or women pedlars, who visited house-wives with bundles of embroidery, linen, garments and clothing – a practice that used to be considered a handy way of preparing the *çeyiz*, or trousseau, for young girls – was one of the main personages of the traditional *mahalle* (neighbourhood).

One can also draw a parallel between the lifestyle and cultural outlook of the *charshi esnafı* – the group culture of the small merchants and artisans – and the religious setting of the *charshi* itself (Sayılı, 1992, p.16):

> The relationship between the bazaar and the mosque in the construction of the Turkish cities cannot be overlooked. The overlap between work hours and prayer times made it necessary for the mosques to be built around the bazaar.

Işın (1985, p.541) lists three structuring elements in the traditional Ottoman life space: the *mahalle*, the *charshi* and the *cami* (the mosque or other religious buildings) and private housing areas. The *charshi* was the centre of commercial activities as well as the administrative offices of the *esnaf*, the tradesmen who manipulated a commercial network that extended beyond the borders of the empire. The consumption norms were defined by religious values until the nineteenth century, when this structure was challenged by imported Western goods which became symbols of social status (Işın, 1985. p.545).

In the nineteenth century, parallel to the changes in the economic life and greater integration with Europe, specialised bazaars and traditional occupations lost their symbolic significance, and consumption norms and practices changed. Consumption patterns, previously homogeneous, shared by rich and poor in the classical Ottoman *mahalle*, proliferated according to the tastes of different social strata and status groups. The upper classes wanted to acquire the aesthetic objects (such as pianos and Western furniture) imported into Istanbul as signs of their social superiority over bureaucrats and other classes in the phase of modernisation (Işın, 1985, p.553).

In the second half of the nineteenth century a number of European retailers – such as Louvre, Au Lion, Bon Marché, Au Camelia, Bazar Allemand, Carlmann et Blumberg, Orosdi Back, Au Paon and Baker – opened department stores in the Ottoman capital and some other major cities of the empire. One of these grand, rich shops, Bon Marché, situated in Pera (the European district of Istanbul) became a standardised name for all similar shops catering to the needs and tastes of a rising Ottoman bourgeoisie (Toprak, 1995, p.27). Bon Marchés became part of late-nineteenth-century Ottoman daily life, as places where the upper classes had access to the Western goods in Galata and Pera. Many novels set in that period mention shopping trips of upper-class Ottoman women to Pera as a planned and special activity for the womenfolk of *konak* (mansion) households. Bon Marchés brought a new experience to shopping, in which the goods were sold not only for their utility but also to cater for the aesthetic needs of customers, starting with shop-window presentation. Consequently, window shopping and strolling in the streets became a pastime and leisure activity in late-nineteenth-century Istanbul. Whereas the traditional *mahalle* lost its homogeneity in living standards and lifestyles, the Beyoğlu and Pera districts emerged as centres of affluence in which an opulent lifestyle was on offer (Işın, 1985, pp.552–3). The split between Europeanised Pera, where the non-Muslim minorities were concentrated, and the Muslim neighbourhoods of the old city became sharper. One could observe the beginnings of the socioeconomic stratification of neighbourhoods in the years before and after the First World War. As Duben and Behar (1991, p.31) comment,

> During the Young Turk period, a small number of wealthy, modern-minded Muslim families began to leave the traditional enclaves of those of their faith in intramural Istanbul for 'apartment life' (*apartman hayatı*), in the new neigh-bourhoods of Nişantaşı and Şişli, which lay north of traditional non-Muslim Pera. This flow continued through the war years and into the 1920s and 1930s. The war years were in many respects a watershed for segments of the old elite.

New habits of consumption, Bon Marché shopping trips, and westernised lifestyles accompanied the growth of a new upper class, an Ottoman bourgeoisie. The early examples of pedestrian arcades, usually called *pasaj* (from the French *passage*) – built in the form of arcades in Pera and later in Şişli-Nişantaşı, and in Kadıköy-Bahariye and Bağdat Caddesi on the Asian shore – were the first venues for window shopping for middle- and upper-class women in Istanbul in the mid-twentieth century.

Compared to strolling in the mall of today, 'window shopping' in arcades was less welcoming and accessible, in that the pedestrian onlookers were not expected to touch goods unless they intended to buy them. Many conflicts arose between sales assistants and potential buyers when the latter handled goods. Even today, in city centres pedestrianised for commercial and cultural purposes the class characteristics of customers are likely to be more homogeneous than in malls. However, women are to be found as shoppers in both. In opposition to the *charshi*, where women were almost always excluded, the open-air markets had more space for women, both as buyers and sellers. Village women, as sellers of their own produce, always had a place in provincial peasant markets. The presence of women as vendors in the periodic open markets in urban centres is, however, a more recent phenomenon.

The culture of consumption in contemporary Turkey: the web of shopping practices

Urban life and culture in the 1990s were marked by the building of malls and entertainment centres in the big cities, and these sites have provided a social space for the development and accentuation of a distinct taste. Nevertheless, shopping is not a uniform experience, even for the upper classes. On the contrary, many different types of shopping outlet co-exist, and each offers a different set of advantages.

Malls – such as Akmerkez, Atakule, Karum and Capitol – are a relatively recent phenomenon in Turkey. In Akmerkez, awarded a prize for the most modern mall in Europe, a vast variety of tastes co-exist. For example, Burger King is next to more traditional Turkish fast food, such as döner kebab or *sultanahmet köftecisi*, and chocolate muffins and doughnuts are sold next to the Saray *muhallebicisi*, selling Turkish milk sweets and puddings. Not only the food, but the cleanliness of the floors, the standards of display, the cafes and even the bathrooms of these malls present ultra-modern, rich and luxurious environments that overwhelm visitors.

Before these malls arrived, Turkey did have individual department stores, such as Yeni Karamürsel and Gima, in which clothing, housewares and even sometimes food were sold under one roof. New outlets, such as Çarşi, Top Avenue and Marks & Spencer, have been opened recently, and are likely to grow in number. Arcades have also existed in big cities for decades, and still have a function today in Beyoğlu, Kızılay, Tunalı Hilmi, Bahariye and Bağdat Caddesi, where a constellation of chain-stores exists.

Enormous hypermarkets, such as Migros, Carrefour, Metro and Beğendik, sell groceries, housewares and even basic clothing to the middle and upper-middle classes, and are mainly family shopping sites.[5] Supermarkets are smaller, and sell groceries for daily consumption. New chains of supermarkets, such as Ismar, have developed through co-operation between non-corporate indigenous entrepreneurs, and have built a widespread network across the country. In addition, neighbourhood-oriented big open markets have emerged to cater to the needs of a particular community, meeting the basic food and clothing needs of fixed-income groups. Neighbourhood groceries and pedlars, small grocery shops, butchers and greengrocers provide 'credit selling',[6] a traditional credit system for the lower-middle classes. They provide convenience for the upper classes, who want goods delivered to their apartments: they order by phone, and have staples, such as newspapers, fresh bread, yogurt and milk, delivered by the apartment-block doorkeeper. In more traditional neighbourhoods, the grocer puts items into baskets hung from windows, in response to the customer's order.

Various forms of door-to-door selling or home visiting also exist. Along with the traditional *bohçacı*, mainly gypsy women, a more modern form has emerged in the last decades, aimed at urban women and practised by companies such as the German Avon and the Swedish Oriflame cosmetic companies. Oriflame had more than 70,000 representatives in Turkey in 1997, indicating the extent of the market and the acceptance of the practice among women. Oriflame is an example of successful international corporate marketing using the services of women in direct selling, thus spreading an ideology of money-making – additional income in the hands of women for their own consumption – as an indicator of success.[7] Representatives provide catalogues and reach customers through networks of acquaintances. In the event of even the slightest dissatisfaction, a 'money-back guarantee' is provided. When a person wants to enter the network, she finds a representative who sponsors her, but she also has to pay an entrance fee. When the new salesperson starts, the sponsor receives a commission on all her sales. It is interesting to note that these are entrepreneurship practices that target women buyers. In a sex-segregated society like Turkey's, it is no surprise that all of these practices are flourishing and finding their niche.

Another contemporary version of the *bohçacı* is the so-called 'suitcase trader', again a case of women selling to women, this time clothing. It is often a mafia-based form of informal trade with Russia and Eastern European countries, and so it is women who act as conduits for this unrecorded international trade. This kind of trade also takes place in more individualised informal networks selling European fashion brands or non-European goods, such as Indian crafts or Japanese technology. The system sometimes involves a chain of intermediaries, sometimes a sole woman who travels to, say, Italy, gets the special orders, and brings them back to sell to customers in the immediate surroundings of either home or workplace.

Especially for lower classes, the main shopping venues are neighbour-hood-based corner shops, grocers, greengrocers and butchers, touring vans, neighbourhood open markets or small-scale markets, or supermarkets. This is due to the limitations of transportation to the centre, and to hypermarkets, which are usually situated outside the city, and also due to the advantages of a personal credit system that operates between shopkeepers and their local customers.

Ayşe and Sencer Ayata's research into housing *sites* in Ankara shows that 40 percent of all the shopping needs in Zafertepe, a *gecekondu* neighbourhood are provided from neighbourhood-based shops. Also, in lower-class apartment-block neighbourhoods such as Abidinpaşa and Keçiören, shopping is neighbourhood based. In Abidinpaşa, the neighbourhood open market is the most popular shopping venue (37.8 percent), and in Keçiören the figure is 23.6 percent. According to the Ayatas' findings, there is an inverse correlation between the level of income and education and the choice of shopping in the neighbourhood.

However, it is possible that in upper-class neighbourhoods close to the central shopping district both the high-priced neighbourhood shops providing a selection of specialities, such as charcuterie or patisserie, and the central shopping district are used more often than in suburban upper-class areas, whose residents do most of their shopping in malls (Ayata and Ayata, 1996, p.104).

Although the choice of shopping facilities differs according to social class, shoppers of the same class may benefit from shopping settings totally different in character. For example, in Etiler, an upper-middle-class district of Istanbul, both the luxurious up-market mall Akmerkez and Ulus Pazarı, an open market bazaar of a type known as a *sosyete pazari* ('high-society bazaar'), cater to the area's needs.

Neighbourhood-based shopping venues provide an informal setting, especially for lower-class housewives, and have comparative advantages over malls, hypermarkets, supermarkets and department stores. While such large-scale shopping units provide product diversity, the convenience of shopping with credit cards, 'one-stop' shopping, and are handy for working women and middle- and upper-class family shopping, neighbourhood bazaars and shops are more convenient for lower-class female shoppers.

The different forms of shopping discussed are not necessarily in competition with each other. On the contrary, depending on the needs of their individual users, each is used strategically and complementarily. There is a web of shopping practices in which the customer obtains goods formally or informally, with the service either of trained shop assistants in high-status department stores or of door-to-door salespeople, with their more familiar ways. All these shopping experiences have something in common: they claim to provide personalised, convenient and reliable service and a congenial shopping atmosphere, whether it is the chain-store's assistant helping a woman to buy a new coat, the Oriflame representative marketing a new lipstick, or the neighbourhood grocer sending a delivery person with a carton of milk to an apartment. Regardless of her social class, these forms of shopping make the shopper feel privileged and special. Although it might be argued that the interaction in the mall or department store is anonymous and less personalised, our interviews have showed us that upper-rank shop assistants and shop managers have remarkable interpersonal relations with their customers, and define their success in those terms.

The changing role of women as shoppers

The woman shopper has recently become the main actor on the shopping scene in contemporary Turkey. The traditional division of labour in household chores gives the responsibility of shopping to men, who are the main breadwinners and usually control the family budget. This practice is still prevalent in small cities and in traditional households in metropolitan areas. Among occupational groups, merchants, the owners of small businesses and farmers tend to retain the traditional pattern of male shopping, these men generally still being in control of all the money in the household. They use mainly open markets or hypermarkets. In such households, the male head of household decides what is to be cooked for the family and visitors.

However, divisions of labour have gone through a transformation in urban areas, especially among the middle classes, whether the wife is employed or not. The rise of the new shopping venues has also transformed shopping practices for women, who have become more important in the making of the new middle-class lifestyle and in urban culture. As Öncü (1997, p.70) argues, 'The homogenising cultural flows of global consumerism have served to produce and re-produce cultural fragmentation at the local level in contemporary Istanbul'. Öncü argues that those in the middle strata in Istanbul have progressively preferred more home-based lives, in their sterilised, orderly and clean quarters, and points to the crisis that the middle classes experience in the era of globalisation, rightly arguing that they feel threatened by this phenomenon and liberalisation:

> Integration into the global economy often strengthens the upper segments of the middle strata at the expense of worsening conditions for the lower-middle class, who are faced with the prospect of downward mobility. Global cultural flows which erode distinctions of high and low culture progressively undermine the symbolic capital upon which a distinctive middle-class way of life is based.

So the markers of distinction are now defined by a variety of social strategies and cultural practices geared towards the ideal home. Öncü suggests that

> ...our 'ideal' home has a money sign attached to it. The significance of contemporary global myths resides in conjuring dreams as commodities, to be bought and sold. What has travelled across cultural borders to Istanbul is the ideal home as a commodity, laden with mythical content through the language of an increasingly globalised advertising industry.

Interestingly, a shopping centre is what the inhabitants of such residential *sites* desire as a sign of middle-class consumerism. Sencer Ayata's chapter in this volume also suggests that women's role in the making of the middle class and in marking the distinction of the middle-class home, family life and lifestyle is central in the 'hierarchy of taste', while men determine the position in the 'hierarchy of wealth'.

It is possible to argue that women have taken over shopping from men in the big cities, just as they pay the bills and do the school trips (Özbay, 1991). Shopping has become part of homemaking and domesticity, especially for the upper and middle classes. This fact could be correlated with the rising number of women car drivers who can go to city malls unescorted. Gumpert and Drucker (1996, p.6) also state that the car becomes the vehicle of salvation for women. The private car is a means for them to move around the city more safely, and shielded from its influences.

Women's access to the household money has also been modified through new practices. Middle-class women can obtain credit cards through their husbands' accounts, giving them both freedom and accountability. In contrast, in the lower income groups women usually function as the budget-makers, and try to distribute limited income according to the various needs of the family and household.

In contrast to the traditional division of labour in Turkey, with shopping being considered men's work because it concerns public space, the modernised middle classes – internalising the Western division of labour, in which men are expected to do paid work and women unpaid housework – now consider shopping to be a housework chore, and therefore assigned to women. Falk and Campbell (1997, p.169) suggests that shopping is mainly a feminine activity, degraded by men. Men and women have different approaches to shopping: women take a shopping trip, while men go shopping for specific needs; women experience shopping as a leisure activity, while men define it in a 'work frame'. This also applies to the Turkish urban middle class.

The mall is a secure, legitimate space for women, which makes shopping both functional and recreational. It has always been the responsibility of women to enhance the status of the family, and shopping is a new facet of this chain of status-making activities. Women appear to shop as individuals, although they actually shop for the household, where they maintain and reproduce the social status through their purchasing. Weekends and nights are family shopping times, in which women exercise certain power over budget decisions and over their husband's time. Women use shopping as a tool to involve husbands more in the daily upkeep of the family and homemaking practices. Also, through family shopping trips women have acquired the power of choice over much of what is bought, and to have access to their husband's income. On the weekend shopping trip, usually women fill the basket and men pay the money.

Through newspapers' consumer rights and shopping information pages, and the emergence of consumer advice bodies and associations,[8] the consumer is constructed as an agent of modernity, and shopping sites become arenas of assertiveness for women. A traditional housewife who has little contact with the outside world can, for example, use the shopping encounter as an area in which to assert herself, by returning a faulty product to the shop.

Malls as democratised social settings

Historically, the Western mall marks the shift from an elite to a mass form of consumption, and is a counterpart of mass democracy, according to Miller (1995). The elements of fantasy, excess and spectacle create an illusion of mass participation and global 'citizenship' (Miller, 1995). According to Shields (1992), the mall provides 'realms of negotiation and empowerment' for the participants.

Shopping in these new urban sites is a total experience for women, including buying, seeing, strolling and eating. It is a space in which to enhance one's collective imagination. The mall is not only for the consumption of goods and services, but is also a place where one shops and constructs and feeds one's imagination of better lifestyles.

These sites can also be considered temples for collective imagination, where sacred, overwhelming, monumental physical construction dominates. It has an aura. You feel you are a part of it. The rich, modern and luxurious landscape enhances your sense of belonging to the urban. By visiting these shopping centres you feel as though you belong to the upper socioeconomic classes, who have access to all these goods and sites. Contrary to the small-shop experience, in which you are expected to purchase things, here you can just hang around, and still feel included. These sites are accessible to people of all socioeconomic groups. The mall is also a family recreation place, a meeting place for youngsters, somewhere they can hang around in. Many parents think the mall safe for their children because at least they know where they are. It is a closed and controlled space in which the young can learn to mix with the opposite sex and be assertive in public space.

On the other hand, malls present a hygienic, sterile, institutionalised environment, one that is well lit, well heated or cooled, in which the relationship between buyer and product is independent of shop assistants. They present a controlled and non-threatening environment to the shopper, 'who can familiarise freely with an item, recognise the need and imagine his/her life with the product' (Gumpert and Drucker, 1996, p.125).

Inside the shops, the counter is abolished and there are various types of display. The absence of a salesperson behind a counter makes the relationship with the goods more direct, the ability to choose being accompanied by an invisible influence to buy. By contrast, in the small shop the process of shopping is mediated through the shop assistant in a more direct, personalised and emotional way. In malls, there is intense energy dispersed into objects of desire rather than inter-personal contact and interaction. In this sense, malls are places where women are relatively free from harassment, unlike when shopping in the street, which still carries a stigma, as a public place. Historically, the 'public woman' has been associated with the non-respectable, the prostitute, segregated from the respectable woman. Women of the streets, street-walkers, were prostitutes, because the open street, with its lack of boundaries and its availability to all, was precisely what created 'promiscuity' in every form. As Gumpert and Drucker (1996, p.6) maintain, women in public places were not only at risk when in the streets, but created risk to themselves and social order more generally.

Connotations surrounding women and the street for centuries characterised women as commodities rather than consumers. In some cultures, the 'good woman' did not venture out into the public realm unchaperoned, as 'nice girls' were kept off the streets and close to home, with the fear that their virginity or virtue or both would be endangered. Women who ventured out were considered street-walkers, belonging to the street, their private lives on display. According to Franck and Paxson (1989), when women are in public spaces they are still defined and perceived in terms of their sexuality, a private role they are never free of. Being on the street has similar, if not worse, connotations for women in Turkey. It is no surprise that, for example, women take a child or a friend along with them when they go shopping. With company, not only does a woman's access to the public become easier – easing the granting of permission from husband or father – but she also communicates the message that she is virtuous and inaccessible to men.

The mall, on the other hand, provides a legitimate use of urban space for women. It is a place in which everything is under the scrutiny of spectators. It is a 'closed open space' in which everything is to be viewed and controlled. Wilson (1992, p.6) argues that the city offers women freedom along with risk: 'woman is present in cities as temptress, as whore, as fallen woman, as lesbian, but also as virtuous woman in danger, as heroic womanhood who triumphs over temptation and tribulation'. The shopping mall is perhaps one chance for a woman to match the male *flâneur* as a free wanderer. As Aksoy (1997) says, the mall is a global town; therefore, we should ask to what extent shopping is an emancipatory practice for women, and to what extent a woman can be free in such an image-directed town. The quotation by the anthropologist Marc Auge (cited in Aksoy, 1997. p.111), from the brochure of the Metro Centre in Gateshead in the Northeast of England – which has more than 28 million visitors a year, 6000 staff and 360 shops in a setting designed according to a town plan and family atmosphere – is the most telling:

> The shopping malls are not confined to space and time anymore. The roots of these centres – in which only the present time is lived – are not in the soil or in a specific geography but in the administration of display, public relations and marketing. Here is an excess of space: The same person can be in Texas, Tokyo, California and Gateshead at the same time. As far as their credits last, people can leave their social identity in the car park and enjoy the personal taste of loss of identity and role playing inside the malls.

In a sense, the mall is a place where one can magically shed a social identity and take on a universal one. Women shoppers can usually get over their feeling of insecurity in a public place through a confidence in the information they gather about goods' quality and price. Also, women usually take time window-shopping, as they feel themselves to be on the scene while strolling in the mall. Hence the mall provides integration for women into capitalist society through individualised gratification rather than communal–societal action.

In Turkey, as elsewhere, the mall seems a place in which differences of class, age and gender do not matter; indeed, it is a democratised space when compared to shopping sites such as the bazaar, the boutique or the department store, not only for the shoppers but also for the staff.

Our interviews with shop managers show that parallel to alterations in the work setting, there have also been changes in the work culture: management ideology, selling strategies and the social conduct of the shop assistants towards shop managers and customers. The shop assistant of a small shop has been transformed into the salesperson in the mall, with a relatively gender- and class-neutral identity. New managerial ideologies at the shop define shop assistants as members of a work team in uniforms carrying the corporate logo. They implement training programmes to impose on the sales process codified, routinised behaviour and speech that necessitates less interaction with the shopper.

According to Reekie (1992), the department store's careful targeting of a female clientele has been replaced by a post-modernist emphasis on diversity and eclecticism. This reformulated consumer culture reaches out to new categories of clientele and searches for new markets among children, teenagers and men. While women's work associated with family shopping has been relegated to more mundane sites of consumption, such as supermarkets, neighbourhood shops and suburban shopping centres, sites of leisure retailing are less feminine in character and target men as customers. In Turkey, although malls target mainly female customers, the pool-rooms recently introduced are designed to appeal to a male clientele.

The gender and class dimensions of shopping encounters

In an earlier project about women office workers and shop assistants (Cindoğlu and Durakbaşa, 1996), we were interested in the different types of discrimination women experience in the area called 'pink-collar occupations', a recently expanding area of female employment parallel to the development of the service sector both in the West and in Turkey. These are also defined as consumer contact occupations, in which stereotypical feminine qualities, such as beauty, attractiveness, docility and service to others, become important assets.

This research was carried out using focus groups and group and individual interviews with office workers and sales assistants in Ankara and Istanbul in 1996. We were interested in focusing on three inter-related issues: social perceptions of women's office and sales work; women's self-perceptions in these jobs; women's coping strategies in the face of harassment.

Office and sales work are feminised occupations involving gendered expectations of job definitions. In our research, we focused on the influence of a number of factors: the organisation of work, in terms of office hierarchies, the scale of the shop, the social-cultural milieu and codes of the workplace, gender stereotypes, and the workers' social class and background. One important question that we dealt with was the extent of the impact of the growing consumer capitalism and the dynamism and proliferation in the area of distribution, marketing and consumption on the internal organisation of shops and the labour force. Inspired by Benson (1996), a study of the history of the department store in America, 1890–1940, we wanted to evaluate how social change was reflected in the shop setting and in the social drama of the actors in this setting: the shoppers, the sales-women and the shop managers.

Benson's study indicates that there has been a shift from a more feminine workplace culture, which emphasised personal service to shoppers, prevalent in small shops run by women to a more masculine business mentality and culture. There has been a corresponding change in the interior design of department stores and hypermarkets to an emphasis on open shelving, tempting arrays of goods, and self-service, in which the display of the goods in an impersonal setting becomes more important.

With England as their subject, Mackie and Patullo (1977), suggest that the pattern of employment in shops has changed drastically, so that in supermarkets the old idea of the importance of service, with its skills, has been entirely replaced by the importance of displaying goods, encouraging a rapid flow of customers through the store, and replacing goods so that the greatest possible tempting array is always visible. In all this, the role of the woman shop assistant has been reduced to that of shelf-stacker and check-out operator.

To what extent is this picture valid for Turkey? Is the status of the shop assistant falling or rising? In our interviews we witnessed a conscious attempt in the managerial ideology of the shops to define the workers in the shop as *satış elemanı* ('salesperson'), much less gendered than the term *tezgahtar kız* ('shop girl'), sometimes disparaged as *tezgahtar parçası* ('counter rubbish'), hinting at low gender and class status. Shop managers openly told us that they preferred salespeople with high-school education and who came from 'well-behaved', preferably middle-class, backgrounds. There are also training schemes that socialise shop workers into the culture of the mall, in which standardised behaviour and etiquette is taught. Along with such an 'egalitarian' managerial ideology, however, we also observed a high turnover and discriminatory practices, such as employing young people short-term, then dispensing with them. Managers clearly indicated that they did not want women who were married or who had children, as they would not be able to adapt to the working hours and conditions of the shop, mainly involving a 12-hour working day, six or seven days a week.

A recent study by the Sosyal Eğitim ve Danışmanlık Şirketi, carried out in 37 shops such as Bennetton, Mudo and Bata, found that 54.7 percent of shop managers were women. This is a very significant number, and our interviews also show that women in this sector are very career-oriented, and work with a real 'protestant work ethic'. Our interviews show that most women in managerial positions in shops perceived the growing area of retailing as suitable for upwardly mobile women. Other findings show that among sales workers, women make up 52.5 percent of the total. The striking figure is the presence of women as cashiers (83.9 percent).[9]

Our findings also show that women experience a certain type of discrim-ination in recruitment and promotion. Young unmarried women are particularly preferred as shop assistants, due to their short-lived work prospects. Among office workers, although state employees benefit from some paid maternity and child-care support, the private sector prefers unattached women without household responsibilities. Along with these job-market characteristics, women also experi-ence different forms of sexual harassment, yet they lack formal and institutional redress. In such cases, managers tended to keep harassed saleswomen out of sight, employing them behind the scenes.

Women try to exploit some of the elements of the traditional patriarchal culture and modernist egalitarian ethic to their benefit in dealing with sexual dis-crimination and harassment in the workplace. Among these defensive strategies, 'de-sexing' the work environment is prevalent. Women are conscious about their appearance, and dress non-provocatively. Another strategy is to utilise kinship codes in the office environment to get respect. They utilise family connections and relations to deal with harassers: one of our informants had threatened the harasser by mentioning acquaintances in high government office.

Encounters between women shop assistants and women shoppers are worth exploring, in order to see the role of gender and class dynamics in the drama of shopping. Douglas (1997, pp.18–19) suggests that 'shopping sites are arenas of cultural contest', with shopping practices showing signs of 'standardised hates', so that 'choosing commodities is choosing between cultures, choosing one and rejecting the others'. We observed that women shoppers, in disparaging products, usually applied strong categories to differentiate the product from themselves, such as, 'How disgusting, fit for a village girl'. In that way, not only do they reflect their dislike of the product, they do so in such a manner as to empha-sise their class status, while devaluing the shop assistant as well.

Another type of encounter in the shopping scene takes place between the 'expert' housewife and the young, usually inexperienced, salesperson. The traditional role of housewife in Turkey includes all kinds of homemaking talents, among them cooking, cleaning and sewing. The Girls' Institutes, as well as People's Centres of the Ministry of Education throughout Turkey, offer extensive formal and informal education to prospective housewives in cooking and sewing. So women who are already expert needlewomen but prefer to buy ready-made clothes are the most critical shoppers. The encounter between the craft-trained housewife and the saleswoman usually takes the form of a contest over how much they know about the product: for example, the cut, style and quality of a garment are discussed obsessively. The contest is as much about the denigration of the saleswoman as the product itself. The hierarchy of age is quite strong in Turkey, and the culturally determined hierarchy among women is likely to be reflected in their conduct towards the usually younger shop assistants. Shop assistants take their revenge by mocking their adversaries over their incompetence in some other area. For example, in our research a shop assistant obsessively told the story of how she teased one of her clients when she used the word *minyon* (meaning 'small', from the French *mignon*) as *milyon* ('million'). She giggled for quite some time at the customer's ignorance. Class conflict is also lived out in such dramas.

We noticed that women in stigmatised occupations, such as secretarial, sales or other consumer-contact occupations, are more aware of their gender because of the gender-typing of occupations, and so react more directly and spontaneously to incidences of harassment. These occupations are perceived as having the connotation of 'sexual service to men' in the public unconscious and male fantasy. Most of our informants related their unease about it. It was interesting to note that women can be quite spontaneous and outspoken about the degradation of their sex status and identity.

In the mall, shop assistants identify themselves as representatives of the various chainstores and labels, and perhaps feel more secure in such an impersonal and regulated work setting. However, workers in fast food restaurants usually work in less secure conditions. The women shop assistants emphasised training as the most important asset in the improvement of their occupational status, professionalising 'service to others' as part of paid labour in a cultural context where these are normally demeaned. Recent developments in the retail sector and management ideologies have successfully rendering the job of 'selling' and 'serving' as a profession requiring certain qualifications.

Conclusion

Shopping practices in Turkey have gone through a great transformation, and we believe that the rise of the malls and hypermarkets played a significant role in this. In this chapter, we have described changes in the homemaking activities of the middle-class housewife and emphasised the gendered aspects of shopping. We believe the mall has afforded, especially for women of the middle and upper classes, the opportunity for a 'fictive' global experience and the freedom of a wanderer in a public place.

We have also analysed shopping in terms of certain dramas that take place between female shoppers and shop assistants. In our view, there is always a struggle involving class and age differences in the process of assessing goods, selling and buying. We have described the working conditions of shop assistants and hinted at various forms of sexual discrimination that female shop assistants face. However, our study also showed that the status of shop assistant is rising with the rise of the mall, especially with rise of standardised in-service training and the more gender-neutral work culture of the mall. In conclusion, the diverse venues for shopping in post-1980s Turkey present us with shifting visions of gender and class in a rapidly changing society.

Notes on chapter 3

1   According to the 1990 census, 59 percent of the population lived in urban areas; Istanbul is the most populous metropolitan area, with 12.9 percent of the total population of Turkey; Ankara is second, with 5.7 percent; Izmir is third, with 4.8 percent. The annual rate of population increase between 1985 and 1990 in Istanbul was 44.78 percent, in Ankara 21.28 percent, in Izmir 30.14 percent. According to the State Statistics Institute Income Distribution Research Report of 1994, 27.5 percent of the national income is consumed in Istanbul, 40 percent in the five big cities of Istanbul, Ankara, Izmir, Adana and Bursa. That means that sections of society with the budgetary means to shop in malls and hypermarkets have increased in these cities. (Sönmez,1997, p.101)

2   In Istanbul, which has the most unequal distribution of income, the most wealthy 20 percent of population receives 64 percent of the city's income (Sönmez,1997, p.102). The poorest 20 percent gets only 4.2 percent. Ankara and Izmir show similar findings; in Ankara, the richest 20 percent gets 47.9, in Izmir the same proportion of the population gets 54.2 percent. The poorest 20 percent gets 5.7 percent in Ankara and 5.9 percent in Izmir (Sönmez, 1996, p.135; Sönmez, 1997, p.104).

3   In terms of the durable goods that Istanbul households own, it is striking to note that 97.4 percent have refrigerators, 83.6 percent hoovers, 73.4 percent washing machines and 90.6 percent colour televisions. (Sönmez, 1996, p.138).

4   A new offer from the banks is the *taksit card*, which allows the holder to pay in instalments when buying from shops that have an agreement with the specific bank. There is also a card issued by a group of different shops that offers payment options and promotions.

5   Domestic corporations in the country, such as Koç, Sabancı, Tekfen, Doğuş, Sezginler and Okumuş, have either entered into the retail sector on their own or helped multinational retailers enter the market by associating with them, either through licensing agreements or joint ventures, as in the cases of Koç Holdings, which owns Migros, or Sabancı Holdings, which has a joint venture with Carrefour.

6   In an interview, the president of Türkiye Bakkallar Federasyonu (the Turkish Federation of Grocers) said that customers in rural neighbourhoods and urban slums were 30 trillion lira in debt to grocers, who also function as a neighbourhood bank. Borrowers cannot be traced, as they are mostly recorded informally as *yukardaki teyze* ('the aunt on the top floor'), *san saçlı bayan* ('the woman with the blond hair'), *maliyeci bey* ('the accountant gentleman') etc. (*Radikal*, 29 April 1998, p.12).

7   'It is very easy to join the Oriflame chain, and Oriflame provides all kinds of sup-
        port for your success. You are under an Oriflame distributor, and an Oriflame
        Starter's Kit is given to you. There are a number of products and publications in
        the Starter's Kit. These publications are a great help in showing how to develop
        your business. Your success is limited only by the targets and effort you specify
        for yourself. Choose great targets for yourself! You will see that many of your
        dreams will come true in time.' (Translated from the Starter's Kit, Oriflame
        Başarı Planı.)

8   In the Milliyet Shopping Catalogue of 19 June 1998, Emre Aköz, editor of the
        shopping supplement of the magazine *Vitrin* wrote, 'The shopping activity has
        developed so much that it becomes a subject for newspaper supplements or
        magazines. *Vitrin*, which has reached readers for more than 80 weeks now, is a
        good example of this; besides we try to have this magazine in your hands every
        season. The speciality of these publications is that they are not merely catalogues.
        They investigate shopping as a social activity beyond 'what to buy?', 'where to
        buy?' and 'how much?', taking into consideration gender relations, culture,
        recreation and stress...I hope you will benefit from our Shopping Guide. If
        we can provide you with a chance to follow the new trends and fashion as well as
        possibilities to buy good quality at a cheap price, we will be happy...'

9   According to the same research, almost 80 percent of the managers are between
        the ages of twenty-three and forty, only 9.45 percent are above forty, and 7.7 per-
        cent are between the ages of twenty and twenty-two. The majority (56.4 percent)
        are quite young, between the ages of twenty and thirty. The findings are not
        divided according to gender (*Radikal*, 25 February, 1998).

References

Aksoy, Asu (1997), 'Küresel Kasabadaydım', *İstanbul Dergisi* 22, pp.111–12.

Ayata, Sencer and Ayşe Ayata (1996), *Konut, Komşuluk ve Kent Kültürü*, T.C. Başbakanlık
        Toplu Konut İdaresi Başkanlığı, Ankara

Benson, Susan Porter (1986), *Counter Cultures: Saleswomen, Managers, and Customers in
        American Department Stores 1890–1940*, University of Illlinois Press, Chicago, IL

Cindoğlu, Dilek and Ayşe Durakbaşa (1996), *İşyerlerinde Cinsiyete Dayalı Ayrımcılık ve
        İşverenlerin Kadın Çalışanlarına Karşı Tutumu: Büro ve Mağaza Çalışanlarına
        Derinlemesine Bir Bakış (Discrimination at the Workplace: An In-depth Approach to
        Women Clerical and Sales Workers)*, project report, Kadının Statüsü ve Sorunları
        Genel Müdürlüğü, Ankara

Dökmeci, Vedia. (1989), 'Batı Alman Şehirlerinde ve İstanbul'da Yaya Ticaret Aksları
        Planlaması', *Yapı* 94, pp.36–40

Douglas, Mary (1997), 'In defense of shopping', in F. Pasi and C. Campbell (eds), *The
        Shopping Experience*, Sage, London, pp.15–30

Duben, Alan and Cem Behar (1991), *Istanbul Households: Marriage, Family and Fertility,
        1820–1940*, Cambridge University Press, Cambridge

Falk, Pasi and Colin Campbell (1997)(eds), *The Shopping Experience*, Sage, London

Franck, K.A. and L. Paxson (1989), 'Women and urban public space: research, design
        and policy issues', in E. Zube and S.G. Moore (eds), *Advances in Environment,
        Behavior and Design* 2, pp.122–46, Plenium, New York, NY

Ger, Güliz and Russell W. Belk (1990), 'Measuring and comparing materialism cross-culturally', *Advances in Consumer Research* 17, pp.186–92

Gumpert, Gary and Susan J. Drucker (1996), *Voices in the Street: Explorations in Gender, Media, and Public Space*, Hampton Press, New York, NY

Gürbilek, Nurdan (1993), *Vitrinde Yaşamak: 1980'lerin Kültürel İklimi*, Metis, Istanbul

Hür, Ayşe (1997), 'Alışveriş Merkezleri', *İstanbul Dergisi* 22, pp.105–107

Işın, Ekrem (1985), '19. Yy.'da Modernleşme ve Gündelik Hayat', *Tanzimattan Cumhuriyete Türkiye Ansiklopedisi*, İletişim, Istanbul, pp.538–63

Kozanoğlu, Can (1995), 'Demokrasinin Beşiği Süpermarket mi?' *Cogito* 5, pp.21–3

Mackie, Lindsay and Polly Pattullo (1977), *Women at Work*, Tavistock Women's Studies, London

Miller, Daniel (1995), 'Anthropology, modernity and consumption', in Daniel Miller (ed.), *Worlds Apart: Modernity Through the Prism of the Local*, Routledge, London and New York, pp.1–42

Öncü, Ayşe (1994), 'Middle class life styles in the cultural geography of post-infitah Istanbul', paper presented at the workshop 'Local Cultures in Global Cities', Boğaziçi University, Istanbul

— (1997), 'The myth of the 'ideal home' travels across cultural borders to Istanbul', in Ayşe Öncü and Petra Weyland (eds), *Space, Culture and Power New Identities in Globalising Cities*, Zed, London

Özbay, Ferhunde (1991), 'Changes in women's activities both inside and outside the home', in Ş. Tekeli (ed.), *Women in Modern Turkish Society*, Zed, London

Özbay, F. (1991), 'Türkiye'de Aile ve Hane Yapısı: Dün, Bugün, Yarın', Mübeccel Kıray'a Armağan. Marmara Üniversitesi Dergisi Özel Sayı, Istanbul

— (1996) 'Evler, Kadınlar ve Evkadınları', in Emine M. Komut (ed.), *Diğerlerinin Konut Sorunları*, Habitat II ön Konferansı, TMMOB Mimarlar Odası, Ankara

Radner, Hilary (1995), *Shopping Around: Feminine Culture and the Pursuit of Pleasure*, Routledge, London and New York

Reekie, Gail (1992), 'Changes in the Adamless Eden: the spatial and sexual transformation of a Brisbane department store 1930–90', in G. Reekie, *Temptations: Sex, Selling, and the Department Store*, pp.170–94, Allen and Unwin, Sydney

Sayılı, Tuba (1992), *Alışveriş Merkezlerinin Gelişimi Sınıflandırılması ve Tasarımını Etkileyen Faktörler*, Mimar Sinan Üniversitesi, Mimarlık Fakültesi, Yüksek Lisans tezi, Istanbul

Serpil, Ahmet, R. Nişel, A. Ağaoğlu and Y. Karapazar (1998), *Bakkaliye Sektörünün Profili ve Rekabet Olanakları*, İstanbul Ticaret Odası, Istanbul

Sönmez, Mustafa (1990), *Türkiye'de Gelir Eşitsizliği*, İletişim, Istanbul

— (1996), *İstanbul'un İki Yüzü: 1980'den 2000'e Değişim*, Arkadaş Yayınları, Ankara

— (1997), 'İstanbul'un Hipermarketleri', *İstanbul Dergisi* 22, pp.101–4.

Shields, Rob (1992), *Lifestyle Shopping: The Subject of Consumption*, Routledge, London and New York

Tokatlı, Nebahat and Yonca Boyacı (1997), 'Internationalisation of Retailing in Turkey', *New Perspectives on Turkey* 17, pp.97–128.

— (1998), 'The State and the Corporate Private Sector in the Recent Restructuring of Turkish Retailing', *New Perspectives on Turkey* 18, pp.79–111.

Toprak, Zafer (1995), 'Tüketim örüntüleri ve Osmanlı mağazaları', *Cogito: Dünya Büyük Bir Mağaza* 5, special issue, Yapı Kredi Yayınları, Istanbul, pp.25–8

Wilson, Elizabeth (1992), *The Sphinx in the City: Urban Life, the Control of Disorder, and Women*, University of California Press, Berkeley, CA

4

Discipline, Success and Stability: The Reproduction of Gender and Class in Turkish Secondary Education

Feride Acar and Ayşe Ayata

Introduction

Schools are not only engaged in the business of 'educating', that is of transmitting knowledge, but are also important agents of social and cultural control. It is also a well-rehearsed argument that, as such, they often function to (re)produce the existing forms of inequality in society (Apple and King, 1977; Margolis and Romero, 1998). Educational institutions reflect a 'philosophy of education' that strives for internal consistency and unity and carries within itself strong elements of a 'world-view' that often incorporates significant legitimisation, if not outright enhancement of existing forms of inequality (Apple, 1971; Willis, 1977; Anyon, 1980; Giroux, 1983).

It is thus to be expected that, in the absence of deliberate intervention, such (re)production would include that of patriarchy which, after all, arguably supports the most pervasive and blatant form of inequality in society, gender-based. Mostly through Marxist theory, social and political science research on education and schooling has long diagnosed, documented and offered criticism of educational institutions' (re)productive ideological function in social and economic inequality. Such critical treatment from a gender perspective, on the other hand, has developed comparatively late in association with the growth of the women's movement and women's studies (Stromquist, 1995).

The formal and informal structures of the education system effective in (re)producing gender inequality cover a wide array of mechanisms and relationships, ranging from authority allocation structures in schools to textbook content, to teacher attitudes and behaviour in the classroom. Today, the need for measures to counteract gender inequalities in all of these areas is recognised internationally as a priority (Platform for Action, 1995).

To put it differently, both the knowledge content transmitted through the curriculum and the 'hidden curriculum' (Jackson, 1968; Willis, 1977; Apple, 1971; Stromquist, 1996), which includes elements such as discipline, school values and norms regarding such aspects of student life as extra-curricular activities and use of language, can and often do function as critical forces in reinforcing or countering gender inequality through the process of gender socialisation.

In processing both the student and the knowledge itself, the school simultaneously engages in constructing and transmitting a hierarchy of knowledge that legitimises and forms the basis of the cultural and social milieu in which gender socialisation, as all else, takes place. Consequently, in the education process, selection, prioritisation and legitimisation of different types of knowledge, along with the context and form of its transition, becomes important. So far as the latter is concerned, the demographic and social background characteristics of the educators, who often become role models to students, are highly salient. They are often the most influential agents of school socialisation, in which conceptions of self and one's place in society are shaped.

The Turkish context

Although there were some earlier attempts during the late Ottoman empire, the foundation of a uniform modern education system based on rationality, scientific knowledge, positivist methodology and a secular world-view was laid in the 1920s and 1930s. This system, often hailed as the single most important achievement of the republic, was designed to turn out independent-minded, free-spirited, intellectually accomplished, emotionally mature generations of young Turks whose self-definitions would reflect liberation from the control of religious and traditional sources of loyalty and an unchallenged commitment to such underlying features of modernism as science, the nation-state and the ideal of progress.

Also in the new education system's philosophy was the notion of equality, particularly of gender. While the state, as a hallmark of its modern character, generally promoted the equality of its citizens, it specifically underlined gender equality as a symbol of the republic's divergence from its Ottoman roots. The symbolic nature of the state's egalitarian gender ideology, nonetheless, pertained mainly to the public sphere and to *de jure* matters.

Through the enactment and implementation of the Law of Unification of Education (LUE) in 1924, efforts were launched in Turkey to create an education system characterised by uniform curricula, designed to ensure universal gender and class-neutral access for all citizens of the republic and to transmit secular and scientific knowledge to all. This law placed all education in the country under the authority of the Ministry of National Education, and in the process abolished any previously existing schools of religious character. Also, courses on religion were eliminated, step-by-step, from all elementary and secondary education curricula in Turkey until the 1930s. (Akşit, 1991; Mert and Bahçacı, 1995: p.18).

The LUE, as a succinct formulation of the republic's education project, also specifically stipulated (Article 4) that 'the Ministry of National Education will establish special (separate) schools to train "civil servants" who will be responsible for fulfiling religious services'. This attempt to confine religious education to the rather limited aim of 'training for religious services', though uncontested in the early days, has remained a controversial issue ever since. With the transition to multiparty politics, from 1945 on, significant deviations from the uncompromising early implementation of the LUE have taken place. One consequence was that the Imam-Hatip schools, originally established in accordance with the 1924 Law on the Unification of Education, were consolidated into the secondary education system through the 1973 Fundamental Law of National Education, as institutions with a mandate to train students to perform religious services as well as prepare them for higher education. It was on these grounds that the then existing 29 Imam-Hatip schools underwent important structural changes and evolved into the contemporary Imam-Hatip lycées (Akşit, 1991).[1]

As the change of their names (from 'school' to 'lycée'), as well as the increase in their numbers and population, signals, these schools came to constitute an integral component of what many considered to be a *de facto* two-pronged (secular and religious) secondary education system, in clear breach of the fundamental principles of the LUE and the constitutionally secular nature of the Turkish state. There is in fact considerable evidence for this argument when the academic performance levels of graduates of Imam-Hatip lycées in the nationally competitive centralised university entrance examinations are compared with those of regular lycées. Imam-Hatip graduates' intentions to continue academic education in the university system in fields unrelated to religion, as well as their success in being placed in the higher education system, has consistently paralleled those of regular lycée graduates since the mid- 1980s (ÖSYM, 1997–2).

Girl students have been admitted to Imam-Hatip institutions since 1972, originally to be trained as preachers (*vaize*) to provide religious services to Muslim women. However, as was clear from their steadily increasing numbers and proportions, over the years these schools evolved into an increasingly favoured alternative to mainstream lycées, particularly for girl students. The preference of girl students and their parents for these schools was mainly due to their comparatively 'virtuous' reputation in conservative communities.

Within the public secondary education system Imam-Hatip lycées are officially categorised under the heading of Vocational and Technical Education, and as such they are supposed to be co-educational. However, this is so only on paper, and all such schools are *de facto* single sex.

In Turkey, all secondary education, public or private, in regular or vocational–technical veins, has been subject to the principles and regulations of the LUE and the Fundamental Law of National Education. This fact, however, does not preclude significant institutional variation in the system. While the existing variety of schools in the public education system has its origins in pre-republican times, it has increased particularly since the 1970s.

Since the late Ottoman period, the offspring of the Western-oriented elite were educated in schools emphasising foreign-language teaching. Many of these schools, originally founded by European and American missionaries, were nationalised following the establishment of the republic, and these mostly private foreign-language schools pioneered Western-oriented, secular and progressive education in Turkey. The emphasis on teaching foreign languages was later adopted by other private schools that also designed their regular curriculum with extra hours of language teaching and science and maths classes taught in the foreign language. In the last couple of decades, the state too has moved towards more foreign-language instruction. A new type of public secondary education institution, called the Anadolu lycée was created, and mushroomed in cities and towns all over the country. These schools have a regular lycée curriculum with reinforced language instruction, and are basically fashioned after the model of foreign-language private schools. The Anadolu lycées and foreign language private schools have come to constitute the elite institutions of the secondary education system in contemporary Turkey.

Besides these regular secondary education institutions, the graduates of which are expected to move on to the university, many kinds of vocational schools established for the purpose of training para-professionals and technicians with specific specialties, ranging from tourism, to electronics, to embroidery, now constitute the landscape of secondary education in Turkey. Among these are the Imam-Hatip lycées mentioned above.

A bird's-eye view of the secondary education system in Turkey finds graduates of a few specialised public lycées called science lycées routinely getting top scores and being placed in the most highly sought-after university programs. It also reveals that in general the graduates of private schools and foreign-language reinforced Anadolu lycées perform better than those of regular public lycées. The relatively low levels of university entrance among regular public lycée graduates, compared with those of foreign-language-teaching institutions (both public and private), can be considered a sign of the deterioration of the rest of the public education system. On average, only half of the graduates of public lycées are successful in gaining entrance to university.

The deterioration of the mainstream public school system owes much to the growing imbalance between the increased demand for these institutions and the public funds made available for education. Education's share of the national budget has over the years declined, leading to increased class sizes, a deterioration in physical conditions and a lack of extra-curricular activities in public schools. Due to the teaching profession's general loss of prestige, and the relative decline of teachers' incomes, the public education system has also found it increasingly hard to recruit high-quality teaching staff.

The study

We want here to take a close-up of the sociological and socio-psychological processes of gender socialisation and identity construction mediated through the formal and informal mechanisms of the different secondary education institutions in contemporary Turkey, as these are reflected in the examples of the three school cultures discussed. These three schools are chosen as cases illustrative of what can be termed 'typical' school cultures of mainstream public and private schools, as well as Imam-Hatip lycées in Turkey. This analysis of the school cultures is particularly geared to understanding how they affect gender identity construction via the values and norms of conduct they support, as well as the formal curriculum they implement.

The school cultures were studied in 1996–7 through interviews with teachers, administrators and students. The schools studied are large, fully developed, well-established secondary education institutions, each with a long history and a very respectable reputation. They are all located in middle-class districts in Ankara; pupils' families range predominantly from the lower- to the upper-middle classes, and recruit their teaching staff from among the best-trained and most qualified members of the teaching community in the country.

What is attempted here is a description of the educational atmosphere of each school, in order to illustrate different aspects of the academic and social milieu. Teachers' testimonies are used as the lens through which these 'images of school culture' are taken. By analysing such aspects of the school milieu as curricular and extra-curricular activities and student–teacher interaction patterns, as well as the teachers' perceptions, attitudes and behaviours as indicators of the hidden curriculum effective in shaping the students' conceptions of self and identity, answers to several critical questions are sought. To what extent, for example, do educational institutions in Turkey actually (re)produce gender inequality, reject, legitimise and/or enhance women's subordination and gender-based discrimination? How, in a society where educational institutions were intentionally designed to foster a rational, secular and egalitarian social order, do schools and teachers function as agents of social control, situated as they are in the midst of traditional, patriarchal and religious gender ideologies?

The Imam-Hatip lycée

The Imam-Hatip lycée we studied is considered one of the best of its kind in Turkey. Entrance to the school was, at the time of the study, by examination. Most of the students came from lower- or middle-class backgrounds. Interestingly, the school was reported to attract more female applicants than male, and on average girls were more successful. In fact, there was a maximum 50 percent quota reserved for girls, on the grounds that this was essentially a vocational school for boys, as girls cannot function as imams. Administrators and teachers stated that many academically promising girls were sent to this school by their very conservative families, who regarded this institution as their daughters' only chance of receiving an education. Curiously, some 'naughty' boys were sent here, for 'discipline'. The overarching feature of the school's culture was the presence of a totalising world-view and philosophy. It is clear that here, at least intentionally, complete control of the student, both inside and outside the school, is desired and attempted. The teachers appear to have internalised this philosophy well, and reflect it in their overall attitudes and behaviours towards students. Often they perceive themselves exclusively as agents of such control.

The philosophy of education adopted here, as one teacher of a religious subject put it, does not view life as 'fragmented' and possibly containing inconsistent dimensions, but rather, as 'a unified whole'. The correct actualisation of this coherent whole can only be achieved by adherence to 'discipline'. To the extent that these themes are present in all aspects of the school's culture, ranging from classes to extra-curricular activities, the observer of the Imam-Hatip lycée cannot help but notice that Islamic values and rules form the basis of the school's philosophy of education.

Sexual segregation and the seclusion of the girls come across as the most visible characteristics of the school culture. Despite the officially co-educational nature of the institution, *de facto* segregation not only discourages interaction between male and female students but also prevents mixed-sex interaction between the teachers themselves, as well as between teachers and their students. As reflected in this female teacher's story, the school observes the segregation rule very strictly:

> A female teacher... was sitting with girls at the cafeteria [when] a boy came to ask or tell her something, and she asked him to sit down too. Then, one of the assistant head-teachers came and was very upset [over what he saw]. He said some highly-uncalled-for things, such as, 'Are you now arranging for girls and boys to meet here?'

According to another teacher, '[In this school], male teachers' contact with women or girls is not considered appropriate, and hence not approved. It can cause rumours.'

Such emphasis on segregation of the sexes, among both teachers and students, is ensured by, among other things, assigning girls' and boys' classes and all activities to different buildings. Furthermore, in each one of the school's segregated buildings there is one staff-room allocated to either men or women. Thus, even if a teacher had classes in one of the opposite-sex blocks, he or she refrained from entering the staff-room in that building. The mechanisms assuring such segregation among teachers are informal rather than official: several teachers have described such a situation as analogous to a woman entering a men's coffee house or a man suddenly finding himself in an all-women tea party.

While such strict sex segregation is considered a 'must' by most, male teachers of religious subjects are the most ardent supporters of the practice. For them, sex segregation, which they define in relation to 'nature' and 'harmony', is an intrinsic aspect of life. Many argued that to put girls and boys in physical proximity to one another would be putting 'fire and gunpowder side by side', to create an unavoidably explosive and dangerous situation.

While the arguments in favour of single-sex education are often found in discussions of education, sociology and psychology in other cultural contexts too, what should be underlined here is that the present case reflects a basic all-encompassing notion of sex-based segregation in all public-sphere activities rather than a pedagogical strategy. As such, it is essentially different from the arguments in favour of single-sex schooling for pupils in a certain age bracket in communities where other forms of cross-sex interaction abound and are in fact encouraged. (Hannan, 1996).

In the Imam-Hatip lycée, both the religiously based justification and the unabashedly patriarchal values that underlie the preference for single-sex schooling are expressed in the words of a teacher, who said, '[in co-educational schools] boys cannot control themselves, thus they cannot fully commit themselves to religion. This would be deliberately putting them on fire [i.e. encouraging them to sin].'

A few teachers have also said that co-education would be detrimental to girls too, because girls would be embarrassed in those classroom circumstances when 'they cannot fully participate, are passive or silent because they are menstruating'.[2]

It is clear that in the Imam-Hatip lycée, teachers' attitudes and values regarding co-education are tied to their preoccupation with young people's sexuality and the salience they attribute to the need to control it. They openly placed this issue at the top of their hierarchy of concerns. While the male teachers of religious subjects were particularly zealous in this regard, others did not appear to hold significantly different views. Furthermore, since the staff of the Imam-Hatip lycée is numerically and culturally dominated by teachers of religious subjects, they are, clearly, the gatekeepers and pace-setters in this institution where the main axis of social and cultural control rests on the control of sexuality.

Beliefs and values about sexuality that are highly gendered and essentialist in nature lie behind the teachers' varying conceptualisations of male and female sexuality. These help to legitimise and reinforce patriarchal teacher attitudes that are basically 'supportive' and 'protective' of boys' and 'limiting' of girls' sexuality. The dominant discourse in the Imam-Hatip lycée attributes the differences between women and men to *fıtrat* ('nature'), as prescribed by Islam, and defines masculine and feminine identities as fixed, unchangeable entities. Being a man or a woman is thus conceived merely as a function of biology, and many teachers adopt an entirely non-challenging, complacent attitude to what is presumed to be natural. This world-view is articulated by teachers through statements such as:

> '[young] men start to experience their sexual identity at a certain point. [From then on] they think about sexuality. Women [on the other hand] are passive, what concerns men [that is sexual drives or needs] do not concern [women]'; 'Women are attractive beings [for men]'.

One teacher of a religious subject even went so far as to state,

> 'Men are active [biologically]. [This is demonstrated by the fact that] men's sperms are active [they move], [therefore] men are much more controlled by sexual desires.'

In this school culture, this kind of biology-based reasoning was so prominent (particularly among male teachers of Islamic subjects) that often boys' relatively lower levels of academic success were attributed to the distractions caused by their sexual awakening. Consequently, boys' unruly behaviour was often thought natural and not controllable by the boys themselves. As expressed by a teacher, 'It is natural for men to commit crimes, it is in their nature'.

Girls' sexuality, on the other hand, was downplayed and not presented as a potentially problematic issue in its own right. While there is a certain subtle recognition of female sexual potency, as expressed by the 'fire and gunpowder' analogy, it is the boys' sexual awakening that needs to be channelled to proper outlets. Girls' sexuality simply enters the discussion as something that should be kept under check so that it does not contribute to the de-railing of male interests, and hence become a threat to social order and harmony. It is important to note that all the Imam-Hatip lycée religion teachers interviewed thought that 'fortunately' it was not difficult to keep female sexuality under control because 'nature' had adequately provided for that. All that was needed was to teach girls to respect religious rules, cultural values, customs and traditions, and to encourage them towards setting up 'a healthy family structure'. This, they all thought, was not very difficult to do, but critical for the creation and maintenance of the desired social order.

Needless to say, dating, flirting and even inter-sex friendships are negatively valued. Male teachers of religion are particularly sensitive on this subject. They entertain very strong convictions about the prevention of such relationships among their students. In fact, any kind of special friendship between girls and boys was considered potentially dangerous and believed to lead to major psychological disorders, fights and even suicides among young people. These teachers saw marriage and motherhood as the most important life goal for girls. Furthermore, marriage was viewed as a lifelong commitment by the woman to her spouse and children. Such commitment, essential to social harmony, could only be ensured by limiting women's sexuality exclusively to the domain of conjugal relationships. Consequently, virginity was seen as a must, and it was believed that a non-virgin could not be committed to her husband with the kind of love and obedience that is expected from a good wife. As one teacher has remarked, 'Premarital sexual experience' is unacceptable in a woman because it may be 'habit-forming'. It is thus shunned as a tell-tale sign of a young woman's future promiscuity.

In addition to the preoccupation with sexuality, the fundamental nature of the school culture in the Imam-Hatip lycée is defined by the overarching importance given to discipline and the need to control the individual. The tendency to associate the control of sexuality with discipline is the primary item on the agenda of the hidden curriculum. Islam is the basis from which the positive and negative sanctions for such values and norms are seemingly derived, at least on the level of theoretical legitimation. Thus it would appear to the observer that, in this school culture, religion is the frame of reference used in settling all issues. Inevitably, in this cultural context, where the age-old religious concepts of 'right and wrong' and 'good and bad' are the backdrop for evaluating the everyday experiences of students and teachers in a modern, urban, middle-class setting, there are difficulties in maintaining a value system that aspires to the total control of the individual. Consequently, there is individual frustration, as expressed by one woman teacher: 'Everything is considered a sin at this school; from [participating in] physical education, to having mixed-sex classes, to not being [properly] secluded and so on'.

'Westernist versus Muslim' is a categorisation extensively used in the Islamist literature of the last two decades and has been the subject of much controversy (Acar, 1991; Ayata, 1991; Güneş-Ayata, 1991). It has also been very much stressed by such representatives of political Islam as the leaders of the now-defunct Welfare Party in Turkey. This dichotomous conceptualisation hangs over the school culture in the Imam-Hatip lycée very noticeably. It is often referred to by teachers and administrators in defining institutional boundaries and in-group/out-group identification criteria. It is interesting in this context, that a female teacher who was not 'covered' complained during her interview that what she found most upsetting was to be accused of dressing like a 'Western woman'; because she felt excluded and morally judged by her peers.

Teacher interviews at the Imam-Hatip lycée also underline an aspect of gender identity creation that is unique to this school culture. The rigidity of sex segregation apparently increases the interaction and strengthens the bonds between same-sex teachers and students. The relaxed, friendly relations between same-sex teachers and students help to alleviate or conceal the experience of the rather harsh overall control experienced in the individual's daily encounters with strict discipline and limitations to freedom. Furthermore, it was claimed that this school culture better accommodates some of the unaddressed, unresolved issues of modern secondary education, such as sex education and mutually supportive family–school relationships, precisely because these are all approached and handled with reference to Islam. Women teachers, for instance, claimed that they can talk with girl students on every topic, including sexuality, so long as the discussion is within the framework of religious laws and values. In fact, they saw it as their duty.

Girl students here can freely enter female teachers' common-rooms, which in appearance and atmosphere rather resemble provincial women's visiting days (tea parties). In the absence of men, female teachers turn this 'public' space into a 'private' one in which women behave, dress and talk freely. In this sense, for women – teachers and students alike – the teachers' common-room assumes a cosy character much like 'home'. Here, they have tea and uninhibited conversations on 'feminine' topics. To this forum, the girl student – who in a sense becomes the 'sister' or the 'daughter' – has considerably easier and freer access than students in general would normally have to teachers' common-rooms in other schools in Turkey.

This rather unusual milieu is often further extended to include the girl students' mothers. Especially for mothers who live in seclusion (tesettür) themselves, and are only able to function in sexually segregated public spaces, this school is a 'safe' and 'accessible' place. They can come and go easily to talk to teachers and participate in parent–teacher events.

The value of this less formal and often more 'self-disclosing' kind of student–teacher relationship, as well as the more 'confidence-building' nature of single-sex education for girls has been underlined time and again in Anglo-Saxon contexts (Mahoney, 1985; Deem, 1984). On the other hand, it has also been argued that despite the distraction element caused by boys' presence, co-education positively influences girls' sexuality and self-image (Lees, 1993) while single-sex schooling by its very nature often affirms gendered identities (Watson, 1997; Arat,1998; Toktaş-Çelik, 1988). Despite such varied claims and not always consistent evidence, it is clear that whether education is mixed or single sex is less important than how a school, through open and hidden curricula, handles gender as a dimension of socialisation (Stromquist, 1995).

It is therefore our contention that, in the absence of any significant cultural and institutional challenges to existing gendered identities, the closer relationships between women teachers and girl students in single-sex schools such as the Imam-Hatip lycées in Turkey can only be expected to further (re)produce inequalities and reinforce conformity to segregationist and discriminatory policies.

In fact, here teachers openly admit to advising girls and boys to choose their occupations in accordance with their *fıtrat*, and not try to contradict it. Furthermore, it is always stressed that the most important *fıtrat* requirement for women is motherhood, a 'natural' extension of which is being 'emotional, sensitive and affectionate', as well as 'weak and fragile'. Clearly this is a gendered, patriarchal and discriminatory educational message that tries to instil in pupils of both sexes the notion that changes in women's roles 'in defiance' of their innate characteristics is not only 'unnatural' but also 'sinful'. The definition of what job is considered compatible with the nature of women has two dimensions. First, the job should not be physically demanding, otherwise the 'fragile' female body will be under strain. Secondly, the job should not necessitate interaction with men, and should be limited mostly to serving women. For example, being a doctor is all right on condition that the rules of modesty and seclusion are implemented in the work context.

The school culture of the Imam-Hatip lycées provides an example of how reliance on religious values and standards functions as a double-edged sword in the specifics of Turkish secondary education. To the extent that religious references are supportive of and compatible with contemporary standards of quality education, religion can, no doubt, act as a major facilitator of improvements in education. The very presence of Imam-Hatip lycées in their current numbers and standards as well the high rates of female enrolment they have bear witness to this. It is, however, when religious doctrine or interpretation conflicts with contemporary ethical concepts of right and wrong that the secular system has internalised, or with fundamental freedoms and modern notions of equality (particularly of gender equality) that an educational culture guided and circumscribed exclusively by religious references creates problems. Institutions that facilitate the construction of gender identities and the creation of a sense of self so defined are particularly threatening to a political order that argues for legitimacy on modern, rational and secular grounds in a socio-cultural milieu that nonetheless harbours what the secular state considers 'hostile' traditional and religious components. The story of Imam-Hatip lycées in Turkey, from the promulgation of the 1924 Law on the Unification of Education to the present, illustrates this dynamic.

The private lycée

The private lycée studied in this research is one of the oldest and most well-established schools in Ankara. It is considered a 'prestige school' by many, and is attended by children of middle- and upper-middle-class urban, educated parents. The school was established in the early years of the republic with the express purpose of contributing to Turkey's westernisation by providing quality education to the younger generations in the new capital. Over the years, the school has grown in size. It is now part of a comprehensive educational complex that includes elementary as well as secondary education institutions. Here science and maths courses are in English, and there is intensive English language and literature training.

Even a cursory observation of the school reveals the highly developed sense of identity and the exceptionally strong 'we' feeling shared by students, alumni and teachers alike. Everyone expresses pride in belonging to this school community. Perhaps as a corollary to such a strong sense of belonging, there is also noticeable social control and pressure for excellence exercised by members of this community. As one teacher said, here 'everyone controls everyone else'.

The teachers express great pride in defining their role in this school as educating young people to become 'enlightened', a term they use as a code for the ideal citizen of the republic, as conceived by Kemalist values, namely well-educated in positive sciences, secular, rational and westernised. Believing these qualities to be the hallmarks of the 'enlightened' person that the school is mandated to create in modern Turkey, they are all extremely concerned about any sign of conservative or religious currents among their students.

Sports and performance arts are major parts of the extra-curricular activities, an aspect of the school culture that is particularly emphasised in this private lycée. Here, extra-curricular as well as academic activities revolve around 'competition' and 'success'; values that define the school culture. The school emphasises participation and competition with other schools mainly in three types of per- formance arts: pop music, folk dancing and theatre. These are all group activities necessitating teamwork and interpersonal interaction among students.

The school has a strong tradition in sports, especially basketball. In addition to a team carrying the school name and originating from among its students which now competes in the national league, its teams regularly enter and win national and international competitions. Such success is viewed as a sign of the school's overall superiority over others. Evidently, the strong 'we' feeling characterising this school culture is further fostered by a fierce spirit of competition in sports.

'Success' is the aim of competition. Both curricular and extra-curricular activities are carried out in a highly competitive manner, and with no less a goal than 'being the best'. Always emphasised in this school culture is to aim for the top: students are often encouraged to 'choose the profession in which they would become a 'star', and are discouraged from choosing 'the professions where they would be average'. As stated by one of the teachers, 'you cannot stay put in this school, you have to be always moving'.

The skills of competition and the drive for success are constantly sharpened and fuelled though formal and informal mechanisms in both academic and extra- curricular domains. Great importance is attached to students' success in national and international science and maths competition, as well as the university entrance examinations. Maths and science teachers in particular devote a lot of time and energy to preparing students for these competitions. Students, especially in their final year, are said to become obsessed with tests and scores.

While the curriculum is highly standardised in this school, all subjects are not necessarily thought to be of equal importance. This private lycée claims supremacy over other schools in foreign language (English), maths and sciences. It is also clear that in the overall ranking of subjects, maths and sciences are generally considered to be harder and more important subjects. Consequently, students who do better in these subjects are assumed to be more intelligent. The school implements programmes among students to bolster talent and achievement in these fields. There are more boys than girls among the science students. Also, among the staff, maths and science teachers are usually considered more valuable than teachers of other subjects, and are often better rewarded. While there are many women teachers of maths and science, a strong male image nonetheless dominates these fields. In other words, it is clear in the school culture that the good student is the science student and the valuable teacher is the science teacher, and most of these are men.

While gender equality is very much part of the rhetoric in this school's culture, it is a fact that girls are often in a secondary position with regard to those science and extra-curricular activities that are the school's 'pride and joy'. As well as there being more boys than girls learning science, sports are dominated by boys: there is a noticeable contradiction between what is preached and what is practiced.

Furthermore, the school's highly competitive and seemingly egalitarian culture exhibits a rather harsh and gender-insensitive evaluation of female performance in general. This is an institution in which not only are the majority of the teaching staff women but also the top administrative positions have a history of being occupied by women. Yet, it also supports an organisational culture where *de facto* demands placed on women in Turkish society and the resulting double burden shouldered by female teachers are not taken into account at all in management practice. This is largely because rules of 'competition' and 'success' for both teachers and students are designed on the basis of rather unrealistic assumptions of gender equality shaped by normative standards of ideology rather than existing realities. Thus the institutional culture of the private lycée, in its commitment to republican ideology, adopts a single undifferentiated set of criteria for evaluating 'success' of boys and girls or the performance of women and men teachers. This is a set of masculine values, often internalised and implemented by high-achieving women themselves. The school culture thus contributes to the reproduction of existing masculinist values and gender-insensitive practices while promoting an abstract discourse on gender equality.

The teachers interviewed in this school define the institution as a 'civilised place'. In operational terms this means a co-educational school where boys and girls and women and men are not physically segregated. However, it was observed that although teachers share mixed-sex common-rooms, there is a sex-based differentiation and tendency to mingle with same-sex colleagues in daily interaction, friendship and association patterns. Similarly, the well-articulated school policy is that girls and boys should have close relationships at school. Consequently, not only are they free to sit as they wish in the classrooms, some teachers even force them to mix, in order to create 'civilised relationships among young people'. Occasional non-conformity to the rules of what is considered 'civilised society', though not openly approved is, nonetheless, often tolerated and attributed to tradition and habit.

Here, the school culture accepts personal relationships among students of different sexes as normal. Dating and flirting are viewed, by teachers, as experiences young people should have so that they can get to know each other better and, as expressed by one teacher, 'get to know his/her prospective spouse and only then marry'. Moreover, teachers often see dating and flirting among students as a positive force for the boys' success. Girlfriends are thought to motivate and encourage boys to study and take classes seriously.

Two aspects of this school culture emerge as distinctive and interesting. One is that as expressed clearly in defining the limits of acceptable cross-sex relationships, the community's needs and standards are expected to take precedence over those of the individual. 'Dating should not be so conspicuous as to distract teachers and other students.' Second, but most saliently, teachers in this school culture discuss the issue of personal relationships among girl and boy students in almost total isolation from such concerns and terminology as sexuality, virginity and promiscuity. In contrast to the preoccupation with the sexual dimension of any conceivable relationship between men and women (or boys and girls) observed in the culture of the Imam-Hatip lycées, here not only is there an obvious preference for avoiding what can be considered explicitly sexual terminology, but an outright reluctance even to establish a link between dating, flirting and sex.

These attitudes on the part of the teachers are familiar to the students of women's history in the Turkish republic as derivatives of an elite cultural heritage in which women's appearance in the public domain is conditional upon the forfeiting of their sexual identities (Güneş-Ayata, 1994; Kandiyoti, 1987; Kadıoğlu, 1993; Durakbaşa, 1998).

It has been argued that the inability of the republican discourse to incorporate women's sexual identity into the conceptualisation of her new 'emancipated' gender identity has essentially weakened this world-view's position vis-à-vis its opponent, the Islamist view (Saktanber, 1997). Similarly, the almost de-sexed perception of relations between boys and girls that teachers in the private lycée entertain can neither be expected to lead to very effective communication between teachers and students nor help consolidate realistic expectations. Both of these problems are identifiable in the school culture of the private lycées, in which realisation of the self as well as relating to 'the other' are processes mediated through the harshly gender-neutral and impersonal media of 'competition' and 'success'.

The public school

In order to understand the educational atmosphere and school culture of the public lycée one has to take into account the social and economic context in which this school is located.

Public schools in Turkey, just like the schools in many other countries, are neighbourhood schools. This particular one was established in one of the middle- and upper-middle-class residential neighbourhoods of Ankara in the 1930s. In time, that location evolved into a middle- and lower-middle-class district of a mixed residential and commercial nature. After the 1970s, some parts of the district came to be surrounded by *gecekondus*, i.e. shantytowns inhabited by rural migrants to the city. Due to these changes in the social class composition of the district, most students in this school are now first- or second-generation rural migrants. Similarly, most of the parents have low levels of education, even if some are financially affluent. While many families in the neighbourhood do not have adequate income to spend on their children's education, as a public school the institution has also, in the recent past, suffered from the cuts in state spending on education. These cuts mainly had implications for mainstream public schools, as opposed to the Imam-Hatip lycées, due to the lack of any revenue from private resources to these institutions. In consequence, this school has double-time instruction, the number of students in the classrooms has increased to a truly unmanageable level and all facilities for extra-curricular activities have been lost. At the time the research was conducted, the school did not even have a gym or a schoolyard. It had been reduced to merely classrooms and courses. In this type of physical set-up, teachers were leaving the school as soon as they finished their classes; and it was not possible to keep the students in school after or even between classes for simple lack of physical space.

Here, we witnessed a social context in which conflicting and strong sentiments co-existed. Teachers interviewed expressed daily disappointments and the extreme stresses and strains resulting from unsatisfactory conditions alongside a passion for life and hopes for a future that they strongly believed could only be secured by education. It was obvious that both the students, who somehow tried to make it in this jungle, and the teachers, who were trying to transmit the values of the society and what they believed to be the 'ideals of the republic' to younger generations, were struggling against insurmountable odds and were often aimlessly 'going through the motions' in rather chaotic surroundings. The teachers were often left ambivalent between trying to understand and 'disregarding' the needs of their students, and oscillated between prioritising their own economic demands and their students' educational needs, while attempting to achieve some kind of equilibrium in the process.

Teachers were always talking of the need to achieve some kind of compromise, rather than reaching any specific goal. The resources at the school's disposal were entirely inadequate and ill-suited to dealing with present-day problems, and the ethical and moral principles needed for guidance were simply not there in a context of rapid change. Consequently, despite the strong emphasis placed on discipline and the commitment to ideals expressed by teachers in their rhetoric, the real situation was, by any standard, difficult, if not impossible, to cope with. It was highly anomic.

Gender issues here, as in other contexts, emerge as very relevant indicators of the school culture. Clearly, in this school there is no sex-based segregation of any kind for either teachers or students. First of all, the space simply does not allow it. Secondly, no one has the extra energy or the interest to oversee inter-sex interaction. In the classes, students sit four to a row; teachers simply do not attempt either to separate or mix them. There are almost no extra-curricular activities in the school, so no specific opportunities for boys and girls to come together. There are no performances, except for the obligatory national ceremonies. There is not even a library in the school. Even physical education classes are a problem. There is one small teachers' common-room and everyone, regardless of sex, uses this space. In this school, there is no opportunity for sex-based segregation; but neither is there any effort to bring girls and boys together.

All the teachers interviewed at this school subscribed to an almost hegemonic discourse of gender equality on the ideological level. There is also nothing to suggest that *de facto* gender-based discrimination is practiced, either with regard to teacher or student participation in the very few in-school activities that exist. With regard to dating and flirting, while some teachers were quite conservative, believing that these activities 'do not have a place at school' and 'are not compatible with school regulations', most were tolerant. Their reservations were expressed mostly along the lines that these relationships should 'not violate the rules of society' or 'should be with the consent of the students' parents'. One teacher put it:

> Close relationships between girls and boys are natural to the extent that they do not disturb the order and interfere with their studies at school.

Another said:

> Girls can have boyfriends in the sense that they need to become acquainted with the opposite sex, which is a very important thing as far as I am concerned. They should at least be familiar with [boys'] different thoughts, attitudes…what is important is that a student should know him- or herself [i.e. should know how to behave].

In discussions of sexual matters regarding young people, as in their responses to questions about the differences between girls and boys, teachers in the public lycée, like their colleagues in the private institution, did not make a single reference to religion or to the so-called 'innate' or 'natural' differences between boys' and girls' conduct.

In this school, the teaching staff has a high turnover rate. Also, during the day they do not stay in the school very long. Thus, there is little chance of developing a 'we' feeling among the staff, and not much reason to identify with the school as an institution. Teachers here do not develop close friendships or co-operative relationships among themselves or with students. In general, both male and female teachers talked about 'distant, cordial' relations between colleagues and basically instrumental interaction with students.

The public lycée is not a competitive place. For instance, the success of students at the university entrance exams is not emphasised as a value or goal in this school milieu. Consequently, 'teaching more', 'teaching better' or 'turning out better graduates' are not high-priority issues in this school. The teachers themselves do not see their position as one of competition in effectiveness of teaching. Similarly, different subjects are not hierarchically conceived. So the teachers have more relaxed and less prescriptive attitudes in recommending future occupations to their students. Many teachers believe that whether or not a subject or an occupation is considered important in society should not be a person's sole reason for choosing that occupation. Material gain, as well as other features of an occupation, should also be taken into consideration. The following quotations reflect the teachers' attitudes in this school, in contrast to those found in the private lycées:

> The occupation should provide the person with a status [but more importantly] a good income;

Never underestimate your occupation, in any case, even if you are a porter... you should be a friendly and respectful one... Be a person who treats people in a manner befitting a human being...

Teachers in this school, in contrast to those in other schools, over and over complained about students' families and teacher–parent relations. The families were usually described as indifferent to their children's education. It is quite common in this school for a teacher or an administrator to call the parents of a student in many times, and have to wait for months for them to show up. It was also reported that parents may show reactions inappropriate to the students' misbehaviour. This prevents better communication between teachers and families. For instance, sometimes when a student's misbehaviour is reported to parents, they respond by trying 'to take the student away from school, to keep him or her at home, to imprison them'. Or on occasions when a student has committed a serious transgression of school discipline such as coming to school drunk, the parents have been known to say 'my child can do whatever he/she wishes'.

At home, most students in the public lycées are exposed either to extreme control or none. They are also faced with significant financial difficulties, since many of them come from poor families in which there is a single breadwinner working for a minimum wage. The student is often expected to contribute financially to the family and to help with housework or family business. The teachers mention that domestic violence against children and other members of the family is prevalent.

The types of indiscipline and disciplinary problems in the school culture of the public lycée quite exceed such conventional educational ones as cheating or misbehaving in classroom. Teachers report cases of drunkenness, drug-taking and prostitution, or a girl student regularly working at a nightclub. Obviously, it is not possible to deal with these problems with the existing regulations or rules of the school. It is clear that the students are often caught helpless in the midst of a situation in which familial problems, parental indifference and negligence cannot be counteracted by a school plagued with material and other shortages. The counselling service in the school is under-resourced and inadequate to deal with the magnitude of existing problems.

Many teachers argue that lately their female students have become increasingly more demanding and ambitious in life. This tendency, although pleasing at first sight, is nonetheless a cause for distress in the eyes of many teachers who question the feasibility and realisability of their girl students' goals under existing conditions. As one teacher put it:

It seems to me that girls are more hardworking recently, there used to be no major difference; [now girls] are more hardworking, more ambitious... [They are always saying,] 'Sir/Ma'am, I'll do it, I'll answer the question' etc... boys remain in the background in their presence; [girls] really care about attending the university.

Such differences can have a number of explanations. First, education is the most important avenue of mobility for girls. Girls can enter into the public arena and prove themselves only through education. It is thus understandable that parallel to the trend in emphasising women's presence in the public sphere, girls are more motivated. Also it is a fact that in Turkey, in recent years, women's efforts have become more influential and increasingly noticeable in public life. In this context, while women's secondary position in society is much discussed in the media and other fields in recent years, there has also emerged a number of highly visible successful women, including a female prime minister, as role models in the country (Y. Arat, 1998). It is to be expected that such developments increase girls' self- confidence as well as boost their expectations and ambitions. Clearly, in the recent past, 'success' for women has come to mean 'success in public life'. This is particularly true for young women and girls from middle-class, urban backgrounds.

Family pressure can also force girls more than boys to prove themselves at school, which is often the only available legitimate public arena compatible with the family. As one teacher put it:

> Girls cannot go out [freely], and at home, probably, they [can] think of nothing [better] than studying.

Or as another argued, 'Girls have a commitment [to family] that has its roots in customs'.

Many teachers also point to the differential physiological and psychological development stages of girls and boys as a factor explaining girls' higher levels of secondary-school success: 'Girls are more mature than boys at this age. It is because of this maturity in thoughts and behaviours that girls are more successful'; 'Boys are always in a mood'.

These facts notwithstanding, many teachers in the public lycée fear that for the majority of their girl students' false hopes may lead to more disappointments.

A rather different aspect of this phenomenon that needs to be mentioned here is that some teachers claim that girls' drive for success is increasing so rapidly that they surpass the boys in everything, including naughtiness and misconduct. To the extent that these are also areas in which young people project their demands and ask for recognition, such developments are to be expected.

In the public lycées, the pursuit of equilibrium and the search for some kind of 'optimal order' is the underlying force defining the school culture. Obviously, an integral part of any order is rules. The absence and volatility of rules causes problems. The public inner-city lycées in Ankara, like so many of their counter- parts in other cities around the world, need to create some kind of stability in the face of tremendous odds. There are the structural constraints of the educational system, its material and non-material deficiencies, increasing expectations of students, particularly girls. And there is the pressure that comes from increasing closure of public education to lower socioeconomic groups. There is the lack of teachers, and their increasing loss of commitment to what has become an unfulfilling career. In this situation of shortages, insecurity, normlessness and disorder, the public lycée is desperately in search of 'a way out', an equilibrium. As expressed by one teacher, the search for consistency, the desire for an orderly existence underlie such equilibrium:

I mean [we need to] reach stability somehow; [this] is very important. The internal moral stability of a person is reflected upon the society. Everyone should have stability inside; it should be established by such an educational system that what the student hears here, he or she should also hear at the private [university entrance preparatory] courses, [and] at home as well. As far as I am concerned, a person should work for him- or herself, then for his or her family, and then for his or her country and humanity as an extension of this.

Conclusion

Analysis of the cultures of the schools discussed here reveals significant differences in class composition, cultural orientation and the mode of socialisation into gender roles between the three types of Turkish secondary schools. The private and Imam-Hatip lycées have successfully created a sense of community and a high degree of commitment to the institutional identity among both students and staff. As forces that help build this sense of identity and the 'we' feeling, the private school capitalises on modernity, social-class distinction, elite status, competitiveness and the high demand for its services from the market.

The Imam-Hatip lycée also enjoys high demand, although from totally different sections of society. This school has also developed a strong sense of identity, fundamentally in opposition to the westernising republican culture of secular public schools.

The public lycée, on the other hand, emerges as the institution in which the 'we' feeling among staff and students is the least developed. Both institutional factors, such as the high turnover rate of its staff and cultural characteristics, like the inability of the institution to define itself in either a positive or a negative relationship of 'belonging' to the dominant or the 'other' culture contribute to this sense of 'identitylessness'. Thus, members of this school community are best described as being in a vacuum, a maze or aimless. The search for meaning and stability characterising this school culture is thus accompanied by an overarching sense of insecurity and lack of self-confidence, reflected in teachers' attitudes and in the expectations and demands of students.

By contrast, the culture of the private lycée is clearly and consistently based on the norms of modern, competitive bourgeois society. Such competition is not only reflected in the attitudes of the administration with respect to the school's relationships to the other schools in the market, but is also reflected in the transmission of an ultimate, competitive ethic to students via both curricular and extra-curricular activities. Positivist science is prioritised in the hierarchy of knowledge adopted by the school. The high value placed on mathematics and science and university entrance exams, as well as on national and international competitive events of extra-curricular activities, such as the performing arts and sports, bear witness to the school culture's emphasis on competition, individualism and modernity. What is more, the nature of education in the private lycée extends this competition to an international level, a further indication of the institutional culture's links with the 'global'. By emphasising natural and physical sciences, the private-school curriculum and culture strengthen links with the outside world, since this is readily convertible knowledge, accessible and easily transmitted internationally. Furthermore, the school's original *raison d'être*, the teaching of English, undoubtedly facilitates integration into the world at large. The school boasts of forming a 'modern/civilised human being'. In many ways its products are indeed 'modern': students radiating a strong sense of individualism, distinguished through a competition and positive-science orientation, with a strong sense of achievement and internalised universal goals and values. Such modernity, however, also incorporates universality, a typical insensitivity to individual or group differences. It is also well known that such gender-blind modernity, claiming to have a universal yardstick to measure everyone, is particularly unfair to women in elevating masculinist values as standards of excellence. The culture of the private school, in fact, reflects this particular deficiency starkly.

The culture of the Imam-Hatip lycées, on the other hand, also carries the undertones of a universal ideology, that of Islam. This universal ideology leads especially the male teachers to be over-confident of their world-view. Religion legitimises their demands for cultural conformity, expressed in terms of Islamic order and harmony. This form of social control is best exercised by sexual segregation, and stresses chastity and honour of girls. The ideology of harmony with nature and creation leads to an idealisation of motherhood and modesty for women and girls. It is obvious that there is no need for a search for any other type or level of knowledge in the school. Islam provides the ultimate knowledge, and leads to ultimate harmony. Thus, the hierarchy of knowledge is, here also, very clearly conceived and transmitted. All curricular and extra-curricular activities have this purpose. Anything that is not conceived as serving Islam is deemed unproductive, unnecessary and to be avoided.

These schools appeal to different segments of Turkish society. The Imam-Hatip lycée appeals to conservative groups from different socioeconomic levels that hold Islamic ideals as alternatives to republican ones. The private lycée aims to educate the children of the educated middle and upper classes of Ankara. The public lycée appeals basically to under-privileged groups. These are the lower-middle classes, working classes and rural–urban migrants. The co-existence of three very different educational cultures in Turkey presents us with differing structures of opportunity and disadvantage for different strata and interest groups in society. The evaluation of this state of affairs depends on the vantage-point adopted.

For some, this is a highly depressing picture, illustrating the failure of republican reforms in the area of education. It is testimony to the 'un-unified' nature of secondary education more than 75 years after the formation of the republic. As such, some would like to read it as the bottom line of a balance sheet that points to the direction in which the Turkish republic's future efforts in education should be stepped up. Others simply view it as proof of the inevitable demise of what they consider to be an outrageous project of Kemalist social engineering. Another interpretation is often voiced by those who see such variety and 'disunity' as reflective of a healthy cultural pluralism essential in a democratic society.

The co-existence of alternative cultures of education, as observed in the three institutions of secondary education here, reflect both conflictual and integrative social forces at work in contemporary Turkey. No doubt, different disciplines can approach the analysis of the situation from varying perspectives, concentrate on different aspects of the phenomenon and come up with a wide array of area-specific recommendations. In this context, the skills, interests and concerns of the authors of this work, who are a couple of sociologists with long-standing commitments to furthering women's lot in Turkish society have inevitably led to this attempt at analysing the alternative secondary education cultures in Turkey in terms of how these influence the construction of gender identities at the crossroads of alternative world-views and social-class backgrounds.

Notes on Chapter 4

1   Although originally only permitted to pursue higher education in the area of Islamic theology, graduates of Imam-Hatip lycées have eventually been granted the right to apply to any and all higher education institutions. Their proportions in different branches of higher education have been steadily increasing over the past two decades. These institutions, like their secular counterparts, comprised middle schools and lycées up until 1997. In 1998, in consequence of the major education reform in the country, the five-year uniform compulsory education system was transformed into an eight-year one. This reform abolished what was considered the lower level (middle schools) of secondary education in the country. In the process, much to the opposition and dismay of Islamist groups and political parties, the middle-school levels (Grades 6–8) of Imam-Hatip institutions were phased out. The reform already appears to have produced a direct effect on Imam-Hatip enrolments, which declined radically in the 1999–2000 school year.

Currently, there are 510 Imam-Hatip lycées in the country. Curriculum-wise, 40 percent of the courses offered to students in Imam-Hatip lycées are what are termed 'vocational' (i.e. courses in different aspects of Islam) and 60 percent are regular secondary-education curriculum. However, it is claimed that due to the presence of a majority of religiously tinted courses among the electives offered, actually 80–90 percent of the curriculum is religion-based (Kuloğlu, 1998, p.117).

2   In religion course classes, girls who were menstruating would not be allowed to recite the Quran. They were asked to come up to the teacher and declare their excuse.

References

Acar, F. (1991), 'Women in the Ideology of Islamic Revivalism in Turkey: Islamic Women's Journals', in R. Tapper (ed.), *Islam in Modern Turkey: Region, Politics and Literature in a Secular State*, I.B.Tauris, London

Akşit, B. (1991), 'Islamic Education in Turkey: Medrese Reform in Late Ottoman Times and Imam-Hatip Schools in The Republic', in R. Tapper (ed.) *Islam in Modern Turkey: Region, Politics and Literature in a Secular State*, I.B.Tauris, London

Anyon, J. (1980), 'Social Class and the Hidden Curriculum of Work', *Journal of Education*, no 162, pp.67–92

Apple, M.W. (1971), 'The Hidden Curriculum and The Nature of Conflict', *Interchange*, vol. 2, pp.27–40

Apple, M.W. and N.P. King (1977), 'What do Schools Teach?', in R.H. Weller (ed.), *Humanistic Education*, McCutchan, Berkeley, CA, pp.29–63

Arat, Y. (1998), 'A Woman Prime Minister in Turkey: Did It Matter?', *Women & Politics*, vol. 19, no 4, pp.1–22

Arat, Z.F. (1988), 'Educating the Daughters of the Republic', in Z.F. Arat (ed.), *Deconstructing Images of 'The Turkish Women'*, St Martin's, New York, NY, pp.157–183

Ayata, S. (1991), 'Traditional Sufi Orders on the Periphery: Kadiri and Nakşibendi Islam in Konya and Trabzon', in R. Tapper (ed.), *Islam in Modern Turkey: Region, Politics and Literature in a Secular State*, I.B.Tauris, London

Deem, R. (1984), *Co-education Reconsidered*, Open University Press, Milton Keynes

Durakbaşa, A. (1989), 'Kemalism as Identity Politics in Turkey', in Z.F. Arat (ed.), *Deconstructing Images of 'The Turkish Women'*, St Martin's, New York, NY

Giroux, H., (1983), 'Theories of Reproduction and Resistance in the New Sociology of Education: A Critical Analysis.', *Harvard Educational Review*, no 53, pp.257–293

Güneş-Ayata, A. (1991), 'Pluralism Versus Authoritarianism: Political Ideas in Two Islamic Publications', in R. Tapper (ed.) *Islam in Modern Turkey: Region, Politics and Literature in a Secular State*, I.B.Tauris, London

– (1994), 'Women in Legislature', *Boğaziçi Journal Review of Social, Economic and Administrative Studies*, vol. 8, no 1–2, pp.107–120

Hannan, D.F. et al. (1996), *Co-education and Gender Equality*, Oak Tree Press (in association with the Economic and Social Research Institute), Dublin

Jackson, P.W. (1968), 'The Daily Grind', in P.W. Jackson (ed.), *Life in Classrooms*, Holt, Rinehart & Winston, New York, NY, pp.33–37

Kadıoğlu, A. (1993), 'Alaturkalık ve İffetsizlik Arasında Birey Olarak Kadın', *Görüş*, vol. 9, pp.58–63

Kandiyoti, D. (1987), 'Emancipated But Unliberated? Reflections on The Turkish Case', *Feminist Studies*, vol. 13, no 2, pp.317–337

Kuloğlu, N. (1998), *Dinsel Eğitim Allah'a Emanet*, Ardıç Yayınları, Ankara

Less, S. (1993), *Sugar and Spice, Sexuality and Adolescent Girls*, Penguin, Harmondsworth

Mahoney, P. (1985), *Schools for the Boys, Co-education Reassessed*, Hutchinson, London

Margolis, E. and M. Romero (1988), ' "The Department is Very Male, Very White, Very Old, and Very Conservative": The Functioning of the Hidden Curriculum in Graduate Sociology Departments', *Harvard Educational Review*, vol. 68, no 1, pp.1–32

Mert, A.B. and Ç. Bahçacı (1995), *Türkiye'de Din Eğitimi*, Türk Demokrasi Vakfı, Ekin Yayıncılık, Ankara

ÖSYM (1997), 'Yükseköğretime Girişte Okul Türü ve Öğrenim Durumuna Göre Başvuran – Yerleşen Aday Sayıları', ÖSYM Yayınları, Ankara

Saktanber, A. (1997), 'Women, Islamism and Politics in Turkey: A Critical Perspective', *Middle East Policy*, vol. V, no 3

Stromquist, N.P. (1995), 'Romancing the State: Gender and Power in Education', *Comparative Education Review*, vol. 39, no 4, pp.423–454

Stromquist, N.P. (1996), 'Gender Delusion and Exclusions in the Democratisation of Schooling in Latin America', *Comparative Education Review*, vol. 40, no 4, pp.404–425

Toktaş-Çelik, Ş. (1998), 'Uzlaşma ve Çatışma: Kız Enstitülerinden Mezun Öğretmen ve Akademisyenlerin Güçlenme ve Direnme Stratejileri', in O. Çitçi (ed.), *20.Yüzyılın Sonunda Kadınlar ve Gelecek*, TODAİE, Ankara

UN Department of Public Information (1995), 'Platform for Action and the Beijing Declaration', *Fourth World Conference on Women*, Beijing, China, 4–5 September 1995

Watson, S. (1997), 'Single-sex Education for Girls: Heterosexuality, Gendered Subjectivity and School Choice', *British Journal of Sociology of Education*, vol. 18, no 3, pp. 371–383

Willis, P. (1977), *Learning to Labour: How Working Class Kids Get Working Class Jobs*, Saxon House, Teakfield, Farnborough

II

CULTURAL PRODUCTION
AND THE PRODUCTION
OF CULTURE

5

Playing Games with Names

Şerif Mardin

The problem

Between 1918 and 1939 Turks embarked on a major identity switch. This involved a change in status, from subjects of a multi-ethnic, cosmopolitan empire to citizens of a republic that set down and affirmed its true Turkishness. For the literate, the transfiguration meant the transformation of the written language from one replete with Arabic and Persian roots to the retrieval (and recasting) of the vernacular and the colloquial, and the shift from a picture of a glorious Ottoman past to the promotion of Central Asian origins. This process was met by Western commentators with either spirited or tacit approval, the change being seen as a step towards Turkish modernisation. Such approval, however, has eluded an important question: how was this transition possible? How did such a major, and successful, transposition take place in a relatively short time? After all, the antithetical quality of 'Ottoman' and 'Turk' was a theme all knowledgeable commentators on Turkey had asserted in the past.

This chapter is a preliminary attempt to explain this transmogrification of literary taste and 'identity', focusing on aspects of the history of the Turkish language. But first, a few clarifications about relevant theoretical frames.

Language

Current theory about the role of language in the rise of modern nationalism derives from Benedict Anderson (1991). This theory constitutes a challenge to the views of the nineteenth-century *littérateurs* that language was constitutive of nationality, i.e. that as an autonomous force it propelled nation-building. Anderson's tack, and he is preceded by others,[1] is that language by itself is not constitutive of anything until it has become a printed language, the twin fruit of capitalism and of the construction of a nation by nineteenth-century intellectuals through the elaboration of the national language.

The idea that intellectuals worked to elaborate a national language is not in itself groundbreaking, having been around for decades. It is also a commonplace for historians of Turkish literature, and the point is not lost on anyone who has graduated from a Turkish lycée. This chapter attempts to study the relation of language to nation-building in Turkey by recasting the debate on language in society. It seeks a middle ground between Anderson and the nineteenth-century language theoreticians in attempting to re-establish some of the validities of language as constitutive in the Ottoman Turkish cultural frame.[2]

The main theme advanced is that despite the imputed use of two antithetical languages in the Ottoman empire – one 'polite', cosmopolitan, and made up of Turkic, Arabic and Persian roots, the other folkic vernacular – a common substratum of 'Turkishness' was maintained across the varieties of linguistic code. This was achieved through the hegemonic position of the cosmopolitan hybrid language of state, which remained 'Turkish' by affirming its difference from the other languages spoken in the empire. Thus observers from Europe could state that the Ottomans spoke 'turc'.[3]

Approaches concerning the link between language and society have been elaborated at a new level of analytical sophistication in studies of the poetic function of language,[4] a development which Anderson completely ignores. In our case, in particular, the concept of 'intertextuality' seems rich in explanatory potential, to unravel the persistence of 'Turkishness' in a language that to this day is characterised as 'Ottoman'. Poetics have already been used with success in the analysis of social structures in Islamic societies, especially with regard to the illocutionary use of language,[5] and it is here that we have to look for the source of the special 'ring' a language can have for a people. Using Ottoman social and intellectual history and poetics opens up novel ways of conceptualising the cultural history of the Ottoman empire at the meeting-point of the eighteenth and nineteenth centuries and, most important, the role of 'Turkish' in nation-building.

Identity

Among contemporary social scientists, the theme of identity has shifted from an approach that examined how, in the course of a lifetime, people attempted to work out a satisfactory self,[6] to one in which it was used to connote the satisfactory integration of a group into a separate community, involving a change in the collective name. But in fact it is possible to have two variants of the pursuit of a collective name.[7] The more modern of these variants, which takes place under conditions of migration from rural to urban areas, can be seen as working at the individual level, where the individual adopts the strategy of greater integration within a group which, in the village, had a much looser grip on him or her.[8] In the second, closer to Barth's work on ethnic groups, a whole group changes its identity markers as a group.

The switch at the 'individualistic' level exists only when social ties have already been loosened to the extent that an individual is liable to be confused, since items of his or her self-classificatory systems are in the process of disappearing.

This individualistic strategy has only been available in recent times, for it is also in recent times that individuals have begun to increase their role as agents rather than simply as units in a collectivity (Giddens, 1991). Richard Handler has shown that as late as the mid-nineteenth century, peoples were evaluated in relation to the set of social networks to which they belonged. In a study of Jane Austen's novels *Persuasion* and *Emma*, Handler (1994) concludes that in these novels

> ... the 'what' of a person refers to characteristics of appearance, manner, mind and situation that have been ascertained from personal experience of the person in question. By contrast, the 'who' of a person clearly refers to a web of social relations that places the individual with respect to family connections and social rank.[9]

In other words – in the nineteenth-century English setting – to *be* is to be placed within a social category. This outside process of placement also determines the subject's self-placement, since the subject also sees him- or herself as part of a collective. This also facilitates this second type of identity switch from one collective to another.

Identity switching

In the history of the Middle East, many groups defined by the names that we give them today, whether religious, ethnic, tribal or linguistic, seem to have operated within these parameters; identity is the collective to which one belongs.

The process of incorporation of one collectivity into another described by Barth is a case in point. A tribal group – for a number of reasons – incorporates itself into another and takes its name. The same name-switching game can be played with ethnic group names, religions or languages. Recent work has shown us how the element of switching has constantly operated in the history of the Middle East.[10] Here, of course, the 'who' is determined from the 'outside', and collectively. Georg Elwert (1997) gives us some examples of the process:

> Some Black Sea Christians in Turkey switched to Islam during periods in this century dominated by 'ethnic exchanges' but maintained the differences declaring themselves to be Alevis. Inversely, the Christian Bogumil heresy in the Balkans increased the clarity of the difference with reference to their Serb and Croat neighbours by switching to Islam when conquered by Ottomans, creating the Bosnians.

Notice the two opposed elements contained in switching: first the change-over, but second the maintaining of the difference even in the change. Thus, while switching occurs differences are not being invented, but maintained, something that should be of interest to proponents of theories of 'imagined communities'. Bruinessen (1977) describes the unbelievable numbers of combinations and permutations of such names that appear in the history of the group that we know today in Turkey as Alevi.[11] But there are limits to such operations, and the limits are set by the number of available names. Although new names appear and old one disappear, there are still a finite number of tribe names, a finite number of names of religions and heterodoxies, and a finite number of names for languages.

One consequence of switching is what may be called the 'exchange value' of a name for the player, quite apart from the symbolic charge carried by each of these names. This brings us to the ramifications of the names 'Turk' and 'Ottoman' through Ottoman history, and the role of their names as identity markers. Difference, as we shall see, will play a central role in this process.

'Turks' and 'Turkish'

The encounter of Ottomans with other 'Turks', i.e. Turkmen or Tatar (in the person of Tamerlane) was not auspicious, the experience being even worse with Mongols whose groups had sometimes overlapped with 'real' Turks. For the Ottoman Sultans – and for burghers as well – the term 'Turk' became one to forget, and was identified with rebellious tribes or country bumpkins. The Ottoman founders were keen to adopt elements of Islamic social organisation that defined urban culture. Doctors of Islamic law were invited to establish urban centres of Islamic civilisation, and Islamic 'private' law was incorporated into early Ottoman society. This was an elaboration of the somewhat superficial Islamisation of the population that entered the composition of the early empire. But a difference remained: 'public' law, i.e. Ottoman 'administrative' law, which addressed aspects of taxation as well as the status of the servants of the Sultan, remained 'Turkic' (post-Mongolian) somewhat embarrassingly so for the less sophisticated Ottoman 'clerics' trained in Islamic 'seminaries' (*medrese*). The founding elites of the empire, in tandem with these borrowings, incorporated some of the vocabulary and the literary devices of the already flourishing Arab Islamic and Perso-Islamic cultures. The name by which the subjects of the Sultan describe the empire in most Ottoman sources, Âl-i Osman ('sons of Osman'), was an Arabic construction. However, a new name, in the ascendancy for some time, 'Rum', or territory of the ex-Roman (Byzantine) empire, emerged, connoting the fact that long before the demise of Rome–Byzantium the Turks were established in the Balkans, that their recruiting of state servants (Janissaries etc) was centred in the Balkans, and that the state apparatus saw the Arabs as different, if not alien. When Sultan Selim I conquered Egypt (1516–17), the Janissaries began to grumble that they had spent enough time in an alien land, and wanted to return to 'Rum'.[12]

The Turkish poet Baki (1526–1600) was later to speak of himself as the teacher of the 'poets of Rum',[13] and this usage can be followed throughout the history of 'Ottoman' literature. All the signs point out that the use of 'Rum' was a polite way of differentiating oneself from Arabs and Persians. A more latent distancing was the continued role played by the Turkish language itself, a role to which I now turn.

Language in republican Turkey

In republican Turkey, in our time, ideological use has been made of a theory of Turkish 'modernisers' that saw Turkish as a language of the peasant or folkic background of Ottoman society. The theme promoted in this context is that there had been a suppression of a Turkish 'essence'. This idea worked in parallel with a policy aimed at retrieving the Turkish vernacular and making it a vehicle of a 'modern' general usage and literature. The most current official explanation for the earlier use of an 'Ottoman' language, purportedly heavily Arabised and Persianised, was that this was a monarchic, elitist plot that created a cultural divide between a palace literature – now described as 'divan' literature – and the people. The responsibility of Ziya Gökalp, a Turkish sociologist who set the frame of nationalist ideology in the republic, for this artless picture is well established.[14] Gökalp's ideas encouraged the creation of a number of official scientific societies, such as the Turkish Language Association (1932), which went on to retrieve 'Turkishness' from folk culture. Following the ideological line of the republic inspired by Gökalp, Agâh Sırrı Levend, a Turkish historian of literature, began, in 1944, to gather materials to recount the history that transformed the simple Turkish – presumably already a well-fleshed-out and seamless whole at the time of the foundation of the empire – into the reprehensible, cosmopolitan, ornate 'Ottoman' of the Ottoman *ancien régime*.[15] Across three editions, in 1949, 1960 and 1972, Levend refined his approach, but the ideological substratum of the book remained in evidence.

Already by the time that the last edition of the book was published (1976), Fahir İz of Istanbul University had contested the existence of a simplistic literary divide in the Ottoman empire. İz showed that there existed three genres in Ottoman prose. First, the simple prose using 'Turkish', i.e. the language of the 'people', then middle prose, more precious but still clear, and finally *inşa* ('rhetoric').[16] He identified *inşa* as the flowery idiom of literatures that went on to create their own esoteric and literary universe (p.1–xvii). İz also showed that the overwhelming volume of Ottoman prose was in the middle prose genre; these never disappeared. He demonstrated that their long-lasting presence in a number of differentiated discourses, such as the literature of mysticism, the educational fare of the Janissaries and popular liturgical song, can be pinpointed.

There were also some fundamental aspects of Ottoman discourse that kept Turkish afloat. Arabic and Persian syntax had never been integrated with the syntax of Turkish in the mix of the three that came to prevail after the fifteenth century in polite usage.[17] Divan or 'palace' literature, once considered the most characteristic and prominent 'genre' in Ottoman literature, turns out to be primarily poetry framed in a set of conventional stylistic patterns, such as the *kaside*, the *mesnevi*, the panegyric and love poetry; all these forms were taken from Arabic–Persian literature.[18] With time, this genre, in which the main aim was to show a sophisticated use of hyperbole, became, increasingly, an end in itself,[19] and in that respect Levend's views concerning the artificiality of 'Ottoman' is justified. But even the practitioners of divan literature often interspersed their conceits with nostalgic remarks about the use of pure 'Turkish' as an ideal to be striven for. Experiments of this type were undertaken by Tatavlali Mahremi (d.1535) and Edirneli Nazmi (d.1548), aiming to use the Turkish vernacular within the frame of divan literature.[20]

In a number of literary sources Turkish was – and described itself as – different from Arabic and Persian, in the sense that the names 'Arab' and 'Farsi' retained the connotation of different cultures. I have shown that 'Rum' was the most polite strategy used in this respect, i.e. both a switch into a new identity, a reference to the Ottomans as torchbearers of Islam and a reminder that these torchbearers were not Arabs. A substratum of Turkish culture was kept by the impediments of vocabulary and syntax in 'Ottoman'. While Ottomans had used Arabic and Farsi in the elaboration of the new polite language, difficulties were constantly encountered on the way to this adaptation. It is reported that when the historian Ibn Kemal (d.1534, i.e. 230 years after the foundation of the Ottoman empire!) began writing the history of the Ottoman dynasty (*Tevârih-i âl-ı Osman*), the ruling Sultan, Bayazid II (1481–1512) entreated him to write in a way comprehensible to higher and lower classes (*havas ve avam*), asking him to be clear (*vazih*) and 'without caring for the affectations of rhetoricians'.[21]

The classics of Islam in Arabic were only read by a small minority of Ottomans, while a large number of these classical works of Islam in Arabic circulated in Turkish translation. An explanation of this somewhat surprising fact is given by the doctor of Islamic law Ismail Ankaravi (d.1631): his grandchildren had complained that the major work on epistolary style which they had to study, the *Telhis of Kazvini*, was incomprehensible. Ankaravi translated the entire work into the Turkish vernacular.[22]

On the other hand, Ottoman everyday Islam was also expressed in the vernacular. The best loved religious text celebrating the birth of the Prophet Muhammad, the *Mevlüt*, by Süleyman Çelebi, was in Turkish.[23] So too were the religious chants that went to the heart of the people, the *İlahi*.[24] Even vaster was the bulk of secular materials in Turkish that constituted the fare of lower classes.[25] In this tradition, texts taken from the written Islamic corpus appeared in manuscripts in Turkish translation, and often took on a life of their own, with additions and corollaries. The *destan* (epic), the *kıssa* (edifying religious story), the vignette (*latife* or *fıkra*) were penned in the Turkish vernacular. It was again in this idiom that the collections of stories of the Persian writer Sadi, as well as motifs from *Kalila and Dimna* and the *Thousand and One Nights* were received in the oral tradition of Ottoman society.

Finally, Turkish was certainly the idiom of the palace. An example may be the account a court historian gives us of the language used by the Şeyhülislâm, the head of the religious institution, at the time of Selim III (1789–1807). The following was the Turkish sentence this dignitary used to express his fears about the Sultan walking incognito in the capital, well-armed and taking pot-shots at whatever he chose. 'Şevketlü Efendimiz tebdilde silah ile gezermiş ve hem tüfenk atarmış. Şevketlü Efendimizin vücud-u humayunu cümlemize lazımdır... Söylesen de o sevdadan fariğ olsun'. Even today, a Turk with a primary-school education would have no difficulty in understanding this palace Turkish.[26] This daily language used in the palace presents an aspect of a wider, latent but hegemonic influence of

Turkish through the many layers in which it was still alive in the 'classical' era of Ottoman history. What is still missing in the history I have attempted to give is how a literature that might have been to a large extent 'Turkish' was able to maintain an identity function at the time when 'Turk' was still used in a pejorative sense. An answer begins to emerge when we distinguish divan literature from the official style. What we find is a latent factor that 'preserved' Turkish even after the banishment of the social identity of the 'Turk' to the margins of social groups. That factor was simply that the official language of the Ottomans continued to maintain a difference from all other languages in the empire. Turkish, the language of administration and of judicial decisions, though interspersed with words taken over from Arabic and Persian, elaborately persianised and arabised, was not Greek, it was not Slavic and it was not Vlach, neither was it Arabic. In other words, the difference maintained by the language was both one connoting the power of the Muslim ruling group vis-à-vis non-Muslims, but also one that distinguished the language from Arabic as the language used in Arab provinces of the empire. Sultan Abdulhamid II, who at one time was thinking of introducing Arabic as the official Ottoman language, eventually had to give up this policy, because of this very penetration of this latent 'Turkishness' into the interstices of administration.

Turkish as a language different from that spoken in the empire kept throughout Ottoman history a 'fresh' substratum of Turkishness, to be revived by Ottoman intellectuals in the nineteenth century. A more ideological frame for this revival was provided by the Turkish republic in the twentieth century. Referring to some of the more fashionable theories of semiotics (Kristeva, 1984), we may conclude that maintaining the difference in the Turkish used by the state, and even by some nostalgic divan *littérateurs*, was an 'intertextual' continuity that had remained effective for centuries.

The potential for the emergence of a form of the Turkish vernacular, its readiness to be plucked out of Ottoman with relatively little effort, was promoted by a number of diffuse social changes that occurred in the various stages of modernisation of the empire. One of these was the little-studied 'localisation' that appears in seventeenth-century Ottoman poetry, and that possibly reflects changes in the urban structure of the empire (*mahallileşme*).[27] More manifest and prominent was the influence of printing, introduced in the Ottoman empire in 1728–9. The first book to come out of this official Ottoman press was an Arab–Turkish dictionary. Usually described with a certain lack of wonder by Turkish sources, the selection of a dictionary to teach Arabic, presumably to scribes who had not the faintest knowledge of the language, as the first text to be printed was extremely important, a deliberate step that highlighted a bottleneck in the promotion of official correspondence at a time when Ottomans were beginning to turn inward to see what they could offer in the competing sciences of the Enlightenment. The same bottleneck may have affected official correspondence, as scribes had to cover an increased number of documents. Manuals of official style were less useful than printed dictionaries, which allowed a more mechanical but also more accurate retrieval of meaning.[28]

In the nineteenth century, these harbingers of a diffuse reaction to the complexity of 'Ottoman' were transformed by an acknowledgment by Ottoman officials of the programme of educational promotion carried out among Western nation-states.[29] Turkish journalism, introduced by the founding of an 'official gazette' in 1831, went on to make a more systematic use of the Turkish vernacular. In the 1860s, the first promoters of private Turkish journalism brought their own contribution, i.e. a new 'journalistic' style aimed at mobilising the literate population towards economic and social modernisation. The same group took the first steps toward the creation of a national literature. Increased contacts with France promoted the adoption of genres like the novel, the most popular of which were in 'simple' Turkish.

In the 1880s and 1890s, a new controversy erupted: a group of *littérateurs* were now denying the legitimacy of Arabic as the foundation of Ottoman culture.[30] Following the Young Turk revolution of 1908, the name 'Turk', already moving up with the times since the 1890s, acquired a new, positive valence enabling 'Turkism' to inspire the official ideology of the Turkish republic in the 1920s and 1930s. The image of the Turk as the country bumpkin was transformed into that of the bronze-bodied, strong, serene and silent farmer carrying his load of grapes door-to-door in the stifling heat of summer. The final step in this extremely complex and cumulative process of retrieval of 'Turk' as the name of language and a people was the Turkish government's 'cleansing' of Arabic and Persian roots from 'Ottoman' and the creation of 'pure' (*arı*) Turkish as an adjunct to the official 'turkic' nationalism of the Turkish republic.

I have used four main tacks to make my point concerning the retrieval of 'Turkishness' from a parent linguistic fund. First, the syntactic characteristics of Turkish precluded an easy fusion with Arabic and Persian. Second, the very volume of the vernacular Turkish circulating in the Ottoman empire worked in the same direction. Third, the daily language of palace officials was colloquial Turkish. Fourth, the parent hegemony of Turkish – even though in its 'Ottoman form' – as the official language of the hegemon kept a 'turkic' substratum in administration. All these forces made it easy to retrieve a Turkish identity in the late nineteenth century. I have not addressed a fifth issue, which appears promising but is too complex to deal with in the present state of Turkish studies, namely a more extensive use of the resources of modern poetics to understand the 'ring' that a language would have when it is put to new, nationalistic uses. A related issue, namely the 'primordial' aspects of language, is currently being revived, once more underlining the failure of the Anderson model as a general explanatory link between language and nationalism.[31]

Thresholds and the autonomous forces of vernacularisation

The 'recapturing' of the latent Turkish vernacular was a task that modernist Ottoman intellectuals set themselves very early. This process went through a number of phases during the nineteenth and twentieth centuries, but none of these have had the detailed attention they merit, and I shall not attempt to correct this weakness of Turkish cultural history here. I shall only address these thresholds to underline that community was set by the very ambiguity of Ottoman as a language. I also want to underline how the almost mechanical working of various facets of vernacularisation impinges on questions relating to modernity. Each one of the stages of 'language simplification' introduces a new dimension of linguistic change, a neglected aspect of the story.

In the historical layering I have in mind, we first encounter the attempts of the architects of nineteenth-century Western-inspired reform, the fathers of the so-called Tanzimat (the name by which historians refer to the redrawing of Turkish society between 1839 and 1876, a period during which much attention was given to issues of language use in the educational institutions established in these years). Already in 1851, a grammar of the 'Turkish language' had been prepared by two of the most senior Ottoman officials, for use by the Imperial Ottoman Academy of Arts and Sciences with a view to enlarging the circle of those literate in Ottoman, an aspect of the attempt to involve citizens in the process of modernisation. The attempt by a new group of journalists with liberal ideas to reach to a wide audience by using a simpler language – a task shouldered by the *littérateur* İbrahim Şinasi in his paper *Tasvir-i Efkar* (founded in 1862) – worked in parallel. Almost simultaneously appears the attempt of Şinasi's contemporary, the poet and liberal leader Namık Kemal, to achieve a goal that can only be described as that of forging a shared Ottoman Turk 'national' literature. Somewhat later, in the short stories and novels of Ahmet Mithat Efendi, one observes[32] an increased number of locutions taken from the domestic vocabulary and discourse of Istanbul households. 'Pure' Turkish becomes even more hegemonic as it becomes the teaching language of the new secular, five-to-eight-year-old schools promoted by the architects of Tanzimat throughout the empire. While both Turkish-speaking Muslims and non-Muslims with a range of mother tongues were accepted in those schools, after 1867 entrants were obliged to pass an examination in the Turkish language.[33]

A third layer of vernacularisation, emerging in the 1880s, which may be judged as the consequence and cumulative effect of earlier phases, was that of new generations of Turks trained in the new colleges (now also including the School of Political Science and the Military Medical Academy). Some of these young men could not any more place themselves in the cultural settings of their fathers. This phase, intimately connected with the building of a literature in 'Turkish', simul-taneously brought in a distancing from the magic garden of Islam, which was now replaced either by suspicion or by a rationalisation of religion and deism. A further form of the vernacular Turkish appears in the late nineteenth century. In the poems of Mehmet Emin it promotes a new view of 'Turkishness' and a conception of the Turkish 'race' as sacred. Soon (1910) the outright use of the Turkish vernacular became a clarion call, in a literary manifesto in the periodical *Genç Kalemler*.[34]

In the era of the Young Turk revolution of 1908–18, controversies regarding the extent to which the vernacular should supersede Ottoman were rife. The focus of the debate, however, was even clearer than it was in the late nineteenth century: it was now about the construction of a cultural identity for the Turkish-speaking population of the empire. For one author the issue was that of the language appropriate to the Turkish *ethnie* (*kavm*) (*ethnie* is a French word used by Smith [1991, p.21] to refer to an ethnic group) and nation (*millet*), which would one day 'have to gather around its own language'.[35] Later, at the time of the inception of the Turkish republic, the focus of the issue of vernacularisation shifted once more. The object was the mobilisation of the population of the republic, a further elaboration of the target of Tanzimat. With the appearance of discussions about the adoption of the Latin alphabet to replace the Arabic, a major new problem appeared, the ability of the Latin alphabet to bring out the symbolic richness of religious texts in Arabic, like the Quran. A focus already adumbrated in the discussions of the 1880s now emerged centre-stage. A leading intellectual, Kılıçzâde Hakkı, stated that it was not 'the Angel Gabriel who brought us the Arabic letters'. Arguable in Islamic terms from the viewpoint of the 'createdness' of the Quran, the argument was still sacrilegious to Turks.[36] The issue of the use of Arabic by Turks also connected with the 'translation' of the Quran, a hotly debated issue beginning with the twentieth century. That a 'translation' of the Quran into Turkish would be a necessary prerequisite for its understanding by literate Turkish Muslims had been promoted at the beginning of the century by the Tatar Musa Carullah Bigi. Ziya Gökalp, ideologue of the Young Turks, had thought in similar terms. For him the vernacular Turkish would not be rich enough if it were unable to share a religious discourse with other Muslim cultures. In the early days of the republic, a number of Turkish intellectuals, encouraged by Mustafa Kemal, set out to produce a Turkish translation of the Quran. Prominent among them were İsmail Hakkı İzmirli and Mehmet Akif. However, in a speech in Bilecik on 5 February 1933, Kemal reminded his audience of the central focus of the issue in the culture of the republic. He had met, he stated, opposition to the Turkification of the Islamic call to prayer, and he added, 'The question is not one of religion, it is of language. One should be quite clear about the fact that the foundation of the Turkish nation will be its national language and national self.' Various attempts were made in the 1930s by the government to 'Turkicise' the call to prayer, ritual and Friday sermons. This last item was the only one that received widespread popular support.

It would seem that it was the double target of cutting modern Turkey's moorings to Arabic, or in a wider sense Islamic culture, and creating a national self that led Kemalist ideologues in the 1930s and 1940s to pursue further Turkification. The further promotion of this trend in literature and scholarly discourse in philosophy and the social sciences has led today to a cul-de-sac and the prevalence of European technical terms in these fields. The rescinding of the Turkish-language call to prayer in 1950 was met by believers in Turkey as victory for Islam. In the meantime, secularist intellectuals continued to use a 'Turkified' vernacular that they filled with 'ur-Turkish' locutions unknown to most Turkish speakers. This is about the stage we have reached today.

Conclusion

The preservation of the resources for the elaboration of a Turkish identity through a number of 'games' of adaptation and disguised hegemonic posture can be traced in the history of the Ottoman empire. The most interesting part of this process, however, is that modernity seems to have diminished rather than increased the opportunities for 'gaming' of this type. Vernacularisation now increasingly appears an irresistible force, and it is this mechanical force that gives the lie to the proponents of theories of cultural invention, such as Anderson. I have followed the transformation that has attended the expansion of vernacularisation, and am well aware of the changes of meaning that each threshold brings with it, but at each stage – and regardless of the actors' positions – the hegemonic, autonomous, irresistible thrust of language has become one that players of games themselves are increasingly forced to confront. In modern Turkey the state's policy of 'purification' of Turkish still exhibits two dimensions of central importance. First, the impoverishment of the language of the intellectuals who, when in need, i.e. often, switch to English. Second, the residue of an earlier, lunatic pursuit for the recovery of a Turkish culture, an exercise which, in its 1930s version, has greater affinity with the Enlightenment's concept of a fundamental, core truth, that waits to be unearthed than with 'inventions' of Andersonian origins.

Acknowledgment

With thanks to Professor Fahir İz, who inspired this chapter but cannot be saddled with responsibility for its contents.

Notes on Chapter 5

1   See, for example, Derrida (1981).
2   See, for instance, Humboldt (1988); also Caussat, Adamskin and Crepon (eds) (1996).
3   Galland, Julien Claude, *Memoire pour Servir d'Eclaircissement et de Supplément aux deux Relations que Mehemet Efendi a fait turc de son Ambassade en France*, Archives du Ministère des Affaires Etrangères, Series Memoires et Documents, Turquie, vol. 10, no 18 (December), cited by Veinstein (1981). Many other examples on the use of 'Turk'/'Turkish' confirming this description appear in European archives and literature.
4   Jacobson (1963); Price (1983); Kristeva (1984).
5   See, for instance, Samatar (1982).
6   Eriksson (1950).
7   Barth (1969).
8   Minnes (1970).
9   Giddens (1991), p.74.
10   Kehl-Brogodi et al. (eds) (1997).
11   Van Bruinessen (1977) '"Aslını inkâr Eden Haramzadedir", The Debate on the Ethnic Identity of Kurdish Alevis', in Kehl-Brodogi et al. (eds), pp.1–25.
12   Ülkütaşır (1979), p.275.
13   Nevzat (1963), p.10.
14   See Tanpınar (1962/1995), p.110.
15   Levend (1972).
16   See 'Insha', *Encyclopedia of Islam*, 2nd edition, vol. III, pp.1241–4.

17   See Deny (1956), 'L'Osmanlı Modern et le Turk (sic) de Turquie', in Deny, Grømbech, Scheel and Togan (eds) (1959), pp.182–258, here p.198.
18   See the discussion in Holbrook (1994).
19   Ibid., p.82.
20   See 'Othmanli', *Encyclopedia of Islam*, 2nd edition, vol. VIII, pp.210–21, here p.213.
21   Bombacci (1965), pp.67–8.
22   Ferrard (1984), p.21.
23   See McCallum (1943/57).
24   See 'İlahi' *Encyclopedia of Islam*, 2nd edition, vol. III, p.1094.
25   See Boratav (1965), pp.42–67.
26   Reported in Uzunçarşılı (1995), p.499n.
27   See *Encyclopedia of Islam*, 2nd edition, vol. VIII, p.214.
28   See Mardin (1961), pp.250–71.
29   See Mardin (1962), passim.
30   See Kushner (1977).
31   See Fishman (1997); as well as earlier statements that language should not be understood as the 'verbal organisation of symbols that mirror an objective world, see Thiele (1995). p.122; also Rorty (1993).
32   Levend (1972), p.168.
33   Kodaman and Saydan (1992), pp.475–96.
34   Levend (1972), pp.272–99; Arai (1991).
35   Kadri (15 September 1327).
36   Levend (1972), p.362, note 404.

References

Anderson, Benedict (1991), *Imagined Communities*, 2nd ed., Verso, London
Barth, F. (1969), *Ethnic Groups and Boundaries: The Social Organisation of Cultural Differences*, Scandinavian University Press, Oslo
Bombacci, Alessio (1965), 'The Turkish Literature', in Boratav (ed.), *Philologiae Turcica Fundamenta*
Boratav, Pertve Naili (ed.) (1965), *Philologiae Turcica Fundamenta*, vol. II, Steiner, Wiesbaden
Caussat, P., D. Adamskin and M. Crepon (eds) (1996), *Le Language Source de la Nation: Mesianismes Séculiers en Europe Centrale et Orientale du XVIII are XIX Siecle*, Mardaga, Paris
Deny, Jean, Kaare Grømbech, Helmuth Scheel, Zeki Velidi Togan (eds) (1959), *Philologiae Turcica Fundamenta*, vol. I
Derrida, Jacques (1982), *Margins of Philosophy*, University of Chicago Press, Chicago, IL
Encyclopaedia of Islam (1969) 2nd edition, Brill
Elwert, George (1997), 'Switching of we-group identities: the Alevis as a case among others', Krisztina Kehl-Brodogi et al. (eds), *Syncretistic Religious Communities in the Near East*, Brill, New York, NY
Ergang, Robert F. (1967), *Herder and the Foundations of German Nationalism*, Columbia University Press, New York, NY
Eriksson, Erik (1950), *Childhood and Society*, Norton, New York, NY
Fishman, Joshua (1997), *In Praise of the Beloved Language: A Comparative View of Positive Ethnolinguistics*, Mouton de Grutyer, Berlin and New York, NY

Ferrard, Christopher (1984), 'The Development of an Ottoman rhetoric up to 1882', Part I, 'The Medrese Tradition', *Journal of Ottoman Studies*, no III–IV

Giddens, Anthony (1991), *Modernity and Self-Identity*, Stanford University Press, Stanford, CA

Handler, Richard (1994), 'Is "identity" a useful concept', in John R. Gillis (ed.), *Commemorations: The Politics of National Identity*, Princeton University Press, Princeton, NJ

Holbrook, Victoria Rowe (1994), *The Unreadable Shores of Love: Turkish Modernity and Mystic Romance*, University of Texas Press, Austin, TX

Humboldt, W. von (1988), *On Language*, Cambridge University Press, Cambridge

'İlahi', *Encyclopedia of Islam*, 2nd edition, vol. III, p.1094

'Insha', *Encyclopedia of Islam*, 2nd edition, vol. III, pp.1241–4

İz, Fahir (1996), *Türk Edebiyatında Nesir*, 2nd ed. (1st ed. 1964), O. Yalçin, Ankara

Jakobson, Roman (1963), *Essais de Linguistique Generale*, Editions de Minuit, Paris

Kadri, Hüseyin Kâzım, in *İçtihad*, 15 September 1327 (28 November 1911)

Kehl-Brogodi, Krisztina et al. (eds) (1997), *Syncretistic Religious Communities in the Near East*, Brill, New York, NY

Kodaman, Bayram and Abdullah Saydam (1992), 'Tanzimat Devrinde Eğitim Sistemi', in Hakkı Dursun Yıldız (ed.), *150. Yılında Tanzimat*, Türk Tarih Kurumu, Ankara

Kristeva, Julia (1984), *Revolution in Poetic Language*, Columbia University Press, New York, NY

Kushner, David (1977), *The Rise of Turkish Nationalism 1876–1908*, Cass, London

Levend, Agah Sırrı (1972), *Türk Dilinde Gelişme ve Sadeleşme Evreleri*, 3rd ed., Turk Dil Kurumu, Ankara

Mardin, Şerif (1962), *The Genesis of Young Ottoman Thought*, Princeton University Press, Princeton, NJ

Mardin, Şerif (1961), 'A Note on the Early Phase in the Modernization of Communication in Turkey', *Comparative Studies in Society and History*, April, pp.250–71

McCallum, Lyrman (1943/57), *The Mevlidi Sheriff of Suleyman Chelebi*, John Murray, London

Minnes, Mattison (1975) 'Islamization and Muslim Ethnicity in South India', *Man*, no 70, pp.404–19

Nevzat, Yesirgil (1963), *Baki: Hayatı, Sanatı, Şiirleri*, 2nd ed, Varlık, Istanbul

'Othmanli', *Encyclopedia of Islam*, 2nd edition, vol. VIII, 210–21

Price, M., (1983), *Forms of Life, Character and Moral Imagination in the Novel*, Yale University Press, New Haven and London

Rorty, Richard (1993), 'Wittgenstein, Heidegger and the Reification of Language', in Charles Guignon (ed.), *The Cambridge Companion to Heidegger*, Cambridge University Press, New York, NY

Samatar, Said S. (1982), *Oral Poetry and Somali Nationalism: The Case of Savyid Muhammed 'Abdille Hasan*, Cambridge University Press, Cambridge

Smith, Anthony D. (1991), *National Identity*, Penguin, London

Tanpınar, Ahmed Hamdi (1962/95), *Yahya Kemal*, Dergah, Istanbul

Thiele, Leslie Paul (1995), *Timely Meditations: Martin Heidegger and Postmodern Politics*, Princeton University Press, Princeton, NJ

Ülkütaşır, M. Şakir (1970), 'Ibn Kemal', *Türk Kültürü*, no VIII (February), pp.39–43

Uzunçarşılı, Ismail Hakkı (1995), *Osmanlı Tarihi*, 4th ed., vol. IV, part II, Türk Tarih Kurumu, Ankara

Veinstein, Gilles (1981), *Le Paradis des Infidèles*, Maspero, Paris

6

'I Dance Folklore'

Arzu Öztürkmen

Had Selim Sırrı Tarcan (1873–1953) seen the outcome of the republican folk dance tradition of the late 1970s, he would probably be most amazed by the new dimensions it took. To Tarcan, *milli raks* ('national dance') had to be invented, modernised and stylised on the basis of folk dance motifs. Today's folk dancers, however, find themselves within a more complex system, a 'supra-genre' of folk dancing referred as *folklor oynama*. Following Adrienne Kaeppler's terminology, this new strand is indeed a 'structured movement system', and it is more rooted in the 'People's Houses' (see below) experience than in the short-lived invented tradition that Tarcan had once proposed. It borrows elements from earlier local dance traditions, but it is also distant from them. With the impact of 'floor patterning', musical instruments and costumes, today's folk dance tradition has grown into a staged popular art form, produced from an economic sector involving not only dancers and the audience, but also teachers, musicians, costume-manufacturers, club managers and school directors. The aim of this chapter is thus to scrutinise the development of folk dance as a 'national genre' through historical processes between the 1920s and 1970s. The relationship between national genres and invented traditions has often been analysed, and their 'national' character has usually been associated with the early nation-building era. Tarcan's invented tradition, *Tarcan zeybeği*, is a case in point.[1] But the invention of *folklor oynama* reveals something different. The tradition of *folklor oynama*, like *Tarcan zeybeği*, has its origins in the early republican institutions, but unlike Tarcan's experience *folklor oynama* is not primarily nationalist in its nature. It is more a product of a historical process that evolved around the agencies of the nation-state, that is of 'nationalisation' itself, and is therefore a national genre in its very nature, without being necessarily 'nationalist'. Given this framework, this study tries to situate *Tarcan zeybeği* in the historical development of folk dancing in Turkey, and explores our perception of the concepts 'national', 'nationalised' and 'nationalist', and their changing meanings in our study of nationalism.[2]

Tarcan's *milli raks*: *Tarcan zeybeği* as an imagined national dance

Dance in the Ottoman context is not a neglected topic. The history of the Ottoman imperial festivals provides us with a fair survey of various forms in which different dance genres were performed, for example ethnic, professional court dancing, grotesque dancing, military dance forms.[3] But the discovery of dance as the representation of an ethnic group or of a nation was new, and came only with the writings of Rıza Tevfik and Selim Sırrı Tarcan. Rıza Tevfik's article 'Memalik-i Osmaniye'de Raks ve Muhtelif Tarzları' ('Dance and its Various Forms in the Ottoman Countries') was published in 1900, and gave a genre-based overview of local dances from the Balkans, the Aegean and the Black Sea region. It drew attention to local dances as expressive of particular cultures, gave early descriptions of some of them, and compared them with European dance genres.

Tarcan's book, *Tarcan Zeybeği*, appeared much later, in 1928.[4] Tarcan, in contrast to Tevfik, was more in sympathy with the new republican regime. But his concept of *milli raks*, although coined in the early days of the republic, was rooted in late Ottoman times, when he was sent to Sweden in 1909, following the Young Turk revolution. Tarcan had in fact developed a keen interest in folk dance as early as 1898. Assigned to an official post in Izmir, he was able to visit villages along the Aegean coast, observe performances of the *zeybek* groups, and participate in their dance events (Tarcan, 1948). When he went to Sweden for training in physical education, he was impressed by the new forms of representation of Swedish peasant dances in urban salons. His most important observation was that in Sweden 'people owed much of their national feelings to folk songs and folk music' (p.17). In his own terms, the Swedish folklorists had 'disciplined' and 'refined' local dances to form a repertoire of national dances, 'excluding some', 'restoring others' and 're-choreographing' what had been selected (p.17–18):

> In this school [in Nees], all the national and local dances have been examined, some of these were totally excluded, some others restored, and the rest re-choreographed to be included in the tradition … I used to perform our zeybek dances, when I attended some family invitations in Stockholm. There, I already decided. On my return to my motherland, my primary task would be to revive the national dances and to give them the status they deserved in society.

He did indeed! He first found six soldiers serving in the Ottoman army, under Sultan Reşad's company. He took them to his own apartment and asked one of his former students to accompany them with his clarinet. The soldiers showed Tarcan some of their *zeybek* figures, which he later described as follows (p.18):

> The arm movements, steps and the knee-bends of those soldiers from Aydın, Ödemiş, Kilizmant, Bursa, did not really resemble one another; they were all the same in essence, but there were small differences in form and movements. They repeated the dance a couple of times, each time they bent their knee at a random time. I asked them why. They told me they performed the way their legs feel it, that this is all innate and not subject to uniformity.

Tarcan was not satisfied with the *zeybek* performances that he observed in areas like Eskişehir, Afyon-Karahisar, Uşak and Manisa. He thought that these dances 'lacked the refinement' seen in Swedish dances (p.19). Moreover, he was confused by the random changes in the timing of the arm and leg movements. Finally, in 1916, he decided to choreograph a *zeybek* dance in a more 'methodological' way, that is with predetermined figures, and a well-calculated beginning and end. Tarcan first picked a *zeybek* folk song, 'Sarı Zeybek', and speeded up its rhythm, while 'preserving the national character of both the song and the dance' (p.29):

> I gave the zeybek's head an upward position and the shape of a pear to his hands, while preserving the particularity of the zeybek dance's attitude and movements. I did not use sharp and rough movements, I paid attention to the harmony between the posture and the movements. I gave a waving movement from the top to the end of the arms.

Tarcan's choreography, with predetermined figures uniformly situated, was in fact imagined as a ballroom dance genre, a dance that could be performed by mixed couples, easily learnable and performed widely. He wanted to eliminate the 'rough' and 'sharp' movements, but also all kinds of improvisation. 'Like the music,' Tarcan stated, 'folk dances ha[d] to have a permanent form' (p.14):

> The content and the goal of national folk dances are extremely important. They are a live expression of people's characteristics, feelings, temperament and moral. It is a must to offer people this noble tradition as a sacred book, once we pass it through an artistic filter. If one does not give permanent forms to folk dances, and if its musical notation and movements are not determined, young people who will get excited by joyful emotions and alcohol in public gatherings, weddings and festivals, will not hesitate to invent new postures, attitudes and even movements as they please.

Teaching his *Tarcan zeybeği* choreography to a mixed group of students, Tarcan also gained Atatürk's acclaim in a performance in Izmir in 1925. According to the Izmir daily *Vakit*, Atatürk asked Tarcan to repeat his performance, and honoured him with the following words (p.3):

> Ladies and Gentlemen! Selim Sırrı Bey has given the zeybek dance a civilised form by reviving it. This master artist's work has matured and come to such a beautiful form that it can be liked and accepted by all of us to have its special place in our national and social life. From now on, we can tell the Europeans that we too have an excellent dance, and we can perform it in our drawing-rooms, representations. The zeybek dance can and must be performed with women in all kinds of social salons.

Atatürk asked Tarcan to repeat his performance, first in a tuxedo and then accompanied by a woman. The image of the national dance was here a social one that could be performed nationally. Tarcan taught his choreographed *zeybek* in the teacher's colleges, and performed it publicly on various occasions. Except for among his students, however, *Tarcan zeybeği* did not find much institutional grounding, which would have allowed it to diffuse nationally, as was intended. Tarcan's students who worked in Anatolia after graduation taught *zeybek* to their students,[5] but these individual efforts did not make *Tarcan zeybeği* Turkey's unique 'national dance', as its founder dreamt. Part of the reason for the lack of dissemination was a dirth of public places in which dance could be 'legitimately' performed. In a context in which there was no 'salon culture', it was hard to establish a social dance tradition. Moreover, individual dissemination of a genre nationwide was almost impossible; with no institutional support, *Tarcan zeybeği* could not go far from where it began.

The People's Houses experience

At a time when Tarcan's students were promoting the *zeybek* genre as a national dance around the country,[6] there emerged another institutional network, namely the People's Houses, which developed an interest in folk dance research and performance. Established in 1932, the People's Houses operated as the semi-official cultural clubs of the Republican People's Party. They survived until 1950, when the Democratic Party came to power.

The interest in folklore was not limited to folk dance in the People's Houses.[7] Folk dance grew, however, to be a more dominant folklore genre elsewhere, being connected to local official celebrations and also representing a particular locality on newly emerging national platforms. One such platform was the ritual cele-bration of the People's Houses' anniversary celebrations, organised each February in Ankara, and gathering folk singers, local folk dance and drama groups for public performances.

The formation of such groups took almost a decade, as the good dancers of particular towns and villages around Anatolia, but also in Thrace, organised them-selves into formal groups. Initially, these groups were organised for performances in local celebrations of national days and festivals, and a number of them (from Çoruh, Black Sea and Balıkesir, and an amateur ensemble of *zeybek* dancers) also performed in the Balkan Folk Dance Festival organised in Istanbul in 1936 (Tan, 1981).[8] The performers in these early folk dance groups have often been criticised for monopolising the dance repertoire by not teaching younger generations. This was partly because being invited to the anniversary celebrations of the People's Houses in Ankara was a matter of prestige and honour, and there was a great deal of competition for places in groups.[9] One exception was the *kılıç-kalkan* ('sword and shield') group, from Bursa, in which an individual was assigned to teach his dance repertoire to younger generations.[10]

The celebrations of national days and anniversaries in the early 1930s and 1940s played a major role in establishing a pattern for the urban folk dance tradition. This pattern consisted of successive presentations of a variety of local dances within a single dance event: in the early 1940s, even gathering dances from the same town was a new concept. The groups that performed at the People's Houses' February festivals usually belonged to the same village or family, typical examples being the group from Pamukçu village in Balıkesir or the Kahramanlar family group from Sıvas.[11] Yet there were also cases of performers from neighbouring villages gathering to represent a particular town in Ankara. Such combinations had further implications: the formation of the new nation-state favoured a definition of locality based on geographical administrative units rather than on ethnic ones. In the case of folk dance, for example, dance names were gradually stripped of the terms referring to particular ethnicities, and were often named after one town, part of the new national administrative system.

Examples of such groupings are numerous: the 'Bursa team' for the People's Houses' tenth anniversary event consisted of musicians and dancers from different villages.[12] The 'Gazi Antep' folk dances were put together by a 'commission of experts' in the Antep's People's House in 1948. The commission not only decided which dances would be included as Antep dances, but also which costumes would be worn.[13]

By the 1940s, folk dance had also begun to be researched by lay scholars, who, following a questionnaire published in *Ülkü*, wrote about local rituals and dance traditions. These accounts were usually very short, listing the names of the dances, the gender of the performers or the context of the performances.[14] Besides these monographs, journals also published articles that directly described the local dance traditions. Addressing issues of history, movement patterns, musical accompaniments and costumes, these articles also included pictures and musical notation at times.[15]

1941 marked an important leap in the way folk dance was performed in Turkey. A group of students from Gazi Teachers College performed in a national day celebration a series of dances from Sıvas, Erzurum and Çorum.[16] This performance was put up by Zehra Alagöz, also trained in physical education in Sweden and inspired, like Tarcan, by the large-scale folk dance representations in Scandinavia (Toygar, 1988). This was the first time that non-natives performed dances from different areas, and for a much larger audience. In a review of this performance, Muzaffer Sözen emphasises that these dances were performed in a 'mixed fashion' (*muhtelit şekil*), meaning that different dances of a same town – in that particular case, Erzurum *bars* – were performed in a row. Sözen (1941) also mentioned the performance held at Ankara People's House, where 'mixed *horons*' and 'mixed spoon dances' were also performed.[17] This was a big hit, drawing ten folk dance groups and a large number of bureaucrats for the anniversary celebration of the People's Houses. According to Şerif Baykurt, the 1941 celebration was conducted in a very special spirit, partly because 1940 had marked the beginning of a series of reforms in the growing People's House network, but also because of the hardships involved in reaching Ankara under tough weather conditions.[18] According to Sözen's review, the programme began with speeches by government officials, including the Prime Minister. Following performances by Aşık Veysel and a chorus of stylised folk songs, a group of dancers performed Karadeniz *horons*, Erzurum *bars*, Mudurnu's spoon dances, Sıvas and Çorum's *halays*, Peçeneks' *miskets* and Ankara *zeybeks* and sword dances.[19] Sözen (1941) depicts the dances, continuing with great enthusiasm:

> All these dances have been performed with national and local costumes, and each was accompanied by special musical instruments. Kemençe accompanied the Black Sea dances, davul-zurna the bars and the halays, and folk songs sung with saz, spoon, zeybek, misket and sword dances. Chosen from different regions of the country, these dances ornamented the People's House's stage

like a beautiful bouquet. The People's House's hall was so full that one could barely stand. For those who watched the national dances even to breathe was impossible, simply because the excitement was so high. With eyes full of tears and with ceaseless applause, that very day, the People's House looked majestic. What had been achieved was not merely the successful accomplishment of a celebration programme, but a true progress in the field of national art nourished by its natural source.[20]

A similar account published in *Aksu* described the 1948 celebration, and illustrated the importance ascribed by the locals to participation in the People's House festival. The journal stated that the Giresun dancers were able to draw the attention of well-known folklorists even when they were rehearsing. The group members were also acclaimed for having 'spread Giresun's touching melodies to every corner of the country'.[21] Those groups that travelled to Ankara for the People's House festivals also performed on other occasions. They often received invitations from universities, the opening of a photograph exhibition or a costumed ball.[22]

There were two important issues that emerged around the experience of the People's House festivals. Firstly, sending a local folk dance group to Ankara for a public performance was seen as an opportunity to promote a particular local image. In this sense, the People's House festivals operated like a marketplace in which new and old towns negotiated symbols to represent their locality. Among many other folk forms, folk dance constituted one such symbol, and certain dances accomplished that association, coupling one town with one particular dance, for example *kılıç-kalkan* with Bursa, *Atabarı* with Artvin, *madımak* with Sıvas. Secondly, this very marketplace formed at the same time a unique ground on which local dances were exposed to one another. This was primarily a visual exchange of forms, as every group only danced 'their' dance, and just 'saw' the others, without performing them. Nevertheless, it was a very important experience that would affect attitudes toward folk dancing and alter the existing repertoires. To succeed on the national platform, each group needed this visual exchange to learn how other groups were received, as well as judging their own reception. There were a variety of reasons for a dance becoming widely acclaimed, among them speed, a sense of drama, and applicability to mixed group performance. In a review published in *Ülkü*, Kemal Güngör, a Republican People's Party inspector, reported his observations of *halay* dances in Çorum and Sıvas. Among those dances, Güngör (1941) praised Çorum *halayı* as having 'very original figures', *İğdeli gelin* as 'worthy of being revived' and condemned *hürürnü* as 'degenerate' because it included 'obscene figures'. Describing *Abdurrahman halayı*, a dance from Sıvas, he explained how the shaking of the body at the end of the figures 'offered a very interesting spectacle'.[23] Similarly, Sözen (1941) reviewed the same *halays* in *Ülkü*, enumerating his favourite figures:

> In both halays, as the dancers release their hands, the harmonic and ordered arm movements in those sections that expressed bravery and heroism are also one of the refined figures which make the dance a much *prettier* spectacle ... As the dancers release their hands in the *yanlama* part, the turn of the group, followed by the putting down of the knee and the hand claps, is among those figures which *strengthened the appeal* of the dance. [Emphasis added.][24]

Sözen's review also invited readers to make the effort necessary to appreciating the *halay* dances:

> ... these dances, which first looked like the repetitions of the similar movements, began to appear refined as one paid attention to them ... the fine nuances which would not catch the eye if one did not pay attention constituted the spirit of the dance.[25]

Since the early performances in the People's Houses, local dance groups have always been concerned about appealing to their audiences. Often, on returning home from Ankara, one of the participants would publish the group's impressions in the journal of their People's House. In an article in *Uludağ*, for example, Turgut Karatal (1944) described how two *kılıç-kalkan* dancers from Bursa had captivated the audience at the 1942 People's House anniversary celebration in Ankara:

> In the beginning, their dancing did not attract special interest, because until the turn of Bursa came, the well-trained national groups of the Kars, Erzurum, Sıvas, Urfa, Kastamonu People's Houses had already won everybody's acclaim with their very successful performances and had fully filled the stage ... but after one or two turns and clashes, the guests were carried away by an excitement which increased from moment to moment. Now, the crowd which was once silent was full of excitement and applauded constantly, as the praising shouts were united into a single voice.[26]

Karatal also quoted from a review published in *Ülkü* on their *kılıç-kalkan* performance. This review was another example of how the author selectively promoted certain aspects of a given dance genre:

> The athletes of the Bursa People's House have enriched this centuries-old Turkish sport with some figures and transformed it into an almost modern dance form. We heard that the sword's sound was similar to the violin's, and that a melody was simultaneously created by the shield. We understood that the Kılıç-Kalkan dance is a sport that also trains our spirits. And we understood that if we elaborate the neglected treasures inherited from our ancestors who ruled most of the world with their taste, delicacy and power, we will see that they are as illuminating and reviving as the sun.[27]

In the reviews in the People's House journals, the issues of order and refinement were more dominantly stressed. It was critical that local dancers manifested order rather than chaos, grace and refinement rather than over-excitement. In other words, uniformity made a representation spectacular. In a review published in *Aksu* (1948), Giresun dancers were praised for 'their success in achieving a regularity and maturity which Giresun should be proud of'.[28] In a review published in *Ülkü*, Sözen (1941) cited Gazi Eğitim Enstitüsü's students, who performed several folk dances 'with great regularity in front of tens of thousands of people'.[29] Uniformity and order also remained a great concern for the collectors or researchers of folk dance. Hüsnü Ortaç praised in his fieldwork report Halil Bakış, a singer from the Uludağ area, for his consistent performance: 'As I was collecting and notating the four songs from Halil Bakış,' Ortaç (1941b) said, 'he repeated each line without changing the rhythm or the melody'.[30]

Concern about order and refinement developed within People's House circles were similar to Tarcan's approach to stylising *zeybek* dances. Tarcan too was obsessed with uniformity, synchronisation and refinement. But his concern was more with individual movements. The reviews of the People's House festivals showed, however, a deeper interest in the group choreography. Tarcan had imagined that his *Tarcan zeybeği* would be performed with a nationally observed uniformity. His invented tradition did not survive widely, yet the ideas of uniformity, regularity and refinement that he foregrounded appealed to a larger public, and found its echo in the People's House celebrations.

After the People's Houses were closed in 1950, the presentation of local dances as part of a 'rich national culture' had already been consolidated. Moreover, there now was an audience, at least among the republican elite in Ankara and Istanbul, that enjoyed the 'idea of folk dancing', if not performing it. Three main stages need to be identified in the shift from a tradition in which local dances were one in which dance became a participatory urban activity. The first of these stages is a continuation of the People's Houses experience, in which private enterprises carried on the tradition of an annual national festival. The second stage involved university students, who travelled from their native localities and enlarged their repertoire with dances from elsewhere. The third concerned the rise of a folk dance market, with its own political economy. In this stage, folk dancing evolved into a new structured movement system, *folklor oyna-ma*, which emerged as a supra-genre, borrowing elements from local dances but incorporating them into this new movement system.

In the footsteps of the People's House tradition: pioneering private folk dance enterprises

The closing of the People's Houses interrupted for a while the tradition of annual folk dance festivals. The first attempt to pursue this tradition came from a private bank, Yapı ve Kredi Bankası. The bank organised a folk dance competition in 1954, followed the next year by the establishment of a foundation, Türk Halk Oyunlarını Yayma ve Yaşatma Tesisi (the Foundation for Reviving and Spreading Turkish Folk Dances). The Foundation's approach to folk dance was not much different from the tradition that emerged under the People's Houses. The dancers were the well-respected performers from individual localities, travelling from there to represent their area nationally. The Foundation had thus evoked the memory of the early People's House anniversaries festivals. The Foundation's by-laws stated an interest in the collection of dances' 'movement patterns, costumes and music', and in documenting them in notation or on film. It also wanted to stylise the costumes and movements to be used in competitions, courses, festivals, celebrations and exhibitions, and to train dance teachers, to support *ballet folklorique*, and to do the necessary publicity for Turkish folk dances in Turkey and abroad. The Foundation took important steps in continuing research and 'discovering' dances that had not been previously performed in a national dance event. If the People's Houses era helped to form a 'national dance repertoire', through their celebrations – by gathering different local dances under a single programme in a pot pourri of 'Turkish folk dances' – the Foundation consolidated this repertoire by continuing the performance frame and including newcomers in that repertoire.[31] The Foundation's domestic publicity coincided with sending folk dance troupes to festivals abroad, a new practice that began with a trip to Italy and Spain in 1950, and to Belgium in 1958 (Evliyaoğlu and Baykurt, 1988). Festivals organised by the Foundation acquired an international character after its sixth year.

These festivals became models for the organisation of other folk dance events, and the formation of new dance groups in different parts of the country. Conforming to the tradition of the People's Houses, the 'success' of the Foundation was expressed numerically by Halil Bedii Yönetken in an article: 48 different dance groups performed nearly 250 different folk dances from 45 localities in the course of the first seven festivals. Yönetken also noted that approximately 12.5 percent of the dances were performed by women only, 25 percent were mixed, and 62.5 percent were performed by men only (Yönetken, 1964–5). Starting with the 1959 festival, some of the dances were performed within a dramatic structure, like a wedding or a village gathering, whose staging required long rehearsals. The Foundation also sent folk dance experts to different parts of the country in order to 'discover authentic dances' never performed outside their native context.[32]

The Foundation therefore continued a tradition rooted in the People's Houses, shifting the festival frame from Ankara to Istanbul, failing to develop a new pattern for the communication of local dance traditions. Very much like the People's House experience, the Foundation opened an opportunity only for a 'visual exchange' of existing dance traditions.[33] With the exception of Gazi Teachers College students who gave a stadium performance in 1941, performing dances not necessarily native to them, folk dancing remained a 'local' enterprise, with performers, usually adults, native to the dances' areas of origin, even if they were performing in Istanbul or Ankara.

Crossing local boundaries: university students and the popularisation of folk dancing

The development of folk dancing into an urban activity was driven by university students, who organised themselves, beginning in the 1950s, into clubs, and began to perform. Born into the invented traditions of republican institutions, but also an invented notion of 'youth', they were accustomed to participating in activities offered by the People's Houses or by schools in their native towns. Most of them had moved into the big cities, carrying with them a knowledge of the dances of their native towns. Student associations like Türkiye Milli Talebe Federasyonu, Türk Halk Oyunları Federasyonu, Türk Devrim Ocakları, İstanbul Üniversitesi Talebe Birliği and Milli Türk Talebe Birliği formed folk dance groups and engaged in public performances, field and festival trips, beginning in the 1950s and continuing on throughout the 1960s. The story of Fikret Değerli, now Professor of Folklore at Istanbul State Conservatory, is a case in point. He moved to Istanbul in the early 1950s, his knowledge of Van dances consisting of observations at weddings and conventional performances in Van's high school during the late 1940s and early 1950s. In 1954, he first joined Fine Arts Academy students in Istanbul performing Anatolian dances. In 1955, he joined Türkiye Milli Talebe Federasyonu (The National Student Federation of Turkey) with a group of students, all natives of Van. The formation of this group was not easy, Değerli recalls, as it was only after long discussion that he convinced other students to take up folk dancing.[34]

In fact, the way dormitories were organised made networking for folk dancing easier for students. Oktay Cengizay, also a student in Istanbul during the 1960s, noted that dorm life was an important factor in encouraging university students to get involved in folk dance activities in the big cities. Dorms were organised on the basis of the town of origin, for example Erzurumlular Yurdu (for natives of Erzurum) or Sıvaslılar Yurdu (for natives of Sıvas). This arrangement made life easier for folk dance leaders to reach natives of certain towns or villages, and to persuade them to teach their own dances to other students. No doubt folk dance activities also served as a solidarity network for those from each locality, and established a sense of pride in their native culture.

University students' folk dance activities were unique in a way that should be emphasised. Events organised by students were the first in the urban context to provide both learning and staging of dances other than those of the organising groups. Although most of the students still had close ties with their towns of origin, they were learning other local dances as well, expanding their repertoire towards a 'national' one. In fact, learning and performing dances from elsewhere was a wholly new experience, allowing not only a visual exchange between different dance traditions – as was the case with the People's Houses and the Foundation – but a bodily one, of exposure to different movement systems. The difference between the Foundation and student organisations became more obvious through the festivals and performances they organised. Local groups participating in annual festivals organised by the Foundation consisted of elderly dancers very conscious of the uniqueness of their own dance tradition. Members of student organisations were not only much younger, but also more interested in displaying the variety of traditions, both for domestic and foreign audiences.

The performance frame of university students' folk dancing was dispersed around a variety of settings. First, the associations held end-of-year performances; they also toured the country performing at particular occasions. Some of the students turned their folk dance knowledge into an asset and taught independently in elementary and high schools, and even in the People's Houses, which reopened in 1963.[35] Yet the most influential form of performance, which carried folk dancing to a more popular level, were the competitions. Following in the footsteps of an initial competition organised by the Foundation in 1954, the National Student Federation, in 1965, transformed the folk dance events held under its annual International Culture Festival into a competition.[36] Other competitions followed, among them Türk Ticaret Bankası's elementary school competitions between 1967 and 1970, and the acclaimed *Milliyet* competitions, beginning in 1970. These latter ones were not organised by student bodies, but involved students in the process as teachers and audience members. Competitions, along with festivals and trips to foreign countries, enhanced through the 1950s and the 1960s the establishment of a dynamic folk dance market. University students operated as an important agency in the making of this market, enlarging their folk dance repertoires and transmitting them to the different layers of urban audience, beginning in 1950. Their way of relating to folk dance was a breakthrough in the transition from locals performing local dances to mixed-locality groups performing dances from a number of areas.

The rise of a folk dance market: schools and folk dance clubs

As folk dancing was revived by university students as an extra-curricular activity in elementary and high schools, there eventually grew a market much larger than the one the students had initiated. Developing since the 1960s, this involved a wide range of actors, including folk dance teachers, musicians, costume-makers, jury members, dancers, administrators and managers of schools and private folk dance organisations, as well as audience members. It was consolidated mainly during the 1970s with the boom of privately founded folk dance groups in big cities. Schools and dance clubs shared musicians and trainers, and thus a very similar repertoire of dances.

There were various reasons for schools' interest in folk dancing. For teachers and administrators, it was a 'representational display event' to distinguish their school from others in the bureaucracy of national education. This is why they usually helped students to participate in competitions and organise trips abroad. But folk dance was also a *sosyal faaliyet* ('social activity'), an extra-curricular activity that brought life to the school community. It was particularly important in establishing co-operative and social relations with parents, and in mobilising them. The relationship with local folk dance was particularly significant. Many school teachers and directors became the pioneering collectors of 'new' folk dances. The dances from Bolu and Afyon-Dinar are a case in point. In Bolu in 1967, Avni Memikoğlu, the local official of the Ministry of National Education, asked Oktay Cengizay to research the dances of the area. He allocated an official jeep, and assigned an elementary school inspector and a woman teacher to accompany him during his research. In Izmir, a private high school, Fatih Koleji, provided accommodation for Fahrettin Şahiner, a local dancer from whom *zeybek* dances of the Afyon-Dinar area were collected.

The folk dance activities of various schools owed their energy also to folk dance competitions started in 1970 by the daily newspaper *Milliyet*. The special research prize also encouraged interest in discovering and performing new dances in urban settings. *Milliyet* competitions were, with a few exceptions, originally held in 11 cities, and encouraged local high schools to perform their native dances, some of them new.[37] From 1977, the Ministry of Youth and Sports also organised competitions. With access to all levels of public education, these competitions addressed not only high schools across the country but also elementary schools, universities, public education centres and the newly founded private folk dance clubs (Tan, 1988).[38]

The growth of competitions during the 1970s also stimulated the emergence of a new sort of institutionalisation in folklore. Independent and private dance clubs, the so-called *folklor dernekleri* ('folklore clubs'), boomed in urban areas.[39] The *derneks* included the term 'folklore' in their titles, yet hardly focused on any folklore genre other than dance. These folk dance clubs drew mostly young people, who discovered in folk dance a new social arena, an opportunity to connect with an urban community made up of others from similar backgrounds. In return for a small membership fee, they had access to a physical activity – one that was legitimate in the eyes of their parents and of the state – to friends, to festivals and trips abroad. Some used these clubs to build careers, careers being often hard to come by: they became the *dernek*'s accountant, stage manager or even teacher in a particular area. *Derneks* transformed into cash the asset of their hundreds of performers: they asked members to perform as amateurs in professional contracts, or marketed folk dance festivals abroad as 'trips to Europe'. Minimising costs with cheap bus trips, shared food and unpaid amateur dancers, they made profits from the small fees collected from their members, or from the honorarium offered by festivals' organising committees.

These *derneks* should be credited most for their socialising impact on young people from conservative backgrounds in urban areas. Bringing together male and female youth in a formal setting, they offered legitimate grounds for week-end activities. As a public event, conservative families found folk dancing more tolerable than any other dance form. Soon, parents and family members became the most consistent audience for folk dance events. In the 1970s, the legitimate socialising that folk dancing offered was a stark contrast to the many politicised youth organisations, and although much youth activity was closely monitored and mostly banned during the late 1970s, the state continued to promote folk dance clubs, and even began to sponsor competitions. This was partly because most *derneks* were not managed by students or young members themselves, but by 'patriarchal' entre-preneurs friendly with the state authorities. From the performers' point of view, *derneks* formed a perfect platform for male–female interaction, through sharing a dance floor, the months-long rehearsal time, or performance trips. They also enabled young people to experience public performance, the ease and simplicity of the movements and the use of everyday clothing in rehearsals adding to the appeal.

For a performer who began folk dance activities in the 1970s, either in schools or clubs, the repertoire was a consolidation of two strands. The first had been formed mainly during the People's Houses era, and comprised local dances that had been widely acclaimed – mainly by the republican elite in Istanbul and Ankara – during the festivals organised by the People's Houses and the Foundation. Some of these dances survived in the new folk dance market (such as *Gaziantep, Kırklareli, Silifke, Erzurum* or *Trabzon*), while others like *Çorum, Konya* and some of the Artvin dances, widely performed in earlier festivals, were eventually excluded from repertoires.[40]

The second strand was a new one, and included dances collected after the 1970s, when the increasing needs of the growing folk dance market forced teachers, managers and directors to distinguish themselves from others either through diversity of repertoire or the use of different styles and new staging techniques.

New demands for the spectacular were met by new offerings. *Diyarbakır* dances became a hit of the 1970s, *Afyon-Dinar* and *Bolu* dances of the 1980s, and then floor patterning became the vogue, offering greater dynamism. Audiences, as much as teachers and managers, exercised their judgement in favour of particular dances. These audiences had changed from the early days of the movement in the 1930s and 1940s, when officials, bureaucrats, intellectuals and inspectors had supported folk dance with a nationalist agenda. Their idea of good folk dance included the display of local costumes through performance in such a way as to project a new image of the republic. The audience that began to form from the 1950s did not comprise only students of Anatolian origins, but also new migrants from rural to urban areas, who still carried strong memories of their traditional culture. In the 1970s, folk dance performances were seen as a new form of urban entertainment: the discovery or invention of a national value for each dance was no longer sought, as it had been in the case of the *zeybek* or the *kılıç-kalkan*; instead, the dance phenomenon was seen as a new national artistic form. These new audiences appreciation was therefore more shaped by staging techniques, fast footwork, engaging melodies and rhythms, heightened drama and size of dancing group.

The emergence of a new movement system: *folklor oynama,* 'to dance folklore'

By the 1970s, the Turkish folk dance repertoire had been consolidated in *derneks* and schools. The 'conventional' repertoire of a group usually consisted of dances from Artvin, Diyarbakır, Edirne or Kırklareli, Silifke, Erzurum, Elazığ, Kars, Adıyaman, Gaziantep, Siirt and Bitlis. Occasionally, new collections would make their appearance, and new collections were added to this repertoire. Performers who joined the activities of schools or *derneks* were exposed to a wide range of dances from different parts of Turkey. Most were not familiar with the cultures from which the dances they performed had emerged. In contrast to the student dancers of the 1950s and 1960s, they were born and raised in cities as the children of the original migrants from provincial Turkey. Either in *derneks* or in schools, they learned dances from a teacher who was not necessarily from the dance's native area. These teachers were pressed by the demands of the new market. They searched for new ways of impressing audiences, school administrators, *dernek* managers and judges. With a few exceptions, the era of discovering new dances had passed. Teachers now had to modify the existing repertoire to impress audiences, and looked for ways of making dances more appealing. Changing the steps was taboo, and possibilities for innovation in the staging were quite limited. One way to make dances more spectacular was to use floor patterns, a technique that created its effect by operating at two levels: first in the organisation of the simultaneous movement of the whole group, and second in the basic steps and arm movements of each dancer.

Floor patterning arose therefore as the best way of giving existing dances a fresh flavour. It offered teachers and performers the chance to innovate without changing the old movements. It added a dynamic quality, although the room for creativity was finite: after all, there were limits to the number of shapes a group could form on stage. The geometrical shapes of the floor patterns – circles and triangles, diagonal or curvilinear forms – had to be repeated eventually. Floor patterning also emphasised the theatrical aspect of the performance, transforming folk dance almost into a popular art and entertainment form. The opening of Devlet Halk Dansları Topluluğu (State Folk Dance Ensemble) in 1975 further legitimised the stylisation of the already canonised folk dance repertoire. Because it was sponsored by the government and frequently broadcasted on national television, the Ensemble strongly influenced the way *derneks* and schools adopted new floor patterning techniques.

After a decade of experience in floor patterning between the 1970s and the 1980s, folk dance circles realised that floor patterning had indeed changed dance steps, and that the use of the same designs for different dance genres gradually produced a series of folk dances that all looked alike. In the 1980s, what remained in the minds of the audience after performances – be they by a *dernek* or a school – was a blurred image of brightly coloured costumes and a variety of changing shapes, rather than the specific movement quality or rhythmic arrangement of a particular dance. From the performers' perspective, memorising the flow of the floor pattern became more important than the basic movements. Teachers would sacrifice perfectionism in an individual dance step, but would not tolerate dancers putting at risk the success of the whole performance by failing to move at the right time to the right place in the pre-determined floor pattern.

Performers, exposed to a number of different dances at a time, eventually developed a mixed conception of the movement vocabulary. Following Adrienne Kaeppler's terminology, they learned a wide range of *kinemes, morphokines* or *motifs*. Kaeppler defined *kinemes* as minimal units of movement with no meaning in themselves. She called a *morphokine* the smallest unit that had meaning in the structure of the movement system, and that could not be divided without changing or destroying that meaning. Organised *morphokines* formed motifs, and the simultaneously and chronologically ordered *motifs* formed the dance itself (Kaeppler, 1967, 1992). Within this framework, dancers in urban Turkey in the 1970s learned in *derneks*, schools or other institutions a large variety of *kinemes, morphokines* and *motifs* from each of the dances they were taught. Given the largely social focus of *derneks* or schools throughout the year-long rehearsal schedule, most dancers did not pay much attention to which town's dances they were performing or to what the movements originally meant. They were more likely to be interested in whether they were dancing next to a good friend, how many times the floor patterning allowed them to appear at the front, or who would watch them in the final performance. As far as the movements were concerned, they perceived the entire dance as a single cultural form, as *folklor oynama* ('folk dancing'), and understood the movements not in the dances' own cultural context, but in their own social context. Following Kaeppler's terminology, the concept of a meaningful movement had a different significance for an urban and a native dancer. Urban dancers were exposed to dances from more than one locality, and their 'kinetic vocabulary' ranged from Kırklareli dances to Artvin dances. On top of that, with the increased emphasis on-floor patterning, it had become difficult to perceive the intricate distinctions between the numerous *morphokines* and *motifs*. Yet dancers could eventually classify similar *morphokines* – each coming from different *motifs* or dances – that cued for them specific parts of the dances they learned. *Morphokines* included pulling the right leg up, bending down, crossing the legs, shaking the shoulders, and were not unique to a single area. The dominant *morphokines* appeared in more than one dance and provided cues for the dancers to memorise a particular *motif* for a variety of dances, leaving the particularities of local dances increasingly indistinct.

Given the dancers' perception of folk dance movements, the canonised repertoire in urban Turkey has become increasingly uniform, until it generated a totally new cultural form, *folklor oynama*, which could not have come into existence in any cultural milieu other than that of the nation-state. In this respect, the Turkish folk dance experience illustrates how the term 'national' can take on a new meaning, one which contrasts with the romantic nationalist definition of the term dominating earlier approaches to dance in Turkey. The enshrined folk dance repertoire of the 1970s and 1980s was national in the sense that it came out of the dynamics created by the consolidation of the Turkish nation-state. In other words, the folk dance that arose in the 1970s throughout urban Turkey was 'national' by its nature, in contrast to promoted folk dance genres, like the *Tarcan zeybeği*, which were imagined to be so.

Notes on Chapter 6

1   *Zeybek* is an Aegean folk dance genre with slow heroic figures. For a discussion of the relationship between folklore and nationalism in the late Ottoman and early republican era, see Öztürkmen (1998).

2   For a discussion of the relationship between folklore and nationalism in the late Ottoman and early republican era, see Arzu Öztürkmen (1998).

3   See And (1976) and Nutku (1972) for Ottoman dance studies.

4   This book was reprinted in the new Turkish alphabet in 1948. The quotations from *Tarcan Zeybeği* are taken from this second edition.

5   Şerif Baykurt, for instance, stated that he learned *zeybek* dances during the early 1930s in Kırklareli from his elementary school teacher İbrahim Bey, a graduate of İzmir Muallim Mektebi, where Selim Sırrı taught (personal interview, 25 July 1992). According to Oktay Cengizay, school teachers continued to teach *zeybek* dances in the Balıkesir area until the late 1940s (personal interview, 14 July 1992).

6   There is an important dimension to the promotion of *zeybek* as a national dance. *Zeybek* belonged to Izmir and its surroundings, places loaded with symbolism from the Turkish Independence War. This dimension may not be a factor in Tarcan's choice of the *zeybek* for the national dance, but it surely found an audience in parts of Anatolia where it was welcomed with its baggage of national memory.

7   Local idioms, folk songs, folk tales and stories were all collected by the People's Houses. For an analysis of the Houses' folklore activities, see Öztürkmen (1996, 1998).

8   The first international Balkan Folk Dance Festival was in 1935.

9   Personal interview with Oktay Cengizay and İsmail Çelik, Summer 1991.
10 See Karatal (1944).
11 Personal interview with Cengiz Aydın, 16 June 1992.
12 See Ortaç (1941b).
13 Personal interview with Ali Çavaz, 11 August 1992, Istanbul. The commission is reported to have been formed by Vakkas Dayı (the leading musician of the area), Ferit Günol (Antep's high school music teacher), Ulvi Can, Vasıf Güllü and Cemil Cahit Güzelbey.
14 See, for instance, Süreyya (1933), Reyhan (1934) and Gök, (1934).
15 See Gazimihal (1946), Hüsnü (1941b), Işıtman (1941), Ortaç (1941a), Özer (1935) and Demirtaş (1937).
16 It seems that two different dance events took place on 19 May 1940, both performed by Gazi Eğitim Enstitüsü's students, one at Ankara People's House, where only Erzurum *bars* were performed, and at the stadium, where dances from the Sıvas and Çorum area were performed along with the Erzurum *bars*.
17 Sözen (1941). The accurate name of the author is Sarısözen, but Sözen is used for consistency with the quotation.
18 Personal interview with Şerif Baykurt, 25 July 1992.
19 *Horon, halay* and *bar* are the names of some Turkish folk dance genres. For a more detailed analysis of Turkish folk dance genres, see Ataman (1975) and And (1976).
20 Muzaffer Sözen, 'Halk Rakslarından Halaylar', *Ülkü*, April 1941, p.112.
21 See, 'Folklor Ekibimizin Ankara Seyahati' in Aksu, vol. 5, no 98 (April 1948), vol. 5, p.1. *Aksu* also reprinted Muzaffer Sarısözen's complimentary review of this performance, which received highest praise for its dramatised dance performance with guns. See Muzaffer Sarısözen, 'Çandır Tüfekli Oyununa Dair!', *Aksu*, vol.5, no.50 (April 1948), pp.2–4. This is a reprint from *Ulus* dated 14 March 1948.
22 See Turgut Karatal, 'Bursa Halkevinin Tahtakıran sistemi Kılıç-Kalkan Cenk Oyunu Hakkında Bir Kaç Söz' in *Uludağ*, no 63 (1944), p.14; Nafi Atuf Kansu, 'Halk Terbiyesi ve Halkevleri', *Ülkü*, vol.17, no 97 (March 1941), pp.3–6; 'Halkevi Haberleri', *Fikirler*, no 165 (1938), p.16.
23 See Kemal Güngör, 'Halk Raksları', *Ülkü*, vol.17, no 100 (June 1941), pp.368–370.
24 Muzaffer Sözen, 'Halk Rakslarından Halaylar', *Ülkü*, vol.17, no 98 (April 1941) p.115.
25 Muzaffer Sözen, 'Halk Rakslarından Halaylar', *Ülkü*, April 1941, vol.17, no 98, p.114.
26 Turgut Karatal, 'Bursa Halkevinin Tahtakıran Sistemi Kılıç-Kalkan Cenk Oyunu Hakkında Bir Kaç Söz', *Uludağ*, no 63 (1944), p.11.
27 Quoted in Turgut Karatal, 'Bursa Halkevinin Tahtakıran Sistemi Kılıç-Kalkan Cenk Oyunu Hakkında Bir Kaç Söz', *Uludağ*, no 63 (1944), p.15.
28 'Folklor Ekibimizin Ankara Seyahati', *Aksu*, vol. 5, no 50 (April 1948), p.1.
29 Muzaffer Sözen, 'Halk Rakslarından Halaylar', *Ülkü*, vol. 17, no 98 (April 1941), p.112.
30 See Hüsnü Ortaç, 'Uludağda Halk Raksları', *Uludağ*, no 45–6, 1942, p.27.
31 See *Türk Halk Oyunlarını Yaşatma ve Yayma Tesisi Senedi*, Istanbul, 1955.
32 For a list of such folk dances, see *Yönetken*, 1964–5, p.7.
33 Ali Çavaz has stated that these early local dance groups also had a certain impact on each other. According to Çavaz's account, the *Meryem* dance of the Antep

region was inspired by *Kıskanç*, a Kars dance, and re-choreographed by Oktay Güzelbey in 1965, while preserving the original steps of the dance (personal interview on 11 August 1992, Istanbul).

34   Personal interview with Fikret Değerli, 15 July 1992.

35   See *Toplum Kalkınması Hamlemizde Halkevleri Semineri*, Halkevleri Genel Merkezi, 1966, pp.111–12.

36   The list of the jury for the international folk dance competition will give an idea on the popularity of this event: Yaşar Kemal, Selmi Andak, Bedri Rahmi Eyüboğlu, Nurullah Berk, Nida Tüfekçi, Ruhi Su, Fazıl Hüsnü Dağlarca and Fikret Otyam.

37   Except for a few occasions, these cities were Edirne, Izmir, Afyon, Isparta/Kayseri, Gaziantep, Adana, Malatya, Diyarbakır, Ankara, Bursa and Istanbul (personal interview with Uzman Sağlık on 11 August 1992, Istanbul).

38   Beginning in 1983, the Ministry of Youth and Sports merged with that of National Education, and from then on the folk dance competitions were organised by the Ministry of National Education, Youth and Sports (Tan, 1988). In the 1990s, this Ministry was again divided into two separate organs, each organising its own folk dance competition.

39   For a list of these *derneks*, see Tan (1988), pp.32–6. For the analysis of their operation, see Öztürkmen (1989), pp.31–51; Özalgan (1984), pp.115–42; BÜFK-EÇY (1987).

40   One came across a number of Artvin dances such as *Polka, Kurt Barı, Kama Oyunu, Kapanı, Berta* or *Sıksaray Horonu* in earlier folk dance programmes, but none of these dances made their way to the conventional Artvin dance repertoire in the 1970s (Ülgen, 1944; Demirsipahi, 1975).

References

Aksu (1948), *Folklor Ekibimizin Ankara Seyahati, Aksu* 5, no 50 (April), p.1

Ali Süreyya (1933), 'Bir Köy Tetkiki: Alucra Kazası Gicora Köyü', *Aksu* 3–4–5–6, pp.29–30

And, Metin (1976), *A Pictorial History of Turkish Dancing: From Folk Dancing to Whirling Dervishes – Belly Dancing to Ballet*, Dost Yayınları, Ankara

Araz, Nezihe (1954), special publication by Yapı ve Kredi Bankası

Ataman, Sadi Yaver (1975), *100 Türk Halk Oyunu*, Yapı ve Kredi Bankası, Istanbul

Baykurt, Şerif (1976), *Türkiye'de Folklor*, Kalite Matbaası, Ankara

BÜFK–EÇY (Boğaziçi Üniversitesi Folklor Kulübü – Eğitsel Çalışmalar Yarkurulu) (1987), 'Folklor Derneklerine Bir Bakış', *Folklora Doğru* 56 (October), pp.33–40.

CHP İstanbul İl Gençlik Kolu (1963), *Halkevleri*, CHP İstanbul İl Gençlik Kolu Yayını, Istanbul, p.4

Çoruh (1938a), 'Çoruh'un Milli Oyunlarından Sarı Çiçek', *Çoruh* 1, no 2 (April), pp.8–9

Çoruh (1938b), 'Ata Barı', *Çoruh* 1, no 4 (August), p.37

Demirsipahi, Cemil (1975), *Türk Halk Oyunları*, Türkiye İş Bankası Kültür Yayınları, Ankara: p.148

Demirtaş, Adnan (1937), 'Ispartada Mahalli Oyunlar', *Ün* 35, pp.486–7

Erdem, Tarhan, and Selçuk İ. Erez (ed.) (1963), *Halkevleri*, Istanbul, CHP İstanbul İl Gençlik Kolu Yayını, p.4

Evliyaoğlu, Sait and Şerif Baykurt (1988), *Türk Halkbilimi*, Ankara Ofset Reprodüksiyon Matbaacılık

Fikirler (1938), 'Halkevi Haberleri', *Fikirler* 165, p.16

Gazimihal, Mahmut R. (1946), 'Ege Bölgesi Oyunları', *Fikirler* 314–15, pp.6–7, 18

Gök, Salim Süha (1934), 'Alucranın "Zil" Köyü', *Aksu* 13, p.13

Güngör, Kemal (1941), 'Halk Raksları', *Ülkü* 17, no 100, June, pp.368–70

Işıtman, Tarık Ziya (1941), 'Bolu'da Milli Oyunlar: Meşeli', *Fikirler* 219–20, pp.19–20

Kaeppler, Adrienne L. (1967), 'The Structure of Tongan Dance', PhD dissertation, University of Hawaii, HI, Department of Anthropology

– (1992), 'Dance', in Richard Bauman (ed.), *Folklore, Cultural Performances, and Popular Entertainments, A Communications-centred Handbook*, Oxford University Press, New York and Oxford, pp.196–203

Kansu, Nafi Atuf (1941), 'Halk Terbiyesi ve Halkevleri', *Ülkü* 17, no 97, March, pp.3–6

Karatal, Turgut (1944), 'Bursa Halkevinin Tahtakıran Sistemi Kılıç-Kalkan Cenk Oyunu Hakkında Bir Kaç Söz', *Uludağ* 63, pp.9–17

– (1945), 'Bursa Köylerinden: Mürseller', *Uludağ* 74 (November–December), p.13

Korkut, Rahmi (1934), 'Köylü ve Köylerimiz', *Aksu* 11

Kösemihal, Mahmut Ragıp (1938a), 'Artvin ve Kars Havalisi Müzik Folkloru Hakkında', *Yeni Türk* 67, pp.253–5

– (1938b), 'Onbeş Yıllık Müzik Çalışmalarımız', *Yeni Türk* 71, pp.452–5

Nutku, Özdemir (1972) *4. Mehmed'in Edirne Şenliği, 1675*, Türk Tarih Kurumu Basımevi, Ankara

Ortaç, Hüsnü (1941a), 'Bursa'da Halk Raksları', *Uludağ* 39–40, pp.53–7

– (1941b), 'Uludağda Halk Raksları', *Uludağ* 45–46, pp.26–32

Özalgan, Haluk (1984), *Zaman-Mekân Eksenlerinde Halkbilimi*, Ülke Yayın Haber Tic. Ltd.

Özer, K. (1935), 'Kalkan Oyunları', *Kaynak* 24, p.507

Öztürkmen, Arzu (1989), *A Survey of the Folk Dance Revival in Turkey*, Masters thesis, Indiana University, Folklore Institute, Bloomington, IN

– (1994), 'The Role of People's Houses in the Nationalisation...', in *New Perspectives on Turkey*, no 11 (Fall), pp.159–181

– (1998), *Türkiye'de Folklor ve Milliyetçilik*, İletişim Yayınları, Istanbul

Reyhan, (1934), 'Akyoma' *Aksu* 1, 9 June, pp.17–21.

– 'Akyoma', *Aksu* 9, 1934, p.21

Sözen, Muzaffer (1948), 'Çandır Tüfekli Oyununa Dair!' *Aksu* 5, no 50 (April), pp.2–4

– (1941), 'Halk Rakslarından Halaylar', *Ülkü* 17, no 98 (April), pp.111–119

Süreyya, Ali (1933), 'Bir Köy Tetkiki: Alucra Kazası Gicora Köyü', *Aksu* 3–4–5–6, pp.29–30

Tan, Nail (1981), *Atatürk ve Türk Folkloru*, Folklor Araştırmaları Kurumu Yayınları, p.7

– (1988), *Folklor (Halkbilimi) Genel Bilgiler*, Halk Kültürü, Istanbul

Tarcan, Selim Sırrı (1935), 'Milli Müzik Nasıl Doğdu?' *Ülkü* 5, no 27 (May), pp.200–5

– (1948), *Halk Dansları ve Tarcan Zeybeği*, Ülkü Basımevi, Istanbul

TMTF (Türkiye Milli Talebe Federasyonu) (1966), *Newsletter of the Uluslararası Kültür Şenliği* (International Cultural Festival), organised by the TMTF on 11 August 1966, TMTF

Toplum Kalkınması Hamlemizde Halkevleri Semineri (1966), Halkevleri Genel Merkezi, pp.111–12

Toygar, Kâmil (1983), 'Folklor Derneklerine Toplu Bakış: I', *Türk Halk Müziği ve Oyunları* 1, no 6, April–May–June, pp.255–7

– (1988), 'Halk Oyunlarımızın Tarihi ile İlgili Notlar', *Milli Kültür* 62 (September), pp.78–80

TRT (Türkiye Radyo Televizyon Kurumu) (1968), *Merkez Program Dairesi Başkanlığı, Türkiye Radyo Televizyon Kurumu Folklor Derlemesi (1)*, TRT Merkez Program Dairesi Başkanlığı, Ankara

Türk Etnografya ve Folklor Derneği (1963), *Türk Etnografya ve Folklor Derneği Tüzüğü*, Ankara Üniversitesi Basımevi, Ankara

Türk Folklör Oyunları ve Estetik Danslar Kulübü (1952), *Türk Folklör Oyunları ve Estetik Danslar Kulübü Tüzüğü*, Ankara

Türk Halk Oyunlarını Yaşatma ve Yayma Tesisi (1955), *Türk Halk Oyunlarını Yaşatma ve Yayma Tesisi Senedi*, Istanbul

Ülgen, Kasım (1944), *Doğu Anadolu Oyunları ve Havaları*, Kars Halkevi Yayınları, Kars

Yönetken, Halil Bedii (1964–5), 'Türk Halk Oyunlarını Yaşatma Ve Yayma Tesisi'nin Hizmetleri', *Orkestra* 20, pp.4–9

– (1966), *Derleme Notları-I*, Çeltüt Matbaacılık, Istanbul

7

The Film Does not End with an Ecstatic Kiss

Seçil Büker

We must analyse German stars, Italian stars, French stars, English stars. We must also confront our 'Occidental' Evolution with Oriental, Japanese, Indian and Egyptian evolutions.

Edgar Morin

Introduction

This chapter analyses the phenomenon of Türkan Şoray's rise to stardom in the context of changing audience tastes and expectations, and the evolution of genres in Turkish cinema. Two stars corresponding to contrasting periods of cinema emerge as symptomatic of these changes. Developing the idea that in the Turkish cinema the Greta Garbo of the pre-1960 elite, Cahide Sonku, was in some sense the opposite of the 'dark girl', Şoray, who after that year became the star of the new urbanites, the products of internal migration, the chapter seeks to demonstrate a parallel between the changing ideological climate and the emergence of the two stars. Thriving after a time in the cities, and overcoming their timidity, the new urbanities chose their star freely – rather than having her imposed on them – and dubbed her Sultana. For she was one of them, the woman for whom they had waited. In the 1960s, social, cultural and economic conditions were ripe for the emergence of a Sultana, and the Turkish cinema, too, was ready to take a dark-browed, dark-eyed beauty to its heart.

A kind of solar performer: a star

In order to analyse the reasons for Şoray's 'sultanate,' I will draw parallels between Turkey's social conditions and the phenomenon of the Sultana. This is a pre-requisite, because it would be impossible to deal with a star without considering the society from which she emerged. After all, stars are the projections of the dreams and aspirations of a society.

Raymond Durgnat says, 'The social history of a nation can be written in terms of its film stars' (cited by Dyer, 1986, p.6). And, according to Molly Haskell, 'Far more than men, women were the vessels of men's and women's fantasies and the barometers of changing fashion. Like two way mirrors linking the immediate past with the immediate future, women in the films reflected, perpetuated, and in some respects offered innovations on the roles of women in the society' (1973, p.12). Obviously film stars are valued in Turkey for many of the same reasons as in other cultures: they offer audiences the vicarious pleasure of identification. However, that an actress in Turkey can turn into a star, or rather into a Sultana, is a reality related to the peculiar conditions of the country. Similarly, the phenomenon of the star turning into a Sultana can only be judged in the distinctive conditions of the 1960s. I have tried to understand how the rules governing the general concept of stardom worked in the 1960s, and how instrumental they were.

The word 'Sultana' was once used to refer to the wives of Sultans, and to elite ruling women. Why would the public accord this title to a star, thus endowing her with this elite status? When we think of the elite, we usually have an image of rulers and governors. History has featured an array of Kings and Sultans. Today, political power generally rests with the heads of state of republican regimes. They decide on behalf of society; in a way, they determine the future of the people.

> However, besides these persons, one finds others, whose institutional power is very limited or non-existent, but whose doings and way of life arouse a considerable and sometimes even a maximum degree of interest. This interest is not related to the consequences which the activities and decisions of these particular individuals (stars, idols, 'divi') can have on the lives and future expectations of the members of society. They belong to another sphere of evaluation [Alberoni, 1962, p.75].

According to Alberoni, stars deserve a specific criterion of evaluation. They are the powerless elite of society and they are charismatic. Max Weber writes:

> By charisma we mean a quality regarded as extraordinary and attributed to a person ... The latter is believed to be endowed with powers and properties which are supernatural and superhuman or at least exceptional even where accessible to others; or again sent by God; or as if adorned with exemplary value and thus worthy to be a leader [cited by Alberoni, 1962, p.78].

A star does not fit into Weber's definition of power and his provision that it is necessary for a charismatic person to be a leader. Alberoni deals with this succinctly: '..."stars" do not occupy institutional positions of power' (1962, p.76). Stars do not have authoritative power, but nevertheless they draw the masses to them. They have their own class of charisma. 'Following Panzini's definition one would understand by this word the phenomenon by which a certain individual attracts, in the eyes of many others, an unconditional admiration and interest' (cited by Alberoni, 1962, p.78).

What are the conditions that make possible the emergence of the star I have defined as the powerless elite? 'Mass media present them any way they please, thus masses deem stars to be attractive, nothing is left to chance and stars are born' (Büker and Uluyagci, 1993, p.14) It is easy to explain the phenomenon of the star with hasty judgements such as these. It is not possible to claim that stars emerged due to certain arrangements peculiar to the system, at least not for the Turkey of the 1960s. The system does not create stars; maybe it just provides candidates, and the audience makes its choice. However 'audiences cannot make media images mean anything they want to, but they can select from the complexity of the image the meanings and feelings, the variations, inflections and contra-dictions, that work for them' (Dyer, 1987, p.5). It is the producer who puts the choice of the audience to use.

The producer has to take advantage of this choice, because for him a star means profits. The presence of a particular star causes doors to open in the market. But in no country is the star chosen by the system (the film industry and its machinations), for the system only suggests the star. The audience identifies with a certain characteristic of the star, be it a physical characteristic, facial feature, or vocal quality. When the system is aware of the predilection of the audience, it adopts it and develops it. The audience generally go to view the characteristics of the star more than the film itself.

Acting ability alone cannot make a star. Generally acting ability has no link with the phenomenon of stardom. Nor does the emergence of fame and image exclusively depend on the films: material about the star in newspapers and magazines sometimes is of greater importance, because what is being said and written about the star is crucial. It is useful for the researcher to scan newspapers and magazines of a given period, especially for the dirt. The spectator, and also the researcher, figure out the image of the star through such material. Films of course support the image, but the star's *doppelgänger* lives in gossip and scandal. The story of the star lives in these texts apart from her real life. Once the image is established, the star has to live up to it. 'To live like a star' becomes an ingrained habit, now that she is an eminent person. She does not have institutional power, but she is more powerful than those who have it, because the audience is captivated by her. Now let us attempt to elucidate those historical conditions which led to the emergence of Sultana.

The etatist elite

It was during the 1860s that Europe first heard the name Young Turks. These men generally belonged to the elite governing class, and although they were identified with the state wished to save it through reforms. They played a major role in shaping the Constitution of 1876, and attempted to fashion a synthesis of European liberalism and the Islamic tradition. In time they separated into two factions, the Liberals and the Unionists. While the Liberals favoured constitutional monarchy, 'The Unionists, members of the secret Committee of Union and Progress (CUP) founded in 1889, viewed the overthrow of autocracy as only the first step towards the social and economic transformation which the constitutional government was expected to carry out' (Ahmad, 1993, p.34). Overthrowing autocracy was not such an easy task, for the Sultan was not only the head of the state but at the same time the religious leader, the Caliph, a figure which a Muslim society would not readily relinquish. The Unionists had three different ideologies: Ottomanism, Islam and nationalism. 'Despite the increasing importance of Turks as the most significant numerical group, Islam not nationalism received the most emphasis; only some intellectuals in the capital took Turkish nationalism seriously' (Ahmad, 1993, p.39). Later the nationalists were to wage war against both the Greeks and the Sultan, emerging victorious to found a republic. The struggle of the Unionists to bring the country into the modern age was thus not in vain. But the world that they aspired to create could only be reached through a capitalist economy, this in turn implying the creation of a bourgeois class. 'Unionism involved creating new classes among the Turks, especially a bourgeoisie which would provide the social basis for the new state' (Ahmad, 1993, p.43).

The republic founded in 1923 under Atatürk's leadership not only abolished the monarchy, but at the same time rejected the entire legacy of the Ottoman empire. It did, however, allow for the bourgeoisie as a necessary adjunct of the modern state, and during the 1950s laid the groundwork for the eventual triumph of this class. Initially, there was no bourgeoisie, and it thus fell to the founders of the republic to carry out the revolution which would create one. 'The Kemalists, who saw themselves as a patriotic group autonomous of all class interests, assumed the task of carrying out a bourgeois revolution *by proxy* [emphasis added], a task begun by the Unionists during the 1914–1918 war' (Ahmad, 1993, p.79). As intellectuals and leaders, they saw themselves as being in a position to decide on behalf of the people. The aim of the Kemalists was to make Turkey into a modern nation-state, one which valued science along with education and a way of life that was modern. A whole way of life had to change, the goal being to create individuals who dressed like Westerners, acted like Westerners, and listened to classical music. 'The first step was expected to lead to the creation of a totally new society, and for such a society they knew that they had to create 'a new type of Turk very different from the Ottoman ...' (Ahmad, 1993, p.77). In 1925, the Kemalists passed a law making it obligatory to abandon the fez and instead wear the European-style hat. Then in 1928 came the law replacing the old Arabic characters with the Roman alphabet. Meanwhile, in 1926, the *sharia* – Islamic canon law – had been abolished. The urban middle class took to these changes, to the point that it could place censorship upon itself. For example, if men and women sat separately, at a gathering, or rather could not arrange to be together, they would caution one another about reverting to the old custom of *haremlik* and *selamlık* (in stately Istanbul homes the men had lived in separate quarters called the *selamlık*, while the women had been grouped together in the *harem*).

It was, however, impossible utterly to ignore the past, and one legacy of the Ottoman empire could not readily be shrugged off. Under the Ottomans, the state had been a dynamic force; and it was thanks to this tradition of centralised government that the face of Turkey changed, at least in the cities, during the republican era. 'The countryside did not change as dramatically, though not for lack of trying' (Ahmad, 1993, p.90). Western culture had no great impact on society as a whole, for the people, the governed, had little in common with the elite, who lived in their own world.

The most salient feature of the Kemalist reforms is that they were imposed from above on the masses by an etatist-elite group. An outgrowth of the Ottoman heritage, the latter, during the early years of the republic, were the only social and political force to be reckoned with. The second feature of the reforms is that they were aimed at creating a society of the Western type [Kongar, 1976, p.106].

In fact, there was a chasm separating the governing from the governed. The elite dressed differently. They listened to the classical Western music newly broadcast by Radio Ankara, and most of them spoke a foreign language, usually French. They believed that Turkey had much to learn from France and its history. 'There were now two cultures: the westernised, secular culture of a tiny but influential minority associated with the bureaucracy, and the indigenous culture of the mass of the people associated with Islam' (Ahmad, 1993, p.92). The Democratic Party, which came to power after 1950, recognised and exploited this alienation between the elite and the masses, enlisting the support of the latter to sweep into power. Many sociologists see this as the beginning of an Islamic resurgence in Turkey.

The etatist elite's candidate for stardom: the blonde

In 1889, the year when the Committee of Union and Progress was formed, Recaizade Mahmut Ekrem wrote a novel called *Araba Sevdası* (*Carriage Love*). The protagonist, Bihruz Bey, is predisposed to fall for a blonde, and when he sees a woman with that colour hair, Periveş Hanım, who also has a sultry look and deep green eyes, he can't help saying, 'Quelle beauté divine!' For Bihruz Bey, who spends the summer in his airy home among the pines at Çamlıca, on the Asian side of the Bosphorous, and winters in a stately home in the city, the coveted fairy girl could only be blonde (*perives* means 'fairy-like'). 'Une jeune fille! Surtout quel goût excellent!' Bihruz Bey finds the *jardin public*, where he strolls of a Sunday afternoon, quite *à la mode*, as is being seen with a blonde. He is struck with her, indulging his fantasies, and that blonde woman becomes the object of his fantasies, and is transformed into an image. He confuses fantasy with reality: attaining the image woman is always impossible, and it holds true for him as well. It is not in dark cinemas that he indulges his fantasies, for at that time there were no cinemas in Istanbul. No, he seeks his image woman in the *jardin public*. As for films, Istanbulites watched their first one in 1897, in a beer hall (Özön, 1985, p.334). For many years, cinema was a step-sister among the performing arts, and the first actual cinema for the showing of films, Cinema-Théatre Pathé Frères, opened in Istanbul only in 1908.

Others, however, soon followed, including: Ciné Éclair (1908), Ciné Oriental (1910), Ciné Central (1911), Ciné Magic (1914). Ten years after the founding of the republic, these cinema names began to be replaced by Turkish ones. Filming of an adaptation from Moliére entitled *Himmet Ağanın İzdivacı* (*The Marriage of Himmet Agha*) commenced in 1916, but, interrupted by the war, it failed to become the first ever Turkish film. Completed only in 1918, it yielded that honour to *Pençe* (*Clutches*), completed in 1917 and immediately released for public viewing. But the first film to have any cinematographic distinction was

Biçan Efendi Vekilharç (*Biçan Efendi, Household Steward*), a lively comedy made in 1921 (Özön, 1985, p.343). Biçan Efendi was an amusing character, and he caught on, so that two more films were made recounting his adventures. So began the Turkish tradition of film comedies, which imposed itself in the early years and persisted.

Another tradition which had an impact on early Turkish cinema was that of the theatre. Indeed, Özön designates the years between 1923 (when the republic was founded) and 1939 as the Stage Artists' Era (1995, p.1). During this time, both the director (Muhsin Ertuğrul) and the actors were on the payroll of the Istanbul Municipal Theatre, and they only did films in the summer months when the theatre was closed, probably just to make extra money:

> Thus not only did they fail to contribute anything positive to film-making, but at the same time they brought their stage-acquired professional habits to the screen, imposing on the cinema the sets, scripts, make-up and diction of the theatre, along with other elements. A style of acting which was overdone even for the stage came across as all the more blatant on the screen ... Moreover, the approach to dubbing introduced by actors who had learned their craft in the Municipal Theatre established a tortured diction which was to stay with us for generations in both Turkish and foreign films, only fading away, at last, in recent years [Özön, 1995, p.23].

This exaggerated mode of acting became an accepted style, adopted unquestioningly even by such stars as Şoray with no theatre training, who had started life as ordinary people. When this style was complemented by the voice of a theatre performer who spoke their lines for them, the resulting whole was unremittingly uniform. But it was also clear that the elite were not pleased with it. While the masses were swarming to the cinemas to see these new stars, the elite preferred the theatre and opera, or to pass the time in evening dress at elegant balls. In addition to the plays performed in the winter months at the Municipal Theatres, plays based on Western originals, it was highly fashionable also to adapt European and American films. In fact, only the titles would be changed, with the content remaining untouched, so that the product was not really an adaptation at all. Scognamillo says that this period marked the beginning of that tradition of adaptation which would eventually reach epidemic proportions (1987, p.39). Films were adapted both from the stage dramas and from films shot in the West. When to this foreign content was added the reigning exaggerated style of acting, it was enough to make a member of the elite shed tears of mirth. In our day, however, when the *arabesk* style has invaded the whole of life, many of the elite look back on these films with nostalgia, finding in them a certain purity and sincerity, regretting somewhat that they were denigrated in the past.

The majority of actresses were stage performers of the day; foremost among them was Cahide Sonku, born in 1916 in Yemen. Her father was a captain in the army who during the First World War settled with his family in Istanbul. Cahide graduated from the conservatory and became a stage actress, and like her colleagues also appeared in films. Unlike them, however, she became a famous film star. Had Bihruz Bey been able to see her in *Bataklı Damın Kızı* (*The Girl from the Marshes*, 1934–5), he would have forgotten all about that blonde in the *jardin public* and given his heart to Sonku. Adapted from Selma Lagerlöf's *Töser fran Stormyrtorpet*, the film featured a peasant girl, played by Sonku even though she had never set foot in a village. 'Audiences took to this film, and the scarf worn in it by Cahide started a folkloric vogue and was even given the name Aysel' (Scognamillo, 1987, p.58). In my view, this scarf was the only thing about the film with which audiences felt an affinity. Certainly they did not feel close to the star, for she was aloof, polite, and what's more blonde. It is hard to detect her eyebrows; only if you look closely can you see them. Sonku managed to conquer the hearts of the city-dwellers. This happened because she looked a lot like the Western woman that the typical republican intellectual had always posited as the ideal. Intellectuals chose to call her 'the Turkish Greta Garbo', 'our own Greta Garbo'. She was the star of the republican ideology, whose adherents were by choice occidentalised, unaware of all the things that they had to repress in order to become westernised. Once again, let us recall Bihruz Bey. He sought the lyrics of a song which he could send to his beloved, and of course it had to be written to a blond. Search though he might, however, he could not find such a thing, until at last he came upon the following, which he did send:

Bir siyehçerde civandir
Hüsnü mümtâz-ı cihandir

This translates as 'The dark girl is a raving beauty, loveliest in the world'. But Bihruz Bey didn't have an adequate command of his own language, and making a complete mess of his bout with the dictionary (at one point he misread a word, found 'yellow horse' and overlooked the word 'horse') decided the lines were written to a girl of fair complexion. It would be fifteen years after the making of *Bataklı Damın Kızı* (*The Girl from the Marshes*) before Turkish film audiences finally found the dark girl actually promised by the poem.

Sonku continued to make films, and in the 1950s established her own company, Sonku Film. It was at this time that increasing migration from the countryside to the cities began in Turkey. She was impassive, and her face did not make any impression on spectators, that is ordinary spectators from the villages trying to find a place for themselves. But the audience who came from the rural areas felt she was beyond their reach, pushed themselves to love her, but felt a bit frightened by her; her cool and impassive face was unfamiliar, she was looking at them, she was remote, so they could not look her in the eye; she was aloof. Because they had not yet come into their own in the city, the fear of the recent city-dwellers could be observed in every aspect of life. They were also ready to love with sincerity.

At this point it would be appropriate to examine the general level of taste among cinema-goers as it relates to internal migration. During the early years, the market was dominated by French films, those of the Gaumont company in particular. 'The French cinema has always been highly popular in Istanbul... Recall that at least until World War II, even American productions were shown with French dubbing, or with Turkish and French subtitles' (Scognamillo, 1991, p.64). In 1929, the French film lost its former hold, for in 1925 American companies had begun to enter the market (Scognamillo, 1991, p.54). If the films on offer, and the films patronised by the public, are any measure, a study by Scognamillo of Anatolian cities indicates that during the 1930s this taste for American films had worked its way across the country.

Relying on the memory of those who were alive at the time, one gathers that in the 1930s cinema halls were as elite and refined places of entertainment as the theatres. At a time when European films dominated – French, of course, but also German and Italian – ushers wore uniforms, cinema-going was a ritual, and when new films started on Wednesday nights at the Melek Cinema in Istanbul galas were held, with men and women in evening dress (Lütfi Akad, cited by Scognamillo, 1991, p.109). One cinema manager in Istanbul during the 1950s recounts that men not wearing suits, or who were unshaven, were not admitted.

It was during these years (the 1950s) that the conditions which gave rise to and nourished such practices began to change.

> Starting in the 1950s, the years when internal migration began and gathered momentum, the city of Istanbul underwent a radical change, which stage by stage overtook the entire metropolis and impacted on cinemas, the cinema-going ritual and cinema manners ... There were galas until 1960, but at them one no longer saw tuxedos, long dresses or furs. The function of the gala had changed, the idea now being to meet the stars of films which might play for one or two nights, and thus to ensure that the films did well at the box-office [Scognamillo, 1991, p.114].

This was a natural outgrowth of the capitalistic transformation that was over-taking the country. The level of taste was declining, and '... films were no longer chosen for an elite audience, but for a much wider one whose numbers were growing daily, as distribution and modes of projection expanded and the wishes of Anatolia increasingly were taken into account' (Scognamillo, 1991, p.72). In my view, whereas in the beginning a more refined taste emanated from Istanbul to Anatolia, after the 1950s the direction of flow was reversed and Anatolia began to impose its level of taste on Istanbul. As will be elaborated later, regional distributors began to order the films they wanted, made with the stars of their choice. 'During the 1956–57 season a cinema in Istanbul which previously had never shown Turkish films began to do so' (Scognamillo, 1991, p.73). As the audiences changed, cinema operators tried to adapt, switching from European films to those made in America and Turkey in an effort to please the new spectators. 'During the 1950s, they advertised in the Istanbul papers, using French to announce the showing of such films as *Nana* and *Cavelleria Rusticana* as they tried not to let the former audience slip away' (Scognamillo, 1991, p.76).

During the 1950s, the Democratic Party emphasised populism and the rule of the people, demanding that political initiative come not from the party but from the grass-roots. It gave priority to the interests of the farmer, offering easy loans and artificially high prices for crops, while tractors and other farm machinery were imported and sold to growers on credit. Construction began on a far-flung network of highways, as new roads connected the villages to the cities. Villages began to look outward, and in the 1950s there began a mass migration from the countryside to urban centres. Kongar maintains that this was not directly tied to industrialisation; that life in the countryside was hard, a fact which he describes as a push factor (1976, p.369). But there was also a force of attraction exerted by the cities themselves, where even if life was not ideal it was far preferable to what the village had to offer. In addition, there were certain cultural values deeply rooted in the society which tended to make the city tantalising. Kongar points out the existence of sayings like the famous 'In Istanbul even the rocks and dirt are made of gold' (Kongar, 1976, p.373). The average holdings per family were not large enough to provide a living, and the situation was further aggravated by a system of inheritance through which holdings were divided up among the sons each time a father died, so that the farms got smaller from one generation to the next, making economies of scale out of the question (Keleş, 1990, p.48). Mechanisation of agriculture was yet another factor conducive to migration, as farm labourers put out of work sought a new life in the city (Kongar, 1976, p.371). They were competing for jobs in the newly developing industry, which, however, could only provide limited employment to these unqualified workers (Zürcher, 1993, p.329).

> To characterise urbanisation which does not stem from rapid industrialisation as 'a transfer from the village to the city of hidden unemployment' reflects an important truth ... The evidence suggests that the massing of population in the cities is 'false and unhealthy' urbanisation. In cities such as Istanbul and Ankara it does not require a very keen eye to note the prevalence, in the service sector, of such jobs as street vending, horse-drawn wagon transport, shoe shining, apartment building superintending, and the like [Keleş, 1990, p.52].

This would be an appropriate place to remind the reader that some of the distinctive boxes in which shoe-shiners carry their polish and brushes have, on the inside, a photo of a Şoray look-alike. Such a shoe-shine box can be seen in Berger and Mohr's *Another Way of Telling* (1982, p.190) As the authors say, '... in the long sequence concerning the impact of the metropolis on an emigrant born in a village, we have used not only images of Paris but also images of Istanbul. All photographs use the language of appearances' (p.134). These people, who subsist through street vending, shoe-shining and other jobs, do not live the anonymous lives ordinarily found in the city, do not act like urbanites, and retain a widely bonded set of relationships. Perhaps this helps them to retain their local and Islamic identity, thanks to which they are happy and manage not to be disturbed by the modernised segment of the city's population. (The latter may be disturbed by them, however, for by now it is the arrivals from the village who dominate in the urban setting.)

> Characterising the Democratic Party as 'reactionary', the 'etatist elite' were also less than enthusiastic about the democratic order which had ousted them from power. The decade from 1950 to 1960 was one of heated debate between the 'etatist elite' and 'traditionalist liberals'. In its war against intellectuals, bureaucrats and the Republican People's Party, the surest weapon of the Democratic Party was its popular support. But when it went to extremes and tried to eradicate opposing groups and views, the gun backfired in 1960 [Kongar, 1976, p.162]

The army seized power. During the 1960s, Turkey adopted a planned economy and set its sights on rapid industrialisation, achieving an economic growth rate of

Idols depicted on shoe-shine boxes

7 percent. When the military relinquished its rule, the etatist elite remained in the ascendant till the mid-1960s, but the people were by now used to liberal policies, and once again that elite surrendered power to the traditionalist liberals.

'The increasingly industrial character of the economy was naturally reflected in the social transformation ... Turkish industry began producing virtually every consumer product which had been imported in the past' (Ahmad, 1993, p.134). Turkey was acquiring the consumer habit, and now looked for a film star to consume. The imported variety would no longer do.

The traditionalist liberal candidate for stardom: the dark girl

As discussed earlier, when Turkey entered the 1950s theatre was the supreme performing art. What, then, had been the contribution of the war years to a style of film narrative based on stage acting. In Özön's view, with European markets closed (due to the Second World War), Turkey began importing films from America and Egypt. The Egyptian films had a great impact on both audiences and directors. They were no different from the films made by theatre people, nor could they have been, since one of the pioneers of Egyptian cinema had been a Turk, Vedad Orfi, who had been trained in the theatre. Thus the influence of Turkish stage directors and performers on the Turkish cinema was further reinforced (1985, p.352).

> More films were imported from Egypt (they were called 'Arab films') than were made in Turkey during the same years. Egyptian films had a profound influence on both audiences and film-makers ... not only exacerbating the unfortunate impact of the stage performers, but leading to a further decline in taste [Özön, 1995, p.25].

Thus a level of taste which had hardly been superlative to begin with worsened even further and became entrenched. Even those who sought a cinematographic language had to use performers and other personnel who had been trained by people whose career was the stage. And let us not forget that audiences had taken to the Egyptian films. Yet despite all these adverse factors, in the 1950s there were directors who managed to develop their own language, men such as Lütfü Akad and Metin Erksan. In the 1960s, such directors turned for their themes to the phenomenon of migration spoken of earlier, and to other social questions. There was even a film treating problems of working-class unionisation, the right to strike and so forth. Of course there was also a batch of comedies and melodramas.

The period was one of enormous expansion in the Turkish film industry. In the context of the problems then concerning the people at large – the population explosion, urbanisation, industrialisation, internal migration, the rapid rise of squatter towns, unemployment, inflation – the cinema was the only cheap form of entertainment available to the masses (television broadcasts had not as yet begun in Turkey). The film-makers, in turn, tried to satisfy this hunger in the easiest, quickest, cheapest way possible. The result was a dizzying pace of film production. Whereas 95 films per year had been made between 1958 and 1960, in 1961 this number rose to 97, in 1962 to 123, in 1963 to 132, in 1964 to 196, and in 1966 to 229. By the last of these years, Turkey had become the fourth most prolific film-making nation in the world, after Japan (442), India (332) and Hong Kong (300) (Özön, 1985, p.368). What was the economic basis for all this activity?

> The producers certainly had no capital, so prior to making a film they would sell its rights to the distributor, who in turn was only willing to invest in performers and types of production which he thought would turn a profit. The distributors literally handed down decrees to the producers. It is an intolerable situation for a nation's cinema to be milked and exploited by regional distributors in this fashion [Okan, 1966, p.26].

During this period the cinemas were filled to capacity. There were nearly 3000 cinemas in Turkey in the 1960s, and the average film was seen by 15 million viewers (Günçikan, 1998, p.1). In Bartin, for example, an average-sized town of ten thousand near the Black Sea, there were in the 1960s four indoor and six outdoor cinemas. Eskisehir, a central Anatolian city with a population at that time of 209,000, had 15 indoor and 16 outdoor cinemas. Here we must draw on Özön to reiterate a significant point: although there were a few directors striving to create their own language, in 1960 the rest were shooting films with male heroes and lots of slang, essentially doing adaptations of foreign films or bestselling novels. After 1960, the emphasis was on drawing-room comedies, adventure stories and comedies of every variety (Özön, 1968). Onaran, on the other hand, notes that in the first half of the 1960s the volume of comedies increased, with all directors preferring this genre. This was when *Fıstık Gibi Maşallah* (*Thank God She's Cute*, 1964), based on *Some Like it Hot*, was filmed with Şoray in the leading role (1994, p.183).

In the 1960s, as the new city-dwellers started to lose their fear, just by chance they encountered someone on the screen who did not scare them or ignore them. They felt good, because they found someone on the screen who was affectionate, looked warm, and they thought they were operating on the same plane. In *Aşk Rüzgarları* (*Winds of Love*, 1960), the male protagonist has three lovers, and does not favour the dark, rather plump one; but the audience does. The audience cheers for the dark girl. The producers heard *vox populi*, and they decided to have her as a heroine of another film. The film *Aşk Yarışı* (*Race for Love*) was made in 1962. A football player who knows nothing about art or literature and an architect who is elegant, refined, classical and cultivated compete for her. As the male stars of the silver screen lust for her, and vie for her favours, the managers of cinemas all across the country competed to show her films. A dark girl fever raged throughout the land.

In the 1960s, magazines and newspapers claimed that she was a typical Turkish woman. The public searched for an idol with certain qualities, found these qualities, and selected 'one of its own'. She conformed to a stereotype of desirability that combined fairness of complexion with a well-proportioned and plump body.[1] She was the longed-for woman, the one who had been taken from them. Finally the audience spotted its Middle-Eastern and rural face on the screen.

Perhaps the strength of the desire to achieve their goal had caused the elitists to choose coercion as a way of instilling the modern identity. According to Uğur, 'the dosage of elegance or refinement which they could absorb had been exceeded' (1991, p.100). Rather than worrying about decency, the new city-dwellers were concerned about going to 1960s comedies that made fun of *parvenus*. The *nouveau riche* class which had emerged with the rise of capitalism were not the same elite who had gone to balls and operas in evening dress. These newcomers fell asleep at the opera (a fact that found its way into some films), and the modern identity was still a remote ideal. It was a source of mirth to cinema audiences that the *nouveaux riches* could not bring off refined activities such as theatre-and opera-going; this was only natural, since nothing in their backgrounds had prepared them for it. Like them, the cinema audiences preferred films and *arabesk* concerts to the opera. The lyrics to those *arabesk* songs were intimate and familiar, as was Şoray. The dark girl had not grown up in an elegant Istanbul home. First she conquered people's hearts as the dark girl, then the dark girl became the Sultana.

In sum, the populist ideals of the Democratic Party (in power in the 1950s) replaced the modernising of the Republican People's Party. Likewise, Sonku, the star of republican ideology, was leaving her place to a new star – the Sultana.

The dark girl follows the rules: the starlet phase

The film magazines got the picture. They claimed that Şoray was more beautiful than the stars of Italian and French films because of her big brown eyes, her expressive face, and her plumpness, wet lips and misty eyes. The audience was captivated by her, the extra weight did not bother them because they loved the soft curves of the Eastern woman. According to the descriptions of the magazines, she was the woman with 'moist lips', with 'misty eyes'.

A film that was to be shot in 1961 featured a scene in which the male character was to kiss the girl on the lips. The two famous stars of the era ended up not accepting the parts because their husbands would not let them. Şoray agreed to the kissing, because she was a starlet still striving to get on. Photographs confirming the kiss appeared in magazines. At this time, Şoray did not refuse to show her legs either. As Morin notes, 'a star's importance is in inverse proportion to the amount of leg shown in her photographs' (1960, p.56). Şoray sits on the sidewalk; she exposes her legs, her underwear shows. A magazine warns 'this is no way to sit'. Şoray's 1961 film *Sevimli Haydut* (*The Loveable Bandit*) has her naked from the waist up. But a traditional Muslim society at least required that nipples be covered, and so her hair hides the nipples. Hair is loose, and she lets it fall over the nipples, but the greater part of her breasts is visible. She is the object of men's desire in the film, and lusted after by men in the cinema.

Şoray obeys the rules of a Muslim country relatively and the rules of the path to stardom totally. She appears in film magazines. She is dying to meet the stars of the era. 'She would like to imitate the star's comportment, but she is obliged to do the reverse: whereas the star flees her admirers, the starlet must look for hers, even create them; whereas the star reveals her soul, the starlet must exhibit her body, offering it as a sacrifice on the altar guarded by film merchants' (Morin, 1960, p.57).

The face is the mirror of the soul

In interviews, Şoray wore dresses that exposed her bare back and tightly wrapped her body. She assumed sensuous poses for photographers. Her face carried a constant smile, and could not really be said to be made-up, but rather heavily painted. As Morin (1960, p.44) writes,

> the make-up which diminishes 'the eloquence of the face' confers upon it a new eloquence. It depersonalises the star in order to super-personalise her. Her made up face is an ideal type. Film make-up does not oppose a sacred visage to the profane face of daily life; it raises daily beauty to the level of superior, radiant, unalterable beauty. The natural beauty of the actress and the artificial beauty of the make-up combine in a unique synthesis.

Who knows what Morin would say if he saw the product of this synthesis in Turkey. False eyelashes, dark red lipstick, heavy powder and a beauty spot constituted the unique but rather kitsch face of the dark girl. But the public loved the face. They could get involved with the dark girl.

Şoray used her face very effectively. She projected her femininity onto her face. Her lips were parted and wet. Her misty, dreamy eyes were arousing. Her face conveyed sexuality. The focus of attention was her face. At random the directors used a lot of close-ups of her face, eyes and lips. This is how Dyer defines the close-up: 'Key moments in films are close-ups, separated out from the action and interaction of a scene, and not seen by other characters but only by us, thus disclosing for us the star's face, the intimate, transparent window to the soul' (1987, p.11). This is what happens when the camera approaches Şoray and lets the spectators take in the details of her face.

The dark girl is now a Sultana, she lays down the law

By the late 1960s, Şoray had become a top star, or Sultana, and laid down her own rules, although she was ignored by the elite and the intellectuals, who espoused the orthodoxy of modernity which had held sway since the early days of the republic. She raised her price. This is the first principle. The contracts had to provide satisfactory criteria of stardom. The public decides whether or not someone is a star; that decision is made at the box-office. She announced that she would be the star of three films a year. This was also the time at which she gave up on short-lived relationships with different men, and moved in with a famous, educated, rich businessman. Letters from him appeared in magazines; we do not even know if those letters are genuine or not, but the most important thing is they were presented as genuine, and readers perceived them as such. In these letters, Şoray's lover addresses her as *Peri Sultan* ('Fairy Sultan') and *Sultan Hanım* ('Lady Sultan'). He was a good mentor, because in a period which lacked professional image-makers, the cleverest lover helped to create the image of Sultana. The audience who read these letters began to think that she might indeed be a Sultana. Now the image of Sultana is her *doppelgänger*. The Sultana's lover was married and he was older than her, but the public took this in its stride. Magazines opposed this relationship, but the public had no qualms about accepting it. This proved Alberoni right: 'One other interesting fact is that the stars are not objects of envy. Further, the elite of the stars is not in general perceived as a privileged class; their very existence is not regarded as a clear and brutal witness to social injustice' (1962, p.87). A society that exercised tight social control granted tolerance to its Sultana. A young woman living with a married man would normally have been simply unacceptable at that time.

Then came the third rule: the Sultana would not take her clothes off and would not show her legs, or even kiss. And Ayhan Işık, who was then known as the King, could not be her leading man. She chose the male star and even the directors; if she wanted she could even change the producer and alter the director as the film was getting under way. One film magazine had this to say about her: 'Now she is the tyrant of film sets. The producer and the male star can only be dependent on her' (*Artist*, 7 December 1965). Reporters were after her, she felt over-burdened and affected dissatisfaction with her reputation, saying, 'I'm tired of my reputation'. The market was flooded with Şoray look-alikes, and she was secure in the knowledge that the glut of starlets would not erode her reputation; she was unique, original, the other dark girls were artificial imitations.

Who did the Sultana compete with?

Three other stars were prominent in the years when Şoray was Sultana. The important point is that they were not *ersatz* dark girls or Sultanas. One was thin, elegant, slender, delicate and blonde. She was the perfect European: her name was Filiz Akın. She seemed to have stepped out of the pages of *Vogue* and to be in Turkey by chance. She should rather have been living in Paris (and indeed eventually did). Magazines dubbed her 'a girl for the salons', 'the pretty girl' of the Turkish cinema, perfectly suited to the role of a blonde, *mignon* girl who had been educated at the best schools. In later years she herself would say, 'I was cute and sweet, but unable to project the image of a sexy woman, which is where Türkan Şoray excelled' (*Kelebek*, 8 June 1992). Şoray, although not blonde, was compared to Marilyn Monroe after appearing in the Turkish adaptation of *Some Like it Hot*, the magazines declaring that she was as sexy and alluring as Monroe. Indeed, Şoray was urged to pose for photographers in the Monroe manner, a request to which she acquiesced (*Ses*, August 1964).

The second important star of the period, Hülya Koçyiğit, was educated, tranquil, serene, restrained; she was a good wife and mother. She was suitable for the teacher image that the republican ideal proposed. She could sacrifice herself by going to backward areas of Turkey. In 1972, a magazine wrote that she could vie with Şoray and the salon girl Akın, ranking her second in a list of four stars (*Ses*, April 1972).

The third, Fatma Girik, was described in film magazines as friendly and affectionate. Men had no room for friends in their fantasies. She was not totally feminine, she was like a tough guy, and she seemed to have the physical strength that had always been associated with men. (Girik was the mayor of Şişli, one of Istanbul's municipalities in the 1990s.). She was *erkek kadın* ('the manly woman'), and known as Erkek Fatma. One historian of Turkish cinema said of her that 'like a jewel, she reflects a simple, unexaggerated doll-like beauty, but it has no element of sexual attraction' (Özgüç, 1988, p.86). Indeed, Girik shunned heavy make-up to give the impression of having stepped in front of the cameras just after washing her face in the morning. In this she was the polar opposite of Şoray, who not only laid on the make-up but also wore false eyelashes.

Şoray provided love and hope for Turkish men. She was their *anima*, the female image of the collective unconscious, just waiting to be developed, like a roll of film. The image stopped being a concept, it found its recipient. She did not dress like a man, or use profanity. Although she seemed gentle, she was not easily led. She was hard-to-get. But her moves, her posture, her smile made her even more attractive than vamps. Şoray did not want to play masculine roles, either in real life or in films. Maybe she knew that men do not indulge in fantasies of such figures. She always remained Türkan Şoray, and played herself. 'Türkan Şoray is cut out for roles in which she is a kind of confection, with half-closed lids and slightly parted wet lips' (Özgüç, 1988, p.97). She can only be placed in the personal actor category:

> The actor who plays himself and whose primary 'talent' is to be himself and nothing more is called a personality actor... This actor, however popular, is incapable of assuming any variety in the roles he plays, for he cannot project the sincerity and naturalness when he attempts to move outside his own basic personality [cited by Boggs, 1978, p.152].

Film magazine headlines claimed that she was 'a woman for all roles'. Actually, she tried really hard to project herself into each and every role. Because of box-office considerations, they gave her, and she accepted, roles that did not fit her personal and physical attributes at all. She 'türkanşorayises' the roles that she plays. She incarnates herself in them.

The eternal virgin

Stars embody dominant values in society and represent social types. Nonetheless, the female type described in Halide Edip Adıvar's novel *Yeni Turan*, a woman devoted to serving society as a teacher or nurse and who puts her femininity aside, also has a place in Şoray's repertoire.

In *Winds of Love*, Şoray comes down from the mountains to the city. In this film she is an idealistic teacher who struggles to start a library at her school, one which will be made up of classical novels and books with an aesthetic appeal. Two men vie for her favours, one a football player and the other an architect.

> At the start of the film our teacher is not very taken with this famous sportsman, who has no education and constantly uses slang, knows nothing but football, leaves the training camp without permission, and spends his time idly in the

streets, sometimes playing ball with the kids. While the neighbourhood girls dream of marrying him, the teacher's dream is to start that library and encourage people to read ... But in the end, although the architect insists that 'our tastes and way of life are beautifully matched', she sits in the stands cheering for the football star whom she has after all chosen [Büker, 1993, pp.4–5].

She may be educated, but rather than give her heart to someone well-read like herself, she joins the common people in the stands by going for a football player.

In *Zorlu Damat* (*The Reluctant Groom*, 1962) she plays a spoilt rich girl who, being rich, decides to buy a fine horse. Here her image is that of someone men do not easily conquer, a girl at the same time determined to have her way. This image of the determined woman is also found in *Kızgın Delikanlı* (*The Angry Young Man*, 1963).

> In this film she plays a determined lawyer who is on the side of the law and reforms not only the man but others who have broken the law. Though her honour is intact, she knows how to preserve her femininity, her womanliness. She is never sexless, nor does she ever adopt a masculine stance [Büker and Uluyağcı, 1993, pp.78–9].

But one who does is addressed as '*bacı*'. Kandiyoti (1993, p.114) touches on the theme of the *bacı*, a word (meaning 'sister') used by men as a form of address to women in order to show that one has absolutely no designs:

> the theme of the sexually unavailable woman, neither a mother nor a sister, the *bacı*, was quite strong in various forms of cultural and literary expression. To choose but one example, the central woman character in the film *Şöför Nebahat* (*Nebahat the Driver*), a popular production of 1950s, is portrayed in a highly unconventional role. She drives a cab, wears leather jackets and a cloth cap, and mingles with the boys. But she is as pure as the driven snow... this portrayal corresponds to that of the 'erkek kadın', the 'manly' woman, who does not have to be 'butch' or unfeminine but simply unremittingly chaste.

Şoray's portrayal never corresponds to that of the 'erkek kadın': she is alluring but coy, not easily yielding herself up. To win her, the man must make an effort and overcome certain difficulties. Nebahat's fellow drivers call her 'Nebahat Abla' ('Older Sister'), and she certainly does not attempt to be alluring. Şoray, on the other hand, is neither *bacı* nor *abla*. 'She so uses her womanliness that men are enchanted and simply unable to utter the words *bacı* or *abla* when speaking to her, since these forms of address stem from blood relationship, by the terms of which sexual dealings are forbidden' (Büker and Uluyağcı, 1993, p.90).

When Şoray plays a lawyer, she roams the corridors of the Courts of Justice, and enters the courtroom, but does not wear a severe suit, although this is the costume appropriate to women in her position in Turkey. About the severe suit, Kandiyoti (1993, p.114) says the following:

> Unlike the veil, which, by concealing its wearer, confirms her unquestionable femaleness, the severe suit and bare face of the woman civil servant can emit powerful messages of sexual unavailability by deemphasising femininity and

projecting a 'neuter' identity. Thus the management of femininity and sexual modesty became part and parcel of the symbolic armour of the 'modern' woman.

But even in this film Şoray does not wear such a suit, preferring a cardigan, feminine dresses with a flower at the collar, or skirts and blouses. When she is sent on assignment to a village, she puts a scarf on her head, thus developing an image which further diverges from that of the 'modern' woman espoused by the republican ideology.

This seems a good point for some remarks on the adoption of 'masculine' identity. In *Aşk Mabudesi* (*Love Idol*, 1969), Şoray sells nuts in a restaurant offering musical entertainment, and to preserve her honour is forced to act like a man, swearing and fighting where necessary. But her 'masculinity' does not annihilate sexuality, as in *Nebahat the Driver* and many other films; here too Şoray remains faithful to her first man, refusing to give herself to others.

'In none of these films is Türkan Şoray divested of sexuality. She continues to occupy men's fantasies, but she retains her honour' (Büker and Uluyağcı, 1993, p.79). In her films, she can remain pure even when playing a prostitute. She is the eternal virgin. In *Cevriyem* (1978), she says, 'I'm a whore, but not without honour,' while in *Asiye Nasıl Kurtulur* (*Saving Asiye*, 1973), the elderly man with whom she sleeps says she is a paragon of honour. Indeed, she is in reality an angel.

The image of the angel is created in her films, made explicit in titles such as *Kara Melek* (*The Black Angel*,1961). Sometimes, when she unwillingly and unconsciously sleeps with a man because something is put in her drink, she is a *Lekeli Melek* (*Tarnished Angel*,1961). But she is still pure and virginal. In *Ağlayan Melek* (*The Weeping Angel*, 1970) she plays a blind, good-hearted girl, and her first man sees her as 'an innocent, pure angel' (Büker and Uluyağcı, 1993, p.83). She sings in a restaurant, and is surrounded by men, yet does not forget her first love. He comes to the restaurant and is smitten by this singer, not recognising her as the woman he had once been with, and tells her that she is an angel without a name. The singer accepts the title, reminding him, however, that she is tarnished. The man then calls her 'The woman who does not stick like glue'. Now the image attached to her is that of the woman who does not run after men.

She is the 'ideal' girl. Whereas she leaves men in peace, they carry a flame for her – although in some rare cases they do leave her. When her husband's life is threatened, she shoots the would-be killers and goes to jail, but while she is there he remarries. At first she thinks of shooting him, but then relents – she knows how to forgive, and will not kill for revenge. So alongside the other images we have that of the forgiving, magnanimous soul. Yet this film also preserves the image of the sought-after woman, as the truck driver who brings her from the village to Istanbul falls hopelessly in love with her, and at the film's end pursues her as she walks off with quick, firm steps.

In *Sultan* (*Sultana*, 1978) Şoray plays a widow with four children who has migrated from the village to the city. Working in homes as a cleaning woman, she is pestered by the minibus (*dolmuş*) driver on her way home: 'What does Orhan say, love me like this is his line' (Orhan Gencebay was the first *arabesk* singer). At night the Sultana goes to the cinema, and in this film-within-a-film we see another *arabesk* singer, Ferdi Tayfur. The audience watching *Sultan* at one point see not the film-within-a-film but the reactions of the audience watching *Sultan*, as the Sultana and her friends are unable to hold back their tears. In real life, many women at that time identified with Şoray; research shows that in general spectators identify with stars of their own sex (Jowett, 1980, p.76). A study carried out in the squatter housing district of Ankara showed that Şoray was the favourite of the women there (Gökçe, 1971, p.144).

By the 1980s, most people simply made fun of all these images and types of behaviour. Emancipated, free women were becoming active in all aspects of life, and they had already learnt to lay claim to their own bodies. How realistic was the imagery that Şoray offered: full of sexuality, faithful to her first man, overflowing with goodness and kindness? This woman was not 'realistic' for the 1980s.

The Sultana decides to be an emancipated woman

In a film set in the village, *Selvi Boylum Al Yazmalım* (*My Willowy Lass in Red*,1977), Şoray plays a woman who in avowing that 'They taught us to be afraid of men' seeks to enjoy the love she now feels. Here she develops the image of a woman who is both strong and determined, who even when abandoned by her husband knows how to stand on her own two feet and raise a child. In 1981, the year she refused to play a prostitute, Şoray directed and played the lead in another village film, *Yılanı Öldürseler* (*To Kill the Serpent*), which, harking back to ancient tales of the East, recounted the story of a woman who is not permitted to marry the man she loves, and is forced to marry one she does not. In this film, Şoray plays a woman who resists – resisting the entire village (society) by refusing to speak to anyone but the man she loves and her son. This silent resistance is magnificent. Later on the Sultana decided to be a 'real' emancipated urban woman (that is, not rooted in fable), but this turned out not to be so easy. In 1981 she was offered the role of a prostitute, a part which it might be argued she had played before. But this time she was being asked to strip like a real prostitute, kiss, moan and portray orgasm. The Sultana was unable to break her mould, and rejected the part, explaining that, 'The role went against the grain of my physical appearance. Interaction between the spectator and the actress forces a certain selectivity on the part of the actress' (*Ses*, 4 January 1981). By that time, however, a director named Atıf Yılmaz had already begun to make films dealing with the problems of women, and they featured an actress (Müjde Ar) who stood for the emancipated woman. The Sultana realised that acting the small town girl would be ridiculous, or sensed that in the future actresses portraying squatter women would have no compunction about moaning and achieving orgasm (for example, *Bir Yudum Sevgi* [*A Taste of Love*], 1984, female lead Hale Soygazi), and that the type of woman they presented would be different from that which she had made her trademark.

Şoray told reporters that 'We can no longer expect audiences to watch the bad films we made back then, for society has changed. In actual fact the rules were not imposed by me, but were perhaps a direction given to my cinema policies by the audience. All of this is now well in the past, and henceforward we must be up-to-date' (*Cumhuriyet*, 20 September 1987).[2] In Şoray's view, being up-to-date meant being 'the living woman', and this in turn implied an awareness of one's own along with a questioning of the self and where one stands.

Interestingly, the process of emancipation in her private life went hand-in-hand with the image she presented in her films from the 1980s, as the Sultana strove to become emancipated in both realms. In *Seni Kalbime Gömdüm* (*And Leave Thee Too*, 1982) she played a woman who questions not only her marriage but also her very existence as a woman, and opposite her the male lead was an actor who, thanks to his role in a television series about an Ottoman Sultan Murat IV, had reached a vast audience. Through this film, the Sultan and the Sultana met and fell in love. Would she be able to say 'No' to the man she had been with for 20 years, and to whom she had been not only faithful, but obedient? Perhaps she would have to first say no on film, and in *Mine* (1982) the eponymous heroine rebels against both her unfeeling husband and society, choosing the man she loves (played by the same stage actor she had become enamoured of before), undressing and making love. Henceforth she would be the questioning woman, who defends her character, her femininity and her sexuality. A prominent Turkish film critic asks her, 'Is Mine Türkan Şoray, or is Türkan Şoray Mine? (Dorsay, 1997, p.148). The real-life Şoray married the stage actor and became pregnant by him, as the magazines and newspapers proclaimed: 'Sultana Türkan to be a mother'.

Şoray had succeeded in moving up a class economically, but she wanted to accomplish this in cultural terms as well, as she dreamed of becoming a stage actress, of studying to develop her potential. At the centre of her life swung a pendulum that oscillated between singing in restaurants and acting on the stage. It swung constantly, unable to stop at either extremity. Although presented with lucrative offers, she has never sung in restaurants, seeing this as a 'lapse' of some sort. On the contrary, she always wished to rise, and while never attaining her goal of acting on stage did marry a stage actor.

With marriage the Sultana moved into her husband's modest home in Ankara, and devoted herself to raising their daughter, the dream woman thus becoming a genuine housewife. In her previous homes, the living-rooms, expansive spaces and furniture had all been reminiscent of a palace, and the public was used to seeing her in such settings in photographs. In her new incarnation she was, needless to say, not content to be merely a housewife, but at the same time went on making films with her husband, with whom she went to bed both in real life and on the screen. But *Bir Sevgi İstiyorum* (*Give Me Love*, 1984) and *Bir Kadın Bir Hayat* (*A Woman, a Life*, 1985) failed to generate interest. This was not only because the dream woman no longer fulfilled public fantasies, but also because the masses had found new idols to worship. This was a time when the *arabesk* culture reigned, and the shoe-shiners mentioned above were now decking their boxes with photos of this type of singer, with whom the masses could better identify and relate to. Whether Şoray chose to live in a palatial home or not, she had now in a certain sense become detached, while in the lyrics of their songs the *arabesk* singers were better expressing the woes and aspirations of the people at large.

When Şoray divorced, the reason given in the press was that her husband could not take the fact that she continued to act like a Sultana. She then made three films – *Berdel* (1990), *Menekşe Koyu* (*Violet Bay*, 1990) and *Soğuktu ve Yağmur*

Çiseliyordu (*Cold and Drizzling*, 1990) – all of which failed to reach a broad public due to the monopolisation of the cinemas by foreign films. Furthermore, as the number of available television channels increased almost daily, the masses preferred to watch films, or the news, on television. Obeying this fashion, the Sultana too began to make television serials, but *Bir Aşk Uğruna* (*All For Love*), an adaptation of *Anna Karenina* which ran on a private channel, was not shown at prime time. Then in 1993 the Sultana played a serpent woman in an adaptation of a folk tale, *Şahmaran*. On her performance in this film, a film critic known for his typically male admiration and praise for Şoray had this to say: 'With her incredible tail, weird costumes and slathered-on make-up, Türkan Şoray struck me for the first time as being *ridiculous* [my emphasis]... She had become a mask woman, and with her extreme stylisation and symbolic approach reminded one of the Japanese Kabuki theatre' (Dorsay, 1997, p.224). Şoray could not be convincing, for she was a mask woman, the mask having been put on in the 1960s, and the mask was so attached to the 'real' that it was now inseparable from it.

In 1987, in the *Hayallerim Aşkım ve Sen* (*My Dreams, My Love, and You*) Şoray plays herself (a famous star) and questions her own acting of previous years. But questioning cannot solve the problem: it is impossible to be redeemed from a phoney gesture or unconvincing dialogue by questioning alone.

When opting for emancipation in *Seni Kalbime Gömdüm* and *Mine*, Şoray used her own voice to achieve a natural effect. It was a great struggle giving up the image that she had constructed over the years. To become a living woman, it is not enough to strip, one must also speak. In Turkish cinema, stars just mouth the words, the dialogue being dubbed by a theatrical actor with sharp diction and an excellent voice. Jarvie (1970) emphasises that stardom is a combination, and that the voice can be an attractive element of this combination. When, for the sake of realism, Şoray gave up an essential part of what made her (the voice of an actress) she did not consider that the lack of a good voice would threaten her. She tried to act in a natural style, but the spectators were irritated by her voice. Having never before used her own voice, she was inexperienced in this realm. For years on end, a voice which was not hers had been part and parcel of the Sultana. (There were essentially three people who dubbed Şoray's voice, chief among them being Adalet Cimcoz, who of the 120 films the actress played in between 1960 and 1970 dubbed 48.) The 'fake' had become the 'natural', and the 'real'. The public was used to perceiving the unnatural as natural, and was surprised to encounter what was really 'natural'. Furthermore, it is difficult to say that this was a new combination, because there was no body language to accompany a natural voice. Şoray had not trained herself to use her body, because she comes from a tradition based on dialogue. In the traditional Turkish cinema, the message is conveyed by means of dialogue, not through gesture. It could be claimed that *mise-en-scène* has switched places with dialogue. The narration is not embodied in images, but dialogue. Şoray has many of these phoney gestures, residues from the era of dialogue. Today, Şoray knows that a good actress needs to create a genuine, convincing character. She carries the Sultana in her very being (or chemistry) like a virus in the blood, so playing an emancipated woman does not work.

In the 1980s, the Turkish film industry had actresses like Müjde Ar, who had internalised the idea of the emancipated woman, did not have any past image to live up to, or had never been the victims of typecasting. Because she really was an emancipated woman, she could defy the censorship board: 'The censorship board is a committee of men, and thus they have the male gaze and they think that cinema and art designate state of being. Whereas, art is our dreams, our future, but this they cannot understand' (cited by Tarik Dursun K., *Milliyet*, 8 March 1987). Being free in all aspects of her own life, it is not too difficult for Ar to play the free woman. In 1984, she starred in a film based on a famous poem. The poem was *Fahriye Abla*. The director, Yavuz Tugrul, discusses the image of Fahriye Abla in the film: 'Perhaps Fahriye is the first woman in Turkish cinema who has to overcome her misfortune and has managed to free herself from prostitution. I do not know if she could be regarded as an ideal but she comes off skid row and becomes conscious of her own love' (cited by Tarik Dursun K., *Milliyet*, 16 March 1987).

It is impossible to read a text without establishing connection with texts that precede it. Eco calls this 'intertextual dialogue', and he defines it as 'the phenomenon by which a text echoes previous texts' (1985, p.170). It could be said that all of the films that feature Şoray form a 'series'. Many of the films tell the same story, presenting the same image. We as spectators know that Şoray is pure, even if she plays a prostitute. We are always sure that she will protect her chastity. If a star or an actress becomes an element of the series, 'salvation' or 'emancipation' are no longer possible. To quote Eco again:

> I would add finally that form of seriality that, in cinema and television, is motivated less by the narrative structure than by the nature of the actor himself: the mere presence of John Wayne or of Jerry Lewis (when they are not directed by a great director, and even in these cases) succeeds in making always the same film. The author tries to invent different stories, but the public recognises (with satisfaction) always and ever the same story, under superficial disguises [1985, p.169].

No matter how much the nature and content of the narrative changes, the Sultana can never be independent of her *doppelgänger*. For some, she is still Sultana, for others she is a has-been, and for a third group she is kitsch. She has to parade in reception rooms, in parties with stock gestures, she has to flash her fake, customary smile to her entourage, and she has to play the adored woman. She graces her subjects, and may be generous while bestowing her attentions, or not. Today Turkey's masses are no longer satisfied to be 'favoured', they want 'justice'. But in a 1985 film in which she starred, the male character can still describe her as a woman who belongs in the palace.

Conclusion

As the republican ideology presented its values to society and tried to impose them, these values were reflected on the silver screen through the personality and the features of the star. Blonde, with slender eyebrows, she was too aloof for the public in general, especially the new migrant city-dwellers. During the 1960s, when these new arrivals began to come into their own and establish urban roots, a Sultana smiled not from the palace but from the screen. Şoray stood for the resurgence of one thing among the many which had been repressed by elitism, and satisfied a deep longing. The public took her to their hearts, for she had appeared at just the right time. Had it been earlier, the *vox populi* would have remained muted, but as it was the broad masses had succeeded in changing the regime itself, in the 1950s, by bringing the Democratic Party to power, and the public could identify with those who governed them. Thus the 1960s were ripe for the star who promised to give back what elitism had pushed below the surface, and the public called this longed-for figure of identification the Sultana.

To be sure, the position of the Turkish cinema at that time also played a role in raising her to the status of Sultana, as the plethora of films shot each year combined with the increasing number of cinemas to bring Şoray's image to the masses. The fact that she played in comedies, a form of entertainment embraced by the public at large, also helped make her popular. To begin with, Şoray obeyed all the rules, even kissing the male lead, but later she took her newly exalted image seriously, imposed her own rules, and began to play the role of Sultana, dispensing grace. By the 1980s and 1990s, however, it was no longer possible for her to be the Sultana of the masses, as social and cultural conditions had changed significantly, along with conditions in the Turkish cinema. Yet Şoray continued in her role, having merged with her *doppelgänger*, playing the Sultana even though by now many perceived this as kitsch.

Notes on Chapter 7

1   An eighteenth-century traveller in Anatolia reports that Circassian and Georgian women would go to great lengths to make themselves attractive to Turkish men. 'These girls have figures that are thoroughly European. They are all fair of complexion, with well-proportioned bodies, but by overeating and making frequent trips to the Turkish bath, they acquire the plumpness so dear to the Turkish male heart' (cited by Hiçyılmaz, 1989, p.16)

2   Here it would be pertinent to note that the Sultana's earlier films are repeatedly shown on television, that the image she built up over the years has been reinforced, and that in her more recent films she has not managed to free herself from the role of 'a woman to worship'.

References

Ahmad, F. (1993), *The Making of Modern Turkey*, Routledge, London

Alberoni, F. (1962), 'The "Powerless Elite": Theory and Sociological Research on the Phenomenon of Stars', in D. McQuail (ed. and trans.), *Sociology of Mass Communication*, Penguin, London

Barthes, R. (1957), 'The Face of Garbo', in G. Mast and M. Cohen (eds), *Film Theory and Criticism*, Oxford University Press, New York, NY

Berger, J. and J. Mohr (1982), *Another Way of Telling*, Granta Books, Cambridge

Boggs, J.M. (1978) *The Art of Watching Films: A Guide to Film Analysis*, Benjamin, Menlo Park, CA

Büker, S. (1993), 'Aşk Yarışlarını da Sporcular Kazanıyor', *Sinema Yazıları* (Yaz 1993)

Büker, S. and C. Uluyağcı (1993), *Yeşilçam'da Bir Sultan*, Afa Yayıncılık, Istanbul.

Divitçioğlu, S. (1991), *Geçivermiş Gelecek*, Bağlam Yayıncılık, Istanbul

Dorsay, A. (1997), *Sümbül Sokağın Tutsak Kadını*, Remzi Kitabevi, Istanbul

Dyer, R. (1986), *Stars*, BFI Publishing, London

– (1987), *Heavenly Bodies: Film Stars and Society*, Macmillan, Hong Kong

Eco, U. (1985) 'Innovation and Repetition: Between Modern and Post-Modern Aesthetics', *Daedalus*, vol.114, no 4, pp.161–85

Gökçe, B. (1971), *Gecekondu Gençliği*, Hacettepe Üniversitesi Yayınları, Ankara

Günçıkan, B. (1998), *Cumhuriyet Dergi*, no 625, p.1

Haskell, M. (1973), *From Reverence to Rape*, University of Chicago Press, Chicago. IL

Hiçyılmaz, E. (1989), *Eski İstanbul'da Muhabbet*, Cep Kitapları, Istanbul

Jarvie, I.C. (1970), *Towards a Sociology of Cinema: A Comparative Essay on the Structure and Functioning of a Major Entertainment Industry*, Routledge & Kegan Paul, London

Jowett, G. and J.M. Linton (1980), *Movies as Mass Communication*, Sage, Beverly Hills, CA

Kandiyoti, D. (1993), 'Gendering the Modern: On Missing Dimensions in the Study of Turkish Modernity', in S. Bozdoğan and R. Kasaba (eds), *Rethinking Modernity and National Identity in Turkey*, University of Washington Press, Seattle, WA

Keleş, R. (1990), *Kentleşme Politikası*, İmge Kitabevi, Ankara

Kongar, E. (1976), *İmparatorluktan Günümüze Türkiye'nin Toplumsal Yapısı*, Istanbul

Morin, E. (1960), *The Stars*, Mouton, London

Okan, T. (1966), 'Türk Sineması'nın Ekonomik Durumu', *Yeni Sinema*, no 3, pp.25–32

Onaran, A.S. (1994), *Türk Sineması I*, Kitle Yayincilik, Ankara

Özbek, M. (1991), *Popüler Kültür ve Orhan Gencebay Arabeski*, İletişim Yayınları, Istanbul

Özgüç, A. (1988), *Türk Sinemasına Damgasını Vuran On Kadın*, Broy Yayıncılık, Istanbul

Özön, N. (1968), *Türk Sineması Kronolojisi: 1895–1966*, Bilgi Yayınevi, Ankara

– (1985) *Sinema: Uygulayımı, Sanatı, Tarihi*, Hil Yayın, Istanbul

– (1995) *Karagöz'den Sinemaya: Türk Sineması ve Sorunları. 1. Cilt*, Kitle Yayıncılık, Ankara

Scognamillo, G. (1987), *Türk Sinema Tarihi: 1896–1959*, Bilgi Yayınevi, Ankara

– (1991), *Cadde-i Kebir'de Sinema*, Metis Yayınları, Istanbul

Staiger, J. (1983), 'Seeing Stars', in C. Gledhill (ed.), *Stardom: Industry of Desire*, Routledge, London

Uğur, A. (1991), *Keşfedilmemiş Kıta: Günlük Yaşam ve Zihniyet Kalıplarımız*, İletişim Yayınları, Istanbul

Zürcher, E.J. (1993), *Modernleşen Türkiye'nin Tarihi*, İletişim Yayınları, Istanbul, 1996

8

Global Consumerism, Sexuality as Public Spectacle, and the Cultural Remapping of Istanbul in the 1990s

Ayşe Öncü

The intensified impact of global consumerism has become one of the major narratives of the contemporary period. Its significance is highlighted by the accelerated shift to post-Fordist systems of production and global experiments in neo-liberal policies. Linked to discussions on the fluidity and flexibility of contemporary consumption forms, a series of arguments about the reordering of temporal and spatial relations have been put forward. And in debates on the 'post-modern' reconstitution of social and sexual identities, consumption has been invested with primary significance as the motor of cultural change. Thus the notion of global consumerism has at once become central to arguments about long-term economic transformation, the shifting contours of political discourse, and the reordering of space, identity and place. This seemingly ever-expanding body of literature, however, has been marked by a persistent difficulty. When couched in very abstract terms, generalisations based on the notion of global consumerism tend to become very thin. The ubiquitous use of the term to illuminate supposedly general factors which apply across societies, and across the field of consumption as a whole, not only hampers an understanding of particular modalities of consumption, but also glosses over issues of place, setting and context in shaping them.

My own aim in this chapter is to engage with the particular and the specific, rather than rehearse the generalities of global consumerism. I will be concerned with a particular facet of global consumerism – the commercialisation of sexuality as a form of spectacle for consumption – in a specific setting, the Istanbul of the 1990s. My aim will be to explore how the opening of sexuality to the gaze, as a form of public display for consumption, has pervaded the everyday lives of different groups in the city, to graft new maps of symbolic meaning onto the established landscape.

Following a keyword: *maganda*

Any attempt to engage with the particular and specific in the realm of consumption studies poses a series of thorny issues. Consumption networks are invariably embedded within broader social and cultural processes. And their extensions are extremely wide-ranging, in both the material and symbolic sense. In practical research terms, this raises the problem of how to make an initial 'cut' into the complex reality of lived experience, and where to stop, given the multiple accretions of consumption in different spheres of everyday life. The strategy that will be adopted here is to focus upon a single keyword – *maganda* – following its shifting meanings and content in its travel from the pages of satirical magazines to mainstream discourse.[1]

Maganda is an invented word which began to circulate insistently and repetitively through daily life in Istanbul in the 1990s – in conversations among friends, in newspaper articles, in television commentaries, captions of photographs in weekly magazines, films and jokes. In everyday speech, its meaning seems self-evident, operating simultaneously as a derogatory label and a stereotype which condenses and connotes an array of socially and morally offensive attributes into a single typification – a *maganda*. As a discursive ideological construct, it appears to activate and gather all accents and nuances of hierarchy and distinction into a total and totalising category of exclusion – the *maganda*. The resonances of the term are strongly gendered – it is 'known' from everyday experience and understood without saying that *magandalic* (the condition or state of being *maganda*) is a distinctively masculine syndrome or affliction.

It is via such keywords that moral/ideological discourses of the moment flood the hidden corners of everyday existence. Using them as a kind of shorthand, we might identify how motifs of large-scale cultural change are not passive backdrops to human relations, but collide with and partly take their meaning from everyday life. The significance of the construct *maganda* resides in encapsulating and bringing into focus how participation in contemporary forms of consumption and narratives of masculinity are interconnected – in ways that are specific to place, setting and context. Inasmuch as the term was 'invented' and gained popular currency at a particular moment in the cultural history of Istanbul, it also provides entry into exploring the power dynamics of global consumerism, as played out in intensely localised everyday life experiences of different groups.

In the following pages, I will begin by offering some broad comments on sexuality as spectacle for consumption in contemporary Istanbul. Then I will turn to satirical magazines as transgressive cultural spaces for the city's youth and venture into this space through the works of a particular graphic artist whose name has become associated with *maganda* cartoons as a distinctive genre of humour. Lastly, I will try to elucidate how the content and meaning of the word has changed in its travel from the cultural space of satire weeklies to mainstream discourse and become incorporated into an ongoing narrative about consumption, sexuality and city life in contemporary Istanbul.

Sexuality as spectacle for consumption in contemporary Istanbul

Consumer capitalism has long been a part of the cultural context in which Istanbulites make their lives. As the country's gateway to world markets, Istanbul's historical trajectory has been inextricably tied to international capitalism. Had it not been so, Istanbul's integration into the global culture of consumerism in the neo-liberal conjuncture of the late 1980s and early 1990s could not have been so swift and explosive. Almost overnight, a dizzying array of globalised images, icons, sounds and commodities flooded the cultural spaces of the city, threatening to overwhelm all established boundaries, distinctions and hierarchies. This was a moment when all the familiar signposts of Istanbul's material and symbolic life seemed to 'melt into thin air', fostering a sense of epochal and totalising transformation.

Under the deepening impact of global consumerism, sexuality was cut loose from its traditional moorings within marriage and family life, transformed into a form of public spectacle for commercial consumption. Sexuality as a form of consumption – decoupled from its reproductive focus and associated with leisure and pleasure – had hitherto been confined to specific sites or quarters of Istanbul, identified as centres of depravity and immorality. Now, images of sensuality and sexuality were everywhere boldly displayed – on billboards lining the thoroughfares of the city, on commercial television screens in the domestic setting of the home, on covers of glossy magazines sold in street-corner racks, or the Sunday supplements of the largest-circulating dailies. And what was opened to the gaze soon became available to buy in a multiplicity of material forms and price ranges. Most conspicuous in middle-class spaces of the city, was the explosive growth of services devoted to grooming and perfecting bodily sexual selves, ranging from an enormous variety of health–beauty–diet–fitness products and centres, all the way to clinics offering the most advanced techniques in cosmetic and plastic surgery. Much less conspicuous, but equally significant, were the trickling effects among low-income populations of the city. In the open-air bazaars which dot the peripheral neighbourhoods of the city, there are now specialised stalls featuring cheap versions of the latest fashions in women's lingerie, doing brisk business alongside innumerable vegetable and fruit stalls and stands of electronic gadgets from Taiwan or kitchenware from Germany.

This was also a historical moment when the dangers of sexuality, publicly flaunted as a form of commercial consumption, emerged as a major focus of public anxiety, and produced an extended discourse on its problems, especially among youth. In a classical Foucaultian manner, a variety of surveillance mechanisms have come into the picture, ranging from well-established police techniques (rounding up 'perverts' and 'prostitutes'; organising raids to discos frequented by youth etc) to the establishment of a governmental council (RTUK, the Radio and Television Upper Council) to classify, interpret and monitor 'offensive content' on commercial television programmes. Municipal authorities were mobilised to impose censorship on visual materials displayed on billboards in the interests of public morality. And a newly created Directorate of Family Affairs, attached to the Prime Minister's Department in Ankara, was delegated with the task of investigating problem areas and developing policy recommendations.

Needless to say, such surveillance procedures associated with the 'official' realm are neither the only nor the most potent form of control over sexuality in contemporary consumer society. They intertwine with a complex web of influences emanating from the market. And in the commercial realm of cultural production, various strands of moral discourse on such themes such as 'excessive consumption', 'excessive materialism' and 'excessive westernisation' have acquired fresh urgency. These have been the perennial themes of Ottoman-Turkish intellectual life for more than a century, and find new echoes in contemporary Islamist discourses, as analysed by Navaro-Yashin and Saktanber in this volume.[2] What has given the past decade a special twist is the way such themes have been taken over by the popular media, and packaged in commercial genres and forms open to consumption by wider audiences. Thus, for instance, on reality shows on television, as well as lifestyle magazines, stories of 'wasted lives' among youth have proliferated. Pathetic narratives of girls who arrive in Istanbul to become television stars or singers and then drift into the trade in vice are of course classic, and have been around for a long time. But they have now been displaced, as favourite tabloid material, with stories about 'children of affluence', who wear designer clothes, frequent expensive restaurants, bars and discos, and celebrate promiscuity in sex and drugs, but eventually end up committing suicide, or are found dead of an overdose in some filthy basement, or fall into the clutches of some religious cult, as a in a recent case, illustrating how 'excess consumerism' breeds 'identity confusion' because it is contrary to Turkish values and ways of life.

Thus for Istanbul's 'youth' or 'younger generations' – between teenage and marriage – the conjuncture of the 1990s opened a window to unlimited consumption for and on sexual bodies, constrained only by financial circumstance. At the same time, the readiness with which the signs, symbols and icons of global consumerism made inroads into the youth cultures of the city – through their own semiotics – meant that the 'consuming young' (*tüketici gençlik*)[3] was constructed as a composite category in the moral discourses of the decade, distilling and objectifying the dangers of sexuality as a form of public display for consumption.

All of the above is of immediate relevance for the purposes of this study, for it is precisely from within the transgressive cultural spaces and rituals of Istanbul's so-called 'consuming youth' that the word *maganda* was invented towards the end of the 1980s. As initially encoded in the ribald and bawdy graphic humour of satirical weeklies, the *maganda* emerged as a figure of derision who is totally oblivious to his own uncouth and offensive masculinity – thus 'interfering' with the moral discourses of the decade, to destabilise and debunk the authoritative codes of 'civility'. By creating the *maganda*, Istanbul's 'consuming youth' took its revenge upon mainstream adult culture – or so it seems with hindsight.

Such a straightforward reading, however, does not begin to capture the kinds of ambivalence and ambiguity *maganda* humour built upon, to achieve such popularity among the young readership of satirical weeklies in first years of the 1990s. Below I will venture into this recent past through the work of a young artist whose distinctive genre of humour and graphic style made him a cult celebrity in the satire milieu. But first, a brief caveat on the satire market itself, and the ways it brings together readers, graphic artists and publishers to map out a distinctive cultural space for the 'young' in present-day Istanbul.

Satirical magazines as transgressive cultural spaces for Istanbul's youth

Graphic humour in general, and satirical magazines in particular, have a lengthy historical lineage in the cultural and political life of Istanbul, spanning more than a century. From the inception of what might be considered an embryonic reading public in the late nineteenth century, humourous line drawings, caricatures of prominent political figures and illustrated jokes proliferated through daily newspapers and various periodicals to gain popularity and acknowledged social significance. And subject to the vagaries of state control and official censorship, satirical magazines have retained their symbolic significance in the political life of the nation, regarded among intellectual circles as a potential means of reaching urban popular classes to simultaneously articulate their grievances and also educate them. That is, until recently.

Over the past 10 years, the publishing life of Istanbul has been dramatically transformed by the global reach of audio-visual culture. A broader discussion of this transformation is beyond the scope of this study. Suffice it to say that the advent of satellite television and deregulation of the state monopoly over broadcasting in 1990 was followed by intense, cut-throat competition among a host of newly established commercial channels, vying for audience ratings and hence advertising revenues. Simultaneously, large daily newspapers, independent family-owned establishments until then, began to change hands. Thus, within a span of three to four years, two gigantic media conglomerates, composed of vertically and horizontally interlinked publishing and broadcasting interests, as well as banks, distribution firms and investments ranging from tourism to condominium construction, were consolidated.

Currently, satirical weeklies constitute a distinctive 'independent' youth niche, in a market that has been taken over by large conglomerates. They proliferate on the news-stands of Istanbul under ever-changing titles – such as *Ustura*, *Hıbır*, *Leman*, *Fırt* or *Zıpır*, their longevity subject to the vicissitudes of a readership between the ages of 15 and 25, and the propensity of young graphic artists to split off and regroup under new titles. New magazines appear and disappear as young readers float from one title to the next, following shifting fashions and their favourite cartoonists. But the low rates of survival and short lifespan of most magazines in this highly competitive market can be misleading. For the total circulation of Istanbul's satirical press has been fairly stable over the past ten years, reaching roughly 1.5 million readers per month, a non-negligible figure in a country where total magazine circulation is estimated to fluctuate between 10 and 11 million. The most popular satirical magazine of the moment, for instance, *Leman*, has a weekly circulation of 100,000, and remains 'free' of advertising. Such a circulation figure, however, implies a broadening of readership base with all the inherent dangers of 'mainstreaming'. It signals the impending flight of younger graphic artists and readership towards new horizons.

The graphic artists who draw for the satirical press are also 'young', with no formal training in art or graphics. The magazines operate as training grounds for young talent, whose creative careers peak around their late twenties, and are considered 'finished' upon marriage. Marriage also marks the moment at which even the most devoted readers lose interest and drift away. So the social boundaries of the satire milieu are defined through the cultural–experiential divide between world of the 'married' and the 'unmarried'. The lived experience of being unmarried in the cultural cosmology of contemporary Istanbul provides a common thread which runs through distinctions of social origin and taste, as well as of gender and age between readers and graphic artists. It also underpins the shared cultural imaginary of 'married-adult-mainstream' upon which the humour content of the magazines is built.

This self-generated conception of being part of an 'alternative', 'anti-establishment' (*muhalif*) world is what renders satirical magazines 'a cultural space', and not simply a market. Survival as an independent venture, 'freedom' from advertising, cheap paper, lack of colour, all carry connotations of being 'alternative' to the other glossy, sparkling magazines (local versions of *Cosmopolitan*, *Marie Claire*, *Burda*, *Playboy* etc.) which stand on the same racks. This is an understanding that is shared by the readers, graphic artists and producers alike. Being a 'devotee' (*müdavim*) means recognising the individualised graphic styles of different cartoonists and being familiar with the street-language they use, as well as the 'characters' they draw. So this is a cultural space defined in terms of 'sharing the same sense of humour' (*aynı mizah anlayışını paylaşma*).

In terms of their content, satirical magazines are an amalgam of spot cartoons, comic strips offering a colourful gallery of characters, interspersed with jokes, footnotes and asides to the reader, as well as columns by popular writers of the moment. Taken together, these provide a continuous stream of conversation, in graphics and in words, which constitute a running commentary on adult life, one that is based on a shared sense of fun, enjoyment of the ridiculous. They are 'alternative', 'irreverent', but not oppositional in the conventional political sense of the term. They thrive on parodies of an adult world which are based on the restricted experiences and codes of youth, and hence remain inaccessible to 'outsiders', that is the adult mainstream. They are not engaged in the business of making a 'statement' to the world at large. They contain no profound statements on the ironies of such global ills as war, poverty, environmental pollution or the like. The situations and typifications they evoke are interwoven with incongruities hidden in the trivia of everyday life, and thrive on offending the aesthetic sensibilities and notions of propriety which govern them. The very 'trashiness' of their humour is part of the sense of fun and ribaldry shared by cartoonists and their readers, a major ingredient in the chemistry which binds them together.

This special chemistry which differentiates satirical weeklies from 'mainstream' humour could perhaps be best be captured through the notion of 'carnavalesque', which Bakhtin used to describe situations of temporary licensed suspension of order. Bakhtin's metaphor of carnival derives from the ribaldry and irreverence associated with popular festivities – mardi gras, faschings, fairs, where formal hierarchy is suspended and the sacrosanct and dignified elements of official serious culture are deprived of their authority through unrestrained festivity and gaiety.[4] It is possible to interpret the Bakhtinian notion of the carnavalesque more broadly, of course, to argue that all humour – pranks, wit, comic-strips, cartoons – builds upon established meanings and common sense categories, and subverts them through play. In graphic humour, the artist accomplishes this by juxtaposing visual signs and symbols from disparate frames of reference, to expose the impurity and arbitrariness of all categories, blurring hierarchical impositions of order to elicit a chuckle. In an instant of surprise and laughter, fragments and emblems are dissociated from one cultural discourse and reassembled in another, conveying the inextricably mixed and ambivalent nature of all cultural life, the reversibility of cultural forms, symbols and meanings. Broadly speaking, all humour 'intervenes' in cultural discourses of the moment, simultaneously invoking and destabilising the familiar. But having acknowledged that all humour contains an element of transgression, it is still important to differentiate – at least in the specificity of Istanbul's graphic humour scene – between 'mainstream' humour adorning the pages of glossy magazines or entertainment sections of daily news-papers, and the hilarious abandon with which all rules of polite utterance are suspended on the pages of satirical weeklies.

Hence, to look for sophisticated plays on meaning in the content of satirical magazines is not particularly meaningful. Their sense of fun is much more situational, often built upon conjuring and capturing the instantaneity of emotions and reactions which are recognisable through experience. Words, expressions and graphic characters are continuously 'invented' to name these experiences, which lose their novelty as they begin to circulate more widely, and are replaced by new ones. Thus what is referred to as 'slang' by the mainstream adult world, and 'restricted code' by social analysts, is very much a part of this process of capturing and 'naming' what is experienced, yet remains unformulated in the discursive realm of the adult world.

From a broader and more general vantage point, the main features I have singled out to describe the cultural space of satirical weeklies, are ones that are associated with a variety of 'youth subcultures' in different parts of the world. Ethnographic studies of youth subcultures, ranging from pop music to clothing fashions, underline how they rely upon networks of small-scale entrepreneurship which reproduce themselves in a frenzy of 'new' styles, as the relentless forces of mainstream commercial culture scour them for images and sounds. But more often than not, these features of youth cultures have been coupled with working-class origins (mainly through pioneering work emerging from the Centre for Cultural Studies in Birmingham in the 1970s) and hence interpreted as a form of resistance or political radicalism. Thus studies of youth subcultures have become synonymous with working-class youth in the broader sociological literature. In the Istanbul of the mid-1990s, the cultural space of satirical weeklies cannot be defined in terms of lower-class origins, however one might define 'lower-class'. Rather, it is based upon and articulates the cultural/experiential world of young people – between teenage and marriage – in Istanbul's cosmos of global consumerism, and constitutes a space of sociability wherein youth from different backgrounds converse through the idiom of graphic humour.

In the light of the above, any attempt to venture into the cultural space of Istanbul's satirical weeklies at a particular moment in time, to engage in 'textual analysis' is a hazardous task. The question of what a 'text' means to its author and to its readers is always a thorny one. When trying to interpret cartoons, this problem is compounded by the play on meanings which is the essence of humour. Further- more, to an outsider, that is an adult unfamiliar with the restricted signs and codes of the moment, the cartoons and comic-strips which pervade the pages of satirical weeklies amount to no more than a set of badly executed drawings, devoid of humour. So what I have to offer below are some general comments on *maganda* cartoons as a particular genre of humour, illustrated by the work of a particular graphic artist, Mehmet Çağçağ, who became a cult figure in the satire milieu of the early 1990s.[5]

Venturing into the cultural space of satirical weeklies through the *maganda* cartoons of the early 1990s

As initially formulated through the non-verbal codes of satirical magazines, the *maganda* is a figure of brute strength, hairy body and unbridled sexual appetites, instantly recognisable by his 'offensiveness' in whatever setting he is depicted – in the home, in parks, in discos, on the beach etc. Rather than representing a socio-cultural type in the conventional sense of the term, the *maganda* articulates, in the graphic language of his creators, a cultural phenomenon that is experienced in the fabric of social existence but remains unstated. Thus when pressed to define in words who exactly a *maganda* is, the graphic artists who coined the term offered the following tongue-in-cheek answer for the mainstream readers of one the major daily newspapers (*Hürriyet* Sunday supplement, 12 January 1992) in the early 1990s:

> *Maganda* is an assault on emotions, an aesthetic aberration. He is an anomaly which corresponds to ignorance, to brute force, to social climbing, to all degenerate values. We created him. He is the animal in us. He is a potential danger. He is hazardous to health. He is the AIDs virus. We allowed him to flourish. He is a stain which cannot be removed. He is like a plastic bottle which never melts, never disappears.
>
> The *maganda* can be from any sex, any class, any race, any occupation. He is contagious, he infects. He can kill you, make you suffer, give you allergies. *Maganda* is universal (unfortunately).[6]

In cartoons and comic strips, however, the *maganda* is almost invariably depicted as an adult male, more often than not in a state of sexual arousal. So while he is an 'aesthetic anomaly'(see cartoon 1) who arouses an 'allergic reaction' in all situations he is present (see cartoons 2 and 3), he is most offensive when sexually aroused (see cartoons 4 and 5). Among the *maganda* cartoons which constituted more than two thirds of all cartoons in *Limon* between 1990 and 1991, for instance, more than half depict him in his *abaza* ('sexually aroused') state. This is when he intrudes, offends, molests, assaults the senses through his warped sexual

Cartoon 1

He: 'Speak up! Where are your erogenous zones? Where's the clitoris [mispronounced 'clitorig']. Apparently there's a G-spot? Tell me where is it, or I'll break your arm. I read it in the papers.'

She: 'How am I supposed to know. I don't know how to read. I swear I don't know. Wouldn't I tell you if I knew?'

Cartoon 2

'The birth of Mevlüt' is cast as a grotesque parody of the birth of Venus. He is pictured complete with gold medallion and hairy chest.

Cartoon 3

He: 'Why aren't your bones crackling, you bitch? Or are you letting others do it?'

She: 'What are you thinking of, Mevlüt'

imagination and the vulgarism of his sexual practices. These are depicted in explicit graphic detail, showing the *maganda* to be devoid of cultural codes which define human sensuality and sexual conduct. Hence the *maganda*'s physical repulsiveness becomes the embodiment of untamed sexual urges.

One possible interpretation for the instant popularity of *maganda* cartoons in the satire milieu of the 1990s is the stark contrast they provide to the glittering seductiveness of sexual images, icons and symbols which pervaded Istanbul during the same period. This was when a whole new range of glossy magazines, from *Cosmopolitan* to *Penthouse* and *Playboy*, not to mention fashion and home decoration magazines, began to compete with each other on the counters of

Cartoon 4

'Sit, sister, it's empty. Come ... come ...'

Cartoon 5

He: 'Come, come, I feel randy again!
She: 'Couldn't you wait five minutes and let me finish the
      dishes'

newspaper stands. Television commercials were rapidly 'internationalised' through joint-ventures between domestic and global advertising firms, acquiring a new patina. And with satellite dishes adorning every other roof, the newly established commercial channels began to beam into living-rooms, projecting onto the screen images of a shiny, clean, orderly world inhabited by good-looking people. The deliberately grotesque graphic style and content of *maganda* cartoons can be interpreted as the antithesis of this world, or as Çağçağ himself put it in retrospect, 'Our answer to the shining, glittering images'. He recollects his youth as a rising artist: 'Cartoons used to flow from my pen. I did not stop to think, I simply drew. I kept saying, over and over, "this is us", "this is what is real".'[7]

But to leave matters at that does not allow us to understand the 'shared sense of humour' upon which *maganda* cartoons are built, or the special chemistry between the young (male) artists who churned them out and their avid readers (male and female) which makes them 'funny'. Because for the reader uninitiated in the cultural world of satirical weeklies, depictions of the *maganda* in a continuous state of sexual arousal are simply obscene, totally devoid of the element of fantasy associated with pornography. What makes them 'humorous' rather than simply offensive is the endless variety of 'everyday' situations in which the *maganda* is depicted, in the intimate interstices of daily existence, in ways that are instantly recognisable. In Çağçağ's words, '... with the *maganda* we went deeper, not simply into the house, but into the bedroom ... we abolished symbolism ... the *maganda* is not symbolic of anything, not poverty, not illiteracy, not ignorance. He just is.' But the prism through which practices in the bedroom acquire 'reality' is precisely the world of glitter and shine which the artist himself describes as 'unreal'. So it can be argued that the pervasiveness of sexuality as a form of public spectacle in Istanbul of the early 1990s has also rendered it visible in the 'privacy' of everyday life situations, no longer taken for granted and unspoken, but recognisable in the realm of public objectivity and open to scrutiny. For Istanbul's youth, this was a moment when the solidity of cultural boundaries separating the experiential world of sexuality (in brothels and back seats of porno-movie houses) and the 'public' universe of gender relations governed by strict codes of untouchability were fractured through the abundance of display for the gaze, and irrevocably shattered by the arrival of 'tourist girls' in growing numbers from the late 1980s onwards. *Maganda* humour is thus the product of a new generation of youth culture in the process of discovering, through the gaze, the aesthetics of practice; and, through tourist girls, the cultural codes of permissiveness.

In cartoons, the fun and enjoyment resides in conjuring an infinite variety of 'private' moments in which the conventional emblems of masculine power (physical strength and sexual drive) are stripped of their authority, and exposed as lacking in refinement and knowledge in codes of sexual practice. Thus in situation after situation, the power and authority vested in the adult male figure is first invoked and then disassembled and cut down to size, through a play on different meanings of masculinity – as drives, as roles and as practices. It is only by keeping in mind the sheer sense of exhilaration which comes when the dominant male figure of the adult world is exposed as being sexually 'illiterate' that it becomes possible to grasp the essence of *maganda* humour. And as such, it can be interpreted as part of the process of destabilising prevailing codes of 'adult' masculinity, among a new generation of youth in the process of negotiating their own.

But of course the *maganda* is not an unequivocally 'adult' figure, but much more ambiguous, which is what makes him fascinating, rather than simply funny, because for the young graphic artists who invented him, and many of their devoted followers, the 'otherness' of the *maganda* is at once an object of ridicule and a source of empathy and subjective identification. To quote Çağçağ, 'The *maganda* is a naïve figure', 'He cannot see himself'. The fact that 'we' (as creators and readers) can recognise him opens the possibility and the desire to be different. But 'we' can only recognise him because 'this is us', 'this is what is real', which contradicts this possibility. It is this ambivalence of recognising one's self in the 'otherness' of the *maganda*, I would suggest, which provokes endless fascination.

Maganda humour, then, is not only about debunking the established codes of 'adult' masculinity or negotiating the cultural codes of 'permissiveness' among a new generation of youth. It is also about experiences of otherness and alienation amidst an abundance of commodified icons and images of sexual fantasy and desire in Istanbul in the 1990s. And in this sense, it is the product of a generation of young men who are discovering that masculinity is now something to be achieved and constantly improved upon, and yet never realised.

At the time of writing, *maganda* cartoons which continue to be recycled in the satirical press are no longer funny, but simply breed boredom. In the rapidly shifting fashions of the satire world, Çağçağ's work is now *passé*. Meanwhile, the word *maganda* has travelled into mainstream 'adult' language, acquiring new connotations in the process of being absorbed into the cultural ethos of Istanbul's middle classes.

The word *maganda* travels into mainstream discourse

In its travel from the graphic language of satirical magazines to the discursivity of everyday speech, the word *maganda* has become a general derogatory label, in, for instance, the lyrics of a rap-song which topped the charts in Istanbul's cassette market in 1991 (Vitamin, Istanbul, 1991):

> How Could You be a *Maganda*?
>
> If you don't spit, belch, or litter the ground,
> Sneeze or sniffle
> Never grow a moustache
> Wear a gold chain necklace
> Open your collar and bare your torso
> How could you be a *maganda*?
> Would it be credible?
>
> If you don't drink or get loaded
> Beat your wife at home
> Make two kids a year
> Hang a gold watch on your wrist
> Harass women on the street
> Molest them on buses and micro-buses
> How could you be *maganda*?
> Would it be credible?[8]

In the lyrics of the song, *maganda* is a label which condenses multiple negative attributes into a single absolute other: belching, spitting, wife-beating, alcohol abuse, verbal harassment, as well as molesting. The *maganda* are now a distinctive breed, with pseudo-racial attributes, whose intrusive presence can be felt on sidewalks, in traffic, sitting in the next row, or at the next table. A second song from the same cassette explains how the *maganda* has now become impossible to avoid in Istanbul (Vitamin, Istanbul, 1991):

A Maganda is a Maganda

In the countryside, in bars, deluxe hotels
Now everywhere in Taksim or Maxim
Jogging, aerobics, bodybuilding
Meetings, clubs, toilets

His soul wooden, his body a tree trunk, his head of pressed straw
Even if he wears a gold saddle, a *maganda* is a *maganda*.[9]

By the mid-1990s, the word *maganda* had entered mainstream language as an all-encompassing epithet to describe and identify a 'publicly' offensive other who actively intrudes to contaminate the public spaces he occupies. Thus the label expanded to capture a new, primarily masculine syndrome, closely associated with nuances of gender comportment in public space – signifying not simply ignorance of proper etiquette, but deliberate offensiveness. To put it differently, the *maganda* are not 'ignorant' country bumpkins who are oblivious to their own lack of polish, but luxuriate in their own offensiveness, simultaneously distasteful (not simply tasteless) and aggressive (not simply vulgar). One last example, this time from journalistic discourse, serves to illustrate how the word *maganda* can lend itself to multiple and often contradictory meanings in its meandering circulation.

The daily newspaper *Hürriyet* (13 December 1995, p.19) allocated one of its back pages to the emergent life styles of the 1990s in Istanbul. Illustrated with aerial photographs of a wealthy new suburb, the write-up informed readers about the exclusive circles of Istanbul, ranging from alumni clubs and conference circuits to imported yuppidom and Islamic suburbs, replete with names of prominent figures. The journalists who wrote the piece, after quoting a series of authoritative sources, claimed that these were the 'post-modern tribes' of Istanbul. In the last section, subtitled 'And the *Maganda*...', they added a conclusion of their own:

> One of the necessary rules in the formation of post-modern tribes is substantial financial worth. The only tribe which constitutes an exception to this rule are the *maganda*.
>
> These *maganda* are members of the *arabesk* culture which emerges when the traditional culture of immigrants to the fringes of megalopolitan Istanbul is fused with urban culture. They do not have a lengthy history. They answer the social needs of the past twenty years.
>
> The coming together of the *maganda* is also an identity. But unlike the other post-modern tribes, they have neither suburbs, intellectual circles, nor labels.
>
> The sense of belonging of this lumpen tribe is established in tribunes, neighbourhood coffee houses and evening strolls on the streets.

The passage above is worth translating, both because it offers one example of how the word *maganda* crops up in journalistic discourse, and is re-defined and re-circulated in unanticipated contexts, but also because the whole passage captures the cultural cosmology of Istanbul in the 1990s. This is an Istanbul in which the experienced world has been transformed through the flow of globalised images and globalised words, providing new scripts through which the familiar is re-interpreted and reviewed. Thus the words 'post-modern' (used in its English-

language form), combined with 'tribe' (translated into Turkish) when assimilated
into the field of experience of contemporary Istanbul, lend themselves to a novel
combination, the '*maganda*-tribe'. But it is only the cosmopolitan academic expert
who can identify the disparate sources and genealogies of the words in the passage
above. In everyday Turkish, the passage above makes 'perfect common sense'.

An evolving urban narrative: the invasion of Istanbul by 'outsiders'

The ease and rapidity with which the word *maganda* has been absorbed into mainstream language deserves further scrutiny. Because the seemingly self-evident,
taken-for-granted meanings of the term are closely bound up with how it is
valorised in public discourse. Its potency as a keyword resides, I would suggest, in
lending coherence to ongoing changes in the realms of consumption, sexuality
and city life, by incorporating them into an ongoing urban narrative – the invasion
of Istanbul by successive waves of 'outsiders'.

The central motif of this narrative – the invasion of Istanbul's cultural
spaces by outsiders who threaten its authenticity and purity – is a familiar one.
In the cultural imaginary of its middle classes, Istanbul has a lengthy history of
'invasion' (*istila*), 'siege' (*kuşatma*) and 'assault' (*saldırı*) by successive waves of
'outsiders', who endanger cherished distinctions of high and low culture. The
discursive-ideological constructions of such outsiders, however, and the labels
evoked to exclude them, have been historically contingent and variable.

Akin to all public narratives, the chronicle of Istanbul's invasion by successive
waves of outsiders operates at multiple registers.[10] It runs through and underpins
a wide range of popular accounts as well as innumerable 'expert' analyses of
Istanbul's social problems, continuously privileging a particular causal chain of
past events, identifying and explaining current issues as well as proposing future
solutions. It also provides an overarching grid of social themes which mediate
between large-scale events and personal experiences of everyday life in Istanbul.
Disparate experiences – lack of running water, encounters with corrupt policemen or difficulties of finding parking – acquire coherence and meaning as part
of the same story. Its potency as a 'public' narrative is thus closely bound with the way
it integrates the very people who are telling, reading or listening as the central
subjects of the story, allowing them to draw upon their own experiences to fill in
the gaps. As such, it privileges and naturalises a particular reality – grounded in
experiences of Istanbul's mainstream middle-class culture – while simultaneously
making contending accounts/narratives seem implausible and chaotic, contrary
to 'fact' as well as 'common sense'. In sum, it is a hegemonic account in the
Gramscian sense of the term, continuously valorised and modified to negotiate the
contours of what constitutes the mainstream, or middle-class, way of life in Istanbul.

As currently narrated in popular as well as scholarly accounts, the chronicle
of Istanbul's 'invasion' by outsiders begins with the arrival of 'peasants' from the
mid-1950s onwards. This was when the word 'peasant' began to lose some of its
positive connotations as the eulogised, authentic core of Turkish nationalism. In

the cultural landscape of Istanbul, peasants were transformed into country bumpkins, lacking in education and therefore the accoutrements of modernity. Thus throughout the 1960s, the social and cultural divisions of city life in Istanbul became solidified (metaphorically as well as physically) around the hiatus separating the 'urbanites', residing in central neighbourhoods of apartment dwellings, from peasants, living in village-like (at the time) squatter settlements on the periphery. In the populist political imaginary of the period, however, this remained a temporary phenomenon, the assumption being that peasants would eventually become 'integrated' into city life – either by becoming modernised, or by developing class consciousness.

This fairly simple storyline became more complicated towards the end of the 1970s, when new popular culture forms flourishing in the urban periphery began to infiltrate middle-class spaces. It now seemed apparent that Anatolian peasants, having lost the purity and authenticity of their traditional folk heritage in Istanbul (but remaining ignorant), had failed to become integrated into cosmopolitan life (but had embraced its crass commercialism). Neither peasant nor urban, they had developed their own half-breed, pseudo-urban culture, which threatened to contaminate and pollute the entire city. In the language of Istanbul's mainstream middle classes, *arabesk* culture had invaded Istanbul.

The epithet *arabesk* denotes impurity, hybridity and *bricolage*, and designates a special kind of kitsch. The word first came into circulation in the early 1970s to describe a hybrid musical genre which emerged and acquired immense popularity among low-income populations in Istanbul.[11] Banned from state radio and television for defying the established canons of both folk and classical Turkish music, by intermixing rhythms and instruments from popular Western and Egyptian music, *arabesk* caught like wildfire in the expanding cassette market of the 1970s. Films featuring famous *arabesk* singers as the star popular hero achieved immediate box-office success in local cinemas on the urban fringes of Istanbul as well as other large cities. In the process, the label *arabesk* acquired a wider chain of associations, denoting a musical genre, a film genre, as well as the cultural habitus and lifestyle of those who enjoy them. *Arabesk*-lovers now belonged to *arabesk* culture – banal, thrashy, but most of all in-between, hence polluted and polluting, to invoke Mary Douglas. *Arabesk* songs, singers and films not only failed to conform to artistically established pure categories of classification, but also contaminated them. Similarly, those who belonged to *arabesk* culture, having lost their moorings in indigenous peasant culture, and begun to mass-consume in ways which combine the material culture of modernity in imperfect and partial ways, belong to neither of the two worlds. Thus *arabesk* culture becomes a placeless phenomenon, both residual and marginal, but also dangerous, because it violates and undermines established hierarchies of taste and distinction in the realm of consumption.

As a form of kitsch urban aesthetic considered vulgar because it imitates with no regard to the original, substituting formica for wood, polyester for silk, the label *arabesk* was originally a derogatory label aimed at low-income populations of Istanbul. From around the mid-1980s, however, the term began to acquire a wider chain of associations, referring not only to the vulgarism of mass consumption among lower classes, but also to a kind of over-consumption symptomatic of newly emergent wealth in Istanbul. The integration of Istanbul into world markets in the era of neo-liberalism has opened new channels of accumulation and upward mobility, creating its own breed of new rich. But this seemed to be a novel kind of 'new rich', devoid of the status anxieties commonly associated with the words *nouveau riche* in French. Instead of trying to emulate refinements of taste, they seemed oblivious to symbolic hierarchies, enjoying their newly found wealth with total disregard for requisite cultural distinctions. In the absence of a name, the label *arabesk* expanded to capture this new syndrome, used not only to refer to the vulgarism (not simply tastelessness) of a new breed of rich, but also, for instance, to a new breed of politician, who disregards distinctions of taste without compunction or embarrassment. Thus, by the 1990s, the term *arabesk* had become an all-encompassing metaphor to describe and identify a general malaise which seemed to plague every aspect of life in Turkish society – *arabesk* democracy, the *arabesk* economy, *arabesk* politicians – all suffering from a condition of indeterminacy and degeneration. In the term *arabesk*, suggests Ozbek (1996), 'we have finally found a name to express the identity problem of Turkish society...'

Concomitantly, however, a new threat of a seemingly different order – the *maganda* – has made its appearance in the cultural scene of Istanbul. To the extent that the label *maganda* is valorised in public discourse by invoking such familiar metaphors as invasion, siege and assault, it becomes part of a continuing narrative whose basic storyline is fairly simple – yet another wave of 'outsiders' who threaten to undermine the civility of Istanbul's cultural life. At the same time however, the construct *maganda* is very much a product of the last decade, encapsulating and bringing into focus lived experiences as well as fears and anxieties associated with sexuality as a form of public spectacle. For the term embodies (literally and metaphorically) the dangers of unbridled, untamed, uncouth masculine sexuality, no longer confinable to specific quarters of the city, but encountered as part of everyday lived experience in public places. Hence its continuous circulation in everyday language, as well as public discourse, signifies a peril that is of a qualitatively different order from the 'impurity' of *arabesk* culture, which signifies a constant influx of large quantities of 'culturally untrained' outsiders. The *maganda* are by contrast natives – a self-perpetuating, self-reproducing product of Istanbul's cultural climate in the era of global consumerism. Their propensity to cross the boundaries of their territorial enclaves (low-income neighbourhoods) to encroach upon public spaces of city life (marked by mainstream middle-class culture) is what makes the *maganda* dangerous. As such, the cultural sonorities of the epithet *maganda* are simultaneously racial, gendered and spatial.

The persistent circulation of the word *maganda* in the public discourse of the 1990s can be seen therefore as part of an active process of re-negotiating the practices of inclusion and exclusion which underpin and shape the cultural topography of the city.

At a moment when sexuality has become commodified as a form of public spectacle, the word *maganda* simultaneously objectifies, engenders and also territorialises its dangers. Thus the constant and persistent threat of *maganda* becomes both a motive and a product of exclusionary practices which are currently re-mapping Istanbul's cultural landscape.

Concluding remarks

Throughout this chapter I have focused upon a single keyword – *maganda* – using it as a vehicle to delve into the intensely localised settings of everyday life in Istanbul in the 1990s. By 'following' the shifting meanings and content of the term from its origins in the satire milieu of the city's youth culture to the discursivity of mainstream language, I have tried to explore how commercialisation of sexuality as a form of spectacle has pervaded everyday lives of different groups in the city, grafting new maps of material and symbolic meaning onto the established land-scape. At the risk of over-abstraction, I will end with a broader point of argument about the significance of urban narratives in lending coherence to the cultural map of cities.

In a metropolis such as Istanbul, the multiple divisions of city life which are constructed in and through consumption processes are not simply a passive reflection of large-scale movements of capital, commodities or cultural flows. They are encountered and made meaningful through 'local' cultural practices. The very multiplicity and diversity of such 'localised' social formations and cultural identities in city space, however, and their shifting contours under the deepening impact of global consumerism, make it difficult to grasp and treat the large metropolis as a single entity. Hence, in the growing literature on global and globalising cities it has become conventional wisdom to reiterate that urban life is becoming increasingly fragmented through growing ethnic, racial and cultural heterogeneity, and progressively divided through social and economic polarisation. There is little doubt that in Istanbul, as in large metropolises in other regions of the world, integration into expanding networks of global consumerism has sharpened existing cultural cleavages as well as generating new polarities. But it does not follow, at least in Istanbul, that the cultural map of the city has thereby lost its coherence for its inhabitants, or that they have lost a shared sense of reality. On the contrary, contradictions generated by the complexity of ongoing changes are encountered and ordered through the familiar storylines of an urban narrative – a collective epic which effaces the underpinning practices of inclusion and exclusion upon which it is built.

As an urban narrative, the social story of Istanbul's invasion by outsiders straddles the boundary between official and popular discourses, selectively appropriating and weaving together elements of both into a single hegemonic–dominant account. It is 'hegemonic' not because it is directly imposed from 'above' in some sense, or because it obliterates all opposition, but because alternative accounts lose their specificity and antagonistic content as they are ultimately mapped and repeatedly circulated as part of the same collective epic. The appropriation of the word *maganda* into the ongoing urban narrative of Istanbul's invasion by 'outsiders' illustrates this 'domestication' process. It also reveals that urban narratives are not a passive backdrop against which unfolding events acquire meaning. They are part of an active process of managing and negotiating contradictory experiences of lived social relations and power con-stellations. Their continuous circulation is part of the boundary work necessary to maintain cultural distinctions which threaten to become blurred unless actively maintained through practices of inclusion and exclusion. To try to put it more simply, 'hegemonic' urban narratives are mobile accounts, continuously in-the-making as part of everyday social relations and practices.

Needless to say, the social story of Istanbul involves a distinctive set of historical mediations and power constellations which are culturally specific in time and place. As such, it is a unique account. But perhaps it is possible to suggest that hegemonic narratives which lend coherence to city space are not unique to Istanbul, but are produced and reproduced as a part of ongoing cultural struggles in different parts of the world.

Notes on Chapter 8

1   In recent work on consumption, the strategy of 'following' commodity-specific chains in various market sectors, or tracing the networks through which specific goods circulate, has become increasingly common. But as Marcus (1995) suggests in his call for multi-sited ethnography, such a strategy need not be confined to traffic in goods. It is possible to 'follow' movements of people as well as symbols or idioms across multiple sites in time and space to investigate their circulation.

2   See, for instance, Mardin, Şerif (1971) on 'super-westernisation'.

3   Beng-Haut (1998) points to a very similar phenomenon in his discussion on globalisation and the spread of consumerism in Singapore, underlining such discursive phrases as 'excessive consumerism' or 'consuming youth'.

4   For discussion on Bakhtin's work in relation to Gramsci's notion of 'common sense', see Brandist (1996). My own understanding of Bakhtin owes much to Mbembe's use of his concepts (1992).

5   My work on *maganda* cartoons of the 1990s grew out of a broader study on various typifications of 'outsiders' in Istanbul's graphic humour scene (Öncü, 1999). I interviewed graphic artists of various ages and generations as part of this project, all of whom talked about their own as well as each others' work. Since I listened to multiple interpretations of *maganda* cartoons during these interviews, and read numerous student papers on them – as the favourite topic in my popular culture courses at the university – as well as reading and enjoying the satirical magazines themselves, what I offer on these pages is not textual analysis in the conventional sense of the term. It could perhaps be described as an effort to 'understand' this genre of humour, in the Weberian *verstehen* sense of the term.

6   In Turkish, the third person pronoun for 'he/she/it' is a single word. I have simply used the 'he' in English. Much of the original wording in this quotation is street slang. My English translations convey the meaning but not the style of expression. The original quotation in Turkish is as follows:

Duygu terbiyesizidir, estetik arızadır maganda. Cahilliğin, kabalığın, sonradan görmeliğin, ne oldumculuğun, yiten, giden, bozulan tüm değerlerin acube karşılığıdır. Onu biz yaratttık. İçimizdeki hayvandır. Potansiyel tehlikedir. Sağlığa zararlıdır. AIDs mikrobudur. Onun büyümesine izin verdik. Lekedir, çıkmaz. Pet şişe gibidir. Erimez, yok olmaz.

Her cinsden, her sınıftan, her ırktan olabilir maganda. Bulaşıcıdır, sirayet eder. Hem öldürür, hem süründürür, hem alerji yapar. Maganda evrenseldir maaalesef.

7　　All references to Çağçağ's personal interpretations of his work are from my interviews with him on two separate occasions in April 1997. He was 32 years old at the time, recently married, and opened a café in downtown Istanbul. Having left his creative years behind, and become part of the 'establishment' himself, he was keen to discuss his 'past' work with me.

8　　Again, my translation of this song robs it of much of its flavour in colloquial Turkish. The original is as follows:

Olur mu Senden Maganda?

Tükürmezsen, geğirmezsen, yerleri hiç pisletmezsen
Aksırmazsan, tıksırmazsan
Bıyıkları hiç uzatmazsan
Kalın Altın zincir takmazsan
Yakanı bağrını açmazsan
Olur mu senden maganda

İçmezsen, kafayı bulmazsan
Evde karını dövmezsen
Her yil iki çocuk yapmazsan
Koluna altın saat takmazsan
Kadınlara laf atmazsan
Otobüste, minibuste fortculuk yapmazsan
Olur mu senden maganda?
Yakışır mı sana?

9　　The Turkish version is as follows:

Kırlarda, barlarda, lüks otellerde
Maksim'de, Taksim'de artık her yerde
Jogging'de, ayrobik'te, body building'de
Toplantıda, kulüplerde, tuvaletlerde

Altın semer giyse bile maganda yine maganda

10　　Following Somers and Gibson (1994), it is possible to think of urban narratives as 'public narratives' which situate historical and current events within stories about the social world, selectively appropriating and emplotting them in a cause–effect sequence occurring over time. But as Linde (1986) has emphasised, in the absence of such 'public' narratives which explain broader social events, it becomes difficult for individuals to produce coherent stories of their lives. To the extent that stories about the social world, that is public narratives, provide an overarching grid of social themes which inform personal life stories, they mediate between large-scale events and individual experiences. At the same time, however, public narratives are collective sagas told from a subject position that is informed by social-class divisions (Steinmetz, 1994). That is, they are ideological, not because they are imposed 'from above' in some sense, but because they operate as part of what Gramsci termed 'common sense philosophy', discrediting and marginalising alternative accounts. My own argument here is that the narrative of Istanbul's invasion by outsiders operates at multiple registers, simultaneously, because it is a hegemonic public account in the Gramscian sense of the word. That is, it is a continuing account which continuously appropriates oppositional views and contradicting events, emplotting them in such a way as to soften and neutralise their antagonistic content.

11   According to Lomnitz (1996), terms such as *naco* in Mexico, *cholo* in Bolivia and Peru, and *mano* in Ecuador have similar connotations of impurity, hybridity, *bricolage*, and designate a special kind of kitsch. He says that these terms resonate with the imaginary of colonial casts, and were originally used as slur words (meaning uncouth or uncultured) against Indians and more generally against peasants, and acquired their currents meanings in the 1970s. The Turkish word *arabesk* was invented and began to circulate in the late 1960s and 1970s. But it has few resonances with the word peasant, *köylü*, who represents the authentic Anatolian core of the Turkish nation. For discussions of *arabesk* in Turkey, see Özbek (1991, 1996), Markoff (1994) and Stokes (1992).

References

Brandist, Craig (1996), 'The Official and the Popular in Gramsci and Bakhtin', *Theory, Culture and Society*, vol. 13, no 2, pp.59–74

Chua, Beng-Haut (1998), 'World Cities, Globalisation and the Spread of Consumerism: A View From Singapore', *Urban Studies*, vol. 35, no 5/6, pp.981–1000

Linde, Charlotte (1986), 'Private Stories and Public Discourse: Narrative Analysis in the Social Sciences', *Poetics* 15, pp.183–202

Lomnitz, Claudio (1996), 'Fissures in Contemporary Mexican Nationalism', *Public Culture*, vol. 9, no 1, pp.55–68

Marcus, G.E. (1995), 'Ethnography in/of the World System: The Emergence of Multi-sited Ethnography', *Annual Review of Anthropology*, no 24, pp.95–117

Mardin, Şerif (1971), 'Tanzimat'tan Sonra Aşiri Batılılaşma', in Erol Tümertekin, Fatma Mansur and Peter Benedict (eds), *Türkiye: Coğrafi ve Sosyal Araştirmalar*, Istanbul

Markoff, Irene (1994), 'Popular Culture, State Ideology and National Identity in Turkey: The Arabesk Polemic', in Şerif Mardin (ed.), *Cultural Transitions in the Middle East*, E.J. Brill, Leiden

Mbembe Achille (1992), 'The Banality of Power and the Aesthetics of Vulgarity in the Postcolony', *Public Culture*, vol. 4, no 2, pp.1–30

Öncü, Ayşe, (1999) 'Istanbulites and Others: The Cultural Ethos of Istanbul's Middle Classes in the Era of Globalism', in Çağlar Keyder (ed.), *Istanbul Between the Global and the Local*, Rowman & Littlefield, Boulder, CO

Özbek, Meral (1991), *Popüler Kültür ve Orhan Gencebay Arabeski*, İletişim Yayınları, Istanbul
– (1996), 'Arabesk Culture: A Case of Modernisation and Popular Identity', in Sibel Bozdoğan and Reşat Kasaba (eds), *Rethinking Modernity in Turkey*, Chicago University Press, Chicago, IL

Somers, Margaret and Gloria Gibson (1994), 'Reclaiming the Epistemological "Other": Narrative and the Social Construction of Identity', in Craig Calhoun (ed.), *Social Theory and the Politics of Identity*, Blackwell, Oxford

Steinmetz, George (1994), 'Reflections of the Role of Social Narratives in Working Class Formation: Narrative Theory in the Social Sciences', *Social Science History*, 16:3 (Fall), pp.488–516

Stokes, Martin (1992), *The Arabesk Debate: Music and Musicians in Modern Turkey*, Clarendon Press, Oxford

9

The Islamist Paradox

Jenny B. White

Identity politics has emerged as a central concept in the analysis of the political culture of contemporary Turkey. Proponents of an analysis based on identity politics suggest that since the 1980s competing discourses of identity, primarily ethnic and religious, have overtaken economic struggle as the defining factor in political organisation and protest (Ayata, 1997; Toprak, 1994). In this essay, I will argue that cultural identity, socioeconomic class and politics are, in fact, inextricably entwined in the everyday context of political action. As a consequence, Islamists are faced with the paradox of trying to create an elite Islamist identity within a populist movement. To do so, activists must differentiate their practice from 'ordinary' Muslim practice, leading to a kind of Islamist elitism. Furthermore, the ability of many activist women to go beyond short-lived, symbolic practice and actually live the lifestyle of the 'new Islamic woman' is limited by the economic constraints of their class. For all these reasons, the 'new' Islamist identity itself is fraught with contradictions about the meanings inherent in its symbols and the practice of the values it espouses. Its politics, in other words, is acted out on socioeconomic, as well as cultural, terrain.

Identity politics is believed to operate hand-in-hand with cultural politics, based on the principle that behavioural styles and tastes in food and clothing are aesthetic distinctions which demonstrate cultural (and thus social) difference and superiority (Bourdieu, 1984). Thus, individuals or groups that desire to change their positioning in society may attempt to do so by strategically manipulating cultural symbols so that they vie with those of the elite for status and legitimacy. More radical yet is the attempt to transform the 'categories of perception and appreciation of the social world and, through this, the social world itself' (p.483). At stake is the right to declare certain identities culturally legitimate, and to determine what is (and is not) civilised behaviour and, thus, socially rewarded.

The focus in identity politics is on cultural strategies and a redefinition and reorientation of the individual rather than the state, a process conceived by some as fundamentally different from political strategies, which revolve around the seizure

191

of political power and changes in the state and legal systems. Thus, Göle (1996) differentiates between two kinds of Islamisation in Turkey, one based on cultural strategies using veiling as a marker of difference and social distinction, and resulting in the creation of counter-communities with new value systems. The other, which she terms 'political Islam', advocates the transformation of society through seizure of political power and the imposition of a new system based on *sharia* law (p.109).

The Islam-inspired Virtue Party (and its predecessor, the Welfare Party[1]) pursued a form of Islamic populism that foregrounded the imagery and rhetoric of an Islamic identity, and focused on the strategic wielding of cultural symbols, such as veiling, in an attempt to attain social distinction. However, the Islamist movement is also very much a political project rooted in issues of social class and, more importantly, in the values of working-class and migrant communities. The seemingly unified identity and symbolic repertoire of the Islamist project is premised upon contradictory impulses: a populist non-recognition of class, status and, to some extent, gender cleavages in the party; the attempt to situate itself as the party of the poor and disadvantaged; and the attempt to re-classify Islamic symbols as elite cultural markers.

Early republican Turkey was mostly rural and relatively undifferentiated in terms of social class. The political elites were characterised less by their economic standing than by their literate education and orientation toward an urban, secular Western lifestyle far from the lifestyle of the rural and provincial population, in which Islam played a fundamental role (Kasaba, 1997; Duben and Behar, 1991). The spread of mass education created career paths that drew people from the cities and provinces into the ranks of the secularist bureaucracy. It also created a cadre of technocrats, managers and other professionals drawn from the rural population, whose values and lifestyles were quite different from those of the Kemalist military–bureaucratic elite. With the introduction of competitive multi-party politics in 1950, these social groups entered political life and took up positions in the bureacratic administration of the state and cities. The values of these new social groups reflected their petty bourgeois and rural origins. They were on the whole less Western and cosmopolitan and felt more comfortable with Islam as a frame of reference for daily life. One of the most successful of this cadre, President Süleyman Demirel, who entered politics in the 1960s, told his party congress, 'I was born in a family that does not sit down to breakfast until the Quran has been read' (quoted in Ahmad, 1991, p.12).

Thus access to political power generally has not been confined to a capitalist elite. One party in particular, the National Order Party, founded in 1970 and the precursor of the Welfare and Virtue parties, represented the economic interests and values of the petty bourgeoisie of Anatolia. Other parties have also followed populist principles, but have alienated the masses with their militant secularism or, increasingly, with their support for economic policies perceived to threaten the welfare of the petty bourgeoisie and the poor.

The opportunity for political advancement, combined with the existence of a strong professional and urban mercantile middle class with roots in small towns and villages, has mitigated against the development of distinct class antagonisms. Class issues thus tend to be expressed in the idiom of cultural differences, particularly regarding the proper role of women in society and of Islam in political and social life, with such issues as women working outside the home and veiling taking centre-stage. In turn, the debates about secularism and Islam are heavily overlaid with class resentments.

The opening of the Turkish economy to the world market in the 1980s and the state's abandonment of its previous role as guarantor of economic security through a controlled economy has created enormous economic dislocations and exacerbated existing differences between rich and poor. Socioeconomic differentiation in Turkey, however, cannot be grasped solely in relation to political and economic domination, but is comprehensible only in relation to community and lifestyles and related structures of power, sources of interest and grounds for moral solidarity (Hefner, 1990, p.25). The traditional social cleavages in Turkey between a conservative Islamic rural lifestyle and westernised urban secular elite were linked to national institutions (the bureaucracy, the military, schools, universities, folkloric clubs etc.) through which the state has tried to propagate its concept of a secular, westernised citizen. Thus, when conservative rural people gained sufficient political mass in the 1980s and began to create an alternative urban culture, their own institutions, and to change the nature of the schools and bureaucracy, the contest was perceived to be one of identity (urban/non-urban, secular/Islamist) to which the other characteristics of the urban poor, such as their class position, was subordinated.

The influence of class is further obscured as communities are cross-cut with other loyalties and sources of motivation: regionalist, religious and gendered. Paul Lubeck, in his study of Islamic political movements in Nigeria (1988), emphasises the inadequacy of either theories of class or cultural explanations to illuminate the behaviour, structure and consciousness of the groups he studied. He concluded that Islamic culture was mediated through the structural and class experience of a group's life. Conversely, subordinated groups resisted economic exploitation by the dominant classes through selective use of Islamic ideology and institutions (p.246). To complicate matters further, Lapidus (1988) points out that Muslim symbols present a moral vocabulary that emphasises communalism, nationalism, solidarity and unity. This focus makes Islamic movements intrinsically hostile to class concepts of political action and effectively impedes the development of class solidarity. Thus, while Islamic belief and behaviour arguably are refracted through the prism of social class interests, and class interests can be addressed by means of Islamic institutions and symbols, the concept of class itself as a motivating factor is denied or obscured by: the focus of Islamic rhetoric on cultural unity; cross-cutting loyalties; and the particular history of the development of class interests in Turkey.

This presents certain advantages – and problems – to a populist political party with a mixed membership of conservative petty bourgeoisie and the working poor and, increasingly, upwardly mobile professionals. Political Islam is able to portray itself as making no differentiations among people on the basis of ethnicity, economic standing, or even whether they are veiled or not. Political action, however, is inspired and mobilised by a great variety of motivations that express the full range of human needs, from the economic to the sexual. The context of everyday life – the situation of Islamist supporters in local and national hierarchies of power and wealth – infuses seemingly unified Islamist symbols with several, at times contradictory, meanings that are then imported into the political movement. In other words, identity politics alone is insufficient to account for the complexity of Islamist political mobilisation in Turkey. The conflicts and nuanced differentiations of motivation deriving from social class and class-situated gender need to be reinserted for a fuller picture.

In the cultural politics of contemporary Turkey, Islamists are attempting to associate such social behaviours as veiling and gender segregation with the meaning complex of urban/modern/educated, challenging social hierarchies that had associated that behaviour in the past with rural/backward/uneducated. This would give veiling the cachet of an elite marker distinct from mass behaviour. These social behaviours and styles also act as unifying cultural markers for the Virtue Party, the Islamist movement's most visible national representative until it was banned in June 2001. However, gender segregation and veiling, as practised in the everyday lives of working-class people, carry multiple meanings derived from the needs, fears and constraints of the urban poor, reflecting gender and class as much as religious or political identity. For these people, daily hardships deriving from unemployment, poverty, lack of adequate infrastructure and educational and healthcare facilities create fundamental conditions within which traditional behavioural forms are the only viable portal to survival. For women in particular, obedience to family, submissiveness, and gender-appropriate behaviour like veiling and segregation are important for claiming the social and economic safety-net of community membership and family support.[2] This too is a form of identity, but it is allied with non-elite, rather than elite, membership, although signalled by the same behaviours.

In a sense, veiling can be effective as a marker of elite status only if it is distanced from the act and implications of veiling in the non-elite environment. For this reason, Islamist activists attempt to distance their own cultural actions from those of the surrounding population by claiming that their own veiling is more conscious, more thought out (*şuurlu*). Islamist intellectual discourse (and academic discourse on that discourse) further supports a distinction between 'conscious' veiling representative of 'cultural politics' and an everyday veiling tainted by competing motivations.[3] Furthermore, veiling as perceived by women (whether elite or working-class) differs appreciably from veiling as understood by men in the Islamist movement. Activist women in the Virtue Party consciously wield veiling and gender segregation as central political symbols to try to forge new social identities and concrete possibilities for women within and outside the movement. The interpretation of these cultural forms by male Virtue Party activists, however, is influenced by the everyday context of veiling and segregation, in which male control over women's sexuality and movement through space has primacy over women's autonomy and control over their bodies.

This contradiction in the political expression of cultural forms can be seen most clearly in the different attitudes of male and female activists to the question of whether women should work outside the home. This is an issue that directly confronts the conflicting meanings of veiling and segregation in two ways: as a means to create a new identity based on cultural forms given social distinction and political force, an identity that would allow women to be veiled but professionally and politically active and physically mobile; and as a guarantee of virginity, the control of male desire, and women's primary place as wife and mother in the home.

The contradiction is given urgency by the fact that there is a great need in working-class neighbourhoods for additional family income. But while the Islamist movement has made room, to some extent, for women to become activists, attend university and work outside the home, other women are denied these opportunities within the same movement. Despite some party leaders' support of women working, male activists and functionaries in working-class neighbourhoods do not support courses to teach women marketable skills. At marriage, even educated Islamist women activists are often asked to stop working by their husbands, particularly after the birth of a child. The distinction between a cultural and a political Islam is thus a spurious one. Beneath the populist rhetoric of 'we are all Muslims', beneath the unified symbolic field, men and women evince different political goals that reflect their distinct cultural experiences of the strictures and opportunities of economic and gender hierarchies.

While politically articulated cultural forms do not necessarily represent the entire culture of a group, nor its entire political organisation, they do provide mutually intelligible symbolic material that has been politically valorised and can support key politico-symbolic dramas (Cohen, 1974, p.132), such as rallies, demonstrations, marches and festivals. These ritualised dramas draw potency from their synchronicity with events occurring in everyday interactions that resonate with the same cultural forms. At the same time, seemingly unified political symbols are contaminated by the meanings that adhere to these cultural forms in everyday life, which may contradict their politically valorised meanings. In this way, the political movement itself may be infiltrated by contradictions.

Culture, Kathleen Stewart (1996, p.5) writes, is 'a process constituted in use', and thus 'given to digression, deflection, displacement, deferral, and difference'. Before classifying, codifying and naming experience to tie down a 'decontaminated' meaning, she urges the re-presentation of the 'texture and density of spaces of desire' (p.26) and a model of culture as a mode of creation and production, rather than a process of selection and classification. 'Meaning', she writes, 'lies emergent in the unfolding of events about which there is always something more to say' (p.58). This chapter tries to reinsert into the discussion of Islamist politics some of the texture of local and political practices, the gaps and multiplicities of meaning, the extrapolations and the contradictions of cultural practice of the same people occupying two places: a social class and a political movement. Imagine desire and obligation projected against a public screen, as in a shadow-puppet theatre. On the screen the audience watches demonstrations, rallies, meetings and speeches. Meanings do not gain clarity in the process, but rather shift and multiply as individual intention is filtered through the structures, possibilities and limitations of gender, class and political action, and shift again as they are perceived by others watching from a different position.

In this chapter, I am concerned with one aspect of the culturo-political complex surrounding Islamist mobilisation in poor urban neighbourhoods, and that is the projection of class and gender-based motivations onto the screen of national politics by a populist political party. In the following pages, I will first briefly address the role of class and gender in the Islamist movement, and then describe and analyse the ritual dramatisation of Islamist politics in a Virtue Party rally and the contradictions contained within it.

The culture of politics

Turkey in the 1980s and 1990s saw tremendous change and transformation. The opening of the Turkish economy and its integration with the world economy, the customs union with Europe, and the development of new markets in the former Soviet territories created opportunities and great wealth for some and unfulfilled hopes and expectations for many others. The government began to privatise industry and dismantle the already thin social safety-net. Prices rose, inflation remained in double figures, unemployment increased as a new wave of rural residents moved into the cities. The new wealth was very visible in Istanbul, the financial and cultural centre of Turkey. A rash of luxurious gated communities and entire new high-rise centres ballooned up throughout the city. In 1982, under the stern eye of the military, which wanted to prevent a recurrence of the violent social unrest of the 1970s, a restrictive constitution replaced the former more liberal document. This stifled the new political demands of various constituencies, from wealthy industrialists to the urban poor. Several avenues of empowerment existed, however. There was a great spurt in growth of civic associations and foundations, the media multiplied, and the electoral system provided opportunities for political participation. In the 1990s members of the business community fielded a party (with limited appeal), the New Democracy Movement.

The segment of the population left behind by the economic transformation found a voice in the Welfare Party, a populist party that emphasised issues like social justice, unemployment, poverty and social security. The poor had moved away from their traditional support for the centre-left parties as well as from the centre-right, both of which were implicated in policies, such as privatisation, that had increased poverty and unemployment among the masses and seemed to support the Western-style development and yuppie lifestyles dominating media discourse (Ayata, 1997, p.70). The Welfare Party rehabilitated concern for poverty, inequality and injustice that had been all but abandoned by the other parties in favour of rhetoric about progress, 'leaping to a new age'. These parties focused instead on issues like Turkey's place in the West and in Europe, the primacy of secularism in social and political life, and nationalist concerns (Cyprus, the Kurdish issue, EU membership).

Since the 1980s, the Islamist movement – I use the term 'movement' loosely, as there are many competing voices and views within it – has decisively inserted itself into the political sphere in the form of first the Welfare Party and then, after it was banned in 1998, its successor, the Virtue Party (White, 2002). A predecessor to Welfare, the National Salvation Party, participated in several coalition governments in the 1970s, but never before in republican Turkey has a religiously inspired party thrown down such strong political and social roots.[4] The network of devout and politically engaged businessmen and industrialists that emerged from the period of economic reform and opportunity in the 1980s provided a stable economic underpinning for various aspects of the Islamist movement, whether in the form of political contributions or the support of charitable organisations, funding of scholarships, or the building of schools and dormitories. In the 1970s, the Welfare Party drew its main support from towns in the under-developed eastern and central Anatolian provinces, and did not do well in the cities (Landau, 1976). In the 1980s, Welfare's voter base expanded to include the urban poor living at the margins of cities (Kirmanoğlu, 1997) who had previously voted for the left-of-centre social democrats. To this has been added the expanding consciously Islamist business community and young professionals. The activists interviewed for this study were residents of Ümraniye, a large working-class neigh-bourhood in Istanbul, with areas of great poverty. In 1994, Ümraniye voters replaced a left-of-centre (Republican People's Party) municipal administration with a Welfare Party administration.

The Islamist movement gained philosophical legitimacy through exposure and discussion of the ideas of Islamist intellectuals in a welter of publications and the media, which included several national and many local television and radio stations. The public utterances of Islamist elites have been subjected to intense analysis (Gülalp, 1997; Meeker, 1991), as have issues of clothing and hair (particularly women's headscarves and men's beards) in the context of markers of Islamist elite status. The distinctive style of Islamist self-presentation is construed as a key symbol of the Islamist movement (Göle, 1996; Ilyasoğlu, 1994), although these styles also have a deep cultural resonance in everyday life not related to the Islamist political project (Delaney, 1994).

The emphasis on the discourse and practices of the elite (or on the elite nature of practices) perpetuates the idea that politics moves out from the centre to engage the periphery, like a motor engaging the cogs of a machine. In some respects, the term Islamist elite is a misnomer, since what is most often referred to is educational status, not necessarily economic status. The two major recent studies of 'elite' Islamist women (Ilyasoğlu, 1994; Göle, 1996) take as their subjects educated women who are politically or professionally active, but whose families are migrants and live in neighbourhoods like Ümraniye. Economic status is referenced in the symbolic association of a particular kind of Islamic dress with upward mobility, but few from a migrant, poor or working-class background have the means actually to move upwards economically, although they may wear Islamic dress. Education, however, is available to the masses, both men and women, thanks to early republican reforms and to some financial assistance by the true economic elites of the Islamist movement, either through direct assistance or by means of foundations and party support. However, women among the Islamist economic elites enjoy a very different lifestyle from the 'elites' of Ümraniye.

Occasionally these contradictions within the party are momentarily exposed, as when the Welfare Party leader Necmettin Erbakan threw a lavish wedding for his daughter at the Istanbul Sheraton Hotel in 1994. The conspicuous consumption made national news and caused some outrage, even among his followers, and may have been responsible for the party losing the 1994 local election in Fatih, one of Istanbul's most Islamist neighbourhoods. In Ümraniye, people who voted for the Welfare Party nevertheless criticised its leader for wasting money. One woman complained that Erbakan had been on the pilgrimage to Mecca several times, when it is only required once in a lifetime:

> How many times does one have to go? What is he trying to show – that he's a better Muslim than we are? And when he goes, he takes his whole entourage with him, his family, and once he even took his grandchild. What is a baby doing on the pilgrimage? Do you know how much money that cost? There are a lot better things he could have done with that money. Like help the poor.

The struggle between Erbakan and Recep Tayyip Erdoğan, the popular mayor of Istanbul, for control of the Virtue Party in part turned on such contradictions within the party and between the party and its supporters: Erbakan's old-fashioned style of elite leadership versus Erdoğan's populism and his image among working-class supporters of being and living 'just like us'.[5]

Use of the term 'Islamist elite' hides these distinctions within the movement between the economic elite and those with limited opportunities, and adds to the mystique of egalitarianism fostered by the movement and the political party by extending the label 'elite' socially downwards to make it accessible to anyone wearing Islamic dress and engaged in political activism or attending university. It also puts social distance between activists and their non-elite background, a distancing necessary if the symbols of Islamism are to be associated with social distinction, status and upward mobility, rather than with their traditional lived contexts. For instance, in her study of 'elite' Islamist women, Göle (1996) insists that the contemporary actors of Islamism are 'not marginal, uneducated, frustrated groups', but rather university students, future intellectuals and professionals, new elites that she says have moved Islam from the periphery to the centre (pp.96, 92). Party activists avoid references to identities forged on the basis of economic position (like *alt tabaka*, lower class) or shared work experience (like *işci sınıfı*, working class), instead preferring terms like poor (*fakir*), actually a bureaucratic category supported by a certificate of poverty issued by the local headman (*muhtar*), and 'the victim sector' (*mağdur kesim*). Both are associated with great shame, and activists take special care when delivering food to 'victim' families that it is not done before the eyes of their neighbours.

Another means of hiding class differences and other contradictions among party supporters is through particularism, referring identity to the level of the individual. The head of an Islamist charity foundation in Ümraniye, an educated, relatively successful businessman, explained that there are no differences among people, in part because they are all Muslims, but also because 'everyone is judged as an individual ... In the foundation, my rank is different, but in other contexts my level (*seviye*) is the same as that of other people. The actual level is that of the person; that is the level within which one finds equal conditions.'

However, although the politics of identity and culture disavow social class, class remains the invisible magnetic pole which repels or anchors culturo-political identities in Turkish society. The simple consciousness of a group's situation in a hierarchy of wealth and power constitutes what Hefner (1990, p.28) calls a self-consciousness of class. This does not necessarily presuppose 'a conviction that those occupying common class situations actually share common interests' or a 'consciousness of kind'. A self-consciousness of class nevertheless remains 'not so much reflected [as] refracted in consciousness, in some cases as alienation and anomie and in others as ethnicity and the motive force of new social movements' (Kearney, 1996, p.146). Class under these circumstances is not a binary concept, or even one that can be fitted into the more refined sociological categories of lower, middle, upper-middle and so on. Rather, class expresses itself as the difference between those who produce more value than they consume and those who consume more than they produce, a definition which allows for the many layers of internal differentiation among producers and consumers of value and the lack of sharp cleavages in contemporary society (Kearney, 1996, p.173). What Kearney calls the politics of general value also accommodates the notion that identities and values indicate the class position of subjects and that people may seek to alter the system of signs that define them, but he argues that this must be seen as occurring within a system of class differences, 'the fundamental, bottom-line economic issue in social life' (p.174).

Motivations for political participation among class-differentiated subjects follow in no small measure from the characteristics of their class position. However, beyond the shared experience of poverty, unemployment, poor health-care, and relative lack of educational and economic opportunities, residents of Ümraniye exhibit the variety of needs, desires, histories and identifications one can expect to find in a neighbourhood of 250,000 residents. That is, among the socially and economically disadvantaged residents, one finds contradictions in the reasons why people supported the Virtue Party, what they expected from it, and in the meanings they attributed to the central unifying symbols and slogans of the Islamist identity. What follows is a dense description of a Virtue Party rally, a ritualised drama in which key political symbols were powerfully brandished to demonstrate and strengthen the party's unity and populist image. The analysis will shift between the politico-symbolic drama of the rally and the more subtle and sometimes contradictory meanings of informal behaviour eddying beneath.

Performing virtue

After nearly two hours of fighting the crowded tumultuous traffic from Istanbul, Sibel[6] and Banu, both journalists, and I entered the city of Izmit and asked for directions to the sports stadium, where a rally of the Islamist Virtue Party was taking place. The rally was called the 'March Toward Virtue Feast', although it involved neither a march nor a feast. Guards were waving cars away from the entrance. Several rows of soldiers and policemen stood at attention at the front of the building. Sibel waved her press pass and caught the attention of some of Istanbul Mayor Recep Tayyip Erdoğan's assistants, who ran over and waved us in. Sibel gave someone the key to the car to park it and we were sluiced into the stadium through a back door.

We were about an hour late and the proceedings had already begun. According to the printed invitation, we had missed some folkloric entertainment, but it turned out that the entertainment had been cancelled in sympathy with the victims of the Adana earthquake which had occurred that morning. In response to Sibel's apologies and queries about whether we had missed the Mayor, our guide, one of the Mayor's staff, a slim, well-dressed man with a very black, round, neatly cut beard and a friendly face, whispered that the Mayor had been delayed and was, in fact, arriving this very moment. We hastened down a grey-walled back corridor and were guided up an entrance into the stands.

We emerged into a dazzling disorienting kaleidoscope of sound and colour. The covered hall, about the size of a stadium at a mid-sized American college, was festooned with large red flags – Virtue Party flags alternating with Turkish ones. Strings of flags were draped tent-like from the centre of the roof. Enormous Turkish flags lined the walls like tapestries. Within this startling blood-red atmosphere, phalanxes of people massed in the stands. The side of the stadium facing me was entirely populated with women in Islamic dress, a palette of long pastel coats, gold flecks on the multi-hued headscarves glinting in the bright white lights. Young women in identical long, light-grey coats and scarves ushered the women to their seats. The stands on our side of the hall and the central area were populated by men, many sporting the rounded Islamic beard and distinctive round-collared shirt of the Islamist. The stadium was completely full. A dull but expectant roar textured the air. It was very bright and very hot.

The assistants made room for us through the crowd, and someone asked me whether I would mind sharing a seat. I agreed, and was handed to a young woman in beige and blue Islamic dress who guided me past the knees of a row of older bearded men. They were sitting not in the plastic stadium seats or folding chairs, but in broad plush upholstered seats along one side of the stage. Sibel and Banu sat at the far end of the row behind me, each, I noticed, in her own seat, although they soon left to go backstage. The veiled woman apologised for my having to share a seat, and added something about not being able to displace the Mayor's bodyguards. I settled myself between the veiled woman on my left and a middle-aged woman with uncovered hair on my right. She was wearing a warm-looking brown suit and identified herself as a member of the Turkish foreign service.

My 'seat' was directly behind Recai Kutan, official head of the Virtue Party, and Recep Tayyip Erdoğan, the Mayor of Istanbul. In the open area on the stadium floor just below us swarmed television and press reporters. Their photographs will show the two party leaders with three women behind them, two of them with uncovered heads, one of them wearing a white, short-sleeved shirt. A long shot would show the three women in a sea of men. As I moved into position to sit, Mayor Erdoğan turned, smiled and extended a hand to be shaken. Next, I extended my hand to Kutan, who had also turned around in his seat. There was a barely perceptible hesitation before he shook my hand, and I remembered too late that some Islamists refused to shake hands with women for reasons of religious purity. The woman to my right nodded pleasantly as I wedged myself between them at the confluence of the two chairs. It was comfortable, but we three just barely fitted. Whenever I moved my hand to take notes, I nudged one of the women. I was sweating profusely. Finally, I was able to look around.

Kutan, a kindly looking white-haired old man, sat quietly by as Erdoğan was continuously besieged with autograph-seekers and people wanting to have their photo taken with him. The mayor courteously signed diaries and invitations and posed for photos with infinite patience, giving each person his full attention. It was clear that people worshipped him; he was the rock star of Turkish politics. The woman to my left introduced herself as Lütfiye. She had a pleasant, round, lightly freckled face with delicate features. We talked in snatches over the noise of amplified announcements and the muted roar of the crowd. She explained proudly that their local organisation had worked for weeks to set this event up. She herself was the press liaison for the local party, although, she added, she did not yet have an official position, but that would soon change. She indicated the stands of women across the stadium and pointed out her sixteen-year-old daughter, a distant figure in white suit and orange headscarf. 'That is my daughter over there,' she announced approvingly. 'She decided on her own to join the [Virtue Party] youth group.'

A small stage was set up at the front of the stadium. Next to the stage loomed a square of at least 20 video monitors stacked together like pieces of a large puzzle. Lütfiye took my hand and whispered that the local Virtue representative (she pointed him out to me, a young man in a beige blazer) had spent two entire days setting up this video presentation. It had been very difficult to get it to work properly, but didn't it look wonderful now. She beamed with admiration. The lights dimmed and every cube in the video puzzle lit up to show a different part of the picture, making a seamless large 'screen'. On this screen appeared images of well-dressed men and women sitting at dinner at a fancy reception, clinking wine glasses. There was some scuttling about around the stage and Lütfiye leaned forward anxiously. Finally it became clear – the sound wasn't working. 'Too bad,' she commiserated, 'all that work.'

But the video itself had a clear enough message even without the accompanying soundtrack. One of the pictured guests at the reception was Prime Minister Mesut Yœlmaz of the centrist Motherland Party. Whenever his image appeared on the screen, the silently watching crowd exploded into a disparaging 'Boo'. For ten minutes we watched the elegantly dressed guests wining and dining on sumptuous displays of food amid silver and crystal on patios and in ornate rooms. Wine flowed; a décolleté bride made a grand entrance through palatial doors. The only sound was an occasional groundswell of 'Boo' as Yılmaz's image appeared, lifting a glass, shaking a hand. Suddenly, the image changed to a desolate place that appeared to be a garbage dump. Small figures approached from the distance, winding among the hills of garbage, bending low to examine the refuse, occasionally selecting a piece and secreting it in the plastic bag each carried. As they approached it became clear that they were children, heads close-shaven against lice, in torn slacks and frayed sweaters that no longer betrayed their original colours but had faded to muddy greens and browns. A garbage truck pulled up and spilled its load; the children sprinted over to examine the new material. As they came closer, they seemed to notice the camera and lined up grinning and jiggling their feet.

The video screens winked out, the lights came on and the host on stage announced the next speaker, the Mayor. The crowd launched to its feet and exploded into a loud, sustained cheer. People – men and women – waved Virtue flags high over their heads and cried out in triumph and jubilation. A chant broke out: 'Turkey takes pride in you'. He started his speech by referring to the film, the outrage of having both of those scenes occurring simultaneously in a country. The crowd roared its agreement. The rest of his speech was straightforward – setting out the Virtue platform. But his delivery was masterful. He thundered, then lowered his voice to an intimate growl. He paused to let his words take effect. He pivoted and addressed all sides of the stadium equally. The overwhelming impression the Mayor gave was that, regardless of whether one was part of a stadium audience or standing next to him while he signed an autograph or shook one's hand, he was entirely, intimately there with the viewer. Dressed in a good-quality but under-stated suit (unlike Necmettin Erbakan, the former Welfare Party leader, with his much-commented-upon taste for bright, expensive Italian ties), Erdoğan projected a combination of powerful resolve and intimacy.

The content of his talk at the Izmit rally consisted of a recapitulation of his successes as Mayor in reshaping and improving the city. This was followed by the five goals of the Virtue Party. Briefly, these are human rights, democracy, free-dom, economic progress and a state based on law. As evidence of the party's respect for human rights he listed price decreases, the provision of water, and the year-round, rather than merely seasonal, operation of the Sea Bus, Istanbul's hovercraft commuter service. These were services for everyone, he pointed out, 'Not making distinctions, differentiations – this is the mark of Virtue'. Human rights were economic rights. Democracy was equated with respect. 'Mesut Yılmaz is not a democrat. He has no respect for people.' 'Either [democracy] will come, or...' and he held that moment, playing with the implied threat, before finishing his sentence, '... or we will continue our struggle for democracy'. Freedom, he went on, meant that people have their rights protected. The centrepiece of this argument was the right to attend university wearing a headscarf. His discussion of economic progress focused on the threat by big business to environmentally sensitive land which the mayor believed was held in trust for the people by the government. He was referring to recent incidents in which a large Turkish holding company sought to obtain rights to build on forested land in Istanbul. Finally, he urged the creation of a state in which laws that are on the books are actually implemented. He emphasised, as have Virtue activists in other conversations, that the present laws of the state for the most part do not need to be changed, but rather need to be implemented equally and fairly.

The mayor ended his speech to wild applause, flag-waving and the chant about his bringing honour to the people. He returned to his seat and was immediately enveloped in a swarm of young veiled women, all in the matching grey coats and headscarves of the youth group that was ushering the event. They were flushed and excited as they proffered bouquets of flowers. Each girl posed with the Mayor while another took the photo. Erdoğan's assistants brought him stacks of albums to sign.

During this interlude, the mayors of Virtue municipalities were asked to gather on stage and receive awards. They were, almost to a man, paunchy bearded burghers. Then Virtue members of parliament took the stage, received awards and filed out. Kutan was announced, and took the stage almost unnoticed. After the Mayor's speech, the crowd had begun to thin, leaving patches of empty seats. Kutan spoke mildly and slowly, with little inflection. People in my row were having conversations with one another. The exodus from the arena speeded up. Kutan was explaining the symbolism of the heart in the Virtue flag. 'We need love. We need compassion. We need affection.' Only Virtue, he insisted, had the five principles, then enumerated them again. Virtue, he intoned, stood for progress and development.

> They ask, are you left, right, mid-left, mid-right. These are artificial differentiations. We are none of these. We want democracy and we are exactly in the middle of democracy... The party that recognizes these desires (*arzu*), the needs of the common people, and meets them, this is the party that will succeed.

In the middle of his speech, I was called away for tea in a back room with Sibel, Banu and members of the Mayor's staff.

The politics of culture

In many ways, the Virtue rally was much like any other political rally in Turkey: the horseshoe-shaped seating, dignitaries in front; the flags and party icons; the speeches, cheers and personality cults surrounding individual leaders; the folk-dance entertainment, with the exception of the Islamist addition of a *mehter* band performance of Ottoman military music, making reference to Turkey's Ottoman past, another central symbolic focus of the Islamist movement. The content of the speeches provided clear political signposts, laid out the path on which all were to walk together, and identified enemies. At the same time, semantic and symbolic elements provided mutually intelligible referents to a shared cosmology and seemingly unified meanings that seemed universal.

Turkey's secularist parties, far from being bereft of such cosmological symbolism, have attempted to substitute what some have called a 'religion' of laicism, the central symbol of which is a representation of Atatürk, founder of the modern, secular Turkish republic. Other than the ubiquitous representation of Atatürk, however, public meetings of the other parties are relatively ambiguous with regard to religious symbolism. At meetings of the Republican People's Party, especially closed meetings attended only by party members and their guests, the consistent symbolic element is the marked absence of religious symbolism – there are no Islamic beards and no headscarves. Public Republican People's Party meetings in working-class areas, however, typically have a mixed audience, with some onlookers sporting headscarves or beards, while others wore short sleeves or were clean-shaven. Men and women sat or stood together, although some groups of local men and women kept to the norms of gender segregation and stood apart.

1997 opening of a women's centre in Ankara, sponsored by the Republican People's Party

Virtue Party Rally in Izmit

Ümraniye women at an engagement party

What made the March Towards Virtue Feast immediately recognisable as an Islamist rally – that is a political rally informed by an Islamic ideology – was the total segregation of the audience, with the notable exception of the five women, including the anthropologist, sitting in the stands behind the party leaders. The second noticeable difference was not so much the dress – people in all kinds of dress attended rallies and events put on by even the most secularist of the other parties – but the homogeneity of the dress.

A third, related but more subtle, difference was the complete absence of markers of social class in the audience. The unifying idiom of Muslim religious identity was underscored by the homogenous clothing style and quality among both men and women and the lack of markers of distinction in seating. With the exception of the plush seats of the first few rows, where the party leaders sat, it was impossible to discern visually any differences in status. The mayors and members of parliament sat on hard folding chairs in the middle section of the stadium, indistinguishable from their neighbours until they stood up to file onto the stage. In opposition to the homogeneity of the party members, however, class was prominently displayed in the video as a divisive national phenomenon. The 'class-less', modestly covered women at the rally provided a severe visual reprimand to the wealthy women in low-cut dresses and bare arms in the film clip. The film also contrasted sumptuous displays of food with gaunt children picking through the garbage. In our discussions, Virtue Party activists often emphasised that, unlike activists of other parties, they 'actually eat with' the people whom they are mobilising or assisting in charity operations. In other words, the personalised nature of Islamist politics is expressed through the metaphor of sharing food, rather than merely distributing it (which other parties do as well). The rally framed oppositions (covered/uncovered, sharing/keeping, equality/unequal differentiation) that vibrated with the accompanying narratives of loss and desire (*arzu*).

Women are the central locus of desire, not only in the traditional sense of sexual shame and danger, but in an expanded referential sense of political, social and economic desire. Likewise, virtue is demonstrated not only by covering (*kapatmak*) the female body to eradicate men's longing, and marrying to channel it, but also by covering or taking care of (*kapatmak* is also used in this sense) the needs of the poor through assistance. The desire for profit ideally is channelled and controlled through love, the desire to rule tamed through the injunction to serve. Virtue is love, compassion and affection. It is also new hovercraft routes and lower prices. Loss does not refer only to loss of virginity and honour, but also to hunger and injustice. Longing is for economic and political justice, not only physical union. Women's virtue becomes national virtue. Desire, projected onto the political screen, sutures the aims of the Islamist elite with the lifestyle of the urban poor, who fear poverty and sexual dishonour and who subsist by means of strong norms of mutual assistance and the control of women's bodies and movement. It is the resonance of the political message with local desire that fuels emotion and support for Virtue.

The virtuous majority

Islamist women manage desire and display virtue by means of a distinctive form of Islamic dress called *tesettür*, which consists of a long, feminine, loosely tailored coat, generally pastel-coloured, and a large silk matching headscarf decorated with abstract motifs that vary with each fashion season. The scarf entirely hides the hair and neck and usually, though not always, the shoulders and bosom. The scarf may be worn without the coat, generally with specially designed suits or dresses that cover the body, and, more recently, among young women, with slacks or even tight skirts. *Tesettür* is more than a style of clothing; it is part and parcel of a lifestyle that ideally encompasses a religio-cultural code of behaviour prescribing the spacial segregation of men and women, appropriate spaces for the movement of male and female bodies in public places and in the home, the proper relationship between men and women, authority of fathers and husbands over daughters and wives, and men over women, and proscribing the interaction of unrelated men and women.

Tesettür, as a form of cultural Islam, is perceived to be not only a marker of difference from the secularist elites, but also from the masses. Implicit in the strategic deployment of symbols to reposition oneself in a hierarchy of social stratification is a rupture from local practice where those same symbols – the disposition of the body, movement in space, and interpersonal relations – are embedded in a community and identity from which the new elites must distance themselves. 'By means of veiling, women try to free themselves from the given conventional patterns of life and yet to differ from traditional Muslim women.' (Göle, 1996, p.130) Activist women acknowledge that their religious devotion is shared by non-activist women of their community, but insist that their brand of Islamic practice is different because it is a conscious practice, rather than one based on tradition. The head of the women's branch of the Virtue Party in Ümraniye: 'My mother is covered (*kapalı*), in traditional covering. Now, our covering is, of course, different from our mothers' covering. Ours is more purposeful, more researched, more conscious (*şuurlu*) than that in our neighbourhood.' Islamist 'counter-communities' try to separate individuals transformed by 'new' Islamist values and sporting newly redefined and valourised symbols from the traditions, values and symbols of the masses.

Despite efforts by the Islamist elite to distinguish *tesettür* and its associated lifestyle from their 'traditionally lived' context and make of them a different 'consciously lived' Islam, *tesettür* remains associated not only with the Islamist movement and Virtue Party, but also with everyday urban life. *Tesettür* is worn by a great variety of women, from middle-class housewives to poor migrants in the urban slums who wish to display modesty, religious devotion, urban cachet and the image (if not always the practice) of upward mobility. Diluting the association of clothing and lifestyle with meaning even further, many modern middle-class secularists, although not veiled, lead consciously Islamic lives associated with veiling. They may pray and practice a modified yet still gender-specific use of public and private space.

Tesettür is also worn by working-class women who do not support political Islam, but rather vote for centrist or left-of-centre political parties. One such is

Samiye, a devout, forty-five-year-old woman with three years of schooling, who migrated from a Black Sea village to Ümraniye more than 20 years ago. She resents the politicisation and valorisation of a clothing style she has worn all her life. 'I've always worn a long coat, since coming to the city... *Tesettür* has been around only the last few years. Before that, people said [someone was] covered... We were Muslims before. Where were they?' She believes that *tesettür* spread because of advertisements on Islamic television stations by the Welfare Party and Islamic holding companies. On the positive side, she explained, she can now buy a coat of requisite length anywhere, rather than having it specially tailored.

Associated with the wearing of *tesettür* is the segregation of women from men, especially unrelated men, both during ritual occasions and in everyday activities at home. Samiye's niece Raife came down from the village for her cousin's pre-wedding all-female henna ceremony. Under her *tesettür* coat, she wore a chic yellow sweater over a long skirt, and the *tesettür* scarf fashionable this year – a black and white leopard print set within a pattern of gold loops. Her mother and father had lived in Istanbul 22 years, but could not make it financially, and the previous year had gone back to their village. She said she was unhappy in the village, but was allowed to come often to stay with relatives. In the village, she dressed for work in the fields, but here she dressed the part of a city girl, in *tesettür*. The banquet room was in the basement of the building, a large room painted on all sides with renditions of folk dancers and landscapes. The women, almost all in *tesettür*, clustered as they went around the room greeting each other and kissing the hands of elders. On the platform a man played an electric organ and sang. Before long, the women realised that the musician was a man and that there were men (including the brother of the bride) walking in and out of the room. There was a ripple of concern. Samiye was angry and exclaimed to the others at her table, 'How dare they have a man here! Don't they know that means no one can dance!' The whispers spread through the crowd. After all, the bride herself was in *tesettür* and paid great attention to not being in the presence of unrelated males, even when she was completely covered. Her white satin gown had a matching turban that covered her hair and bosom. 'She should have known better.' The musician did not leave and the situation worsened.

As the evening wore on, the bride's male relatives came in carrying food and drink, plastic cups of sweet red punch and plates of sweet and salty biscuits, and took away the empty plates and cups. Two lean muscular young men in tight black jeans and white T-shirts lounged about most of the evening brandishing cameras with large flash attachments but rarely taking pictures. They looked like wolves in a pen of sheep. The bride was near tears. Over the objections of her relatives, Raife and a few other unmarried girls danced, wearing their headscarves, but without their coats. The other women were annoyed and bored and, as soon as the henna ceremony was over, began to leave.

The identity of Islamist elites is predicated in large part upon distancing their 'knowledgeable practice' of Islam from the cultural practice of Islamic values, as in the henna party described above. The Islamic social project aims 'to introduce the "real Islam" to social groups with lower levels of education and culture who otherwise experience "folk Islam"' (Göle, 1996, p.113). This distancing can be seen as an attempt at de-proletarianisation. The educated women of the new Islamist elite interviewed in Göle's study (1996)came, for the most part, from conservative migrant families (p.88) like those of Samiye and Raife. They were the activist daughters of migrant communities. In other words, the artificially bounded counter-communities of the Islamist elites generally interpenetrate with the unbounded expanded communalities of the common people. This makes the elite project of differentiating themselves from traditional Muslim women more difficult. *Tesettür* alone is an insufficient marker, since it is worn by a variety of women out of a variety of motivations which elite Islamists would consider unconscious and cultural, focused on domestic gender roles, rather than arising from a conscious motivation based on Islamic activism.

The project of disentangling Islamic activism from Islamic populism is fraught with difficulty and internal contradiction, given the populist nature of the Islamist project and the Welfare/Virtue Party that was its primary vehicle. Some popular Islamist novels and magazines, aimed at an audience of working-class, lower-middle-class and migrant women, focused primarily on Islamic interpretations of modesty, veiling, gender segregation and traditional female roles as wife, mother and homemaker (Acar, 1995). This earned the disapproval of Islamist intellectuals, who disparaged such 'discourses of "cheap radicalism and populism"' as an 'amalgamation of "Islamicisation and proletarianisation"' and 'the birth of an "Islamic arabesque"' (Göle, 1996, p.113), referring to the popular working-class *arabesk* musical style held in equal contempt by secularist elites.

The contaminating convergence of cultural tradition and Islamist symbolism and lifestyle must be controlled in order for an elite cultural Islam to be differentiated and acquire social and cultural legitimacy. Since cultural differences are embedded in class distinctions, the differentiation between common traditional Muslim practice and elite Islamist practice inevitably implies attempts at de-proletarianisation. The most viable avenue for distancing oneself from one's working-class background is education. Groups of *tesettürlü* students thus form self-validating nuclei of young women able to wield their clothing and lifestyle in a 'conscious' way in a public field (university, plazas and roads during demonstrations, the media) uncontaminated by other meanings. Mass meetings of Welfare/Virtue Party activists form another platform on which symbols can retain pristine meanings. Local Welfare/Virtue Party rallies that attract the general public, such as the rally described earlier, are another story altogether. The attendees, despite superficial similarities in dress and purpose which underline the classless feature of Welfare/Virtue's programme, wear Islamic dress for a variety of reasons, practice an Islamic lifestyle to varying degrees, 'consciously' or not, and have differing, sometimes contradictory, motivations for their attendance, activism, or support for the party. It is only *entre nous* or in a neutral public space and as public performance that the image of an uncontaminated elite cultural Islam can be maintained.[7]

In other words, the differentiation of a 'cultural' over a 'political' Islam can be upheld only as long as the cultural is held to be a source of rupture and regeneration of value in its own right, regardless of the exigencies and motivations of social class. If, however, one sees the 'new' politicised Muslim value system not as superimposed on an unenlightened, class-bound traditional Muslim lifestyle, but rather embedded within it, politics and culture merge. Indeed, the attempt to establish an Islamist cultural elite in many ways contradicts the populist Islamist political project.

In this regard, Welfare/Virtue Party populism bore some resemblance to the populism of pre-revolutionary Khomeinism in Iran. The direction of Khomeinism was primarily given by an anti-imperialist middle-class elite positioned against an entrenched power-holding bourgeoisie associated with the West. The Khomeinists mobilised the urban working class, many of them migrants living in shantytowns, who had not been successfully organised by the Iranian left, much as Welfare/Virtue took over the rhetoric and goals of the Turkish left after it had been crushed in the aftermath of the 1980 coup. However, although Khomeinism attacked the establishment, the movement was careful not to undermine private property and the interests of the petty bourgeoisie. After attaining victory over the old order, Khomeinists focused on changing cultural and educational institutions, rather than on changing the economic order. This reflected the ambiguity and contradiction inherent in a movement that wanted to protect the middle-class private property of its elite Islamic leaders, yet strengthen the state's control over society as a whole and provide social benefits to the lower classes that had supported the movement (Abrahamian, 1993). As in Turkey, contradictions between the interests of an Islamic elite and those of the masses were obscured by Islamic symbolism, imagery and rhetoric representing the unity of all Muslims and a classless Islamic society characterised by social justice.

The public expression of shared cultural values is an important factor in the success of contemporary Muslim popular movements because it overcomes, or at least disguises, community factional and class divisions. A common cause, perhaps a public protest, crystallises the sense of a city- and nation-wide Muslim identity and community consciousness (Freitag, 1988). Organisational cohesion, however, is not a given. In Turkey it was supplied by the Welfare/Virtue Party, providing a public structure within which complex and fragmented Muslim communities could express class issues within an idiom of social solidarity and co-operation, rather than class antagonism. Nevertheless, differences within society (whether they be gender, social class, ethnic or sectarian) means that the fit among symbols, organisations and interests is bound to be imperfect (Lapidus, 1988).

Subjects of desire

Another manifestation of the implicit contradiction between conscious activist intentions and traditional cultural expectations hidden under the canopy of populism is the different constructions of women's rights, privileges and motivations by activist women and their male colleagues within the Welfare/Virtue Party. While many activist women I interviewed in Ümraniye were engaged in the Islamist project in order to carve out new areas of autonomy within the traditional expectations of their community, male Welfare/Virtue Party activists in the next office were motivated in part by a desire to reinforce traditional female roles and to enhance their own autonomy vis-à-vis women, for instance, by supporting polygyny, which is illegal in secular Turkey.

Female Welfare supporters were responsible for getting out a large part of the vote for Welfare. In the month before the 1995 elections, in Istanbul alone, the Welfare Party's women's commission worked with 18,000 women and met face-to-face with 200,000 women (Arat, 1997, p.67). The women were very much interested in using Welfare/Virtue as a vehicle to advance the position of women, particularly through education and work outside the home. As a female Welfare Party activist in Ümraniye put it, 'I too used to be just like other women in this neighbourhood. I sat around and ate and talked, ate and talked. But now I've found myself. I've become active and productive.' She firmly believed that women should work outside the home, get an education, and enter the professions.

Female Welfare supporters were extraordinarily successful in popular mobilisation, and it is widely acknowledged that they were in large part responsible for Welfare's success in working-class neighbourhoods like Ümraniye. They worked person-to-person, building cells of local women attached to the Women's Branch which, in turn, was guided by the party and took its direction (and much of its financial support) from there. However, almost no women were represented in the party administration and the women's branches and commissions had no formal status within the party.[8] Male party activists generally answered questions about the lack of women in the party's formal administration by retraining the question on the issue of banning headscarves in university. This deflected internal division and emphasises the artificial unity of political symbolism. The issue also was avoided by reference to democracy: a government that refused education to women on the grounds of their wearing a headscarf was undemocratic. However, when pressed about the importance of education for women, male activists stated simply that women's main role was to be mothers and homemakers, and that women should be educated because that would make them better mothers.

Within the party, there were contradictory views about whether women should work outside the home and whether they should receive training to do so. In an interview,[9] Istanbul Mayor Erdoğan underscored his belief that women should be fully involved in social and political life, but with several reservations:

> Some work is not suitable for women; it goes against their delicacy, like the work women did behind the Iron Curtain: working in construction, laying roads and so on. It's natural for them to do other work. They could even be those who manage managers... Women's right includes political work. But I support struggle (*mücadele*), not a quota system... A quota means you are helping people; it's an insult to women.

On the other hand, the Mayor also believed that 'Working at home is safer for women. They often get no insurance when they work outside the home; if they are young, they may be molested in workshops and other workplaces. This way they aren't oppressed by the employer.'

I asked him whether this meant he believed all women ideally should work at home. He shook his head emphatically and explained:

Those women who have the talent and the education, those who are engineers and so on, anyway find work. If women have graduated from high school, they should be able to work. But for the others, staying at home at least gives them the possibility of making their own trousseaux [with money earned from the sale of handicrafts]. But it's a stopgap solution. You can't solve the unemployment problem that way.

Both the Mayor and male activists, in other words, differentiate between women who are educated and may work at a profession and women who are not educated and would be better off at home than in a job where they could be oppressed and molested.

However, local male activists in Ümraniye in their discussions and in practice added the requisite that even educated women's first priority is husband, home and children, and that they should stop working at marriage or after the birth of a child. I know of several cases in Ümraniye where educated professional women and activists were required by their new husbands or husbands' families to remain at home after marriage. In some cases this resulted in greatly constrained mobility, including being required to ask permission to leave home to visit nearby family and friends or to shop at the grocery. A common theme in popular Islamist fiction is the quandary faced by Islamist women when they marry and lose the 'voice' they had as activists, students and professionals (Ilyasoğlu, 1994). Non-Islamist women's popular fiction also takes up this theme.

Although activist women in Ümraniye agree with the idea that women's first responsibility is to make a home for her husband and children, they also have very firm ideas about the need for education and work, and not only to make a woman 'a better mother'. A female activist in Ümraniye: if a girl's family doesn't send her to school, 'what will that girl do at home? ... She'll go either to a textile workshop or wait at home for her fate (kısmet). That a man should come, see her, like her, and found a nest [start a family]. Why should it be like that? [She will sit at home and] be a consumer, not a producer. But if that girl finishes high school, finishes university, maybe she will work somewhere in some area, and find herself contributing to the country's economy by working.'

In Ümraniye, Welfare/Virtue Party-administered municipal offices were staffed by veiled secretaries, several of whom were computer experts. They designed and published the municipality's reports and booklets. The municipality handed out slick self-presentations (put together by the veiled secretaries) and magazines, newspapers and brochures giving party and municipal news. Male activists distributed these to cafes, barbers' shops and local stores, places frequented by men. When I asked the men how the information got to the women, they answered that the men could bring it home if they wanted to. There were segregated computer classes for female students, generally veiled. Although the women were very active in low-level party political mobilisation, the party's Women's Branch was not formally incorporated, a fact which irked some of the women activists. Despite the central symbolic representation of women in the party and the availability of computer courses to students, there were no courses offered through the party or the Welfare/Virtue municipalities to teach married women or housewives skills that would allow them extra income, even income from work at home. There were only traditional handicraft courses; the women could sell what they made in the courses at occasional small fairs set up for that purpose.

This was in direct contrast to the policy of the previous administration in Ümraniye, led by the Republican People's Party, which set up 'People's Schools' to teach women typing, sewing, literacy and other skills with the express purpose of making the women financially more independent and physically mobile (White, 1996). The Welfare Party, when it took over the municipality, had closed down many of the programmes (offering such services as skills classes, meeting rooms, kindergartens and, in another neighbourhood, refuges for battered women) that secularist and feminist women's groups had set up on property owned by the municipality. In the case of privately owned premises, other tactics were employed, for instance sending in squadrons of veiled women to pray in the meeting rooms and hallways, discouraging other women who would have used the services.

I asked the head of an Islamist charity foundation in Ümraniye (which worked in tandem with the Welfare/Virtue municipal governments) why, given the widespread poverty in the neighbourhood, the foundation or party didn't open courses for women to learn skills they could use to earn money for their families. He replied that they tried to take care of the women's money problems through the men. 'Women's duty is to take care of the home and children. There is no need for women to work to earn money, and therefore no need for courses like that.' When I pointed out to another male activist that the men were often unable to pay even for schooling for all their children, but that if mothers could earn money they would be able to send their children to school, his answer was that people had to live within their means. Later, Erdoğan and the head of the charity foundation independently explained to me their view that the municipalities and foundations could do only so much because of the widespread poverty and unemployment, that it was a system-wide problem that could not be solved by training women to work.

Nevertheless, on the subject of work and women's place in social life, the principles guiding the male party ranks in Ümraniye seemed to contradict the principles motivating the activists of the local women's branch. Such a contradiction was flatly denied by the women, who insisted that if there were Virtue Party men who thought that women shouldn't work, it could only be their personal opinion, not party policy.

The question of *sharia* law, also an avowed desire of some male Virtue supporters and functionaries in Ümraniye, although there was no consensus as to its meaning or implementation, was also dealt with by women activists through denial and personalisation. 'We are already living *sharia*,' explained one highly placed woman activist. 'I wear the veil – that is *sharia*. I pray – that is *sharia*.' When asked whether she would consent to being a man's fourth wife, she scoffed and exclaimed, 'What woman would consent to anything like that nowadays'. By contrast, a highly placed male activist in Ümraniye: if a man committed adultery, he wouldn't be guilty, rather 'the state would be guilty for not allowing him to marry a second wife'. He argued that men and women both had sexual needs that may not be satisfied by only one person and that caused them to seek out additional people to satisfy this legitimate need. If the state forbade it, it forced people to commit a crime that could be avoided by giving permission to marry more than one person. This 'right' did not apply to women, even though they may have the same needs. 'Because women bear the children and it is crucial to know whose child she is bearing...she can't be with more than one man.' Many other male activists I spoke to in Ümraniye shared this desire for *sharia*, although each projected onto it his own preoccupations: *sharia* to bring legal justice, *sharia* to stamp out corruption, *sharia* to stop economic exploitation, *sharia* to 'protect women from exploitation'.

Even though women in Virtue's Women's Branch did not have the power to affect the party's practices, for instance, by opening the courses they would like, they still believed that the party would give women the opportunities they sought. After all, they pointed out, they themselves, through their party activities, became independent and competent, left their houses, 'found' themselves. At the Virtue rally, three women sat on two chairs in a place of honour. At one level, this was an elevation of women and an expression of the party's avowed principle of not making distinctions (between men and women, veiled and unveiled women, social classes, ethnicities and so on). On another level, it was an indication that, while women were given status in the party, this was done in a circumscribed manner. They were not given access to administrative or financial decision-making, except within their own tightly organised but autonomous hierarchies. Women were elevated over other women, but were not placed in an equal position (or elevated over) men. Several hierarchies were in play simultaneously that both supported and obscured the gender hierarchies in everyday life, from which activist women tried to distance themselves.

The place of the cultural other

Tesettür indeed became a marker of distinction and of upward social mobility, even if the reality was different and the motivations 'impure'. That is, it is a political symbol that unified members of the Islamist movement and Virtue Party. It also hid class differences among members of the party and was, itself, a symbol of upward mobility and an urban lifestyle. The women activists desired mobility – social, physical and professional. Yet *tesettür* also signified the opposite of mobility: the proper place of women is in the home. For male Ümraniye activists, in particular, veiling symbolised women's reserving their beauty, their attention and their labour for their husbands and family. They categorically resisted the idea that women could or should work outside the home after marriage. This corresponded to the reality of non-political life in much of Ümraniye, where women were under the protection of their family and under the authority of family males. They worked for their family and did not travel far afield from their homes, especially after marriage.

The party projected an ambivalent message: the Mayor supported women working, but women were only loosely incorporated in the party structure and, at the time of my study, there were no women in the highest positions. Much as Lütfiye, a central organiser of the Izmit event, had no official position but was seated in a place of honour behind the party leader, sharing her chair with a marginal although equally honoured foreigner. Nevertheless, as members of the audience and in terms of political activity, women in Virtue were partners with men. They were, in many ways, more visible than male activists. During the same time period as the Izmit rally, hundreds of women in *tesettür* demonstrated in front of universities and marched on the capital, Ankara, to demand the right to wear headscarves at university. Yet during a public lecture presentation arranged by the Ümraniye Welfare Party municipality in 1997, the two women who attended were seated behind a bookcase in a dark back corner of the room where the male audience sat. Despite the populist, classless attributes of the Izmit rally audience, the official leadership of the organisation lay with men. Only token or marginal women (journalists or foreigners) were seated by the hand of power. Informal activism and formal leadership were gender-segregated fields of political action.

In one respect, attempts to distance a new Muslim culture from traditional Muslim culture, and thus elevate it in social status, have made visible an alternate path for upward mobility. This has been facilitated by the activist and 'missionary' roles (Göle, 1996, p.112) that became available to women as the political Islamist movement expanded its activities. Women's activism and training also was supported financially by Islamic businesses and foundations. However, the path to actual economic and social advancement is closed to most men and women. And even women who have taken advantage of the educational, training and activist opportunities offered by the Islamist movement live tradition-bound lives that are in many ways similar to those of their mothers. Change is severely limited by lack of money and education, but also by conflicting gendered desires that are projected onto the political screen as unequal hierarchies of power.

The concept of identity politics, as distinct from political Islam, is insufficient to explain the nuanced contradictions and myriad interpolations of political action and daily practice. Socioeconomic class continues to be important as an organising principle, although not as a 'consciously felt subaltern collective identity' (Kearney, 1996, p.174). Although the Virtue Party did not use the discourse of class, it was clearly organising its political agenda around class issues. Equally clearly, these were issues to which the urban poor responded. Political mobilisation of Islamists in disadvantaged neighbourhoods like Ümraniye reflected the entire spectrum of needs that arise in such an environment, including the different needs and aspirations of working-class men and women. These were projected onto the party and imported into the political process contradictions and instabilities.

However, political mobilisation also derives impetus and direction from the connection between political action and local culture, not only from a disconnected centre imagined as uncontaminated 'elite' life scenarios. The performance of political action engages symbolic forms that resonate with the social drama of everyday life where men and women act out their needs and aspirations.

Acknowledgements

This research was funded by the Institute of Turkish Studies, the University of Nebraska, and the Social Science Research Council. I would like to thank Ayşe Çağlar, Lourdes Gouveia, Deniz Kandiyoti, Augustus Richard Norton, Sutti Ortiz, Ariel Salzmann and Kathleen Stewart for their helpful comments on earlier drafts. I am solely responsible for the ideas contained within.

Notes on Chapter 9

1　This chapter is based on ethnographic research carried out in Istanbul between 1994 and 1998. The research period covered the tenures of both parties. Thus, reference may be made in the text to one or the other party.

2　Kandiyoti refers to this as the patriarchal bargain – protection and security in exchange for submissiveness and sexual propriety (1988). Women's labour for her family and her community also builds a portfolio of mutual obligation on which she can draw when necessary (White, 1994).

3　See, for instance, Göle's interviews with elite veiled Islamists (1996), who are represented as standing for the movement.

4　This was furthered by the fact that in the 1980s the military, with the support of the Özal government, encouraged the building of mosques and expansion of religious education. The military hoped Islam would be a socially unifying force that would heal the societal rifts that precipitated the 1980 coup and that would counter a perceived communist threat.

5　The Welfare Party was accused of advocacy for Islam and banned in January 1998. Erbakan, the leader of the party at the time, was banned from political activity. Later that year, Erdoğan was sentenced to a ten-month jail term and banned from politics for life. He was accused of having called for religious insurrection during a campaign speech in 1997 when he read a verse from a poem written in the 1920s by Ziya Gökalp, a nationalist hero: 'The mosques are our barracks, the minarets are our spears, their domes are our helmets and the faithful are our army'. Both he and Erbakan were still considered leaders of the party by their followers, despite their lack of formal position.

6　Pseudonyms are used throughout, except for party officials.

7　The economic and intellectual elites that finance and guide the movement need not fear cultural contamination since their elite status is unassailable. In any case, they too generally remain *entre nous*.

8　Although this can be attributed to state laws forbidding political parties from forming special interest branches.

9　With the author, 29 June 1998, Istanbul.

References

Abrahamian, Ervand (1993), *Khomeinism: Essays on the Islamic Republic*, University of California Press, Berkeley, CA

Acar, Feride (1995), 'Women and Islam in Turkey', in Şirin Tekeli (ed.), *Women in Modern Turkish Society*, Zed Books, London, pp.46–65

Ahmad, Feroz (1991), 'Politics and Islam in modern Turkey', *Middle East Studies*, vol. 27, January, pp.3–21

Arat, Yeşim (1997), 'Islamist women challenge the boundaries of citizenship,' *Human Development Report: Turkey*, The United Nations Development Programme, Ankara, p.67

Ayata, Ayşe (1997), 'The emergence of identity politics in Turkey', *New Perspectives on Turkey*, no 17, Fall, pp.59–73

Ayata, Sencer (1993), 'Continuity and change in Turkish culture: Some critical remarks on Modern Mahrem', *New Perspectives on Turkey*, vol. 9, Fall, pp.137–48

Bourdieu, Pierre (1984), *Distinction: A Social Critique of the Judgment of Taste*, Harvard University Press, Cambridge, MA

Cohen, Abner (1974), *Two-Dimensional Man: An Essay on the Anthropology of Power and Symbolism in Complex Society*, University of California Press, Berkeley, CA

Delaney, Carol (1994), 'Untangling the meanings of hair in Turkish society', *Anthropological Quarterly*, no 67, October 1994, pp.159–72

Duben, Alan, and Cem Behar (1991), *Istanbul Households: Marriage, Family and Fertility, 1880–1940*, Cambridge University Press, Cambridge

Esmer, Yılmaz, 'Parties and the electorate: A comparative analysis of voter profiles of Turkish political parties', in Çiğdem Balım et al. (eds) (1995), *Turkey: Political, Social and Economic Challenges in the 1990s*, Brill, Leiden, pp.74–89

Freitag, Sandria B. (1988), 'The roots of Muslim separatism in South Asia: Personal practice and public structures in Kanpur and Bombay', in Edmund Burke III and I. Lapidus (eds), *Islam, Politics, and Social Movements*, University of California Press, Berkeley, CA, pp.115–45

Göle, Nilüfer (1996), *The Forbidden Modern: Civilization and Veiling*, University of Michigan Press, Ann Arbor, MI

Gülalp, Haldun (1997), 'Globalizing postmodernism: Islamist and western social theory', *Economy and Society*, vol. 26, no 3, August, pp.419–33

Hefner, Robert W. (1990), *The Political Economy of Mountain Java*, University of California Press, Berkeley, CA

İlyasoğlu, Aynur (1994), *Örtülü Kimlik: Islamcı Kadın Kimliğinin Oluşum Öğeleri*, Metis Yayınlar, Istanbul

Kandiyoti, Deniz (1998), 'Bargaining with patriarchy', *Gender and Society*, vol. 2, no 3, pp.274–90

Kasaba, Reşat, 'Kemalist certainties and modern ambiguities', in S. Bozdoğan and R. Kasaba (eds) (1997), *Rethinking Modernity and National Identity in Turkey*, University of Washington Press, Seattle, WA, pp.15–36

Kearney, Michael (1996), *Reconceptualizing the Peasantry: Anthropology in Global Perspective*, Westview Press, Boulder, CO

Keyder, Çağlar (1993), 'The genesis of petty commodity production in agriculture: The case of Turkey', in Paul Stirling (ed.), *Culture and Economy: Changes in Turkish Villages*, The Eothen Press, Huntingdon, pp.171–86

Kirmanoğlu, Hasan (1997), *Refah Partisi'nin Yükselişinin Ekonomi Politiği*, Istanbul Bilgi Üniversitesi Araştırma Merkezi, Istanbul

Landau, Jacob M. (1976), 'The National Salvation Party in Turkey', *Asian and African Studies*, vol. 11, no 1, Summer, pp.1–57

Lapidus, Ira M. (1988), 'Islamic political movements: Patterns of historical change', in Edmund Burke III and I. Lapidus (eds), *Islam, Politics, and Social Movements*, University of California Press, Berkeley, CA, pp.3–16.

Lubeck, Paul, 'Islamic political movements in northern Nigeria: The problem of class analysis', in Edmund Burke III and I. Lapidus (eds) (1988), *Islam, Politics, and Social Movements*, University of California Press, Berkeley, CA, pp.244–60

Meeker, Michael (1991), 'The new Muslim intellectuals in the republic of Turkey', in Richard Tapper (ed.), *Islam in Modern Turkey*, I.B.Tauris, London

Stewart, Kathleen (1996), *A Space on the Side of the Road: Cultural Poetics in an 'Other' America*, Princeton University Press, Princeton, NJ

Toprak, Binnaz (1994), 'Women and fundamentalism: The case of Turkey', in Valentine M. Moghadam (ed.), *Identity Politics and Women*, Westview Press, Boulder, CO

White, Jenny B. (2002), *Vernacular Politics: Islamist Mobilization in Turkey*, University of Washington Press, Seattle, WA

— (1997) 'Pragmatists or Ideologues: Turkey's Welfare Party in Power', *Current History*, vol. 96, no 606, January 1997, pp.25–30

— (1996) 'Civic Culture and Islam in Urban Turkey', in Chris Hann and E. Dunn (eds), Civil Society: Challenging Western Models, Routledge, London, pp.143–54

— (1994) *Money Makes Us Relatives: Women's Labor in Urban Turkey*, University of Texas Press, Austin, TX

Yavuz, M. Hakan (1997), 'Political Islam and the Welfare (Refah) Party in Turkey', *Comparative Politics*, vol. 30, no 1, October, pp.63–82

III

SHIFTING IDENTITIES
AT HOME AND ABROAD

10

The Market for Identities: Secularism, Islamism, Commodities

Yael Navaro-Yashin

In the 1980s and 1990s, every issue has been politicised in the medium of consumable style, regardless of its ideological orientation: from antiracism, antisexism, and antihomophobia, to evangelism, antiabortion, and right-wing antigovernment stances.

George Yudice, 1995

Consuming 'culture'

'Culture' has too often been conceptualised as distinct from the domain of commodification[1]. Anthropologists have written numerous ethnographies of the disruption or transformation of 'culture' through the incoming forces of capitalism. Like the concepts of structure and change, products of binarism, the categories of 'culture' and 'economy' too have been pit against each other to overlook their inherency. When 'culture' has been too easily mapped onto 'what is local', 'economy', even after centuries of capitalism all around the globe, has been associated with 'what is Western', and therefore with what is 'external' to and what supposedly contradicts 'authentic local culture'.

From a perspective which would separate out 'culture' and 'economy' into different disciplines in the social sciences (anthropology and political economy respectively), different historical periods (tradition versus capitalist modernity), and different places (the Middle East, for example, versus the West), it would be possible to simply study Islamists in contemporary Turkey as representative of 'culture' and secular-westernists as the handmaidens of the capitalist 'economy'. This would be a perspective which imagines 'culture' to be manifested originally outside political economy, or which perceives the economy to be an ensuing appendage upon or an interruption of a formerly pristine domain of 'culture'.

This ethnography of consumerism and contemporary politics of culture in Turkey questions such binarist approaches to society and history, which end up reproducing, sometimes by default, positivist notions of 'culture'. This chapter presents a social history of the political economy of culture. Political economy, focused upon through the medium of commodification, is studied as a domain of construction. Constructionists have too often studied the imagination of 'nations', 'cultures', and 'identities' in idealist terms, as if these categories materialised in our consciousnesses and were then applied to produce historical events. Construction, however, is also about political economy, or, to put it differently, political economy is intrinsic to the construction of cultures. For, as easy as it seems to raise our consciousness about the constructedness of our political categories, it is difficult to change the political economic conditions of such construction.

This chapter studies the manufacture of the veil and of the portrait of Atatürk as central commodities and symbols of cultural identity in contemporary Turkey. I use the term manufacture to refer not only to abstract imagination, but also, literally, to production in real and tangible terms. Following the work of Stuart Hall (1990), what follows is an ethnography of the production of culture. I argue that secularist and Islamist identities in contemporary Turkey are products of manufacture. They are not original and essential, even though they are experienced as such. In other words, they are not reflections of some primordial 'Turkishness'. A number of students of nationalism in Turkey have pointed to the centrality of gender in the making of politics of identity.[2] Some have analysed the symbols of veiling and Atatürk as central markers of cultural identity.[3] And yet, no one has done an ethnographic history of the actual manufacture of the symbols of 'veil' and 'Atatürk' in the real and imagined terms of everyday life. Based on fieldwork conducted in the Islamist veiling sector, in marketplaces for religious commodities, in public centres for the manifestation of politics of identity, and among secularists, this chapter aims to be a prolegomenon to such an endeavour. If the 'veil' and 'Atatürk' have become central signifiers/symbols in the contemporary politics of identity, what sort of social history brought this about?

Politics of culture between secularists and Islamists in Turkey in the 1980s and 1990s developed in the context of a consumer market influenced by globalisation. So central was consumerism to the social life of this period that political conflicts were organised, expressed and mediated through this medium. Islamist movements have mostly represented themselves in reaction to commodity cultures which spread Western lifestyles and values. Equally, certain scholars of Islamism have studied the movement as an expression of a 'critique of modernity'. My observations of the mainstream of the Islamist movement in Turkey have been otherwise. Commodification proved to be a context and activity historically shared by Islamists and secularists alike, rather than being a domain that divided them. There certainly were variations within secularist and Islamist modes of consumerist practice. And yet, it does not hold ethnographically to associate commodification with westernisation, as if it were necessarily antithetical to local practices of Islam or to a movement that organises itself around the theme of the sacred.

Commodification had a central role in the shaping of this particular politics of culture. I argue that the realm of Islamist and secularist cultures was already and from the beginning commoditised. It is not that commodification disturbed formerly genuine identities. Rather, Islamists and secularists consumed and felt their identities to be genuine, making the very opposition 'genuine/false' obsolete. Commodification had much to do with the reification of certain symbols, like 'the veil' and 'Atatürk', as emblems of 'identity'. Pitting consumable signifiers against one another, commodification had a role in transforming the politics of culture into a war over symbols.

In the 1980s, cultural identities were packaged up to be assumed in commodity form. Battles over political difference were waged through the medium of consumption. As Islamists came to forge identities in distinction from secularists, they thought about their habits of use and modified or radically changed the sorts of things that they bought and sold. They wore different clothes, they ate only certain kinds of food, they frequented particular shops, they started special businesses of their own. The rise of the Islamist movement in popularity and power is indissoluble from the development of specialised businesses for 'Islamic goods' and the formation of market networks for believers. Islamists came to define themselves as having an 'identity' (*kimlik*) in assuming new things for consumption that they represented as 'of the lost Islamic past'. The creativity that went into the making of political activism was co-handed with market innovation.

When Turgut Özal came to power in the mid 1980s, he did so in simultaneously addressing the secular bourgeoisie in the metropolises and the believing businessmen of smaller cities in Anatolia. Özal set Turkey's course for privatisation, for a massive intrusion by multinational companies, a free market and foreign goods. Things that were never found in shops in Turkey until then became quickly commonplace. Turkey's economy underwent what was later called 'the boom time'. As television was privatised, the advertising industry took a new shape, having found an invaluable resource. New businesses started in turn, introducing further new products to the consumer market.

Özal's economics followed the lead of three years of martial law under a military government, this being the first elected government after the coup of 1980, and Özal had ambiguous relations with the generals, who disapproved of his connections with Sufi orders and religious communities, and were skeptical of his bold moves towards economic and political liberalisation. Yet Özal managed his relations with the army in order that the army kept the law and order for the economic reforms to take hold.

Public life was transformed in the Özal period with the development of young urban professionals. In the aftermath of the coup, when most of the student leaders of the left were still in prison, a new culture of learning developed in universities, where students predominantly opted to study business administration, economics or marketing. 'Success' was re-advertised as of greatest value, and the making of lots of money was highly prized. Opening one's own business, getting married, owning a house, a car and home appliances, travelling on holidays and being financially comfortable were marked out as the mode of contemporary being and aspiration. Television ads paraded families who had 'made it'. Happiness was measured on a scale of buying and easily consuming. Those young people who 'successfully' completed their studies in business or related subjects went ahead to work in the newly privatised media companies, the increasing number of advertising agencies, banks and businesses. Restaurants, cinemas, clothing chains, bars and cafes in the city multiplied. Istanbul was quickly remade in this period to serve an expanding lifestyle.

Yet changes did not take place in the lives only of the secular urbanites. The state's economy under Özal was also (and especially) geared to the advantage of the businesses of the religious in smaller cities of Anatolia. Özal himself came of a conservative religious family from Malatya. His family had strong ties with a branch of the Nakshibendi Sufi order and he had formerly been a member of the National Salvation Party, which was later to be transformed into the Welfare Party. Özal's aim was to channel resources to this category of Turkish capital as well, to revive the market by bringing Muslim capitalists, businessmen and small traders to compete with the secular bourgeoisie, with their more enduring ties with Western-centred capitalism. While the advertising and culture industries of the secular mainstream grew in that period, an extensive market also developed under the management of religious businessmen, some of whom were Islamists. The culture and values of the Özal period also influenced those who identified with Islamists.

Turkish businesses were now engaged in a massive export drive, even though, due to the free-market policies of the new government, the import of foreign goods always exceeded exports. And businesses were not only involved in trading with foreign countries, but also in investing as multinationals abroad. Muslim capitalists, as specially encouraged by the Özal government, were forming their own conglomerates as well. The Kuralkan group, for example, and İhlas Ltd, produced all sorts of items, from cars to biscuits. In time, Muslim capital came to compete in almost all sectors of the economy, producing paint, ceramics, timber, soap, detergents and petroleum, along with almost everything else that was marketable. When advertising certain products, such as food and clothing, these new or expanded companies introduced themselves as moral from an Islamic point of view. That was what differentiated them from the companies of secularists. Some 'Muslim companies' presented themselves in the market by claiming higher values: following the dietary prescriptions of Islam, not investing in interest, not serving food to employees during the month of fasting, reserving money for charity (zekat),[4] producing good quality products, and making 'just' profits. The Ülker biscuit, for example, was claimed to contain no lard, leaving the older Eti brand in the cold. Many of these 'Muslim companies' in time turned into self-managed multinationals.

What was significant about the consumer culture of this period was its close links with the politics of identity. As conservative small-town capital-holders grew to become small urban shopkeepers or founders of bigger metropolitan companies, they created a market for their lifestyle and ideology. They were able to develop their capital by following the logic of contemporary capitalism. Yet they also geared their energy to the making of an alternative market for goods for those who felt alienated from the religiously forbidden (haram) or westernised goods that had dominated arenas of consumption. As they leaned on the financial strength brought by investing in all areas, these companies also made sure that all the needs of 'a Muslim', as they defined him or her, were specially met.

The veil as commodity

A most important good that was brought to the marketplace by Muslim business-people in Turkey was the veil.[5] More than other consumer items produced in Muslim companies, there was an overload of symbolic interpretation around the veil and its many versions. In the 1980s, Turkey's textile industry had grown to be highly competitive in the world market, selling Europeans their preferred styles at good prices. But clothing businesses also developed in the Muslim sector of the economy. The rise of the Islamist movement in the 1980s and 1990s in Turkey was integral to the creation of a market for headscarves, overcoats and veils for women. Several companies sprung up, then, to produce and sell all sorts of clothing items for women who 'covered'.[6] There were certain clothing shops that were cheap, and geared to the basic needs of women of low or average incomes. Such shops would be placed in the side- or backstreets of neighbourhoods inhabited by Islamists, rather than on the main streets. The colours of overcoats would generally be plain, dark blue, dark green, black or brown, in either cotton or polyester.

However, most shopkeepers interviewed said that women who wore Muslim dress did not prefer cheap veils and overcoats, that they especially bought good-quality things and paid the price, since this was the most important apparel that they thought themselves to be investing in. Young Islamist women, especially those who attended university or had jobs outside the home, liked not to dress from such side-street shops, but from those with more stylish models of head-scarves and coats. In 1994, when I was doing my research, specific colours were in fashion among covered university students: light pink and lavender, all the shades of purple, pastel blue and green, shady yellow and grey. Students carefully matched the colour of their *türbans* (as a version of headscarf came to be called in the 1980s) to that of their overcoats, in the fashion that they took onto the streets at that time.

Islamist women students had also developed a liking for a special kind of cloth for overcoats, of stoned silk. These particular *pardösüs* ('overcoat', from the French *pardessus*) as they were called, were not cheap. In 1994, when I did a survey of veil shops in the Fatih and Unkapanı districts of Istanbul, overcoats in stoned silk were 3.5 million Turkish lira (about US$50 at the time), expensive for the average budget in Turkey. Those made of pure silk were 4.5 million. One could also find cheaper coats for 2 million, made of cotton, and others that were partly made of wool for 3–4 million. Those stoned silk *pardösüs* fashionable among Islamist women students were not made of locally produced cloth. Stoned silk was promoted in Islamist shops as a 'foreign product' (*yabancı mal*), with the intent of inferring better quality. The veils and overcoats that were in fashion among Islamist women students, defended as representative of 'local culture', 'the local past' and 'local values' were made of English cloth.

Veil shops introduced their products as heirs of 'the past'. A woman who worked in a headscarf company in 1994 said that they had started trading in head-scarves 20 years ago. 'The headscarf's past lies in Ottoman times,' said she, arguing that there had been a break in the use of the item in the republican period, until it was picked up again in the 1980s. She read an Islamist narrative of Turkish history into the veiling apparel in her shop window. This particular headscarf

shop was one among 30 in a bazaar of covered women's clothing (*tesettür giyim*) in Unkapanı, Istanbul. Some of these headscarf and overcoat companies had brand names that evoked Islam: Tevhid, for example, referring to unity under one God, Ihvan, signifying Muslim brotherhood, or Hak, using one of the names for God.

A shop attendant here recounted the history of the market for veils in Istanbul. He noted that he and his boss had started their own particular business 25 years ago, when such brands as Mesture or Tekbir in veiling were not yet around. They used to make veil models to special order at that time. They had only so many customers, and produced overcoats on request. Most of the time, they prepared other sorts of clothing. Later, when they saw that there was a developing market for clothing for believing women, they went straight into that business. By that time the conglomerates Mesture and Tekbir had started to mass-produce headscarves and overcoats, and people were buying ready-made goods on the market. In time, covered women even began to be discriminating about the brand (*marka*) they chose, comparing quality and style with one another:

> In the end, we had to modify our styles to match those that were being invented by the big veiling companies. We had to do that in order to remain in the market. We try to reproduce those popularised designs with less cloth so that our prices could still be competitive beside the monopolies' price cuts. Plus, clothing is not like food. You have to change things in order to keep getting customers, in order for them not to get bored. For example, silk was in fashion last year. Everyone wore that until they had it up to here with silk. Then, one of the big companies put the stoned silk models on the market. That is what is in fashion this year. We now have to produce that, too.

This merchant's story is illustrative of the commodified quality of covered women's clothes.

Another trader of Islamist clothing in the Unkapanı marketplace for veils had his own understanding of proper covering. 'There can be no such thing as "fashion" [*moda*] in Islamic covering,' he said:

> If you are covering, you will not pay attention to showing off or ostentation. Aren't there those who do? There are, of course. The Tekbir company, for example, has created a fashion for veiling. They saw that there was demand and they started to do the trade. Of course, you will dress beautifully. The others [secularists] are dressing pretty. Aren't you going to dress pretty? In Islam, there is the commandment to cover, but to cover in a pretty way. The condition in covering is to conceal the contours of the body. You have to wear wide and loose-fitting clothes, in other words, and never tightly-trimmed ones in public. Sometimes I do get women who ask for tight models in overcoats. But those who cover with knowledge and good conscience would not do that.

Producers and sellers of 'Muslim women's clothes' had agency, and a role in the shaping of what proper covering was about. Trading and the economy were not compartments apart from the making of contemporary Islamist identities.

The market for headscarves, overcoats and veils had extensions all over Turkey, as in parts of Western Europe. The shops in Unkapanı sent most of their products to cities and towns, especially in Eastern Anatolia. There was less

demand for headscarves and overcoats of this sort, shopkeepers noted, in the
Aegean region of Turkey. On the other hand, a great demand for veils came from
Germany. Many Turkish workers and immigrants there had taken up the head-
scarf, looking for the specific brands that they liked from Turkey.[7]

One of the contexts for the rising Islamist movement in Turkey of the 1980s
and 1990s was the free market in commodities. As a culture of excessive consumption developed among the mainstream secular middle class, especially in
the metropolises, so did Islamists of a small-town Anatolian background define
their difference by organising other strategies of use. Companies and shops of
people of differing cultural and social backgrounds came to compete with one
another in the same capitalist market. And distinction, quality and morality in
goods was now defined around the rubrics of the politics of identity. Secularists
were ultimately 'different' from Islamists because they consumed different
things. The habitus of consumption became a central marker of internal cultural
difference in Turkey.

Secularist commodities

Until the market for Muslim identities developed, secular mainstream textile
companies did not accentuate the cultural symbolism of what they exhibited in
their shop windows. There were buttoned shirts, sweaters, short skirts, stylish long
skirts with vents up to above the knees, low-cut and stretched blouses introduced
as under the name *badi* (the Turkish transliteration of 'body'), all sorts and colours
of jeans, long dresses and short dresses. In the 1980s, Turkey's mainstream textile
companies came to compete with Italian and French brands in producing
'European' clothing. A number of big clothing companies, such as Mudo and
Yargıcı, began to hire their own designers. Some acquired world renown, like Zeki
Triko, which advertised its women's bathing suits and bikinis by paying the world's
top models (like Cindy Crawford) to pose for its internationally distributed
brochures. As certain European multinationals began to use cheap Turkish labour
to produce their goods, these Turkish-owned textile companies were beginning to
show Europeans what they liked to wear.

But initially, these expanding Turkish textile companies introduced their
goods as the norm for 'what is worn in the modern world'. Until the Islamist market
for clothes developed, Turkey's secular mainstream companies did not over-
interpret the culture that they in fact produced. The clothes exhibited in the chic
boutiques of posh neighbourhoods in Istanbul, as well as the variations and copies
sold in smaller and more modest shops in other parts of town, were introduced as
'standard' clothing, or as 'contemporary' wear, contrary to the advent of Islamist
textiles. The associations of 'culturalism' were objectified onto the clothing
practices of Islamists, the ways of secularists being constructed as neutral or
devoid of symbolism and history.[8]

In the mid-1990s, when I was doing my research, the now established secular
companies had started to define themselves as producers of a 'secular lifestyle'
(*laik yaşam tarzı*) and a 'civilised identity' (*çağdaş kimlik*).[9] They presented themselves

as heirs of Atatürk's Hat Reform, instituted in 1925 against the wearing of the
turban and fez by men in Turkey. These companies were carrying Atatürk's values
into the present. If secularist women in Atatürk's time wore skirt-and-suit sets
(*tayyör*),[10] their granddaughters would wear the clothes produced by these companies: jeans, dresses, blouses and skirts. In symbolically attacking the 'Muslim
companies', these 'secular companies' began to present their items as the apparel
of 'modernity'. To be modern (in Turkish secularist language, *çağdaş*), one had to
dress in the ways prescribed by the mainstream textile industry. Some companies
even attempted to colonise the meaning of the headscarf: the modern way to wear
a scarf was around the neck, not over the head. Photos of women with stylish
scarves around their shoulders were sent to press. That was 'the modern look'. 'The
modern woman' was to be distinguished from 'the backward Islamist woman' in
the discourse of the secular mainstream textile companies, according to what she
consumed and especially what she wore.

Women's clothes were most highly symbolic in a market war over identities.[11]
Yet there were other items in the market for 'modern' or 'Atatürkist' identities
that were crafted by secular mainstream businesses and shops in reaction
to Islamist consumer goods. At the height of conflict with Islamists, Atatürk
paraphernalia was put on the market. In 1994, after the Welfare Party's election
victory in municipalities, one could find all sorts of things on the market with
Atatürk's image on them. There were pins of Atatürk to be attached to one's coat,
sweater, or blouse as brooches. Atatürkist women and men began to wear these *en
masse* to be even more visibly distinguishable from Islamists. There were silver-
coloured pins with Atatürk's portrait, as well as golden-coated ones. One could
now find these in most little shops in the market. Traders in Istanbul's informal
market, with their makeshift little counters on pavements, now sold Atatürk
pins along with pins of the grey wolf, symbol of pan-Turkism. There were now
commodities to label every identity. As the well-advertised celebrations of Republic
Day 1994 drew to a close, other sorts of Atatürk paraphernalia also appeared in
shops. There were posters, framed portraits, postcards and pictures of him to be
found in every style, shape and colour. One image of Atatürk was especially popular,
in which he was presented in white shirt and black suit and tie, pointing up to the
sky, and therefore to 'progress', with one finger. On important secularist public
commemoration dates, such as Republic Day (29 October) and the anniversary of
Atatürk's death (10 November), mainstream secular newspapers, such as *Sabah*,
Hürriyet, and *Milliyet* distributed free posters of Atatürk to their readers. Framed
copies of Atatürk's 'Sermon to Youth' ('Gençliğe Hitabe') were on sale, as were
those of the 'Tenth Year of the Republic March' ('Onuncu Yıl Marşı').

In time, wearing such Atatürk paraphernalia became quite widespread in
society. State employees, for example, angered by the rise of Islamism in public
institutions, attached such things to their uniforms to show their reaction to
the Welfare Party. School teachers, working women, business women and men
displayed 'the profile of Atatürk' on themselves, semiotically defending their lifestyle against that professed and practiced by veiling Islamist women. Secularists
began excessively to decorate their offices, their homes and themselves with
images (in object form) of Atatürk. A small bust with one of his sayings inscribed

underneath, along with one of his characteristic portraits in the background, a flag of Turkey to one side, and a pin on one's suit became an ordinary way to fill one's space with material culture.

Atatürk paraphernalia has a history that predates the politics of secularist and Islamist identities in the way it took shape in the 1980s and 1990s. In the 1930s, when Atatürk was head of state, foreign sculptors had been hired to make and erect big statues of him in the newly constructed boulevards of Ankara, as well as in Taksim Square in Istanbul. In time, Turkish artisans also took up the pursuit, sculpting statues of marble or cement for all the schools and public offices of the country. Today, the most frequently encountered statue all over Turkey is still that of Atatürk.

Mehmet İnci was among the first Turks to produce statues of Atatürk in the period between 1936 and 1940. His son, Necati, who still practices his father's profession in a studio in the Maltepe district of Istanbul, originally built in 1942, recounts that 'That standard look that you are accustomed to see in Atatürk statues was first created in my father's studio as a mould.' Indeed the İnci statue studio produced the portraits of Atatürk in army uniform, as found in front of military institutions; as the first teacher of the Latin alphabet to Turkish youth, as encountered in front of many schools; on top of a rearing horse, as in public squares; dressed in bowler hat, tail-coat and cloak, near cultural institutions; and taking his first foot step in Samsun to start the War of Liberation, as seen on hill-tops all over Turkey and northern Cyprus. There were hundreds of Atatürk statue studios in Turkey, but this one was one of the first. According to Necati İnci, until the Welfare Party took hold of Istanbul's municipalities the main demand for Atatürk statues came from municipal leaders: 'Welfarists are not putting up statues of Atatürk in every public site that they reconstruct, as the old municipalities used to'. At the time of my interview with him, he was still sending statues to schools and offices of the state, but he noted that there had been increased interest from the private sector. More and more Atatürkist organisations and secular-minded owners of companies and shops were placing orders. The moulds in the studio had lived through almost all of Turkey's republican history. Statues had been produced in an artisanal way, funded mostly by institutions of the state. Yet what was happening in 1994 was different. There was now great demand for Atatürk statues from private businesses eager to reproduce Turkey's secularist project into the future. The shop was not fit for the mass-production required by the new politics of identity. The market for Atatürk figures was slowly being encompassed by commodification.

There is now a fully fledged commodity market for both Islamist and secularist identities in Turkey. Any study that isolates the politics of culture from the consumerist context in which it was produced in the 1980s and 1990s would be misguided.[12] As new goods were put on the market by companies trying to lure their customers towards innovation, new forms of 'being' or 'identity' were shaped as well. Businesses began to craft and sell 'Turkish authenticity', whether secularist or Islamist. Consumers assumed that there was 'authenticity' in what they wore and ate, although market-produced.[13]

Istanbul's new marketplaces

In the 1980s, a new kind of market was introduced to Istanbul (see Chapter 3). Modelled on the multistorey shopping malls of the US in their Western European variants, major marketing centres were constructed in the heart of the city. Located in the Bakırköy district of Istanbul, Galleria was the first such structure to be erected. The shopping mall targeted the newly rich inhabitants of the luxury apartment complexes in the Ataköy neighbourhood. Other customers would be able to reach Galleria by car, conveniently using the vast underground car parks.

When it first opened its sliding doors to customers, thousands of people flocked to see what it was about. One floor, as window-shoppers were to observe, had been reserved for chic boutiques with mostly Western-sounding brand names, displaying fashionable European-style clothes. There was a shop for socks and stockings of all sorts, and one for expensive women's underwear. High-heeled shoes in all their fantastic variations were arranged in the window of another, alongside fashionable dresses, trousers and accessories.

The mall's newest visitors were shocked to see the price-tags attached to items. Many of them did not have the means to acquire the goods displayed. Indeed, at first, many just went to look, curious to see what was presented as 'the modern way to shop'. Families of four, five or more from shanty neighbourhoods bordering Bakırköy walked to Galleria, some women in the headscarves they had taken up after migrating to the city, to promenade about in the new department stores. One floor of Galleria was most crowded of all. American-style fast food from Mexico, China and Italy was sampled by excited little children and grown-ups who wanted to experience 'modernity'. Young waiters and waitresses, hired for their 'European' looks, tall and slim with blue-green eyes and light-coloured hair, served hamburgers and fries in their brightly coloured flashy uniforms.

In time, Istanbul's middle-to-upper class integrated Galleria into its shopping habits. More structures of this kind were put up across the city. Between the upper-class neighbourhoods of Levent, Akatlar, Etiler and Ulus was erected an imposing Akmerkez, with more than 40 glossy stores mirroring back the rays of the sun, standing out in Istanbul's otherwise lower-rise silhouette. A similar mall of this kind was built, finally, on the Anatolian side of the Bosphorus, under the name Capitol, to attract the well-to-do of the districts of Kadıköy and Erenköy.

The vast shopping arcades were introduced as emblems of a modern and civilised life. Spending time in such spaces, waiting to get to the top on escalators, walking through the glittery shop windows, and being served in the in-store cafes of clothes shops, people would come to sense what it felt like 'to be in the West' or 'to live like a Westerner'. 'Europe has come to Istanbul', many shop-goers said appreciatively. The malls were advertised with temporal symbolisms. They were promoted as belonging to 'the new times', 'contemporary' or 'up-to-date'. These were the spaces that would lead Turkey into a future of 'civilisation and prosperity', in this construction.

In 1994, the mainstream secular newspaper *Hürriyet* published a series of articles describing Istanbul's shopping malls. Akmerkez was promoted as 'an up-with-the-times (*çağdaş*) shopping centre, beyond the year 2000'. 'Since it was opened ten months ago, the centre has drawn people to itself, has become part of life,' the article noted, concluding that 'people are experiencing civilisation in these spaces'.[14] The heralds of the new markets spoke through a discourse of progress that they assumed was shared by their target customers. These shops, 'like Europe', looked to the future. And there was nothing, from this point of view, that could be better than moving Turkey with the times.

Islamist publications represented the new shopping malls in a different way. The Welfare Party's press organ, *Milli Gazete*, captioned a photograph of Capitol:

> Turkey has two faces: the rich and the poor... The rich shop in giant shopping centres and spend loads of money. They easily waste the money that they easily earn... These people who are obsessed with trademarks pay twice, thrice or five times as much money for things of the same kind and quality that they could buy elsewhere for less... In Turkey, which is claimed to have jumped a century ahead, the rich get richer and the poor are further crushed, more impoverished.[15]

The new shopping centres were compared with the informal market of the Topkapı district of Istanbul. By contrast, in Topkapı, the writer noted, 'you won't find those who have fetishised trademarks. Those who shop here give priority to covering and cleanliness. This is what befits civilised (*medeni*) people.'[16] Another Islamist publication, the *Aksiyon* news weekly of the *Zaman* newspaper likened Capitol to a 'temple of consumption'. The author of this piece began his critique of the new consumerism with a social history of the market in the Ottoman empire. He was interested in nostalgic comparison. When the doors of the Grand Bazaar were opened in the morning in past times, a prayer would be read against trickery, he recounted, citing the *Encyclopedia of Old Monuments* as reference:[17]

> For many centuries, the ethical values of our bazaars comprised disinterest in profit, of contentedness, and of sufficing with little. The trader who had got his first customer for the day (*siftah*) would send the next to his neighbour who hadn't. The richness of our spiritual and moral life used to extend from our homes and temples to our bazaars. Until the second half of the nineteenth century, our bazaars existed in times when the customer was not harassed by sellers and when the word for stealing was not in dictionaries.
>
> Customers were also different in that period. It was considered detestable to buy something that exceeded one's need. People knew their accounts in that period and there was no such thing as credit cards. In those times when quality products could be found cheap, bargaining was first in the list of deplored manners. In those times, when there weren't fast-food stalls, bowling rings or cafes, local tastes and traditional values were in the forefront in the markets.
>
> Not too much time, only a century, has passed since then. People learned about exports and imports and got caught in the magic of the free market. Globalisation and transformation started to shape peoples' lives. And giant shopping centres took the place of covered bazaars.[18]

In such Islamist ethnographies of Istanbul's new markets, narratives of progress in the secular mainstream press were countered with nostalgia. Islamists identified themselves with 'an earlier era', which they idealised as morally superior. Those of them who critiqued the 'rise of consumerism' as they called it, professed to keep a distance from the values of the 'new times', idealised by the beneficiaries of the economic boom. And Islamists differentiated themselves, in their public discourses, from those they constructed as 'westernised secularists', not only in temporal affiliation but also in social status. As *Milli Gazete*'s juxtaposition of 'the rich and the poor' illustrates, certain Islamists associated the shopping centres with the economic power of the wealthy.

Shopping malls were received in Turkey through the prism of a politics of culture polarised between secularists and Islamists. Those secularists who might otherwise have criticised the advent of a new style of consumerism found themselves defending the malls against an Islamist culturalist critique. Likewise, well-off Islamists who wanted their life habits to include the new malls saw that they were taking positions against them in their public discourse. At the level of public pronouncement and statement, secularists and Islamists appeared to be opposed on the issue. In time, those malls which did not at first use secularist symbolisms in their packaging and advertisements started to use pictures of Atatürk in their hallways and on products.

In December 1995, right before national elections were to take place, the entrance corridor of Akmerkez looked different. Behind a glossy glass curtain were lined up black-and-white portraits of Atatürk, enlarged to four times life size. The Welfare Party was expected to win the elections, and almost everyone who followed polls was aware of this. The managers of the mall advertised where they stood in the politics of identity: on the side of secularism. While Atatürk in his own time had built the state-owned clothing industry, supported by the public Sïmerbank, in 1995 the pioneers of Turkey's integration into the free market were reinscribing the definition of 'Atatürk' to mean conspicuous consumption. Yet the pictures of Atatürk did not appear peculiar to those seeing them on visits to the mall. Here, they thought, they were living a modern lifestyle, the course Atatürk had set. Fearing an Islamist disciplining of the everyday, many secularists domesticated at least the semiotics of 'Akmerkez' and its like, making them part of their 'identity', even if they could not afford to shop there. The mall came to represent the epitome of secularist, in opposition to Islamist ways of carrying on with everyday practices of life.

Yet, over-interpreted as they were, shopping malls have not yet swallowed the whole market domain of Istanbul up, as they seem to have in parts of the US. Different kinds of shopping are still available in Istanbul's many neighbourhoods. I could, at this point, direct my ethnography straight out of the mall and into the lower-key sector of small trading in Islamic goods. As the writer of *Milli Gazete* had done, I could move to contrast Akmerkez with the simplicity and modesty of shops of religious commodities in the district of Eyüp, for example, where religious shopkeepers show prayer mats, turbans, robes, non-alcoholic perfumes, rose water and the like on make-shift counters on the pavement. Certain cultural critics of Istanbul have taken up such rhetorical comparisons, interpreting Istanbul to be a 'dual city, *alaturka*', with posh suburbs on the one hand, and shanty neighbourhoods on the other. This portrayal of Istanbul's residential panorama is too simplistic. It glosses over the realities of life for those who live in cheap apartment housing, in old urban neighbourhoods, and in well-settled shanties. A dualistic narrative of Istanbul's history of class relations is worrisome also because it produces a tendency to interpret every political conflict flatly onto the distinction between the very wealthy and the very poor. Asu Aksoy and Kevin Robins map the secularist/Islamist distinction too easily onto such a dualistic narrative of class, in which the former are written to represent the economically privileged to the disadvantage of the latter.[19] Class-based polarisation is in Istanbul's contemporary history. Yet this cannot be breathed right into the secularist/Islamist conflict. The narrative of class difference that is there in Aksoy and Robins's work is quite common in the political discourse of Islamists, many of whom represent themselves as the economically disadvantaged. The Welfare Party got most of its votes from Istanbul's shanty residents in municipality elections and, like other populisms, has been presenting itself as 'the voice of the poor'. But, as my account in this chapter has begun to illustrate, the Islamist movement is implicated in a politics of capital, wealth and consumerism as well. The Welfare Party derived its strength through financial support from Muslim capitalists. So rather than going to Eyüp to visit the little shops on the sidestreet by the mosque, as a dualistic narrative of shops and identities would do, I will move my narrative of Istanbul's markets to the shop windows of Islamism, the wave of consumerism to which the Eyüp shops are now connected.

The Islamist department store

Right beside the Fatih branch of Benetton is the shop of Turkey's biggest Muslim apparel company: Tekbir, Inc.. Centrally and well located on the main street of Fatih (a neighbourhood preferred by religious families) and right across from the Fatih mosque (one of Istanbul's biggest), Tekbir has its shop window. *Tekbir* is the Islamic word for a call to cry 'God is great' (*Allahüekber*). The *tekbir* precedes the call to prayer (the *ezan*) and the performance of the *namaz*. In their demonstrations in the 1990s against secularist institutional measures aimed at religious life and politics, Turkish Islamists took up the habit of calling for *tekbir* after every public pronouncement. Like other shops for covered women's clothing, and like Islamist publishing houses, this company took up a religious word as its brand. One did not have to think too hard to make the connection. As *tekbir* asks all believers to pronounce the greatness of God, so would the dresses and apparel sold in the shops of the company named after it.

A visit to the shop revealed two display windows, open to the gaze of pedestrians, above which was the emblem of the company: Tekbir, Inc. (Tekbir, A.Ş.). In the foreground of the windows was a television and video that constantly played a tape of models wearing the company's tailored scarves and overcoats. Beside the television stood several dummies, displaying the clothes. The mannequins had been positioned with their backs to the shop's windows, their heads looking down, in an attitude of Islamic modesty. Each modelled a Tekbir veil. The colours of the overcoats varied in their rich maroons and light greens. On the backs of the models' heads were shown Tekbir's colourful headscarves, and here, on Fatih's main street, women were viewing the display of this most popular veil company.

In November 1994, I interviewed one of Tekbir's owners, in the Fatih branch. Mustafa Karaduman, head of the group, was born in 1957 in a village in Malatya. He was a fellow townsman of the late president Özal. As he recounted his life story, he moved to Istanbul in 1969 after finishing elementary school, with only 100 lira that his father had borrowed from a neighbour. He entered the textile industry as middle ironer, but quickly advanced to become final ironer, machinist and tailor. After some years, he started a sewing studio with his brothers, in which they sometimes styled veils to order. Tekbir was now owned by these eight brothers. The company had donated 200 million lira in alms (*zekat*) that year, had paid 15 billion lira of tax to the state, but did not work with any banks, refraining from receiving interest, as commanded by Islam.

Karaduman sat behind the cashier counter of the Fatih shop as we were talking. His shop attendants, all covered women, came and went, asking him questions, bringing things to show him. They addressed him in the familiarised 'Brother Mustafa'(*Mustafa abi*), and might have been his relatives. Customers interrupted our conversation as they came to pay. Karaduman was the owner of a multinational company, yet, unlike the secularist owners of conglomerates of the same size and capital, he sat as cashier in one of his shops. Tekbir's employees knew their boss personally.

Karaduman narrated his world and vision:

> We started our business before the community of believers had expanded. In the years when we began, there wasn't a market sector for covered women's clothes. We created the sector. It hadn't an infrastructure or market at the time. 'Since we are Muslim, let us produce what befits our beliefs,' we said. We started the business in 1978. Within three years we were organising fashion shows (*defile*). In the Turkish market, we were the first to introduce the ready-to-wear black veil (*çarşaf*).[20] In the beginning, demand was not obvious; shops were not used to this business. In the 1970s there were traditional firms who made dresses for those who covered. But these were very limited.
>
> There were women who decided to cover after seeing the varieties in our exhibition. We worked on this concept in our advertisements: we used the images of covered women as doctors, students and business executives. Women thought that they would be forced to enter a sack if they practiced Islam. We broke this conception. All organs of the media had to admit that covering is beautiful. What preachers could not accomplish through their sermons, we were able to communicate through our shops and fashion shows.
>
> We do not only aspire to influence fashion in Turkey. We would like to make a mark on world fashion. We believe that Turkish people can give a direction to the world, too. If all people in the world are creative, so are we. We are going to spread all over Europe. We are going to change the flow of the world. How did the mini-skirt spread worldwide? Likewise, we will spread covering to all of the world.

Karaduman was very ambitious. His rivals were not other veil companies, which his company had largely out-competed, but the clothing companies of secular Turkish businessmen. Like them, he would speak to the fashion world of 'the West'. Tekbir's models would be liked so much that they would be preferred to the models, styles and fashions of Yves Saint-Laurent, he said. And he professed to have achieved this. His company had shops in nine cities in Germany and one each in the Netherlands, Belgium, Denmark, France, Australia, the US, Lebanon and Saudi Arabia. Karaduman channelled his neo-Ottomanist aspirations through the medium of multinational capitalism:

> In Europe, they think *tekbir* is the word for 'covering'. When you go to buy gas in Turkey, you do not ask for gas, but for Aygaz, don't you?[21] And likewise, when you ask your grocer for butter, you say that you want Sana.[22] Like this, in Europe they say that they want Tekbir when they are looking for covered women's clothes.

One could be sceptical of Karaduman, with the bragging tone in his account. Yet, it should be clear from these excerpts how much Karaduman's Islamist aspirations are accompanied by a version of capitalism with westernised aspirations.

Karaduman professed to be doing business in accordance with the prescriptions of Islam, differentiating himself from secular businessmen. He said, for example, that his company did not derive any interest from its money, interest, the profit from lending money, being forbidden in Islam. He claimed to be practicing commerce under a higher order of ethics, and maintained that his company had separated itself from the rules of the world market. He claimed, also, to be paying more than the minimum wage to workers on the shop floor. Above all, his self-declared mission was bring to the market the apparel of a higher life ethic.

As the manager of the most popular veiling company in Turkey, Karaduman had a specific definition of the proper dress and manners of 'the Muslim woman':

> In Egypt and Algeria, the veiling sector remains amateur. When Arabs come to visit Turkey, you see that all the shape of their bodies is out in the middle. The purpose of covering is to keep the garment long enough to reach your ankles and your wrists. The shape of the back or of the breasts should not be obvious. The headscarf will cover all the hair and the neck. The Egyptians order cloth and overcoat models from France. The Frenchman does not know what covering is. He sends the narrowest model of overcoat. Now the Egyptians are demanding products from us.
>
> When you develop a model for veils, you will think about the culture and climate of the country you are designing it for. Plus, everyone has to abide by the fluctuations in fashion. As European clothing models are not for the covered, we cannot benefit that much from them. But we do follow yearly fashions in colour. You can do anything you want with colour as long as you do not compromise on the precepts of Islam with regards to proper covering. The framework put forward in the Quran is this: the contours of the body will not be visible.

Tekbir's owner closely followed the waves of fashion, as produced and reproduced by Turkey's secular clothing companies, sought after in Europe. He aspired to no less a worldwide prestige or personal capital than those companies, and he shared their modern capitalist practice and outlook. Yet he wanted to achieve these aims by the alternative route of 'Islam', in the way that he and his partners defined it. He understood, he said, that women refrained from the veil because it was not beautiful. Women preferred to wear 'open' (açık) clothes because they felt that that was how to look pretty.[23] Tekbir set out to show, however, that veiling could be more beautiful than open clothes. Women could look good and fashionable, and, most importantly, modern and upper class, while also observing Islam.

Karaduman claimed to have had a role in popularising covering among Turkish women. He was outspoken in his political support of covered students who were being ousted from university classrooms and were organising demonstrations in protest. He was active in the making of the politics of culture between secularists and Islamists. Covered women students had become the centre of focus in this politics:

> We are with the covered girl students with all our hearts. If they want to cover as their belief demands, they should be able to. These girls are not covered by force; they are doing it because they want to. You cannot force anyone to cover or to do the *namaz*. When headscarves were outlawed in universities for the first time, some open girls (*açık kızlar*) stood beside their covered sisters in coalition. When we saw this, we gave them gifts of headscarves as a spiritual gesture. They said that no one else had shown them support of the sort.

Indeed, I had observed in other Islamist demonstrations that Muslim apparel companies were distributing headscarves to the demonstrating students free. That Tekbir had influenced the construction of the modern Muslim woman's look had already been suggested to me by owners of smaller veiling businesses. Tekbir indeed paved the way in the market for headscarves, in time turning into the most popular outlet for covered women's clothing. The company's managers have been influential in the constitution of 'Muslim womanhood' in contemporary Turkey.

In the 1980s, the Institute of Higher Education (YÖK), attached to the state's Ministry of Education, formally forbade the wearing of the headscarf in university classrooms. Veiled woman students took to the streets in widespread demonstrations. In return, the Institute had to modify its definition of the sort of covering that was to be disallowed. Black veils (*kara çarşaf*) would unquestionably be banned. However, the *türban* (derived from the French word *turban*, for scarf) would be permissible. In this construction, the *türban*, which is colourful, bright and stylish, modelled on the scarves that European women threw around their shoulders, would be tolerated, as representing a relatively more 'civilised' (in its modernist Turkish sense) mode of covering. And it was Tekbir (along with other producers of headscarves) who realised the Institute's definition of 'modern covering', producing ready-to-wear *türbans* that complied. The image of the modern covered woman would be available, now, for consumers. In fact, producers of the *türban* were realising the Kemalist state's modernist aspirations. Women were to be modern even if they wanted to veil. Or, women could veil *and* be modern if they used the *türban*. This would be a specific (religious) kind of modernity, but modernity (and capitalism) it would be, nonetheless.

And yet, Tekbir's owner still claimed to have been inspired by 'the past'. He presented his company's clothes as 'authentically Islamic', versions of the clothes worn by Turkey's Ottoman predecessors before the institution of Atatürk's clothing reforms in the mid-1920s. Karaduman used every means to present his clothing styles as replications of 'the original Islamic way of covering'. He was in fact creating images that would satisfy the quest for 'authenticity' among covered women who wanted to be 'modern'.

The trademark of Islam

Tekbir reached its clients through well-advertised fashion shows. Indeed, the company to a certain extent modelled its practices on those of similar companies owned by secularists in Turkey. These shows were central to the making of fashion and the creation of a clientele, as Karaduman had observed. After our meeting, he gave me an invitation to a Tekbir fashion show.

The show was held in November of 1994 on the ground floor of the Tekbir Store in Merter, an industrial district of Istanbul reserved for textile companies. The space was small, too small for the number of spectators. The organisers had made an attempt to segregate seating and standing room (*harem-selamlık*). They had tried to construe a proper 'Islamic' way of watching a show, men on one side, women on the other.

Yet, even before the show began, it turned out to be difficult to implement this separation. There were more women in the audience than men, and not enough space in the women's section. So some of us were sent to stand behind the men. Girls ran to talk to their fathers, women who had forgotten to mention something to their husbands or male friends walked right into the men's section, children ran back and forth. The segregation was only theoretically in place.

Most of the women in the audience were covered, although none of them wore the black veil. Few women were open, sitting beside their covered relatives or friends. There were older as well as younger women. It seemed that women had come to the show as an outing for the weekend. In the middle of the fashion hall was a T-shaped podium for the show. The seats on the right-hand side of the podium had been reserved for journalists, and indeed there were reporters from a number of television channels, including those of the secular mainstream. Cameras were trained first on the audience and then at the models, as they took to the stage. On the other side of the podium were male guests.

Above the well-lit podium was inscribed the much-advertised brand Tekbir, lit by spotlights. The company's logo read, 'The world's trademark in covered women's clothing' (*Tesettürde Dünya Markası*). Through the mist of artificially produced smoke appeared a couple of professional models. Both were dressed in fantastic-looking clothes, covering their bodies from head to toe. As the poignant rhythm of the music of the film *1492* was heard in the background, the models began to trot, discreetly moving their hips from left to right on their column-like legs, supported by high-heeled shoes. The audience applauded in amazement and enthusiasm. Bright-coloured silken covered-wear, with full headgear, left only a blue-eyed, much-made-up face uncovered. Models who normally exhibited underwear, bathing suits and 'western' clothes to the secular bourgeoisie in big hotels around the city had now come to sell covered clothes to those who wanted to follow an alternative fashion.

'Mashallah! Mashallah!' cried old people in the audience, 'God has blessed you!' At first, the eyes of the viewers beside me were directed at the faces of the professional models, big blue mascara-laden eyes, lip-lined mouths, thin and small noses, carefully plucked eyebrows. And then, 'Look at that waist,' one young woman beside me gasped, 'I will throw myself over a flight of eleven stairs,' she exclaimed. She was expressing her sense of feeling small beside the majestic-looking models. 'Wow! Look at that face! I am looking only at the faces, not at the clothes,' another covered woman remarked. 'These women are seducing me,' one woman declared amidst repressed laughter.

'Black and White,' announced the male voice on the loudspeaker that introduced the next selection. And again through artificial vapour appeared well-covered mannequins, this time in combinations of black-and-white headscarf and overcoat. The last show was a display of 'Inspiration from the Ottoman Palace'. Models, their faces covered to only reveal their light-coloured eyes, strutted along the podium in extravagant clothes. 'This is how women dressed in the Ottoman harem,' the announcer said. Richness shone out of the embroidered cloth, matching the pearls and gold on the bodies of the models. Tall, thin, blue-eyed women's beauty, as institutionalised in Turkey's mainstream fashion industry, grinned through the turbans designed for the morally conscious. During the show, the model that received the most enthusiastic applause was the one who wore a black silk veil that covered the whole body, including the nose and the mouth. The facial section of the veil had been decorated with golden-coloured accessories, and the blue eyes of the model were highlighted.[24] Those blue eyes, that represented 'modernity' to Turks, were employed not only in the secularist fashion industry, but also in Islamist sectors that aspired to be Muslim and modern: blue-eyes with a black veil could be combined in this address to the world of contemporary Turkish symbols.

As the models walked by, I noticed that much of their outline could be discerned through the clothes. Their full breasts, string-like waists and thin columnar legs imposed themselves through their 'Islamic' clothes. 'Does this fit with Islam?' I asked a covered woman who was standing to watch beside me, 'these tightly-sewn, narrow gowns that disclose the contours of one's body?' 'Well,' said the perplexed-looking woman, for a while unable to find an answer to satisfy my uncovered head, 'this is homewear, you know, only to be worn beside one's husband and relatives.' 'But all these men are watching these models here,' I said. 'Doesn't that contradict the laws of Islam?' One covered woman who heard my question nodded in agreement. The first woman, again perplexed, said, 'They are doing this now to introduce the clothes. Normally people wouldn't wear these clothes in public. I am also a trader, you know. And a trader has to exhibit his products. This man is doing this and he is doing it well.'

After the show was over, the models quickly dressed back into their normal clothes: tights, mini-skirts and high-heeled boots. They then sprang out of their dressing room, waving their blonde hair about amidst the covered audience that was helping itself to lemonade and cookies. 'How do you feel about appearing in a show like this?' I asked one of the models in the dressing-room. 'I did this once last year and I could not hold back my tears as I walked on the podium,' she said.

'I am an Atatürkist, you know. But it is undeniable that people are wearing these things. And I am a professional, so I am doing this.'

Outside, in the reception room, I spoke to three older women who had watched the show. 'The models looked so much prettier under covers than they did in their tights and mini-skirts when they came out,' one of these women said. 'That is the gist of the matter. Take it that way,' she said. Another of the women said, 'My daughters are not covered. At a time like this, it is hard to tempt young women to cover themselves. This sort of show proves to young women that they can be beautiful, and perhaps even more beautiful, when they cover themselves in the Islamic way.' And she continued:

> Poor girls in the midwifery section of the Medical School are not being allowed to enter their laboratories. They are discriminating against us. You know, I covered myself when I was 39 years old. Until then, I had lived my life in nightclubs with saz, play and drinks.[25] One day, I decided that enough is enough. I would go on the *haj* and really transform myself.[26] After I wore the headscarf, one day I went to the clothing store where I always used to shop. The woman who always helped me there did not recognise me and treated me like someone who wouldn't be able to afford buying anything from that store. Only because of my scarf! No one can know anyone's money or belief. They always discriminate against us like this.

This woman was probably quite wealthy, given that she used to spend her life in nightclubs, could afford going on the *haj*, shops in expensive stores, and is disturbed when mistaken for someone from a lower class. What shook her the most was the loss of a visible class identity, in assuming the headscarf. She liked the Tekbir fashion show because the styles exhibited by the models allowed her to maintain her middle-class identity as she turned to religion. Unlike radical Islamist critics of consumerism and materialism, this woman had no qualms about spending to reveal her status. She was content, now that she could reconcile her social position with her identity as a believer. This was an attempt to render the veil a symbol of higher class, rejuggling the symbols of class and distinction.[27]

'It was very beautiful, spectacular!' one of the three women said. When I queried about the compatibility of the show with Islam, one of them was taken aback, exclaiming, 'You are not disturbed by such shows when uncovered women do it and you are when we do it! Why shouldn't we the believing community benefit from the good things (*nimet*) of the world?' A young woman I spoke to after the show also seemed very appreciative: 'We have to keep abreast of our times,' she said. 'If our grandmothers wore black veils, we cannot do that today. Perhaps we need to compromise a little. But no, in fact I don't think we are compromising in anything.' As we were chatting, one of the models, dressed again in her own clothes, appeared on the stage in tights, high-heeled boots and a black leather jacket. She jumped over the podium steps, made her way through the crowd of covered women and walked out to wait for a cab. The young woman I was talking to glanced curiously at her nonchalant attitude. After all her appreciative comments on the whole event, she couldn't hold herself back from an aside: 'I don't think they should come out like this in these clothes.'

There was a mixed feeling among the women audience of the show about the value of the enterprise. Many of the women enjoyed very much what they saw. They liked the idea that they could look pretty, rich, modern and fashionable as they practiced their beliefs. They watched, as they compared their own figures with those of the models put on a pedestal. Women had gazed attentively, scrutinising the models' looks, clothes and styles of walking. There were some women who wondered whether the exhibition as an event fitted with Islamic ethics. There were yet others who turned the exhibition into a fruitful context for political activism: during the reception that followed the show, some women were campaigning for the midwifery students who had been thrown out of university classrooms for being covered. They were collecting signatures in support of the students and in protest at the state university administration. The show was an important site for the manifestation and shaping of a politics of identity.

Islamist periodicals gave the Tekbir show a mixed reception, once again. Some newspapers, especially those that were affiliated with the Welfare Party, like *Milli Gazete* and *Yeni Şafak*, published appreciative reports on the event, referring to 'the increasing number of women who cover'. But in examples of the more radical Islamist press, the newspapers *Vakit* and *Selam*, there were brutal critiques of the event.[28] Atilla Özdür, columnist in *Vakit*, drew attention to the fact that the Welfare Party's youth organisation (Milli Gençlik Vakfı) had also organised fashion shows of this sort for covered women.[29] This radical Islamist was categorising Tekbir along with the Welfare Party and the mainstream of Islamism in Turkey. He was arguing that, for the most part, Turkish Islamists were integrating Islam with the capitalist system. Karaduman had asked several religious leaders (*hocaefendiler*) to give *fetvas* (to pronounce their religious opinion) on the clothes produced by Tekbir. The columnist in *Vakit* called those preachers to stand forward and repeat whether such models and behaviour were fitting in Islam. Özdür's piece was foregrounded by a critique of capitalism, as a system which solicits growth in market goods in order to prevent crisis. This analysis was followed by an exegesis of Tekbir:

> Turkey, as part of the capitalist world, has entered that atmosphere. Whatever their religion may be, people are unable to keep from adapting to the rules of capitalism in their trading relations. This is a reality...
>
> The 'Tekbir' Clothing Company has been organising fashion shows for the last three or four years. These were followed by much discussion, for and against, in public. In these fashion shows, woman models were dressed covered and were sent to strut before the curious gaze of onlookers; women and men in the audience sat together in rooms that turned into the hot cubicle of public baths [*halvet*]; hundreds of millions [of Turkish lira] were given to luxury hotels, the cost of which was cut from tax statements; and prices on covered women's clothing rose as a result.
>
> We analysed the event as an activity to enhance consumerism and resolve the crisis of marketing in capitalism. We opposed these fashion shows on the grounds that they eroded a thrifty philosophy of life and the Islamic principles of modesty, asceticism, and abstention from worldly pleasures.[30]
>
> These fashion shows were approved by Muslims who submitted to the hegemony of capitalist relations of business ... In democracies, the majority is deemed to be right. We have remained in the minority. We have been defeated in front of the reality that one cannot be Muslim without being a capitalist.

What is the solution? There is no solution to this. For a lifestyle which befits a Muslim, one which emphasises abstention from worldly pleasures, would paralyse all markets. If you were to remove the consumerist practice of fashion shows, the capitalistic structure would be destroyed.

We are either, once and for all, going to remain under this wreck or we are going to, as long as we live, be entrapped in imperialism's vicious circle of debt in continuing to sell Islam to one another.[31]

The text of this critic's review of Tekbir fashion shows was imbued with references to Marxist language on 'capitalism'. This radical Islamist was lamenting the incorporation of Muslim ethics into the logic of a consumer market. There were others, however, who argued against Tekbir, comparing Karaduman's justifications of his shows with Islamic sources. In a reader's letter published in *Vakit* and *Selam*, Ismail Uzun argued against Tekbir's definition of Islamic propriety. No religious leader, according to this reader, would sanction a show featuring modelling women, watched by a mixed company of men and women. He had his definition of 'proper Islamic covering' in turn, one which he defined in opposition to Tekbir's:

> The principal purpose of covered women's clothing is the prevention of moral degeneration. It is meant to keep women from arousing carnal sentiments in men. In this situation, it is not right for professional models who normally pose in bathing-suit shows to be exhibiting covered women's clothes.[32]

Karaduman, in an interview on an Islamist radio station, had made a reference to Ayşe's life as wife to Prophet Muhammad, noting that she had watched a sword and shield show with the Prophet. He had wanted to legitimise the Tekbir shows on the grounds of *sünnet*, of following the lifestyle of personalities of the first centuries of Islam, the era know as 'the Time of Bliss' (*Asr-ı Saadet*) by Islamists. The writer of the letter in *Vakit* argued against Karaduman's interpretation of Ayşe's actions. According to him, 'Ayşe watched a sword and shield show through a window beside the great prayer room only in standing behind the Prophet and leaning her head on his shoulder'.[33] He was pitting this reading of Ayşe's life against that used by Karaduman to defend his shows, with references to sections of the Quran and to sources on life in the Time of Bliss. What Tekbir was doing in the name of Islam contradicted these sources: 'Tekbir's clothes and manner of trading are inappropriate from the standpoint of Islamic observance of the Prophet's ways of life [*sünnet*]'.

So, there was contention, within the Islamist community itself, about the value of veiling exhibitions. Some radical critics distinguished their understanding of Islam and covered women's clothing from that promoted by Tekbir. Yet on a broader level, suggested one of the radical critics, it appeared that Tekbir enjoyed greater success than its opponents. Its clothes were extremely popular among Islamist women. Covered students attended its shows as a basis for their political cause. Tekbir had an important hold over the market.

It was not only Islamists, of course, who were using exhibition in the politics of identity. In fact in the very week in November 1994 in which Tekbir held its fashion show in Merter, another fashion show was taking place at the Cultural Centre in the Harbiye neighbourhood of Istanbul, this time for secularist politics.

It was November 10, the anniversary of Atatürk's death, and two Atatürkist organisations, the Culture and Arts Foundation and the Mustafa Kemal Organisation, had organised a show narrating the history of the bowler hat, as introduced by Atatürk for Turks in the first decade of the republic.[34] Through this show, 'The Hat is a Story', the secularist organisers wanted to revive the spirit of the hat reforms, as instituted in 1925 against the wearing of the fez and the turban by men. In the same move, Atatürk also prevented the wearing of the veil by women. No Turkish men now wear the bowler hat, but the organisers of the show were using the hat as a symbol of 'civilisation', in their terms, to counteract Islamist women's headscarves. 'The hat', in this rendering, when worn by mannequins on display, represented 'being up with the times', whereas 'the veil' was a sign of 'backwardness'. In this promenade of models, too, the politics of identity was at play. Producers of new versions of the classical bowler hat, and long gowns, constructed these as 'contemporary' and 'modern' clothing (çağdaş, in secularist language), in an attempt to make their case against Islamists. They were at the same time introducing and advertising their companies' styles, as available in Istanbul's fashionable boutiques and department stores.

The fashion show has a longer history in Atatürkist institutions than in Islamist ones. In fact, fashion shows as such were started in Turkey under the auspices of the Girls' Institutes, founded in the 1920s and 1930s to promote European-style dress among Turkish women. Students in the Girls' Institutes would produce the sort of clothing fashionable in Europe at the time, synthesising it with Turkish motifs and embroidery.[35] The Institutes, of course, were there to institutionalise the hat reform, and no clothing produced in them included head-scarves of any sort for women. Students, who designed and sewed the dresses under the supervision of their European-trained instructors, would then exhibit their work in front of their mothers, fathers and relatives, as well as the republicanist bureaucratic elite. Institute-tailored clothes were in vogue among the wives and daughters of bureaucrats. However, the modes of display practiced in the early years of the republic in the Institutes was qualitatively different from those used in 1994 by secularist or Islamist fashion companies, which operate in the late-twentieth-century context of the free market for commodities.

The force of symbols

The claim to be representative of a 'past Ottoman and Islamic reality' was what gave the Tekbir fashion show its legitimacy and force. Indeed, the exhibition of veils and headscarves could not have appealed to morality if it weren't for the revivalist argument. The announcer presented the products under titles like 'Inspiration from the Ottoman Palace'. Tekbir's Chief Executive had called religious leaders (hocas) to endorse (to give fetvas) the propriety of the company's veils. Karaduman and his brothers wanted to do business in the 'Islamic' way, and when they spoke about their enterprise, they referred to the lifestyle of the Prophet Muhammad and to relevant Islamic sources. The organisers of the fashion show wanted it to stand for 'Islamic morality' and to be representative of 'the Islamic past'. The ambience of the display hall was also pre-planned as 'moral' from an Islamic point of view, women being segregated from men. There was an attempt, then, to 'authenticise' (in this case, 'Islamise') the viewer's space too. Unlike much of the world outside that hall, Tekbir's architecture of space aimed to create 'what befitted Muslims'.

And yet, in the staging of the event there were problems in representation. Despite the efforts of Tekbir's management neatly to compose the space and action of the show, nothing turned out quite so neat and orderly. Despite efforts to separate by gender, in practice women and men kept visiting one another in the spaces reserved for the other gender. Children kept running back and forth. When there wasn't enough space for women, women were directed to stand behind a row of men's seats. People were not used, in their everyday lives, to separate themselves from one another by gender in this way. Tekbir had attempted to create a representation of 'Islamic authenticity' even in the audience space, but had difficulty maintaining this representation's unity of referent and referred.

Things were likewise 'messy' on the podium. Karaduman had likened his set-up to the story of Ayşe, who had watched a show while leaning on the Prophet's shoulder behind a window. He did not want his fashion show to be distinguished from the real life of the Prophet and his wives. The models presenting the clothes were all dressed up to conceal their body-shapes, leaving only the face or eyes and the hands in the open. Tekbir's Chief Executive had his own understanding of proper Islamic apparel for women, and his proposition was that his company was producing it. Women watching the show wanted to think like the management of Tekbir. Indeed, many of them showed their enthusiasm through applause, and they defended the show, the event, the company and the specific clothing models in the name of Islam. They had enjoyed themselves, and they wanted to think that it was indeed 'true' that they could dress up beautifully like this and still be Muslims.

However, women also made asides expressing ambivalent thoughts and feelings. They expressed their intimidation by the tall and thin models. They weren't sure whether it was right for the men in the audience to be watching the models exhibit Islamic homewear. At the end of the show, the models, now dressed in their own clothes – black leather jackets, mini-skirts, boots – and with uncovered wavy blond hair, walked up from the backstage onto the podium and in through the reception room, where the audience was helping itself to tea and biscuits, on their way out. Covered women who were chatting there did not like the appearance of the models' revealing clothing, having just watched them display Islamic modesty. The models who had been 'representing Islam' on the podium had stated their allegiance as Atatürkists backstage, and had trotted through the hall at the end in their own clothes. The problems with the representation were obvious even to the women in the audience who wanted to believe in it. Radical Islamist critics in the press made more direct references to the problems of the Tekbir affair.

The Tekbir fashion show made claims to 'authenticity'. The managers were presenting their clothing models as 'alternatives to the world of fashion'. Unlike the 'open' clothes worn by unbelieving Turkish women, Tekbir clothes were modelled on the 'reality of Islam'. Tekbir's motto was 'the trademark of Islam'.

The company was attempting to monopolise the representation of Islam. And it was certainly successful. Despite a number of critical reviews of the fashion shows in radical Islamist newspapers and radio stations, Tekbir clothes were indeed extremely popular among covered women, and more so than any other brand or model. And like the women who had watched the fashion show, many of the company's customers wanted to believe in the representation. The confusion of the women in the audience was accompanied by a more ardent effort on their part to hold onto the representation as a symbol of 'reality'.

This was happening in spite of the women's at least partial awareness of problems with the Tekbir representation of 'Islamic clothes'. People in the audience questioned the certainty of Tekbir's representations, and there were critics who queried the validity and legitimacy of the whole enterprise. Islamist women were not totally immersed in a discourse that works through mechanisms of representation. They expressed confusion, they reflected on what they watched, they thought it through and elaborated.

However, there was still an effort to keep the representation in place, despite ambiguity and questioning. As noted above, Tekbir products were extremely popular, and the company made large profits. Plus, there was immense effort and goodwill on the part of covered women in their defence of Tekbir clothes and the like. That the representation was not so neat and orderly, and that there was awareness of the mess, did not lead to a popular rejection of the products. On the contrary, there was mass consumption. There was something else, then, that sustained the force of the representation even when its viewers and consumers thought it unreal. The representation kept toppling over itself, but was still effective. How?

It was difficult for Islamists to put the world about which they were nostalgic on show. At every turn, it was too obvious that the representation did not match reality and that the representation had taken on a life of its own, as symbol. Yet, there was reluctance among the audience, despite at least partial consciousness of the fakeness of representation, to admit that the representation was problematic. Women in the audience mostly wanted to hold onto the representation as if it stood for a greater reality of 'Islam' and 'Turkish authenticity'. They wanted to believe in the representation even if it was difficult, in practice, for the representation's poise to be maintained.

What was happening here was quite complex. The signifier 'veil' had assumed such significance and power that it no longer mattered too much for consumers of Tekbir products whether the representation, as such, was a construction. As a construction, no less, 'veil' had power, potency and a life of its own. Now women consumed 'veils' in and of themselves, rather than for what they stood for. The struggle for Islamic life and politics had been diluted, in the process of consumerism, into a struggle for 'the veil' alone. It was no longer required of signifiers to even produce neat effects of reality. Tekbir veils did not have to represent 'Islamic morality' in an unproblematic way for them to be popularly worn. Veils were only signifiers now, not requiring the other half of the orderly binary pair (a signified). The veil had been transformed into the purpose itself in the politics of Islamist identity in the Turkey of the mid-1990s. The historical context of commodification (the 1980s and 1990s) had much to do with the manufacture and reification of the symbol of 'the veil', in opposition to that of 'Atatürk'. The politics of identity was transformed into a politics over symbols in the context of consumerism.

In order to elaborate theoretically the force of representations of headscarves even when their constructedness is obvious to their consumers, I will turn to the work of Jean Baudrillard. In 'The System of Objects', Baudrillard writes about the phenomenon of the 'pure signifier, without a signified, signifying itself'.[36] He develops this concept in order to distinguish his approach to 'the commodity' from that of Marxist philosophers of need. Marxists critiqued advertising for producing 'artificial needs'. They differentiated these from those needs that they deemed 'authentic'.[37] In contrast, Baudrillard argues that 'in the logic of signs', or in the consumer society that he studied in the late twentieth century, 'as in the logic of symbols, objects are no longer tied to a function or to a *defined* need'.[38] And there is consumption nonetheless.

The headscarf has been interpreted by Islamists as a representation of 'Islamic chastity', 'the holy past', and 'Turkish local culture'. That the representation does not neatly pair up with the ideal is obvious to many women who cover. It appears, as Baudrillard would have noted, that the signifier 'headscarf' has through this taken on a life of its own, living by itself even beyond its problematic representation. The veil has a social life,[39] a different one now, as signifier. It does not simply refer to female religiosity or belief. It has gained meaning in and of itself, and almost independently of belief. It symbolises itself, and in itself refers to the politics of identity, opposed to secularists and the 'secularist state'.

It is not the labour value congealed in the veil-as-commodity that disturbs radical Islamist critics of commodification. It is rather the supernatural value (the sacred, religious value) that is congealed. So the veil, for Islamists, is the apparel of a religious fetish. The problem for radical Islamists arises when it is turned into another kind of (commodity) fetish. However, that perhaps is precisely the point: that in the age of commodification, the veil takes on a different meaning, rather than remaining the apparel of belief. It takes on added significance in itself ('it', rather than 'belief', becomes the fetish; or, rather than remaining a symbol of belief, 'it', the symbol itself, becomes significant (the signifier in and of itself) where politics is waged over the symbol more than over its content.

The market for identities

With the ethnographic material in this chapter, I have attempted to illustrate that the politics of identity of secularists and Islamists in the 1980s and 1990s has been involved with a history of commodification. At every turn of political activism, 'identities' were expressed through the medium of consumer goods.[40] Above, I have given examples of secularist and Islamist commodities, as packaged for use and displayed. The creativity and innovation that goes into the bringing of new goods onto the free market left their mark on the shape of the politics of culture. Identities are, to an important extent, produced in the context of a marketplace. This does not diminish their personal or existential meaning and potency. Yet, through an analysis of 'the market for identities', I wanted to recast the claims of this potency to 'authenticity'.

What is most curious is that as market production continues, activists for secularism and Islamism all argue the respective 'authenticity' of their habits of life and use, both positions countering one another with contradictory narratives of 'Turkish authenticity'. Both are two versions of nationalism, and both seek to establish primordiality and close affinity to 'the culture of Turkey', the words of activists for 'identity' carrying weight because they lay claim to 'originality'. In the 1980s and 1990s, the market was a powerful determinant of the shape of 'authenticity'. 'Identities' are not 'real' in the essentialist sense for secularists and Islamists, but constructions, and one important site for the manufacture of our contemporary notions of 'self' and 'culture' is the market.

Turkish Islamist intellectuals' writing on 'Turkish identity' is a critique of westernisation that can instructively be compared to anthropologies which reify 'native culture'. In their public discourse, radical Islamist intellectuals have mostly associated consumerism with the culture of westernists in Turkish society. In much contemporary Islamist writing, secularists are portrayed as 'fake' or 'simulations of the West'. In contrast, Islamists struggle with one another over the meaning of properly 'being oneself' as a Muslim and a Turk. In this reading, secularists are not 'authentic'. They have mutated to repress their former true selves in adopting Western ways of living. Central to the Islamist critique of 'secularist inauthenticity' is secularist habits of consumption. Islamists reproach their opponents for using 'foreign' and religiously forbidden things.

In this chapter, I hope to have illustrated that a habit of consumption is not only in the everyday life of Turkey's secularists, but also, to a determining extent, in that of Islamists. Islamists have come to identify themselves as such by buying and using things distinct from those used by secularists. There is a claim here to be consuming things that are closer to the Turkish Muslim's 'true self'. The overcoats made of English silk are only one example of an 'Islamist good' that is hard to place among 'the Western' and 'the local', 'the foreign' and 'the Islamic'. The *türban* in itself is the best example of an Islamist use of a product of the modernist measures of a Kemalist state. When they have orientalised themselves and attempted to present themselves as 'modern', Islamists have drawn more inspiration from secularists and from the West than they have from the Islamic and Ottoman past. Similar ambiguities exist in products emblematised as 'secularist'.

Islamist social critique too easily maps the lifestyle of Islamists onto that of Turkey's poor or Turkey's economically under-privileged. The associations of wearing 'Western clothes' and leading 'westernised lifestyles' are too easily conflated with 'Turkey's wealthy' in this political discourse. Accordingly, westernisation was imposed on 'Turkish society' by 'elites'. And, even though 'the elites' developed a lifestyle 'foreign to Turkey', 'the rest of Turkey' (also referred to by Islamists as 'the other Turkey') kept to 'its values', or has attuned itself to its true conscience since. Islamists have projected all sorts of lifestyles that they defined as 'improper' onto 'Turkey's rich'. 'The real Turkey' or 'the culture of the people', as Islamist intellectuals have often said, is not about using 'Western things'. A binarist discourse on class went hand-in-hand with Islamists' politics of identity.

This chapter has contested Turkish Islamists' attempts to map a specific construction of 'Islamic authenticity' onto 'Turkey's subaltern'. A certain popular and mainstream branch of Turkish Islamism (incorporating the core group of the Welfare Party and its supporters) is interested not in overturning class distinctions per se, but in expanding the domain of middle-class taste and lifestyle to include norms expected of the believing Muslim.

A certain definition of 'modernity' has indeed been associated with high status.[41] Yet, mainstream Islamists are not countering class stratification or the class system, but the symbolic references of 'high class'.[42] They counter not 'modernity' as such, but its definition. They would like 'modernity', as a marker of class, to encapsulate the signs of Islamic life too for a woman wearing a veil to be perceived as 'upper class' as well.

As I have tried to show, a believing class of capitalists has developed in Turkey, and the Islamist movement has taken its shape in conjunction with the activities of this group. The class of Muslim capitalists is different in many ways from the secularist bourgeoisie. The latter have a longer history in Turkey's urban centres, more entrenched ties with sources of Western capital, and are descendants of a longer lineage of wealth. Most Muslim capitalists come from the conservative established families of small towns or cities across Anatolia, and if they now live in the metropolis, they are the first or second generation to do so. Yet they form a class of capitalists, nonetheless, even though, as I have illustrated in my description of the Islamic marketplace and the Islamist company, with specific and different business practices. Muslim capitalists, just like their secularist counterparts, have created a market for consumption, and a prolific one at that.

To reiterate my points, secularists and Islamists in contemporary Turkey are implicated in the same capitalist consumption market. The politics of identity between these communities developed in the shared context of Turkey's unification with a worldwide free market of commodities and goods, and what is significant now is that Islamists are as active as secularists in the making and shaping of this market.[43]

Notes on Chapter 10

1   Kopytoff (1986) distinguishes culture from commodification (p.73).
2   See, for example, Kandiyoti (1996) and Göle (1991).
3   See, for example, Aynur İlyasoğlu (1994) and Ayşe Durakbaşa (1987).
4   *Zekat* is one of the five precepts for being a Muslim. It refers to giving alms to the poor.
5   Another central commodity of the market for 'Islamic identity' fashioned by varieties of Muslim capital was the book.
6   I use the term 'covered' as the literal translation of the local Turkish term (*kapanmak, kapalı*) for veiling.
7   For an ethnography of Turkish women's headscarves and xenophobia in Germany, see Mandel (1989).
8   As I note here, there was a tendency among secularists to view their lives as supra- or extra-cultural. Secularists thought that they had transcended 'culture'

to meet a 'global' (European) norm. The approach can be compared to that of Ruth Frankenberg (1993), who studied 'racialised identity' not among black, but among white, American women. Also see Darini Rajasingham's (1993) study of white British women's ways of othering.

9   The term *çağdaş* in secularist Turkish usage literally means 'contemporary' or 'modern', suggesting a state of being up with the times or of keeping abreast of progress. In daily usage, however, in the 1990s, *çağdaş* came to mean 'civilised' in the Eurocentric sense of the term. A particular section of society, those who associated themselves with Atatürk's vision, over-used the term in reference to themselves and their aspirations, in contradistinction to Islamists. Note that one of the biggest Atatürkist civic organisations is called Çağdaş Yaşamı Destekleme Derneği, or the Society for the Promotion of Civilised Life.

10 In early republican years the *tayyör* was adopted by young nationalist women as the proper modern dress for the nation's new Turkish women. For this, see Durakbaşa (1987).

11 See Göle (1991) and İlyasoğlu (1994).

12 George Yudice (1995) makes a similar observation.

13 For an excellent critique of discourses of 'authenticity', see Vincanne Adams (1996).

14 *Hürriyet*, 18 October 1994, p.7. The Turkish original for my translation of the last sentence is striking: 'İnsanlar burada çağdaşlığı yaşıyor'.

15 *Milli Gazete* 2, 7 November 1994, p.1. The article was making a reference to Turgut Özal's phrase 'çağ atlamak', with which the leader of Turkey in the former decade had promised that he would make Turkey 'jump a century ahead'.

16 Ibid. Note that the writer of this article is attempting to appropriate the terms of 'being civilised' to the ways of ordinary believers. He does not use the word *çağdaş* to imply 'civilised'. He rather uses the older Ottoman-Turkish word *medeni* to describe the lifestyle of frequenters of the Topkapı market. In this definition, a more modest life in an Islamic sense of the term is what being 'civilised' is about.

17 *Aksiyon*, 10–16 December 1994, pp.32–5. I would here like to draw attention to the similarity between this nostalgic discourse of an Islamist intellectual with versions of anthropological critiques of modernity. Deniz Kandiyoti (1996) cautions us against this sort of coincidence in 'Contemporary Feminist Scholarship and Middle East Studies'. Likewise, Hammoudi (1993) draws attention to the coincidence between colonial and post-colonial discourses on what is authentic to a Muslim society (see p.viii). My intention in this article is to illustrate the embeddedness of Islamists in the everyday practices of the 'modernity' (here understood as market-oriented capitalism, materialism and consumerism) that they critique.

18 Ibid., p.34.

19 See Aksoy and Robins (1994), in which the phrase 'dual city, *alaturka*' appears on p.71. The following quote may give an idea of these critics' narrative: 'In their differences, in the contrast between the villa new towns and the *gecekondus*, we can see the growing polarisation that is making a dual city'.

20 Here Karaduman is referring to the veil (*çarşaf*) in distinction from the head-scarves and overcoats (*türban* and *pardösü*) worn by most Islamist women in Turkey today. The black veil, made of one piece of cloth from head to toe, is worn by religious women who want to refrain from ornament in their covered clothing.

21 Aygaz is a standard gas brand in Turkey, pretty much a monopoly. Karaduman's example can be compared to the common use of the word 'xerox' in the US for photocopying.

22 Sana is a standard brand of butter in Turkey, used very widely.

23 'Open' is my literal translation for the common Turkish adjective for women who do not cover (*açık*).

24 The reason for the increased applause for the model who wore the black veil in particular can be interpreted in the following way: the fashion show was taking place in the midst of other secularist discourses about the 'backwardness' of 'the Islamist headscarf'. Secularists frequently used 'the black veil' (*kara çarşaf*) as symbol to critique 'the position of women under Islam'. So when the model at the Tekbir fashion show appeared so beautiful in the black silken veil, Islamists in the audience rose up in enthusiasm. For the applauding Islamists, this was a rebuttal of the secularist discourse. The people in the audience, along with Tekbir, were re-writing the meaning of the signifier 'black veil', in Turkey's public culture.

25 The saz is a Turkish musical instrument used in Turkish folk and classical music.

26 The *haj* (the pilgrimage to the holy sites in Mecca) is one of the five prescriptions of Islam, required for the Muslim who can afford it.

27 See, for example, Bourdieu (1984).

28 The newspapers *Milli Gazete* and *Yeni Şafak* have wider circulations than *Vakit* and the weekly *Selam*. *Milli Gazete* is read by many supporters of the Welfare Party, those who influenced the victories of the party in municipal and national elections. *Yeni Şafak* is the newspaper of Islamist intellectuals who are in dialogue with leftist and secularist intellectuals. Generally, *Yeni Şafak* has been supportive of Welfare. *Vakit* and *Selam* are radical Islamist newspapers, both of which are quite critical of Welfare for being too pragmatic and modernist, and for compromising on the requirements of Islam. One of *Vakit*'s main editors, the popular Islamist intellectual Abdurrahman Dilipak, wrote a column criticising the wedding of Necmettin Erbakan's daughter. The wedding was held in the Istanbul Sheraton, and although the bride's dress was covered, it was highly extravagant.

29 Such shows were not only organised by Tekbir. The Welfare Party also organised them all over Turkey.

30 The Turkish words that Özdür used in this section to describe Islamic principles were *tevazu*, *zöht* and *takva*.

31 See Atilla Özdür, 'Bu son yazıdır', in *Vakit*, 11 November 1994, p.4. The original Turkish of the last of Özdür's statements on 'selling Islam' is *birbirimize İslam satacağız*.

32 İsmail Uzun, 'Tekbir Giyim' in Dikkatine', *Vakit*, 16 November 1994, p.13. A re-print of this article appeared in *Selam*, 28 November–4 December 1994.

33 Ibid.

34 For an account of this exhibition, see the news piece in the secular mainstream newspaper *Sabah*, 11 November 1994, p.33.

35 For a historical ethnography on the Girls' Institutes and their students, see Navaro-Yashin (2000).

36 Baudrillard (1996).

37 Ibid., p.41.

38 Ibid., p.44 (emphasis his).

39   For the concept of 'social life' in reference to commodities, see Appadurai (1986).
40   Alfred Gell (1986) observed that 'consumption involves the incorporation of the consumed item into the personal and social identity of the consumer... think of consumption as the appropriation of objects as part of one's personalia' (p.112).
41   See Kandiyoti (1997).
42   See, for example, Bourdieu (1984).
43   It would be interesting to compare contemporary Islamists' discourse on secularist traders with early republican Kemalists' discourse on non-Muslim traders in Turkey. Indeed, Islamists have been accusing secularists of being 'compradors' of sorts. In nationalism in the Middle East, cultural difference has too easily been mapped onto difference in access to financial resources. In early republican Turkey, the wealth tax (*varlık vergisi*) was forced onto non-Muslims to create a Muslim-born Turkish capitalist class. Non-Muslims who were not wealthy suffered much from this measure. We need more complex, ethnographically based assessments which do not get mingled in nationalist discourses or their contemporary variations. Kandiyoti (1998) points us in new directions in conceptualising the relation between wealth and cultural difference in the Middle East.

References

Adams, Vincanne (1996), *Tigers of the Snow and Other Virtual Sherpas: An Ethnography of Himalayan Encounters*, Princeton University Press, Princeton, NJ
Aksoy, Asu and Kevin Robins (1994), 'Istanbul between Civilisation and Discontent', *New Perspectives on Turkey*, no 10 (Spring), pp.57–74
Appadurai, Arjun (ed.) (1986), *The Social Life of Things: Commodities in Cultural Perspective*, Cambridge University Press, Cambridge
Baudrillard, Jean (1996), 'The System of Objects', in *Selected Writings*, ed. Mark Poster, Polity Press, Cambridge (originally published 1968)
Bourdieu, Pierre (1984), *Distinction: A Social Critique of the Judgment of Taste*, Harvard University Press, Cambridge, MA
Durakbaşa, Ayşe (1987), 'The Formation of "Kemalist Female Identity": A Historical-Cultural Perspective', MA dissertation, Boğaziçi University
Frankenberg, Ruth (1993), *White Women, Race Matters: The Social Construction of Whiteness*, University of Minnesota Press, Minneapolis, MN
Gell, Alfred (1986), 'Newcomers to the world of goods: consumption among Muria Gonds', in Arjun Appadurai (ed.) *The Social Life of Things: Commodities in Cultural Perspective*, Cambridge University Press, Cambridge
Göle, Nilüfer, *Modern Mahrem: Medeniyet ve Örtünme*, Metis Yayınları, Istanbul
Hall, Stuart (1990), 'Cultural Identity and Diaspora', in Patrick Williams and Laura Chrisman (eds), *Colonial Discourse and Post-Colonial Theory: A Reader*, Harvester Wheatsheaf, New York and London
Hammoudi, Abdellah (1993), *The Victim and its Masks: An Essay on Sacrifice and Masquerade in the Maghreb*, University of Chicago Press, Chicago and London
İlyasoğlu, Aynur (1994), *Örtülü Kimlik*, Metis Yayınları, Istanbul

Kandiyoti, Deniz (1996), *Gendering the Middle East: Emerging Perspectives*, I.B.Tauris, London and New York

— (1997), 'Gendering the Modern: On Missing Dimensions in the Study of Turkish Modernity', in Sibel Bozdoğan and Reşat Kasaba (eds), *Rethinking Modernity and National Identity in Turkey*, University of Washington Press, Seattle and London, pp.113–32

— (1998), 'Some Awkward Questions on Women and Modernity in Turkey', in Lila Abu-Lughod (ed.), *Remaking Women*, Princeton University Press, Princeton, IL

Kopytoff, Igor (1986), 'The cultural biography of things: Commoditisation as Process', in Arjun Appadurai (ed.), *The Social Life of Things: Commodities in Cultural Perspective*, Cambridge University Press, Cambridge

Mandel, Ruth (1989), 'Turkish Headscarves and the Foreigner Problem', *New German Critique*, no 46, 27–46

Navaro-Yashin, Yael (2000), ' "Evde Taylorizm": Cumhuriyetin ilk Yıllarında Evişinin Rasyonelleşmesi', *Toplum ve Bilim* 84: 51–74

Rajasingham, Darini (1993), 'The Afterlife of Empire: Immigration and Imagination in Postcolonial Britain', PhD dissertation, Princeton University, Princeton, NJ, 1993

Yudice, George (1995), 'Civil Society, Consumption, and Governmentality in an Age of Global Restructuring: An Introduction', *Social Text*, vol. 14, no 4, 1–25

11

'We Pray Like You Have Fun': New Islamic Youth in Turkey between Intellectualism and Popular Culture

Ayşe Saktanber

Introduction

On 25 February 1998, thousands of students from different universities holding different ideological views ranging from leftist to nationalist rightist, and Islamist to liberal democrat rallied around a single cause for the first time in the recent history of Turkey. They had organised a large demonstration in Istanbul to protest at a new circular from the Ministry of Education banning headscarves and beards in universities. This circular also covered Imam-Hatip Schools, where religious education is at the very centre of the curriculum. In the last five years, there have been an increasing number of violent confrontations between students with differing political views, although these have not been on the scale of pre-1980 clashes. Such a gathering of students around a single cause should therefore be seen as an important development both for Turkish youth and Turkish political culture.

Although this proscription targeted Islamist students in general, women constituted the main target, if we consider that not all male Islamist students let their beards grow. However, not only Islamist groups but almost all university students, regardless of political affiliation, treated it as repression by the state, stemming from military pressure on both the government and the Higher Education Board. Two days after this first demonstration, on 27 February, the leftists and nationalist rightists (known as idealists or *ülkücü*) withdrew after the declaration by Istanbul University's Rector that the ban would be postponed. However, Islamist groups continued the protest, marching to Beyazıt Square with thousands of covered young women students at the front and men bringing up the rear.

An incident from that demonstration shown on prime-time news was particularly striking, since it showed with full metaphorical irony the state of modern Turkish culture and politics. The visual narrative of this news story went like this: in their colourful silk headscarves, with others in tightly closed black veils, thousands of female Islamist students were gathered in Beyazıt Square. Then, a small plane appeared, showering thousands of leaflets on the crowd, the white paper glistening like the tail of a paper dragon. Students reacted spontaneously by applauding, not knowing, however, what the leaflet was about. Their applause seemed sarcastic, in that they probably thought this a warning by the state about their protest. At that moment, we, the audience, were informed that this was a Turkish Air Institute plane co-operating with the national postal service, PTT, to let people know that the PTT was providing a free service for people to send faxes to the English-language weekly *Time* in order to elevate Atatürk from second to first place in their survey to select the most influential people of the twentieth century (in which hundreds of thousands of Turkish Internet users had participated to vote for Atatürk, and after a long struggle with the Greeks had at least managed to keep him in second place!). When the reality was known, however, we saw in the next scene the discontent and indifference of those covered students, who were well aware that the cameras were trying to capture their reaction. Nevertheless, the last scene of the report was rather telling. As none of the students would read this leaflet in front of the cameras, a small boy apparently not yet in his teens was filmed carefully reading the text, mispronouncing the name of the weekly and reading the name of Mustafa Kemal Atatürk with the due pride and reverence he had doubtless learned in school. We learned during the same report that this flight's coincidence with the demonstration was entirely accidental: it was organised by the PTT because this was the last day of voting; the plane's route had not been specially selected either. What made this event most interesting and ironic was its spontaneity. Moreover, through the comments and facial expressions of the newsreader, Ali Kırca, we were made aware, though briefly, of the bizarre yet bitter conflict between love of Atatürk and Islamic reaction.

For my part, among a series of alternative readings, one in particular immediately suggested itself. I interpreted both the content and the image of this episode as a graphic depiction of Turkey's predicament, which can be formulated as 'modernisation from above, Islamisation from below'. In this particular case, quite paradoxically, 'below' was the university students, the most promising section of the young, to whom Atatürk had entrusted the republic in his famous speech to Turkish youth. However, in this demonstration these Islamist students, as is well known, were not against the Turkish state as such, but rather Kemalism as the official ideology of the republic and its westernising project. All the same, they conveyed their complaints not only to the Turkish state and society, but also to international institutions that are indeed Western in character, such as the UN, virtually calling on its Secretary General to see their situation: for instance, a poster in English proclaimed, 'Annan, come and see, big Saddam is here!' All this can also be interpreted as what I call the panoramic narrative of modern faiths, global assertions and local values that Islamic youth creates, both to build an identity and represent their 'otherness'.

The newly acquired images and characteristics that can be observed in Islamic youth in Turkey cannot and should not be explained, of course, merely within the limits of a set of given political actions and ideological discourse. This is actually what has usually been done to understand both the Islamic and the wider youth culture as a whole in Turkish society.[1] Hence, as a consequence of such a restricted perspective, which should be interpreted as one of the political heritages of three military interventions in Turkey – in 1960, 1971 and 1980 – the ties of youth with politics are either loosened or, at certain historic junctures, virtually cut altogether, either through depoliticisation or imprisonment. Moreover, in spite of a tolerant adult rhetoric about youth in Turkish culture, the young are either associated with irresponsibility, idleness and even foolish hedonism,[2] or else charged with heavy, albeit theoretical, responsibilities centred around heroic themes like saving the country and the nation, or, as potential adults, the task of building a decent future both for themselves and their parents.[3] Since, above all, the irrationality of youth is a given in Turkish culture, it is also thought that this period, with its transient and unreasonable hopes and desires, should be got through as quickly as possible.

However, the youth of any society create various cultural forms, whether economic or political, produce new styles of appearance, behaviour and language, and develop new ways of communication, expression and representation, which, significantly, they actualise in the course of their everyday life. Moreover, the young develop tactics to create their own space, subverting the meanings of, and developing several 'resistance rituals', to the parent culture determined by the powerful few who strategically determine life places, such as public institutions and marketplaces, buildings and their surroundings, and the general framework of the urban landscape.[4] The young also contribute to the enlargement of popular culture as a whole, as well as to the intellectual life of a society, and may develop their own subcultural forms inasmuch as they are not only the consumers of cultural forms and products but also their producers. In this respect, within the framework of a broader youth culture, Islamic youth can be treated as a subculture; yet, as there is no homogenous Islamic youth in Turkish society, it also becomes possible to identify subcultures within that grouping.

In order to distinguish any subcultural form among Islamic youth, I argue that first and foremost we should develop a perspective through which the general characteristics of Turkish Islamic youth can be portrayed, since, although that grouping constitutes one of the most central issues of Turkish public life, it has not yet been studied as a culture in its own right – or, more specifically, as what I call a panoramic narrative, produced by Islamic youth to express and represent an identity oscillating between intellectualism and popular culture. Rather, Islamic youth is reduced to a mere manifestation of a political ideology which posits itself against the state and its secular regime. It is true that political ideology plays a great part in the formation of Islamic youth culture, yet I will argue that a political discourse by itself cannot be sufficient to sustain any social practice, and thus cannot create a culture. It can, at best, provide a broader cognitive framework through which boundaries between what is to be believed and what is not can be negotiated in a dialogue which also includes negotiations on procedures for forming identities and lifestyles. However, insofar as Islamic youth is seen as the product of a wider political movement, that of Islamic fundamentalism, the deviancy usually ascribed to youth has also been applied to Islamic youth. In other words, in Turkey, where, unlike many Muslim societies, the dominant, official cultural forms – and also parental ones – are largely secular in both their constitution and manifestation, Islamic youth is not only differentiated from the parent culture as such but also from other youth, who have no politicised religious affiliation. Moreover, the term Islamic, which I use to identify a particular youth culture, does not merely refer to a religious identification as such. This grouping is not called Islamic simply because its members are much more pious than other Muslims, but because they also search for an alternative Islamic life politics and new social order.

Class, in addition to political orientation, has also constituted the basis of studies done on youth in social sciences: political views and positions are seen as the reflections of the complex negotiations that youth makes with class culture. In the context of highly industrialised Western capitalist societies – be they late-modern, post-modern or globalised *in toto* – since the working classes have been the progenitors of youth subcultures, their political challenge has been framed as a critique of the hegemonic culture of capitalist class society in general, and the experience of divisions and contradictions within working-class culture in particular. However, in their pioneering work, *Resistance Through Rituals*, Hall and Jefferson (1976) have argued that youth are 'doubly articulated' to class and to age, differentiated in class terms and from their own parents. Yet, in this line of inquiry, the complex characteristics of these emergent youth subcultures were not overlooked either, and, as Hebdige (1979, p.126–7) has pointed out:

> individual subcultures can be more or less 'conservative' or 'progressive', integrated into the community, or extrapolated from it, defining themselves against the parent culture…these differences are reflected not only in the objects of subcultural style, but in the signifying practices which represent those objects and render them meaningful.

Similarly, concepts like homology and *bricolage* became central in an attempt to understand inner dynamics and resistance forms of these youth cultures. The concept of homology aimed to show that, contrary to popular myth, subcultures are not lawless forms but can be characterised by an extreme orderliness, in the sense that each part is organically related to other parts and, by such a fit between these parts, the members of the subculture can make sense of the world.[5] The concept of *bricolage*, on the other hand, entailed argument about how some forms of discourse (particularly fashion, for instance) can, as a new form of resistance through style, be radically adapted, subverted and extended by subcultural groups to erase or subvert their original straight meanings.[6] In the case of Islamic youth, such a subversion would involve the headscarves of young women and girls, as well as other items in their dress codes, insofar as such modesty codes do not simply denote their confinement to the private sphere. This also keeps alive the gender aspects of analyses of youth culture, in addition to the question of the emancipation of women and the ways in which young Islamist women subvert it by rejecting the concept of gender equality, replacing it with an Islamic under-standing of gender equity. Nevertheless, this understanding does not prevent women from becoming the symbol of Islamic youth, which is usually not the case in other, particularly Western, youth cultures.[7]

We must bear in mind, however, that class-based analyses about Western youth culture cannot be uncritically applied to the Turkish context. Social life in

Turkey is not demarcated by the type of class culture that must be addressed in analyses of youth in highly industrialised Western societies in general and the British society in particular whence literature has originated. There is no comparable working-class culture in Turkey, and the challenge that Islamic youth poses to the existing social system and culture cannot be evaluated merely as a 'symbolic class war' either, in the sense that the fighters will 'lose in the long run and end up as victims anyway',[8] by way of adjusting themselves to ongoing lifestyles as Islamic youth grow older. A perspective of marginalisation, generally suitable for a study of youth culture, can be as problematic. The marginalisation of youth is usually construed, as Amid-Talai aptly observes, 'by either subsuming its particularity within, and hence attributing it to, a more general Other, or exoticising the youth culture before it has been counted as sufficiently different to be cultural in its own right'. By this logic, she says, 'youth, it seems, have two choices: either they can be different because they are Quebecois, Algerians, Nepali, English etc, or they can shout their difference'.[9]

Islamic youth in Turkey sometimes 'shout', as in the example above, but most of the time, to meet their individual needs, they try with varying degrees of success to produce a culture by copying and modifying both Western and Eastern cultural forms,[10] as well as global images filtered either by the media or personal experiences.

Intellectual purity and the joy of faith: safe ways of posing social distinction

In the winter of 1990, while embarking on fieldwork on the Islamic way of life, I was inspired by an unexpected encounter to study Islamic youth at a later stage. In the course of my fieldwork, I met many young men and women (or, to use the preferred term in Turkish for unmarried young people, girls and boys) who were either at high school or university or else preparing for the university entrance exam, and a few who were employed just after graduating from high school or attending vocational courses. Moreover, in the later stages of that study, I also conducted focus-group interviews, especially with university students (separated according to gender of course). My first encounter with a group of female university students living in one of the dormitory apartments of the urban complex (called *site* in Turkish)[11] in which I carried out my study[12] has never lost its thought-provoking brightness for me, providing both the inspiration for the present study: 'We pray like you have fun', the title of this chapter, was uttered by one young woman during that encounter, and approved of by her friends. This not only marked the distinction they wanted to draw between themselves and others, but also indicated how they marked this boundary.

A group of four female university students had knocked on the door of a woman I was interviewing to ask whether she needed anything from the supermarket. We talked and, due to the interest they showed in my study, we immediately made an appointment to have tea after finishing the interview. I was so eager to see as many people and places in this *site* as possible that I cheerfully agreed to see them, despite feeling exhausted by the current interview. One hour later, they dropped by, and instead of going to their house we had tea in the home of the interviewee, whom they addressed as *abla*.[13]

They seemed quite cheerful and friendly, and also curious about me and my project, engaging in lively chat as if they had known me for a long time and had a close intellectual affinity. It was obvious that, as university students, they regarded me, a relatively young woman researcher from a respectable university, as someone familiar. In addition, I believe my prior acceptance by a woman whom they trusted as a very pious *abla*, though not as intellectual as themselves, encouraged this warm atmosphere. This encounter, free of any considerable difference in ideology and world-view could have happened between any young female university students at any time or place.

They confidently started to speak about their lives in that *site*, providing autobiographical detail and taking pride in their status as achievers who, in spite of modest family backgrounds, had managed to enter university education and transcend the expectations of both their close environment and the wider society, that pious Muslim girls become traditional passive housewives. They were social achievers who had not only taken necessary action to step into both intellectual and professional life but also to break out of their traditional class ties, while still remaining true to their religious duties and customs, the observance of which is particularly evaluated in the narrative of Turkish modernity as traditional. In this way, they were also in a position to criticise the current Turkish political system and society, and take an oppositional stand towards both. This was how they liked to represent themselves, and how they perceived their place and identity in wider society.

On the one hand, they seemed extremely hopeful and optimistic, but on the other they felt a deep resentment of the criticism directed at them by secular sections of society. Nevertheless, a strong sense of contentment about their personal situation went hand-in-hand with a sense of social distinction attained through their perception of themselves as being on the 'true' path. This path was not contaminated by the blind emulation of Western lifestyles, which, in their eyes, were completely ignorant of the human essence emanating from God's will and blessing; they rejected the seductive idleness of an irreligious life marked by personal indulgence, listening to meaningless Western music, watching illusory and also risqué movies, dancing in nightclubs, and flirting on street corners or in silly Western-style pubs and cafes. Instead, they preferred to spend time enhancing their knowledge of religion, science and social matters, and helping those in need of both moral and material support who had lost their enthusiasm for leading a proper, honest life as a result of the unbearable pressures of a pitiless, chaotic and unjust social system. More importantly, Islamic observance, the five-times-a-day prayer rituals and other practices of worship, seemed to function for these young people as a source of refreshment and strength while struggling with the bluntness of their world. Such withdrawal from mundane activities, however routine, provided them with insight and the space to enhance both their personal maturity, in the sense of being on the true path, and their feeling of belonging, in the sense of being part of a wider social network, the Islamic community. They claimed to derive a great deal of satisfaction from the ritualistic actions in their lives, that is, the performance of daily prayers (*namaz*) before God, and from the ablutions that precede these, all of which can only be done because of God's mercy.

These girls, like others whom I met later, were not, however, averse to light chat and giggling, which usually take place among female peer groups, over boys, fashions, beauty, soap operas (though relatively conservative ones), and the goings-on in Turkish magazine life, especially with regard to stars of what is called in vernacular Turkish 'classical Turkish music', like Emel Sayın, Muazzez Abacı and Ahmet Özhan. They were also quite knowledgeable about other media products, such as television talk shows, comic books and cartoons, music videos and the like. However, they were quite careful, in making the effort to criticise, to distinguish themselves from, the habitual consumers of those products. Despite their member-ship of this relatively secluded *site*, they were not closing their eyes to outside influences, although they were trying to be very selective about what they read and watched, and where and how they spent their leisure time. Thus, they were very eager to create leisure activities which complemented their religious beliefs and needs. As I have stated elsewhere, such activities ranged from organising reading and discussion groups, to coming together to write small parodies of Western-style lives, and to singing hymns, as well as participating in charity activities and *irşad* ('guidance') studies.[14] Most of them were also quite careful to attend Islamic plays and movies, which were quite few in number at the beginning of the 1990s. They also tried to read as much as they could from the Muslim intellectual literary genre.

However, this striving for a kind of personal intellectual purity among these young people should not be judged unexpected. On the contrary, I will argue that this has been a characteristic of Islamic youth culture from the early 1980s in Turkey, and has become one of the major concerns of the many scholars who focus on the new Islamic literacy as the most remarkable feature of emerging Islamic political activism. A group of relatively young men have been extensively recognised and studied as Muslim intellectuals, constituting the loci of this new literacy and becoming the role models of those, especially among the young, who also strive to be counted Muslim intellectuals, a term that we owe to Michael Meeker[15] and to his distinguished studies on a number of Turkish Muslim writers. These intellectuals have broken new ground in Turkish intellectual life with their 'surprisingly erudite literary, philosophical and political texts', produced from within an Islamic discourse. Meeker lists their main characteristics as follows: their prose is contemporary Turkish, and their writings critical and reflective; they share a similar social and educational background with their audience; and they appeal to their personal experiences, which their readers are likely to share, and often attempt to reach conclusions which serve as an orientation for personal thought and action. Although they may pronounce on past or present political issues or insist on political activism, they do not speak for specific tactics, groupings and parties. They are strongly against justifying Islamic principles from a Western perspective, rejecting the question of how accommodation is to be reached between Islam and the West. This constitutes the main difference between these writers and earlier Islamist thinkers of the late nineteenth and early twentieth centuries. Finally, and most importantly, by attempting to develop authentically

Islamic versions of Western concepts and institutions, they believe that the feeling of inferiority before the power of the West can be overcome (Meeker, 1994, p.153–4). Moreover, Meeker also depicts the portrait of what he calls 'a new kind of believing audience in Turkey' (p.159), as follows:

> The audience of Muslim intellectuals, which did not exist in any appreciable number only a few decades ago, is itself a product of the Westernising policies in Turkey. Like the Muslim intellectual himself, his reader is a believer who is likely to have had a secular education, may hold a higher degree, may know something of a European language, may have visited Western Europe, has read bits of Westernist literature, philosophy, and social history, and is familiar with progressivist and modernist ideologies. In effect, both writer and reader are 'Republican Muslims', believers whose outlook has been decisively shaped by the secularist institutions of the Republic and the Westernising of Turkey [pp.161–2].

Another common characteristic of the authors that Meeker particularly studied was that they all live either in Istanbul or Ankara, but were 'born into a family of provincial townsmen or officials or attended provincial primary and middle schools'.[16] Yet, as Meeker has demonstrated, they all managed to gain a reputation as Muslim intellectuals, not only in Islamic circles but also in those of most of their secular counterparts. Moreover, the work of some, in particular the poet İsmet Özel, and their evaluation of their personal situations and of developments in the Turkish polity and culture have been hailed, for instance by Mardin (1991), as the signals of a bottom-up social change, as opposed to that so long imposed upon Turkish society from above by the modernising forces of the Turkish state.

Although some Islamic women's magazines appeared in the second half of the 1980s,[17] the female counterparts of these Muslim intellectuals did not appear as intellectual figures in their own right until the beginning of the 1990s. However, when they started to appear in that men's world of Muslim intellectual life, these women highlighted 'the headscarf issue' in their books and articles about the identity, status and the role of Muslim women. This has constituted the most salient problem of Islamic female youth, and hence, as is usually argued, has become the banner of Islamic political activism in both Turkey and other parts of the Muslim world.[18] Like the men, they have not hesitated to share their personal experiences with their audience, but they emphasise the struggle that they have had to engage in as 'covered' women. Furthermore, unlike the men, they have also provided a basis for a much more concrete inquiry into the question of how to maintain Islamic family life, self-development, class identity and, thus, what we may call Islamic taste and style.

Although in terms of their social and educational background they show no significant differences from their male counterparts, their exclusion from several public institutions, professional activities and intellectual circles has been much more dramatic then men's, to the extent that it is not only their alternative intellectual identity but their physical appearance which is targeted. While fighting against this, they also criticise the role attributed to Muslim women by both Muslim men and conservative Muslim women, who tend to see the role as merely that of homemaker and mother, aspiring at best to a comfortable middle-class life, and who undermine the self-actualisation of Muslim women by preventing their participation in public life. In short, they support the intellectual self-development of Muslim women as long as it does not harm the fabric of Islam.

The examples both male and female Islamic youth have received from these intellectuals, both male and female, have helped the development of an image of what an ideal modern young Muslim should look like, of what activities he or she should be engaged in, and how to enhance his or her own Muslim identity. This has also helped to constitute the image of not only a 'highly literate' Islamic youth, but a very ambitious one, knowledgeable in both religious and non-religious matters, aware of contending paradigms in social, economic and political matters and philosophy, as well as the history of both their own nation and the West. This image has freed them from any feeling of inferiority vis-à-vis both the West and the westernising forces in their own society.

At this point, I will once more argue that if one way of doing this has been to develop an intellectual identity through the usual channels, the other has been to build a distinct alternative lifestyle. The latter, however, has not been as easy to create as an image of intellectual elitism produced in an already defined intellectual atmosphere.

Negotiated pleasures: images, sounds and motions mediated by Islamic cultural codes

With the realisation of an Islamic way of everyday life in urban Turkey as part of the revitalisation of Islam, suitable aesthetics, manners and practices have also appeared. I argue that this has given rise also to the emergence of a popular culture which is mainly Islamic in character. It can sound quite paradoxical to talk about an emergent popular culture with Islamic characteristics, to the extent that in modern Turkey, the term 'popular culture' particularly refers to urban culture (though there is no such thing as urban which does not contain elements of the rural or provincial), but not as such to *halk kültürü* ('culture of the people'), which in Turkish usually refers to what is understood as 'folk culture' in English. However, since the urban visibility of Islamisation is also a relatively new phenomenon in republican Turkish society, it becomes clear why there is a need to talk about something like an emergent Islamic popular culture. On the other hand, if, as John Fiske (1994, p.24) argues, 'the popular is a shifting set of allegiances that cross all social categories such as class, gender, age, race, region and so on', it can, therefore, better be described 'in terms of people's felt collectivity rather than in terms of external sociological factors'. That is, feeling above all Muslim and entering into a set of allegiances as a Muslim is sufficient to belong to a felt collectivity centred around Islamic deeds and thoughts, and thus form an Islamic popular culture.

Here, again, the meaning of Islamic may vary according to the degree of enunciation of a broader Islamic language and behaviour. However, insofar as there is no dominant popular culture, rather an interplay between what is 'dominant or subordinate' and what is 'similar or oppositional' (p.24–5), it is possible to talk about an Islamic popular culture as such. In other words, Islamic popular culture, like any other popular culture, is something fluid, open to change, and with no stability. This is not only because it is commercialised, with commodities produced and distributed by a profit-motivated industry,[19] but because, again as Fiske (1994, p.23) argues, 'to be made into popular culture, a commodity must also bear the interests of the people, since popular culture, no matter how industrialised, is not merely consumption, and cannot be adequately described in terms of the buying and selling of commodities. Popular culture is an active process of generating and circulating meanings and pleasures within a social system.' On popular culture, I will finally say that, of course, it does not necessarily cater solely to youth, but youth constitutes the majority of both its consumers and producers. The young are the most active in creating new forms, as well as interpreting and reinterpreting the old ones, and also in developing oppositional practices, tastes and habits, and thereby in creating a popular youth culture.

Nevertheless, if popular culture is the art of 'making do' with what the system provides, as Michel de Certeau showed us,[20] the variety of what the system provided was quite limited in form and content when the prototypes of today's Islamic popular culture first started to appear at the beginning of the 1970s. These were mostly produced with rather ideologically determined artistic aspirations. Thus, literature and cinema appeared as the first areas in which the Islamic youth of the time tried to make their mark. Actually, the project of building a so-called Milli Sinema (National Cinema) had been discussed since the early 1960s by youth rallying around the National Turkish Student Union (Milli Türk Talebe Birliği). Today's well-known Muslim film directors and critics, such as Yücel Çakmaklı and Salih Diriklik, started to take their place in the intellectual cinema market while they were quite young, and the first Islamic film company, Elif Film Kollektif Şirketi, was established in 1968.[21] In 1971, the first commercial Islamic feature movie, adapted from the cult novel by Şule Yüksel Şenler, *Huzur Sokağı* (*Serenity Street*), was filmed by Yücel Çakmaklı under the title of *Birleşen Yollar* (*Crossing Roads*). This met with considerable commercial success, largely due to its leading man and woman, Türkan Şoray and İzzet Günay, the most popular film stars of the time. From this film on, the most favoured themes of Islamic cinema have tended to be the encounter between the good, modest and authentic traditional person and the degenerate, alienated and bad modern one. Such films emphasise the suffering experienced by people because of this, and especially that of the young, who unintentionally and inevitably fall in love with each other, and the discovery of the true path by the misguided modern person, even if this comes too late for a happy ending.[22] Thus, such a dichotomising approach, which pits the old/good against the bad/new, has also been linked with the theme of the sufferings of Muslims under an unjust, non-Islamic system. *Minyeli Abdullah*, which was shot in two separate parts in 1989 and 1990 by Yücel Çakmaklı, became another classic of the Islamic genre. This film, adapted from the eponymous novel by İsmail Hekimoğlu, was much more explicit in its theme of suffering for the struggle to maintain one's Muslim faith.[23] What we saw in the 1990s was slightly different from before, in the sense that overt confrontation between the Islamic and the Western/secular began to be portrayed in a much wider social context and through a greater variety of personalities. *Yalnız Değilsiniz* (*You Are Not Alone*), a film by Mesut Uçakan, a younger successor to Yücel Çakmaklı, is a good example, in that it reflects in a much more detailed way both the political atmosphere and the problems of Islamic youth in the 1990s. In this film, a personal tragedy is located in the social conditions which surround individuals, as in *Minyeli Abdullah*, but an attempt is made to associate the actual motifs with the recent realities of Turkish social life. Thus, this film, like *Minyeli Abdullah*, pulled into the cinemas thousands of people who, by accident or design, would not normally have gone. The aim of those who earlier described themselves as making National Cinema or, later on, as making 'cinema sensitive to Islam' was, and still is, 'to fill the moral void' created by the denial of a place for Islam in society in general and in Turkish cinema in particular. In addition, there have been recent and noted efforts in Islamic cinema to attain religious sublimation via Sufi mysticism, or *tasavvuf*. Hence, the concept of Düş Sineması ('Dream Cinema'), for instance, came into being in the 1990s as an attempt to interpret what Bediüzzaman Said Nursi said about dreams and reality, and also the analogy he drew between films and dreams.[24] Directors like Tarkovsky and Kieslowsky are the exemplars for those who hope to convey Sufi messages in essence and form, and develop a new Islamic language of the cinema. However, for the time being, these two different elements are very careful not to be hard on each other, or direct severe criticisms on even the undeniably rigid social typologies which are developed in Islamic films, as sketched above.

In the context of cinema, the important point is that in the 1990s the positive and negative personality types developed in several Islamic publications, sermons and conversations (either in private gatherings of various religious orders or public meetings) have come to be depicted on the screens in a much more 'concrete' way, and have helped in the emergence of a 'hyperreality' in the sense that Baudrillard (1983) coined the term. For, in this specific case, the social contrast between modern and traditional produced through several texts, like those movies and novels, becomes more real than the real, and replaces the reality itself.[25] This, however, forms models to be publicly discussed and rehearsed at the personal level, while also allowing people to derive productive personal pleasures from these images of the human condition. Similarly, television serials and movies, cartoons and comic scripts, as well as the 'small media', like Islamic postcards, graffiti, stickers and posters started to appear in the market, thereby constituting an important aspect of Islamic popular culture.[26] Rather than being original innovations, however, these appear to be duplications of the forms prevalent in general youth culture. What is new here for Turkish society, where religious purity prevails even in daily conversations – except for some vignettes, like Bektaşi anecdotes[27] – is that not only is the application of certain religious motifs and codes to new popular commercial forms – such as small media, that have nothing to do with conventional symbolic religious commodities, like Arabic religious calligraphies for wall decoration or prayer beads and good-luck charms – even sold on the tables of street vendors, but also the commodification of religious motifs and codes for irony and satirical amusement.

Contrary to such novelties, it can be said that Islamic youth in Turkey has usually followed the protest tradition which first appeared within leftist circles – organising solidarity sessions in large venues with live music, poetry reading, posters and slogans. In such gatherings, there is only one major difference: young women and men sit separately and, apart from occasional swaying to the rhythm of the music, no one ever dances. However, it should also be noted that both during and after the Iranian Revolution such spectacular manifestations and representations also started to be used among Islamic youth, yet they can also be seen as part of a good old leftist revolutionary tradition.[28]

Today, it has also become possible to talk about 'green pop' – Islamic popular music – and 'green serials' – Islamic romance novels.[29] Although Islamic romance is not a new genre, the fact that some recent publications are seen as risqué even in non-Islamic circles is quite a novelty. An important aspect of this literature is that the novels are treated, even by their authors, as 'guide books' for youth, and Islamic youth in particular, on proper intimate relationships or marriages, experiences they may have in romantic relationships and so on. Therefore, the proclamation of Islamic messages, or messages at least not inimical to Islamic ethics, is said to be the ultimate goal of Islamic film-makers, novelists and musicians. Although this appears as a meta-language through which these people explain their course of action, if we accept the axiomatic assumption of Bourdieu (1984) about popular culture, it becomes easier to understand why some texts are widely consumed despite their didactic nature. Bourdieu suggests that popular texts refuse any distance between aesthetic and everyday life, and that, thus, their popularity lies in their closeness to the everyday experiences of the people. In this respect, it can be said that, through popular texts, an aesthetic of popular life is created which meets the cultural experiences and social aspirations of the people. The emergence of the popular music genre known as *arabesk* is a good example of this. If, as is widely held, *arabesk* music, which synthesises Western and Turkish music through an Egyptian influence and has lyrics expressing the desires and frustrations of urbanising people, emerged as the voice of people caught between Western and local/Eastern lifestyles,[30] it becomes easier to understand the essence of the emergent green pop, which is a blend of Islamic hymns (*ilâhî*), militaristic/*cihad* songs (*marş*), folk ballads (*türkü*) and *arabesk*. This kind of music is also fragmented and, although it does not constitute a new musical genre, its various forms, including a highly Western 'New Age' variant, seem to be an important part of Islamic popular youth culture. Another interesting phenomenon to note is that in the airplay of the various private radio stations catering to Islamic people and/or youth, folk ballads tend to predominate. It is especially interesting to observe that the Islamic young, however urbanised, are inclined to listen to folk songs not necessarily as a mere extension of their family backgrounds but rather as a consequence of their search for an authentic identity. Similarly, the lyrics of many green pop songs are either written to protest at the oppressive influence on Muslims of the unjust, non-Islamic order of this mortal world, or to show solidarity with the Muslims of Bosnia, Chechnya and Palestine.[31] One can also hear songs, such as 'Yeni Dünya Düzeni' ('The new world order'), in which Muslims are warned that participation will result in oppression, 'Bir Avuç Dolar İçin' ('For a fistful of dollars'), or 'Ayasofya' (the former 'Haghia Sophia'), which criticises the present museum status of the eponymous mosque, or 'Kalbimdesin' ('You are in my heart'), said to be dedicated to the Prophet Muhammad.[32]

All these popular texts are as fragmented and diverse as other popular texts, but their common feature is that they are all mediated, by and large, by Islamic codes. Nevertheless, non-Islamic texts are also available to Islamic youth, and some, especially the intellectually celebrated, are highly favoured among those who are careful to identify themselves as being outside Islamic party politics. Especially members of Nurist groups (followers of one of the biggest Muslim religious orders in Turkey, derived from the Nakşibendi religious order led by Bediiüzzaman Said Nursi [1876–1960]) – whether those belonging to Fethullah Gülen's community, those affiliated to *tarikats,* or political parties, or those free from such connections, who call themselves radicals – are keen readers of the books of Gabriel Garcia Marquez and Louis Borges, and listen to Pink Floyd, as well as to Yusuf Islam (the former Cat Stevens), and New Age music. They also adopt some behaviours of non-Islamic youth: calling, for example, light chat, mostly 'stag-talk' among men, *geyik muhabbeti* has became common among Turkish youth since the late 1980s. This terminology, I think, was brought into Turkish youth slang from American slang due to its phonetic resemblance to 'geek talk'. This same youth, especially those who describe themselves as radicals, are often students in the better universities in Turkey, and thus are more prone to global influences than others. However, for example, these same young people do not omit to participate in Friday prayers, just like more conservative Islamist youth, though they prefer to form alternative flexible communities and *mescids* ('prayer rooms'), rejecting ordinary mosques, which they see as the mosques of the state, which they equate with the 'Other'.

As any youth grouping does, the Islamic young know how and where to find each other. However, since they do not frequent restaurants and bars, they usually rally around certain bookshops and meet in particular tea gardens and coffee-houses, or at the meeting rooms of certain *evkaf,* as well as both in their dorm-like bachelor apartments and family houses. Unlike non-Islamic youth, they are careful to celebrate religious feasts and holy days, although this is not done merely out of respect for their elders but also for their own amusement. They are quite careful, however, to display a serious, cool appearance in public places, especially when among non-Islamist people. Laughing loudly or making rude jokes, cuddling each other, and making fun of others is rare among Islamic youth. Rather, they prefer to maintain a distant, if not defensive, bearing corresponding to a state of being 'cool' among Westernised Turkish youth. They also like to show how fluently they can use terminology from both Ottoman and modern Turkish, as well as Arabic.[33] In public, the girls seem to be much more serious, and even more vigorous than the boys. They also dress in a much tidier and more fashionable manner than their male counterparts – perhaps because, as I pointed out at the beginning of this chapter, they and their headcovers have become the symbol not only of Islamic youth and popular culture but also of the Islamic movement as a whole.

Images, sounds and motions mediated by Islamic cultural codes that I draw upon in this section as part of a popular Islamic youth culture are also negotiated pleasures experienced by Islamic youth in Turkey in their effort to build a distinct identity. Their excursion among different paths of intellectual/popular, local/global, modern/traditional, however, gives this state of negotiation a nomadic character. Fiske (1994, p.24) asserts that people have to produce nomadic subjectivities because of the necessity of negotiating the problems of everyday life within a complex, highly elaborated social structure and realigning their social allegiances according to the necessities of the moment. The necessity of negotiations to handle not only the problems of everyday life but also the problems of identity is also evident for Islamic youth. Yet, experiencing a kind of 'fixed' identity, like being first and foremost a dedicated Muslim and trying to preserve it throughout several social allegiances, may not lead to the production of subjectivities that are nomadic in the sense that Fiske refers to. However, being both between intellectualism and popular culture, and between the dominant and subordinate, Islamic youth can be said to be experiencing such a 'nomadism', even if the borders of the lands in which they roam are mainly demarcated by Islamic rules and precepts.

Some concluding remarks

The effect of Özalism on Turkish popular culture has been extensively discussed by young Turkish writers.[34] Common themes include the changes in economic perspective, and in the moral orientation of Turkish society as a result of rapid economic integration with the world markets, or, more specifically, that the liberal understanding in Turkey is that the end – 'making it' – invariably justifies the means, as well as the end of the vestiges of Kemalist corporatism and the calling into question of secularism. Perhaps the ending of the monopoly of Turkish Radio and Television (TRT) in 1990 was the most important of these social ruptures, in that it eventually entailed a considerable change in the narrative forms conveying social and political messages to the public. Thus, for the dissemination of Islamic messages and the creation of its popular cultural forms, the commercialisation of television and radio played an important role.[35] I would also argue that the success of the Welfare Party in the municipal elections of 27 March 1994[36] helped Islamic popular culture to find several new opportunities to enlarge its space. Moreover, this encounter with power, perpetuated by the Welfare Party's leadership of the 1996–7 coalition government, gave Islamic cultural codes greater prominence in public life than ever before. This entailed the deployment of cultural symbols as the principal weapons in the battle between Islamic and secular forces in society, a conflict which not only fostered the rapid commodification of cultural symbols but also, and more importantly, facilitated the accessibility and availability of Islamic cultural products. Here, by cultural products, I mean not only consumption goods such as books, cassettes, postcards, clothing and decorative items, but also public places such as parks and gardens, tea and coffee houses, and cafeterias in the shopping areas or districts of the city in which there were previously no such places catering for Islamist customers. In other words, what we have observed in the 1990s, in addition to television and radio broadcasts available for individual consumption, has been the proliferation of other cultural products mainly designed for collective use, in large part due to the financial and moral support of Islamists occupying positions of power.

In Turkey, the expansion of Islamic civil society has always gained impetus in line with the political power of Islamic forces: Muslim and/or Islamic NGOs are likely to increase their influence as well as their number as a consequence of having organic relations with governments and municipalities. However, despite the possibility of their direct or indirect access to power, Islamic circles can manage only to a certain extent to realise strategies to create their own places in which Islamic youth can maximise their own space. Perhaps, unlike their secular counterparts, Islamic youth tends to behave in harmony with the powerful – as long as, of course, the powerful also adhere to Islamic principles. Actually, at this point, it should be noted that Islamic youth with Nurist leanings, for instance, can fall out with Nakşibendis when the latter are in power and vice versa. It is also true to say that in terms of popular culture, aside from the main differentiation revolving around the axes of Islamism and secularism, the main differences within Islamic popular culture itself become observable in their encounter with power, whether Islamic or not. Here, for instance, republican nationalistic discourses appear to be a differentiating characteristic between the Fethullah Gülen branch of Nurist youth groups and Nakşibendi youth as such, as the former has tended to rely upon nationalist discourses and symbols such as love of country and the flag more eagerly and overtly than the latter. Otherwise, different Islamic groups, whether they identify themselves simply as Islamic or as Nurist, Süleymancı, Nakşi, Caferi, radical or whatever, generally share similar tastes and styles in cultural products.

Thus, radio stations, television channels, newspapers, magazines, music groups, novelists, film-makers, commercial operations and publishers, as well as certain districts and public places in the city, can be dominated by different Islamic groups, who develop different discourses to form different political narratives and related ways of doing things, but they may continue to use similar Islamic cultural codes. In this respect, anti-secularism, anti-Kemalism and anti-westernism constitute the common sentiment which unites different Islamic groups. I have tried to emphasise the parameters of such a commonness throughout this chapter in order to explore the basic premises of an emergent Islamic youth culture in Turkey. I argue that it is only on the basis of such an attempt that further studies aiming to differentiate between particular subcultural groups among Turkish Islamic youth can be carried out.

Another important note to make as a concluding point is that, recently, Islamic youth has started to find some supporters from non-Islamic youth when a common stance is maintained against the various manifestations of these 'isms' enumerated above and against certain governmental pressures, like the example I gave at the beginning of this chapter. On the other hand, a distance becomes evident between Islamic and non-Islamic youth due to the former's insistence on using the society's conservative cultural codes and on shutting themselves off from non-religious alternative lifestyles and other kinds of personal or group ventures, and due to their criticism of sexual permissiveness and mixed-sex friendships. For Islamic youth too, the generation gap can pose a problem, particularly when parents do not approve of their children's Islamic identity and they desire to maintain an Islamic way of life. Despite some shared tastes and popular cultural forms, Islamic youth's understanding of entertainment and a good time is considerably different from that of their secular peers. This applies especially to sex segregation, a practice which has been struggled against since the establishment of the republic. The Islamic young are over-cautious about any kind of bodily expression, other than presentational codes regarding veiling for girls and beards and hair for boys, and, in the same way that they carefully avoid dancing, Islamic youth, both male and female, seems not to be interested in sport, apart perhaps from martial arts like karate and judo. Although this point may be deemed unimportant compared to others, I think Jane Desmond (1993–4) is right when she argues that bodily 'texts' are as important as other cultural texts in terms of furthering our understanding of how social identities are signalled, formed and negotiated through bodily movement, including all forms of dance, theatrical performance and ritualised movement. In this sense, Islamic youth restricts its bodily texts mainly to the genuflection of ritual prayers, except for those who are adherents of religious orders where music and dance accompany *zikr* rituals.[37] Humour constitutes another problematic area for Islamic youth, to the extent that didacticism rather than flexibility dominates the discourse in the humour market which caters to Islamic youth. Here again, moral restrictions about the mingling of the sexes, as well as other rules distinguishing the sacred from the profane, which decide what is and is not morally corrupt, define the scope of humour for Islamic youth and the humorous cultural texts that cater to them.[38]

It seems that when Islamic youth is considered, two axes of orientation, one vertical (paradigmatic) and the other horizontal (syntagmatic), have to be taken into account. By the vertical axis, I refer to a scheme of internal, religious–intellectual self-development aiming to reach the higher levels of faith and God's mercy. By the horizontal axis, I refer to the scope of activities and practices that allow Islamic youth to develop popular Islamic cultural texts and practices. In other words, by the latter I am referring to a given set of ways of operating and 'making do' in the course of everyday life. The intersection point of these two axes constitutes the moment where the vertical, faith, coincides with the horizontal, or everyday practices, which together shape the narrative structure of Islamic youth. This, I hope, clarifies what I mean when I suggest that Islamic youth culture should be studied as a panoramic narrative of modern faiths, global assertions and local values as embedded in everyday practices. Political action and ideological discourse are thus inseparable parts of these cultural texts/dialogues. The reason I suggest seeing the whole process as a narrative stems from my agreement with the argument of Michel de Certeau (1984, p.77–8) about the theory of practice and narration, according to which practice cannot be dissociated from narration. As I understand it, first and foremost, in order to be actualised, any practice needs its own story time. Therefore, how the actions of Islamic youth are put into a story form, as intermingled with the incentives of faith, intellectualism and popular culture, gains a specific importance in the investigation of how the memory, reasoning and imagination behind these actions are narrated as they flow within time. Finally, I will argue that in the narrative of Turkish Islamic youth, the question of whether it is worth telling captures one of the basic features of narrative structure, that which Bruner (1991, pp.11–12) calls 'canonicity and breach'. In his view, the important component of a narrative, the one that makes it worth telling, is the breaching of the 'legitimacy' of the canonical script as such. In the case of Islamic youth, this is done by the breaching of the legitimacy of some of the canonical script of the republic, in particular its principles of secularism, westernisation and gender equality. Thus, whether interesting or not, as long as the narrative of the Islamic youth manages to be unusual or innovative, in other words manages to breach that canonical script, it becomes tellable. Nevertheless, as for the other side of the story, the extent to which Islamic youth are able to breach the legitimacy of the canonical script of Islamic fundamentalism will also show us how innovative they can actually be, and make their story worth telling.

Acknowledgment

I shared my interest on Islamic youth culture with students who participated in my seminar on 'Cultural Analysis of Media Texts' in the Department of Sociology at METU during the 1997–8 Spring term. Here, it is a pleasure for me to thank them all. They made invaluable contributions to the enlargement of my knowledge and insight with their enthusiasms and lively discussions. Among them I would particularly like to mention Nur Savaşcı and Nuh Yılmaz, as well as my former thesis student Elif Daşcı, whose meticulous survey of Turkish Islamic feature films, and the interviews she conducted with different members of Islamic cinema circles enriched the scope of this study.

Notes on Chapter 11

1   A recent study conducted by the İstanbul Mülkiyeliler Foundation Social Research Center for the Konrad Adenauer Foundation constitutes a rare exception, in the extent to which its aim was not only to explore political aspects of the behaviour of youth in Turkey, but also social aspects and to a certain extent some cultural aspects. However, although by the time this paper was written the study had not been published, it does not specifically focus on Islamic youth either, though it analyses some of the religious tendencies of the youth. Konrad Adanauer Foundation (1999), *Turkish Youth 98: The Silent Majority Highlighted*, Ankara.

2   See, for example, Doğan (1994), the study published by the Ministry of Culture as one of its reference books.

3   For instance, Şerif Mardin (1978) showed how, in the decade up to 1980, hero-worship and heroism, especially in the name of saving the country, affected the behaviour of youth participating in violent confrontations, as members of leftist and rightist groups.

4   I borrow this idea of difference between the place and the space, in the sense that people use strategies to create places and tactics for spaces, from Michel de Certeau (1984, pp.35–36, 37), who employs these concepts as part of his analyses about the ways in which people cope with a given system in the course of every-day life. For example, he argues that 'By contrast with a strategy... a tactic is a calculated action determined by the absence of proper locus ... The space of a tactic

is the space of the other. Thus it must play on and with a terrain imposed on it and organised by the law of a foreign power... In short, a tactic is an art of the weak.'

5   Willis (1978).

6   Ibid.

7   For a long time studies on youth have almost always been about masculinity, and consequently the gender dimension of the subject was subsumed beneath a perspective saturated with boys' behaviour and styles. For an account criticising such approaches, a pioneering study, see, for example, McRobbie and Garber (1976). Also, for an early feminist critique of subcultural studies, see McRobbie (1980) and (1991). See also Michael Brake, 'The Invisible Girl: The Culture of Femininity Versus Masculinism', in Brake (1985). Among a few exceptional studies which particularly focus on female Muslim youth or include them, see, for example, Fuglesng (1994); also Davis and Davis (1988). Also see a re-evaluation from this study (1995).

8   See H. Wulff, 'Introducing youth culture in its own right, the state of art and new possibilities', in Amid-Talai and Wulff (eds) (1995), p.3.

9   Amid-Talai, Vered, 'Conclusion: The 'multi' cultural youth', in Amid-Talai and Wulff (eds) (1995), p.224.

10   See Mardin(1994).

11   For a broader definition of the term *site*, see Introduction in this volume.

12   See Saktanber (1997) and (forthcoming).

13   Although the term *abla* is used to address an older sister, it is used also for older female neighbours and friends.

14   Saktanber (1994), pp.113–14.

15   Meeker (1991) and (1994). I am, of course, aware of the fact that this term was first coined by W. Montgomery Watt (1963) in his famous study on Al-Gazali, yet here I point to the specific use of the term in the contemporary Turkish case.

16   Meeker (1994), p.159. Meeker (1991) focuses especially on İsmet Özel, Ali Bulaç and Rasim Özdenören as examples of Muslim intellectuals; however, Abdurrahman Dilipak, for example, can very well fit the same account.

17   See Acar (1991) and (1995). Also, see in the same volume Arat (1995).

18   For example, Cihan Aktaş, one of the most influential Islamic female intellectual figures, among others like Fatma Karabıyık Barbarosoğlu, Zekiye Oğuzhan, Nazife Şişman and A. Zeynep Tozduman, started to publish her books from the second half of the 1980s, but has she only become known to a wider audience since the 1990s. See Cihan Aktaş, *Kadının Serüveni* (*Adventure of the Woman*), Istanbul, 1986; *Sistem İçinde Kadın* (*Women within the System*), Istanbul, 1988); *Tanzimattan Günümüze Kılık Kıyafet* (*Clothing from Tanzimat to the Present*), Cilt 1, 2, Istanbul, 1989, 1990); *Tessettür ve Toplum, Başörtülü Öğrencilerin Toplumsal Kökeni Üzerine Bir İnceleme* (*Veiling and Society: A Study on the Social Backgrounds of Veiled Students*), Istanbul, 1992; *Modernizmin Evsizliği ve Ailenin Gerekliliği* (*The Homelessness of Modernism and the Necessity of the Family*), Istanbul, 1992; *Mahremiyetin Tükenişi* (*Exhaustion of Privacy*), Istanbul, 1995. Also see Fatma Karabıyık Barbarosoğlu, *Modernleşme Sürecinde Moda ve Zihniyet* (*Fashion and Mentality in the Process of Modernisation*), Istanbul, 1995; Aysel Zeynep Tozduman, *Islam ve Batı Gözüyle Kadın* (*Women with the Eye of Islam and the West*), Istanbul,

1991, Nazife Şişman, *Başörtüsü Mağdurlarından Anlatılmamış Hikayeler* (*Untold Stories from the Victims of Headcover*), Istanbul, 1998; Zekiye Oğuzhan, *Başörtüsü Günlüğü* (*The Journal of Headcover*), Istanbul, 1998.

19 For an argument on the production of culture and its relation to the commercialisation of symbolic goods in the Turkish Islamic context, see Chapter 12.

20 See de Certeau, Michel (1984), '"Making Do" Uses and Tactics'. Also, see in the same volume his arguments on 'Popular Cultures: Ordinary Language'. For what he calls 'the very ancient art of "making do"', among many examples he provides one quite suitable for the point that I want to make here. De Certeau argues that we need some operational schemas to be able to carry out our daily lives. These "ways of operating" – ways of walking, reading, producing, speaking, etc ... are similar to "instructions for use", and they create a certain play in the machine through a stratification of difference and interfering kinds of functioning. Although the uses and tactics that an African immigrant employs in France are given as the example here (p.30), I believe it fits well to explain the situation of anybody who is supposed to "find ways of using the constraining order of place or of language" whether this language be his/her own or this place his/her native town.'

21 See Diriklik (1995), p.26.

22 In the four years after *Birleşen Yollar*, Yücel Çakmaklı made a series of movies such as *Çile* (*Ordeal*, 1972), *Zehra* (1973), *Oğlum Osman* (*Osman My Son*, 1973), *Memleketim* (*My Home Town*, 1974). In all of them, the problems of the 'over-westernisation' of youth constitute the main theme, in lower and upper classes, the stories being set both in Turkey (Istanbul) and Western countries like Germany (*Osman My Son*) and Austria (*My Home Town*), which allowed him to make overt comparisons between the local and foreign, namely the European. In all these movies, the hero or heroine finally finds the true path and converts or returns to Islam after experiencing a great deal of suffering at the personal level due to rootlessness and alienation from to his/her own local, namely Islamic, cultural values.

23 The setting of this novel, as well as the film, is not Turkey either (see note 22) but Egypt, which allows both the author and the director to convey their messages about the repression and violence that the state imposes on Muslims. This also provides an opportunity to show the association between westernisation as such and colonisation, which took place in Egypt. A similar point is made by Mardin (1994, p.xi) for the setting of the novel.

24 See Yalsızuçanlar (1994) and Kabil, Şasa and Yalsızuçanlar(1997).

25 For such an interpretation of 'hyperreality', see, for example, Best and Kellner (1998).

26 I must note that Islamic stickers are quite a new product for the Islamic cultural market. On the other hand, it was in 1993 that for the first time I came across Islamic 'graffiti', in the form of small postcards, prepared so that they could be attached to things, at a Religious Books Fair held under the Kocatepe Mosque, the largest mosque in Ankara. In 1998, some bookshop and stationery shop owners in Ankara reported that since there is no demand for these specific postcards their production stopped. Nevertheless, to find a seven-volume series on Islamic graffiti is not surprising. Köşk (1997).

27   These are stories said to be told by the dervishes of the Bektaşi order, which are ironically yet politely contemptuous of orthodoxy and are common among the Alevi people as well as people who support religious free-thinking rather than conservative Sunnis.

28   See, for example, the chapter in Fischer and Abedi (1990), pp.335–79.

29   New Islamic pop music is discussed by İsmail Safter as 'Tears and Holy Wars in Cassettes' and 'Green Pop of Hizbullah in the South-East' in the Turkish daily *Radikal* (14–15 October 1997). One month later, in the same daily, a serial appeared under the title of 'Islamists Love Bestsellers', also calling the subject 'green love', prepared by Şebnem Aksoy and Pervin Kaplan, *Radikal* (5–6–7 November 1997). Since green is widely accepted as the symbolic colour of Islam, these new Islamic popular cultural products are allegorically labelled in the Turkish media as 'green pop', 'green love' etc.

30   See, for example, Özbek (1997), for example pp.212–17. In her analysis, she particularly examines the songs and lyrics of the cult figure of Turkish *arabesk* music, Orhan Gencebay. For a very comprehensive analysis on *arabesk* music in Turkey, see Stokes (1992).

31   The band called Grup Kıvılcım (Group Spark) and their cassette *Çeçen Dansı*, (*The Dance of the Chechen*), as well as *Sızı* (*Grief*), the cassette of solo artist Ömer Karaoğlu, and *Şehidler Kervanı* (*Caravan of Martyrs*) by the group Menzil (Destination) can be given as examples of this style. There are, of course, others who define their music as 'slow-rock', like Aykut Kuşkaya, whose most famous cassette is *Umut Sancısı* (*Agony of Hope*); his music is often compared with Ahmet Kaya, a widely known 'protest' pop-music star among youth with neo-leftist leanings. (At the time this article was written Ahmet Kaya had not emphasised his Kurdish identity, and, depending on the reactions he received from pop music circles, he had not exiled himself voluntarily to Paris either).

32   I selected these songs from the cassette *Bir Güneş Doğuyor, 1* (*A Sun is Born, 1*), produced by three young Islamist men whose portraits on the cassette cover somehow attest to their Islamic identity. As any Turkish observer would say, they are definitely neither rock nor pop stars, but ordinary modest young Muslim men.

33   For the emergence of such a blend in Turkish language as a relatively new trend and how it appears a necessity for Islamic intellectual expression, as well as the vernacular usage, see Chapter 5.

34   See, for example, Gürbilek (1992); Kozanoğlu (1992), (1995) and (1997).

35   For a very resourceful discussion on the effects of the commercialisation of television on cultural politics in general, and on Islamic politics and cultural codes in particular, see Öncü (1994). On a similar subject, for a more general assessment of the diminishing effect of the state on the media in the Middle East, see Norton (1999).

36   In this election, the Welfare Party won the municipalities of 28 big cities, including Istanbul and Ankara, and in the latter the same success was also achieved in the elections of 18 April 1998 by the Virtue Party, the successor of the Welfare Party.

37   Although it differs in action and performance in general terms, religious *zikr* is praising God with recitation of litanies, the act of glorifying God. It is also understood as a dervish religious service. However, in the history of Islam, certain

religious orders like the Nakshibendis appeared as a distinct order, differentiating themselves from others with purging music and dance in their *zikr*. See, for example, Schimmel (1986).

38   In 1980, Necdet Konak started publication of a comic magazine called *Dinozor* (*Dinosaur*), and others, like *Çıngar*, *Cümbüş* and *Flit*, followed this example after 1990, but did not survive more than one or two years. However, a magazine called *Ustra* (*Razor*), published between 1994 and 1997, became the most famous of them all, mainly because of its creator, Hasan Kaçan, a prominent Turkish caricaturist who was previously known as a leftist but was converted to Islam at the turn of the 1990s. Upon conversion, his main concern became to create a type of caricature which would distance itself from what he called the exploitation of sexuality, nudity and sexual perversion.

References

Acar, Feride (1991), 'Women in the Ideology of Islamic Revivalism in Turkey: Three Islamic Women's Journal', in Richard L. Tapper (ed.), *Islam in Modern Turkey*, I.B. Tauris, London

— (1995), 'Women and Islamism in Turkey', in Şirin Tekeli (ed.), *Women in Modern Turkish Society*, Zed Books Ltd, London

Aksoy, Şebnem and Pervin Kaplan, 'İslamcı Aşk', *Radikal*, 5–6–7 November 1997.

Arat, Yeşim (1995), 'Feminism and Islam: Considerations on the Journal of Kadın ve Aile', in Şirin Tekeli (ed.), *Women in Modern Turkish Society*, Zed Books Ltd, London

Aktaş, Cihan (1986), *Kadının Serüveni*, Girişim, Istanbul

— (1988), *Sistem İçinde Kadın*, Beyan Yayınları, Istanbul

— (1989/90), *Tanzimattan Günümüze Kılık Kıyafet*, vols 1, 2, Nehir Yayınları, Istanbul

— (1992), *Tessettür ve Toplum, Başörtülü Öğrencilerin Toplumsal Kökeni Üzerine Bir İnceleme*, Nehir Yayınları, Istanbul

— (1992), *Modernizmin Evsizliği ve Ailenin Gerekliliği*, Beyan Yayınları, Istanbul

Amid-Talai, Vered and Helena Wulff (1995), *Youth Cultures*, Routledge, London and New York

Barbarosoğlu Karabıyık, Fatma (1995), *Modernleşme Sürecinde Moda ve Zihniyet*, İz Yayıncılık, Istanbul

Best, Steven and Douglas Kellner (1998), 'Exploring Modernity, Post-Modern Theory: Critical Interrogations', in Arthur Asa Berger (ed.), *The Postmodern Presence* Walnut Creek, London, Altamira Press, New Delhi

Baudrillard, Jean (1983), *Simulations*, Semiotext, New York, NY

Brake, Michael (1985), *Comparative Youth Culture*, Routledge & Kegan Paul, London and New York

Bruner, Jerome (1991), 'Narrative Construction of Reality', *Critical Inquiry*, no 18 (Autumn), pp.1–21.

Bourdieu, Pierre (1984), *Distinction: A Social Critique of the Judgement of Taste*, Routledge, London

Daşcı, Elif (1998), 'The Impact of Islamic Ideologies on the Turkish Cinema: A Study on the Popular Products of Milli Sinema between 1970s and 1990s', unpublished MA thesis, METU, Ankara

Davis, Susan S. and A. Douglas Davis (1988), *Adolescence in a Moroccan Town*, Rutgers University Press, New Brunswick, NJ

— (1995), '"The Mosque and Satellite": Media and Adolescence in a Moroccan Town', *Journal of Youth and Adolescence*, vol. 24, no 5, pp.577–93

de Certeau, Michel (1984), *The Practice of Everyday Life*, University of California Press, Berkeley, CA

Desmond, C. Jane (1993–4), 'Embodying Difference: Issues in Dance and Cultural Studies', *Cultural Critique*, Winter, pp.33–63.

Diriklik, Salih (1995), *Fleşbek: Türk Sinema-TV'sinde İslami Endişeler ve Çizgi Dışı Oluşumlar V I (Flashback, Exceptional Incidents and Islamic Apprehensions in the Turkish Cinema-TV*, Söğüt Ofset, Istanbul

Doğan, İsmail (1994), *Bir Altkültür Olarak Ankara Yüksel Caddesi Gençliği (The Youth of Ankara's Yüksel Street as a Subculture*, T.C. Kültür Bakanlığı Milli Kütüphane Basımevi, Ankara

Fiske, John (1994), *Understanding Popular Culture*, 6th edition, Routledge, London and New York

Fischer, Michael M.J. and Mehdi Abedi (1990), *Debating Muslims: Cultural Dialogues in Postmodernity and Tradition*, University of Wisconsin Press, WI

Fuglesng, Miniou (1994), *Veils and Videos: Female Youth Culture on the Kenyan coast*, Stockholm University, Stockholm

Gürbilek, Nurdan (1992), *Vitrinde Yaşamak (Living in the Shop Window)*, Metis, Istanbul

Hall, Stuart and Tony Jefferson (eds) (1976), *Resistance Through Rituals*, Hutchinson, London

Hebdige, Dick (1979), *Subculture: The Meaning of Style*, Routledge, London and New York

Kabil, İhsan, Ayşe Şasa and Sadık Yalsızuçanlar (1997), *Düş, Gerçeklik ve Sinema (Dream, Reality and the Cinema)*, İz Yayınları, Istanbul

Konrad Adanauer Foundation (1999), *Turkish Youth 98: The Silent Majority Highlighted*, Ofset Fotomat, Ankara

Kozanoğlu, Can (1992), *Cilalı İmaj Devri (Polished Image Age)*, İletişim, Istanbul

— (1995), *Pop Çağı Ateşi (Pop Age Fire)*, İletişim, Istanbul

— (1997), *Internet Dolunay Cemaat (Internet, Fullmoon, Fethullah Gülen Community)*, İletişim, Istanbul

Köşk, Sadi (ed.) (1997), *Duvardan Duvara Yazılar (Wall to Wall Graffiti)*, 7 vols, Istanbul, Vural Yayıncılık

Mardin, Şerif (1978), 'Youth and Violence in Turkey', *European Archives of Sociology*, no 19, pp.229–54

— (1991), 'The Just and the Unjust', *Daedalus*, vol. 120, no 3, pp.113–29

— (ed.) (1994), 'Introduction', in *Cultural Transitions in the Middle East*, E.J. Brill, Leiden

Meeker, Michael M. (1991), 'The New Muslim Intellectuals in the Republic of Turkey', in Richard L. Tapper (ed.), *Islam in Modern Turkey* (I.B.Tauris, London and New York

— (1994), 'The Muslim Intellectual and His Audience: A New Configuration of Writer and Reader among Believers in the Republic of Turkey', in Şerif Mardin (ed.), *Cultural Transitions in the Middle East*, E.J. Brill, Leiden

McRobbie, Angela and Jenny Garber (1976), 'Girls and Subcultures: An Exploration', in Stuart Hall and Tony Jefferson (eds), *Resistance Through Rituals*, Hutchinson, London

McRobbie, Angela (1980), 'Settling Accounts with Subcultures: A Feminist Critique',
     Screen, no 34, pp.37–49.
— (1990), *Feminism and Youth Culture*, Hyman, Boston, MA
Norton, Augustus Richard (1999), 'The New Media, Civic Pluralism and the Slowly
     Retreating State', in Dale F. Eickelman and Jon W. Anderson (eds). *New Media in
     the Muslim World: The Emerging Public Sphere*, Indiana University Press,
     Bloomington and Indianapolis, IN
Oğuzhan, Zekiye (1998), *Başörtüsü Günlüğü*, İz Yayınları, Istanbul
Öncü, Ayşe (1994), 'Packaging Islam: Cultural Politics on the Landscape of Turkish
     Commercial Television', *New Perspectives on Turkey* (Spring), pp.13–36
Özbek, Meral (1997), 'Arabesk Culture: A Case of Modernisation and Popular
     Identity', in Sibel Bozdoğan and Reşat Kasaba (eds), *Rethinking Modernity and
     National Identity in Turkey*, University of Washington Press, Seattle, WA, and London
Safter, İsmail, 'Yeşil Pop', *Radikal*, 14–15 October 1997
Saktanber, Ayşe (1994), 'Becoming the 'Other' as a Muslim in Turkey: Turkish Women
     vs Islamist Women', *New Perspectives on Turkey*, no 11 (Fall), pp.99–133
— (1997), 'Formation of a Middle Class Ethos and its Quotidian: Revitalising Islam in
     Urban Turkey', in Ayşe Öncü and Petra Weyland (eds), *Space, Culture and Power:
     New Identities in Globalising Cities*, Zed Books, London
— (Forthcoming), *Living Islam: Women, Religion and Politicisation of Culture in Turkey*,
     I.B.Tauris, London
Schimmel, Ann-Marie (1986), *Mystical Dimension of Islam*, The University of North
     Carolina Press, Chapel Hill, NC
Stokes, Martin (1992), *The Arabesk Debate: Music and Musicians in Modern Turkey*,
     Clarendon Press, Oxford
Şişman, Nazife (1996), *Başörtüsü Mağdurlarından Anlatılmamış Hikayeler*, İz
     Yayıncılık, Istanbul
Tozduman, Aysel Zeynep (1991), *İslam ve Batı Gözüyle Kadın*, Seha Yayınları, Istanbul
Watt, Montgomery W. (1963), *Muslim Intellectual*, Edinburgh University Press,
     Edinburgh
Willis, Paul (1978), *Profane Culture*, Routledge & Kegan Paul, London
Yalsızuçanlar, Sadık (1994), *Düş Sineması (Dream Cinema)*, ISAV, Ankara

12

Pink Card Blues[1]: Trouble and Strife at the Crossroads of Gender

Deniz Kandiyoti

Introduction

Few social groups can boast the visibility and media attention that male-to-female transsexuals have received in Turkey in recent years. At one point, hardly a month went by without some feature in a popular magazine or a television interview. The cartoonist Latif Demirci captured this frenzied interest with his depiction of an apartment block in a notorious backstreet of Istanbul. Through each window, a transsexual could be seen being interviewed, filmed or recorded, with a queue of journalists waiting in the street outside and being invited to be patient by building janitors. A recent book offering vignettes on modern Turkey devoted an entire chapter to an interview with Sisi, a famous transsexual.[2] More intriguingly, the popular magazine *Kim* featured an article that appeared to be recording a complaint by the male gay community about these flashy upstarts, voicing an attempt to distance themselves from them.[3] Their contention was that millions of homosexual men, the true heirs of Ottoman tradition forced into retreat after post-Tanzimat westernisation, were having to lead secretive lives for fear of being found out, while a handful of transsexuals were making quick money from prostitution. Whatever the scale of this urban phenomenon, it appears to have caught the public imagination and stirred up an almost voyeuristic curiosity.

It was not merely their entrance into the arena of public debate that aroused my interest in transsexuals. My previous work had led me to explore various facets of gender ideology in Turkey, primarily in relation to the subordination of women. It was not long, however, before I realised that the institutions shaping and reproducing hegemonic masculinity were central to the maintenance of relations of power and hierarchy in the society as a whole.[4] Dominant constructions of masculinity define the standards against which other masculinities are evaluated, and some may emerge as the bearers of subordinate identities. Being born male and having to craft a female self inevitably opens access to the 'backstage' of gender ideology, to aspects of the cultural 'small print' that may easily remain hidden from view for those who have experienced their gender as somehow 'unproblematic'.[5]

It was with a view to uncovering this often contradictory and ambiguous small print that I initially approached my subject. The meaning of the transgression implied by transsexualism had already become the subject of a heated controversy among feminist theorists. Some, like Raymond (1979), saw transsexualism as the product of a society with strictly bipolar gender roles, and denied the possibility that transsexuals could ever truly share the experience of womanhood, going as far as accusing them of being implicated in the oppression of women. Other writers also evaluated transsexualism as a reinstatement of the most stereo-typical notions of femininity and heterosexist understandings of the meaning of womanhood.[6] Others, on the other hand, contended that transsexualism as well as other cross-gender phenomena had the potential to unsettle the rigid binaries of male and female and presented subversive possibilities, challenging our dominant understanding of sex and gender.[7] The more far-reaching implication of these various positions was that the fundamental distinction between sex, as a biological given, and gender, as culturally acquired, which underwrote so much of con-temporary feminist theory was being re-examined and contested.[8] 'Sex', as Butler (1993, p.2) put it, 'is, thus, not simply what one has, or a static description of what one is: it will be one of the norms by which the 'one' becomes viable at all, that which qualifies a body for life within the domain of cultural intelligibility.' Sex itself could, therefore, be evoked as a cultural norm which governs the materialisation of bodies.

It was also clear to me, however, that the complex processes of identification, inclusion and exclusion that go into the formation of sexed subjects are historically and culturally specific. From this perspective, the appearance and cultural regulation of trans-gender phenomena, which are by no means new, must be understood in their local contexts. In a rare contribution on hermaphrodites in Islamic medieval law, Sanders (1991), for instance, notes an absence of anxiety about homosexuality which pervades European texts on hermaphroditism, but an extreme concern about maintaining the 'gendered integrity of their world', hence painstaking efforts at correctly classifying and gendering the ambiguous body for the purposes of its appropriate insertion into Muslim ritual and into the formation of social and familial ties. In contemporary ethnographies, local examples range from the *xanith* in Oman, male transvestites who do not necessarily tamper with their male genitalia,[9] to the *hijra* of the Indian sub-continent, who do.[10]

I shall argue in this chapter that transsexualism in Turkey is a uniquely modern possibility, both as an identity and as a medical category (above and beyond the role of the medical establishment in producing transsexual bodies). My argument will unfold on three different levels. The first will involve an investigation of the legal–administrative framework for the regulation of gender in contemporary Turkey and the medical discourse which defines transsexuals. This account will be cross-cut by the narratives of some transsexuals on how they categorise them-selves and each other, and what constitutes 'passing' as a woman. The second will be a description of transsexuals as part of an 'illegal' urban subculture with its own networks of support and communication and its own coded dialect. Finally, I will insert the recent visibility of transsexuals in Istanbul into the broader context of increasing globalisation of images and fashions, the politicisation of identities and a growing entertainment sector ranging from strip-clubs to street prostitution. Transsexuals in Turkey, as elsewhere, appear as the unsettling harbingers of a new urban scene; the mega-metropolis where everything is on display and for sale, a new arena where the landscapes and, especially, the nightscapes of Istanbul, Rio, New York and Bangkok may begin to shade into one another.

What does it take to be a woman

In Turkey one's properly documented identity matters a great deal. Much black humour revolves around tales of mistaken or misrecorded identity.[11] However, the acquisition of an identity card is for the most part a routine and uneventful matter. The format and appearance of these cards changed some years ago. When I handed in my rather drab, unisex grey notebook to receive my new identity card under plastic cover, I hardly noticed that its colour was pink. This is not the case for the many men who have to build intricate life strategies around the acquisition of this precious commodity, the pink card which provides the legal affirmation of their new identity as women. The legislation that has made this change possible is of relatively recent origin. It was based on the precedent of Bülent Ersoy, a popular singer who applied to the courts for a legal recognition of his identity as a woman following a sex-change operation in London. Eventually, a new article was added to the 29th clause of the Turkish Civil Code in 1988, stating that, 'In cases where there has been a change of sex after birth documented by a report from a committee of medical experts, the necessary amendments are made to the birth certificate'.[12] This was the outcome of a lengthy legal battle dating from 1981, at which time the military regime then in power had a particularly uncompromising stance on any form of social deviance.[13] Despite these changes, the medical and legal preconditions for sex-change surgery have not yet been fully worked out, creating areas of uncertainty, tension and potential medical malpractice. Şahika Yüksel made a strong case for the recognition of transsexuality (as distinct from transvestism and homosexuality) as a *sui generis* category, and for the legalisation of sex-change surgery after an appropriate interval for psychotherapy and concerted medical opinion.[14] Illegality opens the way to unscrupulous forms of medical practice for profit, and may compound the difficulties of an already stigmatised group. Indeed, an article titled 'Butcher of Travestis' in the magazine *Aktüel* revealed that some transsexuals were subjected to castration, rather than vaginal reconstruction, under local anaesthesia in hurried and unhygienic conditions. The victims refer to themselves as *duvar*, literally meaning 'walls', and consider their sexuality irreversibly blighted.

There is little doubt that the existence of transsexuals as an increasingly visible group raises a host of uncomfortable questions concerning the accommodation of a deviant minority to a generally conservative society, especially in the morally and existentially loaded realms of sexuality and gender identity. This is captured in a book of short stories by the gifted gay writer Murathan Mungan (1987), featuring a poignant tale titled 'The Tears of Love or Rapunzel and the Vagabond'. A tough cab-driver, Efkar, falls desperately in love with a beautiful young man, Ümit, who reciprocates his feelings. They have an intense and passionate love affair but problems arise as the illicit nature of their relationship and the attendant social pressures intrude into and erode their peace of mind. Efkar, who cannot bear the pressure any longer and wants to 'regularise' their status as a couple, demands the ultimate sacrifice of Ümit as a token of his love: a sex-change operation. Ümit complies but is abandoned by Efkar nine months later; he returns to a sad life of heavy drinking and she becomes a prostitute.

One of the most noteworthy features of this tale is the contingency of its out-come. The factors that finally lend it inevitability are exogenous and result from societal pressures over which the protagonists feel they have little control. One senses a yearning for a different world in which they could live happily ever after without having to alter their bodies. The authorial voice is that of a male gay expressing the despair of a persecuted minority.

This stands in stark contrast to both medical discourse and the narratives that some transsexuals construct about themselves. The medical diagnosis, based on *Diagnostic and Statistical Manual*, third edition, presents transsexualism as a form of deep-seated gender dysphoria which is distinct from both transvestism and homosexuality, the signs of which may appear early in life and require corrective surgery to restore the patient, who may be given to intense depression and suicidal tendencies, to better mental health.[15] The causes of this condition are considered to be primarily endogenous and there is no ambiguity over patients' desire to rid themselves of the physical characteristics of their biological sex. The legal path to obtaining a new identity card goes, in principle, through at least two years of living as the other sex, with psychotherapy, progressive hormone treatment, breast implants and genital surgery only after an evaluation by a team of medical experts. In practice, however, most transsexuals apply for their new identity card *post facto*, after either having undergone sex-change surgery or being at an advanced stage of hormone therapy and cosmetic surgery. They have to initiate a court case with a petition for a change of identity cards. Referral to a medical authority acting on behalf of the court follows, and a committee of experts establishes whether the applicants are of sound mind and whether their biological sex con-stitutes a serious threat to their mental health. Obtaining such a report opens the way for a legal change of identity. They also undergo a thorough post-operative medical examination, in which features such as depth of the vagina are evaluated, before being finally issued their pink card.

The actual trajectories of transsexuals may, in fact, be extremely diverse, and there appears to be no self-evident 'end-point' for their reconstructed identity. In local parlance, they are referred to as *travesti*, the more common colloquial appellation being *dönme*.[16] They refer to themselves as *lubinya*, a term which is part of a broader subcultural vocabulary to which I shall return later. Most work as prostitutes. Whatever the diversity of their experiences, however, there are some striking commonalities in their reports of the phases that lead to 'passing' as a woman. Sevda,[17] who has just undergone sex-change surgery, recounts her different phases as follows:

> I was active as a gay from the age of 16. When I became a transvestite, my hormone and cosmetic surgery were not advanced enough to conceal my beard and my

features. This is when I went through my *frapan* phase.[18] I used to compensate by wearing very high heels, short skirts and lots of make-up. As I become more confident about my body, I felt I could be less exaggeratedly feminine.

Hale, who looks like a plain, petite woman in her thirties, has had no surgery at all, and has achieved remarkable results on hormone therapy only. She says, 'Hormones love me. Look [wobbling her breasts, which are clearly not silicone implants], they are mine, all natural. I also don't have to wear any make-up.' I had to admit that her skin, body posture, bone structure and general appearance could have fooled me. She smiled contentedly. This is the ultimate achievement, becoming *doğal* ('natural'), when you can afford not to wear any make-up and to go around in plain, workaday clothes. Nuşin achieved this stage quite a while ago. She walks in wearing a T-shirt, jeans and sandals, without make-up and long, loose auburn hair. She pulls out a newspaper article about her ongoing litigation with a man she had hit with her car, in which she is described as 'a young housewife'. She also shows me her pink identity card. She has clearly made it. She is in the

Sevda looking in a hand-mirror (picture Mary Robert)

club circuit in Europe and is affluent enough not to have to 'work' while she is in Istanbul. She, nonetheless, has her newspaper article ready at hand as the ultimate affirmation of her success.

Many transsexual narratives mirror the determinism of medical discourse when it comes to talking about the inevitability of the path eventually chosen. Hale, who led a sheltered life in the provinces, reports that she always knew she wanted to be a woman: 'I remember being 12 years old and going to bed praying "Please God let me wake up as a woman". Of course, then I didn't know it was possible'.[19]

Ayça started hormone treatment when she was 14, and got her sex-change surgery when she was 18. She was in a relationship with a man, which made it easier for her. She had no doubts at all that she did what she had to do, and spoke disparagingly of those who have spent time in therapy groups: 'What they do there is waste your time and hold you back. What they are really trying to do is to turn you around and talk you out of it. I always went private and never bothered with any of this.'

Nonetheless, there are constant attempts to sort out the 'fakes' from the 'real' transsexuals in a world where unreconstructed male prostitutes also work as *travestis*. Pointing to a window across the street, where I discern two silhouettes, Ayça comments, 'These guys over there ... They only do it for the money. They don't go in for the hormones or anything like that. If you look at them up close you can see they barely attempt to conceal their beard. They even think that when they save enough money they will go back to where they've come from and get married. It's not so easy, of course. Anyhow, we don't talk to them.' Everyone present nods in assent.

What is it that makes a 'real' woman? Hale, who is unoperated, is one of those highest on the scale of 'natural' femininity, and most self-assured in this respect. She has been in a long-term relationship with a married man whose family knows about her. Sevda, who looks much more masculine, provides a clue when she describes the following incident: 'I was involved in a traffic accident with a friend who was covered in blood. When they finally took her away, I fainted. In the end, the doctors paid as much attention to me as to her. It was awful, but I consoled myself thinking that at least these were womanly feelings (*kadınca duygular*).' Looks may be important, but psychological femininity is the ultimate goal, since it is the successful performance of the feminine that qualifies one for womanhood.

These feelings and attitudes are carefully monitored and cultivated, and comments are freely exchanged about an individual's state of readiness for the 'final' operation. Nuşin, for instance, thinks that Sevda may have gone for it too soon. A visiting male gay friend, Hasan, comments: 'She had a perfectly good life as a gay. But when her mother remarried and left town and her grandmother took her in she had to work, and started out as a transvestite. Then she went on to this. For a whole year I stopped talking to her. But now I have to accept it.' Hasan's comments indicate that he sees Sevda as having exercised a choice – one that was partly prompted by her circumstances but one he may also have experienced as disloyalty to her male gay persona. Sevda, herself, is quite sure that she wants a woman's body, but recognises it takes practice to become a woman, and especially to achieve a female orgasm: 'It will require a great deal of concentration at first. But my doctor explained that it is possible'.

Sevda also acknowledges the force of peer pressure once you have embarked on the pursuit of feminine perfection. There is merciless teasing (*koliye almak*), preferably in the presence of boyfriends, to cause the victim maximum embarrassment. She recalls an incident in which someone tossed a razor blade into the lap of one of the girls while she was in the company of a man, with the comment, 'Darling, your beard is showing'. Appearance becomes a subject of constant preoccupation, fine-tuning and sometimes bitter rivalry and envy.

Writing on *travestis* in Salvador, Brazil, Cornwall (1994) comments, 'The juxtaposition of male and female attributes forms part of the allure of the *travestis* and defines the value of the commodity they sell'. Indeed, many shun the sex-change operation as they may be required to perform as men; their feminine appearance acts to mask homoerotic desire and helps middle-class customers to enact macho roles in public whilst indulging their hidden fantasies.

Sevda concedes that her sex-change operation may have cost her quite a few clients, but she didn't care, as she was in love with a man who helped pay for her surgery. In any case, those who have embarked on hormone treatment claim to have lost the full use of their male genitals and become 'without function' (*fonksyonsuz*). Nonetheless, they freely acknowledge that they continue to serve a purpose: 'Never mind, even if it is good for nothing, keep it there. The sultan with a handle (*kulplu sultan*) is better than one with none.' Sevda confided later that many are, in fact, fully functional and able to fetch high prices. When pressed on this question, she muses on the ambiguities of male desire and the fact that being women-with-a-difference makes them better suited to understand what men really want: 'After all, we are of male origin (*erkek kökenli*), and we know everything that turns them on'.

Ayça suggests, however, that there may be 'fake' transsexuals, those who felt pressured into making tactical decisions about their identity: 'It got particularly bad under the military regime, you know. They were carted off to police stations and had their hair cut off and were beaten. Some were exiled to Eskişehir. After that, many had to mutilate themselves (*kendilerine kıydılar*).' Being caught as a prostitute with a pink card may have been bad enough, but looking like a woman and producing a blue card was quite another matter. Due to a loophole in the law even post-operative transsexuals could not be arrested as prostitutes if they still had a blue card; they were therefore rounded up and released again, but not before being subjected to severe beatings and humiliation.[20]

Military service, a compulsory stage for all adult men, is generally avoided through the production of a medical certificate bearing the comment 'psycho-sexual deviation'. In personal terms, this may provoke a breaking-point in familial relations. Sevda's father wanted her (him) to enlist at the age of 18, even though she was an excellent student clearly headed towards university education, because he felt the army might 'sort him out'. He threatened never to speak to her again if she didn't enlist; she didn't and they have never spoken again. The only one present during our conversation who had done military service was Nevin, who said she did it out of choice: 'I could have got out of it with a medical certificate, but I did it out of obstinacy. At first, I was harassed by the men, so I finally decided to go to the commander. I said, 'Sir, I am gay, but with your permission I would like to complete my service'. He was a devout man who never missed his prayers. He called the corporal and said, 'Corporal, I entrust this boy to you. See to it that no harm comes to him.' After that, I never undressed in front of the men and showered in the officers' bathroom. I really had a very easy time.'

It should be clear from the foregoing that a whole continuum of identities may co-exist under the broad label of *travesti*. I was able to discern only three, although there may conceivably be others: those who are assumed to impersonate women for profit, but are anatomically untransformed (this comes closest to transvestism proper, which involves cross-dressing only, but is not normally defined as 'opportunistic'); those who may have been 'forced' into tactical choices to undergo surgery by social coercion or the expectations of a partner; and those who claim to be or want to become 'real' women and may be at different stages of the sex-change process. It is not hard to imagine how these categories may, in fact, interpenetrate, and how individuals may end up negotiating their identities in the context of the opportunities available to them or the obstacles put in their way. A caring partner may help defray the costs of cosmetic surgery, a hostile family may push a gay towards a *travesti* working life, a good network of friends may provide crucial tips and guidance on the road to successful transformation. Of these, induction into the transsexual subculture is most crucial to daily survival, since most individuals are alienated from their families, and only have their wits and each other to rely on. However, the boundaries of the subculture are by no means clear-cut, resembling a porous network of individuals weaving in and out, both in and outside Turkey.

Backstreets and working lives

Ayça is just back from a season in clubs in Switzerland. She works as a stripper, and shares her impressions of the Moroccan, Filipino and German transsexuals she has met. She also has views about the preferences of customers of different nationalities: 'The Germans want fully operated strippers. The Yugoslavs and Italians may prefer those who have a penis, so I sometimes have to use padding'.

Nuşin has lived in Germany for many years, and worked in several European locations. She makes comparisons between Turkey and Holland: 'This place here is really backward. What does it mean to have to lean out of windows and call out 'Psht, psht' to attract attention? There everything is out in the open, civilised.' She projects herself as cosmopolitan and sophisticated.

Whatever actual individual levels of exposure to the outside world may be, there is an unmistakeable sense of a wider community 'out there'. Some Filipinos come to Turkey for surgery because it is cheaper, the more affluent from Turkey may prefer to go to London. News travels fast: about new clubs, better surgeons, magazine articles, television programmes. Daily life, on the other hand, appears intensely local, and revolves around a particular neighbourhood in Istanbul. Rented flats are shared; some live and work in the area, others have residences elsewhere and only come here to work. There are no pimps, just land-lords and landladies to pay and the police to look out for. Each finds her way to the district in a different way.

Sevda commented on her feelings of loneliness and depression when she decided to leave home: 'Then I met Engin, who had been aware of the Taksim district two years before me. I had very few men friends because I was gay. And it really showed. I didn't know anything then. I was 19. Then she started introducing me to people and took me to Yeşil Bizans.[21] I started feeling much better. I didn't know there were places where gays could go. I was finally in a place where I could get the teachings of gay life [the last two words were spoken in English]. I have now been working as a prostitute for the last year and a half.'

Introduction to 'the life' usually takes place under the guidance of a more experienced friend who knows the ropes. An intense communal life of mutual visiting, nursing after surgery, cooking and sharing meals, telephone calls, visits to the hairdresser and swapping anecdotes creates the impression of a self-contained world. When I heard the word *madi*, I also realised that I had come across a foreign vocabulary; I was informed that it simply means 'ugly'. Transsexuals use their own coded language, with a small vocabulary of about 50–60 words. They claim it is based on gypsy dialect with traces of Spanish, Latin and possibly Armenian. It

Blondie at the window (picture Mary Robert)

conveys crucial information about the ages of men (*sorsak* for the really young, below 15, *manti* for those younger than 22, *lacho* for those between 23 and 30, *balamoz* for those over 40, and *puri* for the very old), money units, appearance and a range of activities.[22] 'It's our secret language. We use it when we don't want to be understood. All sorts of people come here. We don't want to seem crude.' A crucial distinction is also made between *gacı* ('woman') and *has gacı* ('real woman', the term for genetic females). The term reserved for those on the way to becoming women is *lubinya*.

Despite a superficial impression of inward-lookingness and boundedness, there was also a sense of total openness, of people coming and going at will, of friendships forming and dissolving. Some displayed a real sense of mission about enlightening others about who they really are, undoubtedly prompted by the fact that transsexuals have been in the public eye; some have been interviewed on television, others have become rights activists, and a few have made it to stardom, fame and fortune. A term that keeps recurring is *bilinçsiz* ('without consciousness'), to refer to those who can't tell the difference between gays, transvestites and transsexuals, and hold hostile attitudes to all. Ayça demonstrates this didactic urge when she recalls her reaction when they asked her to strip before actually giving her the pink card; 'In fact, I didn't have to. I had already gone through all the committees and the court, collecting the card was a mere formality. But I thought to myself, never mind, let them see me, they may become more enlightened (*bilinçlenirler*), I have no problem with that.'

The police harassment that transsexuals report being subjected to partly relates to their work as prostitutes. 'What else is there to do?' retorts Sevda, 'I was studying in a university department which required one of the highest entrance examination points. Do you think anyone would give a job to someone like me? Anyone with a bit of conscience must realise there is nowhere to go for us. We are seen as good for one thing only: sex. I saw a television film once showing two transsexuals running a shop – an antique shop, I think – in England. I thought to myself, 'Isn't that incredible? They actually have an ordinary job'. I would much rather be a working woman than do this. I do want to try something else. I might train as a beautician and work on film sets, or with television or something to do with entertainment. It would have to be a marginal environment though (*marjinal bir ortam*) to cope with someone like me.'

She concedes, however, that few around her have the same resources: she has higher education and knows a foreign language. It is unlikely that others could have many options. Besides, they could never achieve the same levels of income; in the summer of 1995, they charged an average of one million lira (then roughly US$20) for a fifteen-minute session, and saw at least five customers a day. Cosmetic surgery is extremely expensive, and so are the rents, and the temptation to buy expensive clothes is hard to resist, but there are examples of those who have made judicious savings and investments and are now comfortably off. They can live off the rents of their property, and transsexual landladies are known to charge higher rents, 'because they know what we do and how much we make'.

There is a definite hierarchy of preferences in ways of making a living within the profession. 'For a member of the third sex [Sevda's own term], the best way to make a living is to work in clubs abroad. The money is good and you meet all sorts of people.' There are considerations of prestige, remuneration and safety involved in the choices one makes. The most hazardous way of working is going for *oto-stop* (hitchhiking, stopping passing cars). 'I remember in my former neighbourhood, older boys used to get into two or three cars at night and say; 'Let's go to Beyoğlu to beat up some *dönme*. That was their idea of fun. It doesn't happen as much now. The police intervene.' Clubs may be marginally more dangerous than working out of apartments, since they are still the customers' turf. Besides, a performer's card is needed to be allowed to enter clubs. Working out of apartments, though safer, means attracting passers-by by leaning on the window-sill, sometimes for such long stretches of time that bruises develop on the elbows. It also means being able to afford rent. The rent paid for the apartments varies as a function of their distance from the street; the higher up you go, the cheaper the rent gets. There may be regulars, and in some cases longer-term boyfriends, but the majority are casual customers. Occasional police raids punctuate the life of the street.

> Within two minutes all the lights go out, there's no one left at the windows, it all happens in a flash. They sometimes do break into flats. On one occasion, the police arrived when we were out. My flatmate was an experienced woman, she had taken the precaution of having the door reinforced so they could not break it down. They demolished the wall instead. We had the place assessed for damages – of course, that cost money – and sued. The case is still in progress. That was an illegal entry, an assault on domicile.

In the summer of 1995, there was a sense of stand-off, and accommodation between the street-dwellers and the forces of law and order. Police raids had an almost ritualistic feel, suggesting a well-established routine of protection and pay-offs. However, the foothold transsexuals had in this neighbourhood revealed itself to be extremely precarious. A year later, in the summer of 1996, when the UN Habitat II conference was hosted in Istanbul in the luxury hotels surrounding Taksim Square, stray dogs and transsexuals bore the brunt of the major 'clean up' operation that preceded the event. Transsexuals were evicted *en masse* from the backstreets of Taksim and dispersed throughout the city, keeping in touch through the clubs, hairdressers and cafés they frequent. Recalling the event, Tülay describes a military-style operation, the police using fire-ladders to break into flats through the windows, with triggers cocked; a first-floor flat was set on fire. 'They behaved as though they were expecting to meet with armed resistance,' she comments. An officer nicknamed Süleyman the Hose (*Hortum Süleyman*)[23] was widely rumoured to bring an almost fanatical zeal to the operation and to be waging an all-out war against transsexuals. The inhabitants of the neighbourhood were said to be collaborating with the police force despite the fact that they fraternised with the girls and rented them flats. There were also suspicions that club owners had started resenting the fact that too much business was being transacted on the street. Tülay felt, nonetheless, that the transsexuals were partly to blame for this state of affairs:

> Before the street used to run on a set of unwritten rules. 'New' girls were not allowed to stand at windows for two or three months, and were trained by the

older ones. There were no more than two girls in a flat and they took turns at the windows. Then there was an influx of younger 'inhabitants', generally male gays who went around in drag. There were sometimes four-to-five girls to a flat, and they started to behave more provocatively to attract the attention of passers-by. Some even showed their breasts. They brought it upon themselves.

Tülay, who is in her fifties and one of the oldest inhabitants of the street, went back to her village in Yozgat, where she is well accepted by her family, during the 'troubles', but returned out of a sense of solidarity. She claims to have done her best to advise the younger set: 'You are eating bread from this job, so don't push your luck. Believe me, I have seen many periods of curfew (*sıkıyönetim*)'. She concludes sadly, 'The sluts misbehaved and now the ladies must suffer'.

At the street level, the transsexual community appears to be totally embedded in local developments, and is constantly buffeted by the ebb and flow of events and the way these are mediated through policing practices. This is, however, a misleading impression, since transsexual identities in Turkey are articulated against the background of a much broader international framework of gay and trans-gender politics, on the one hand, and the circulation of images, fashions and commodities, on the other.

The local and the global: permeable boundaries and negotiated identities

In the opening paragraphs of this chapter, I referred to a striking cartoon by Latif Demirci, without commenting on its provenance. This cartoon was forwarded to me in England by trans-gender activist Phaedra Kelly with the request, 'Could you translate this for me?' To my shame, I never did, but could not help but ponder on the extensive nature of the networks in the international trans-gender community. An air of cosmopolitanism permeates the transsexual community in Istanbul. Sex-change surgery takes some across national borders, and news travels fast on new procedures and techniques, and on better cosmetic surgeons. So do opportunities for jobs in the entertainment industry. There are some foreign transsexuals either living in Istanbul or just passing through. Role models for fame and achievement do not only consist of local idols like Bülent Ersoy, but are also drawn from the West, as in the case of the fashion model Tula, who is held up as the epitome of success. In the course of our conversations, I was asked for back copies of *Roses*, a Manchester-based transsexual magazine, even though few read or speak English. Smart dressing accompanies acute brand consciousness and a flair for the latest fashions.[24]

There is a sense in which the debates I referred to earlier about whether transsexualism reinscribes or challenges gender dichotomies appear somewhat spurious in a context in which identities are defined as heterogeneously and conjuncturally as they are here, and in which both possibilities might, therefore, co-exist. Some transsexuals yearn for conventional female roles, while others call themselves feminists. The way identities are crafted depends a great deal on the overt or implicit political reference points adopted.

Many, with their dreams and materialistic aspirations for a fast track to fame and fortune, capture the cultural mood of post-1980s Turkey to an uncanny degree. The indistinct boundaries between the urban underworld, the world of prostitution, and that of the entertainment industry encourage such dreams of mobility and betterment. An awareness of the short shelf-life of their youth and looks motivates some to seek committed partners who will 'set them up' with a flat of their own or even some capital. The knowledge that maternity is foreclosed as an option gives a hard edge to calculations about future financial security.[25]

Few, however, are willing to inscribe themselves in a broader search for voice and legitimacy, or overtly to politicise their trans-gender identities. Demet Demir, who was a student militant as a male, and is a member of the Human Rights Association, has been trying to find such a voice, and received acknowledgement through an award from the International Gay and Lesbian Human Rights Commission based in New York. However, the Association of Sexual Rights and Liberties in Turkey, which started as a fragile coalition of gay and feminist activists, seems to have foundered on the rocks of internal dissent. At first, they encountered the reluctance of some male gays to 'come out'. However, the real parting of the ways came about during a human rights conference at which a leading male gay activist accused transsexuals of trying to modify the laws simply in order to practice prostitution freely, and of riding the sexual liberties bandwagon for purely opportunistic reasons. This wounded the transsexuals deeply, and he was in turn accused of trying to claim a 'respectable' identity for male gays at their expense. As the article in *Kim* referred to earlier seems to suggest, there may indeed be an attempt by male gays to go 'mainstream' by recovering their lost identities through an interrogation of the Ottoman past. Like all identity politics, that of male gays may be going through a phase of rediscovery of the self through the establishment of an identity with reference to a long, if submerged, national past. Transsexuals are placed in something of a no-man's-land with respect to such claims.[26]

An even more puzzling event was the 'flag incident', which highlights the slipperiness of the surfaces upon which identity politics is inscribed in contemporary Turkey. A newly founded political party, HADEP, witnessed at its first congress in July 1996 an incident which raised a furore: the Turkish flag was taken down by some participants. In protest, many streets were festooned with the slogan '*Bayrak inmez, ezan dinmez, vatan bölunmez*' ('The flag flies, the call to prayer never ends, and the motherland remains undivided'), inspired by the local branches of the MHP, with known anti-Kurdish positions. A leading male gay activist who had attempted to found a green party in Turkey hung a Turkish flag at the door of Claudia Roth, the representative of the German Green Party in Istanbul, as if to chide her for being more active as a pro-Kurdish sympathiser than as a Green activist. This incident was the subject of multiple interpretations in the transsexual community, including the possibility that the gay activist might be trying to ingratiate himself with the authorities by establishing his 'nationalist' credentials. That the tensions between cosmopolitan libertarianism and nationalist respectability should appear to haunt a community as marginal as that of gays and transsexuals in Turkey was a discovery the implications of which I am still uncertain about. What appears certain, however, is that the establishment of gendered personae, even when these represent major infractions of dominant cultural codes, are always cross-cut by other markers of identity, and remain captives of the broader discursive universes of which they form a part.

Conclusion

I hope to have shown that the identities of male-to-female transsexuals in Turkey are crafted through complex interfaces between their personal biographies, the economic and political pressures of their immediate milieu and the more distant backdrop of international trans-gender and human-rights politics. The category of *travesti* itself emerges as a heterogeneous one encompassing a wide range of physical attributes and sexual practices. The interactions of *travestis* with state apparatuses at critical junctures of their lives – when applying for new identity papers, trying to avoid military service or being handled by the police force – communicate powerful messages of their stigmatisation as a deviant minority. It would be worth investigating the extent to which the category of 'coerced' trans-sexuals is the product of just such pressures.[27] On the other hand, the images of fast-track living, glamour and consumption that they project, as well as the market networks in which they circulate, from boutiques and nightclubs to society surgeons, encapsulate the post-1980s mainstream, with its emphasis on material success and 'making it fast' (*köşeyi dönmek*) to an uncomfortable degree. There appears to be a specifically Turkish mode of living transsexuality, and it may not only be the ambiguities of their gender and their illicit pursuits that account for the fascination they exert, but a more subterranean unease about the cultural sub-texts they allow us to glimpse.

Notes on Chapter 12

1   This was the title given by Mary Robert to a photographic exhibition she held in Paris on male-to-female transsexuals in Istanbul. It was her exciting photographic work that inspired me to explore the back streets of Istanbul in June 1995 and July 1996. See our photo essay 'Transsexuals and the Urban Scene in Istanbul', *Middle East Report*, vol. 28, no 1 (Spring 1998). I am also grateful to Şahika Yüksel, who, as a psychiatrist involved in group therapy with transsexuals of both genders, shared her important observations with me, and to İskender Savaşır for his insightful comments on the sexual liberties movement in Turkey. I would also like to thank Phaedra Kelly, who runs International Trans-gender Affinity in the UK, for making me aware of international solidarity networks in the trans-gender community. Finally, my special thanks go to Demet, Sevda and others for being such incisive and sophisticated commentators on both their own lives and on Turkish society.

2   Kelsey (1996).

3   Oya Özdilek, 'Muazzam bir eşcinsel sanat, kültür ve geçmiş', *Kim*, February 1996, pp.98–101.

4   Kandiyoti (1995), (1994) and (1997). For an elaboration of the term 'hegemonic
     masculinity' see Corrigan, Connell and Lee (1985).

5   This is not to suggest that the gender identities of genetic males and females
     who experience greater continuity in their gendered personae are non-
     problematic, but rather that the existential or psychological problems they may
     experience do not generally entail their redefinition and reclassification in legal
     and administrative terms.

6   S. McNeill (1982), Vern and Bonnie Bullough (1993).

7   Garber (1992), Butler (1986).

8   For a discussion of this shift in positions, see Nicholson (1994), who argues for
     a thorough historicisation of the notion of sex and sexuality, and accuses writers
     such as Raymond of 'biological foundationalism'.

9   Wikan (1977).

10   Nanda (1990).

11   For instance, the well-known story of the late humourist Aziz Nesin, *Yaşar, Ne
     Yaşar Ne Yaşamaz* (*Yaşar Who Neither Lives nor Doesn't*) tells the tale of someone
     who is unable to prove he is alive, in truly Kafkaesque fashion. Similar tales
     of women called up for military service and men unable to enlist abound.
     Events take a more tragic turn when contacts with the bureaucracy turn into
     unalterable fate.

12   *Resmi Gazete* (*Official Gazette*), Amendment to the 29th clause of law no. 743, the
     Turkish Civil Code, 12 May 1988, 19812. This item of legislation may appear as
     more advanced than that of many European countries, where the original
     record of one's sex of birth is not thus obliterated. I hope to show throughout
     this article that in Turkey the pressures towards the elimination of ambiguity in
     matters of gender are very high, and may have influenced this outcome.

13   *İlmi ve Kazai İçtihatlar Dergisi*, vol. 22, no 253 (January 1982), page 911–913,
     provides the details of the ruling, stating that the decision as to whether or not
     the complainant, who merely has the appearance of a woman, really is a woman
     is a medical matter. The complainant's appeal was therefore rejected on the
     grounds that further medical examination was necessary. Two dissenting opin-
     ions to this ruling are particularly noteworthy. They insist that there is no neces-
     sity for further investigation, since the complainant was born male and lived
     as a male beyond puberty: 'the sex-change operation was a wanton, wilful act
     the consequences of which the complainant would simply have to endure.'
     'Otherwise,' the text goes on, 'this would make it possible for every man wishing
     to benefit from the advantages of being a woman to achieve this by taking on the
     role of a woman. There is no doubt that this would alter the equilibrium of
     nature and destabilise and confuse the value judgments of society' (p.913). I am
     grateful to Muzaffer Menteş for providing me with this legal document.

14   Şahika Yüksel, *Cumhuriyet*, 13 February 1988, p.2.

15   The *Diagnostic and Statistical Manual of Mental Disorders* (*DSM*) of the American
     Psychiatric Association, which is subject to periodic revision, is also used in
     Turkey as the basis of psychiatric diagnoses. It is noteworthy that the diagnostic
     categories have themselves become a subject of controversy, and that lobbying
     by gay activists in the US resulted in the abandonment of the term 'perversion'

in relation to homosexuality. It is also worth noting that it is only in the third edition of the *DSM* (Washington DC, 1980) that the category of 'transsexualism' appears for the first time, under the label 'Gender Identity Disorders' in the section on 'Psycho-sexual Disorders'.

16   This term literally means 'convert', to denote someone who has changed religion. It is more commonly associated with the followers of Sabatay Sevi, a self-appointed Jewish messiah in the seventeenth century, who eventually converted to Islam with his community. The *dönme* are assumed to have kept a distinct identity.

17   These are fictional names, although the accounts that follow them are not.

18   From the French word *frappant*, meaning 'striking'. It is also used in Turkish slang to indicate an eye-catching, vampish appearance.

19   An interview with the surgeon by Mary Robert revealed that the reconstructed vagina preserved the existing nerve paths of the penis and that various techniques exist to maximise sexual response. A Turkish doctor claims to have pioneered a new technique in this respect.

20   A particularly dreaded practice is called 'being taken on an adventure' (*macereya takılmak*). Normally one can only be held in custody without charge for 24 hours. There are, however, seven police stations in the Beyoğlu district in which transsexuals operate, and they may be transferred from one police station to the next, making it very difficult for their lawyers to catch up with them. They may be released after a period of physical and verbal abuse.

21   Yeşil Bizans ('Green Byzantium') is the name of a café which used to be run by gay activist İbrahim Eren, founder of a green and sexual liberties party named Radikal, for which he was jailed. At the time, he used to champion the rights of transsexuals, but there has since been a parting of the ways between the male gay and transsexual communities.

22   Among which the term *kolileşmek*, which translates roughly into being made into a parcel, and refers to having sex, and *üçlemek*, which refers to concealing the unoperated penis by means of wrapping it around the genital area and keeping it in place by means of surgical or bandage tape.

23   A nickname earned by the use of a plastic hose to beat transsexuals.

24   I am grateful to Shahla Haeri for pointing out to me after a slide show by Mary Robert how thoroughly Western Istanbul transsexuals looked. This is not a minor point, since the *hijra* in India and the *xanith* in Oman wear national dress. The images on which Istanbul transsexuals model themselves are taken from *Playboy*, *Hustler* or fashion magazines, and no attempt is made to impersonate exotic Eastern beauties. This, however, is generally in keeping with the styles cultivated by popular singers or other entertainers in Turkey.

25   Sevda, who was in love with a young man doing his military service, knew, for instance, that his family would force him into a marriage afterwards and that she could bear him no children. She finally ended up with another man with whom she was not in love, but who 'set her up' in a nice flat.

26   It was, nonetheless, pointed out to me that just around the corner, in Başkurt Street, there existed a brothel in the nineteenth century that offered beautiful boys only. The transsexuals were thus signalling that they inscribe themselves in this past of homoeroticism.

27   The only other reference I have come across indicating the broader existence of such a category was in reference to China, where some male gays claimed to have been forced into sex-change surgery (BBC World Service, 8 July 1996).

References

Bullough, Vern and Bonnie Bullough (1993), *Cross Dressing, Sex and Gender*, University of Pennsylvania Press, PA
Butler, Judith (1993), *Bodies That Matter*, Routledge, New York
— (1986), *Gender Trouble: Feminism and the Subversion of Identity*, Routledge, New York
Cornwall, Andrea, (1994), 'Gendered Identities and Gender Ambiguity Among Travestis in Salvador, Brazil', in A. Cornwall and N. Lindisfarne (eds), *Dislocating Masculinity: Comparative Ethnographies*, Routledge, London
Corrigan, Tim, Bob Connell and John Lee, 'Towards a new sociology of masculinity', *Theory and Society*, vol. 15, no 5, 1985
Garber, Marjorie (1992), *Vested Interests: Cross-dressing and Cultural Anxiety*, Routledge, London
Kandiyoti, Deniz (1995), 'Patterns of Patriarchy: Notes for an Analysis of Male Dominance in Turkish Society, in Şirin Tekeli (ed.), *Women in Modern Turkish Society*, Zed Press, London
— (1994), 'The Paradoxes of Masculinity : Some Thoughts on Segregated Societies', in A. Cornwall and N. Lindisfarne (eds), *Dislocating Masculinity: Comparative Ethnographies*, Routledge, London
— (1997), 'Gendering the Modern: On Some Missing Dimensions in the Study of Turkish Modernity', in S. Bozdoğan and R. Kasaba (eds), *Rethinking Modernity and National Identity in Turkey*, Washington University Press, Seattle
Kelsey, Tim (1996), *Dervish: The Invention of Modern Turkey*, Hamish Hamilton, London
McNeill, S. (1982), 'Transsexualism ... can men turn into women?', in S. Friedmen and G. Sarah (eds), *On the Problem of Men*, The Women's Press, London
Mungan, Murathan (1987), *Kırk Oda (Forty Rooms)*, Metis Yayınları, Istanbul
Nanda, Serena (1990), *Neither Man, nor Woman; The Hijras of India*, Wadsworth Publishing, Belomont
Nicholson, Linda (1994), 'Interpreting Gender', *Signs*, vol. 20, no 1, pp.79–105
Raymond, Janice (1979), *The Transsexual Empire: The Making of the She-male*, Beacon Press, Boston
Sanders, Paula Sanders (1991), 'Gendering the Ungendered Body: Hermaphrodites in Medieval Islamic Law', in N.R. Keddie and B. Baron (eds), *Women in Middle Eastern History*, Yale University Press, New Haven
Wikan, Uni (1977), 'Man Becomes Woman: Transsexualism in Oman as a Key to Gender Roles', *Man*, vol. 12, no 2, pp.304–19

13

A Table in Two Hands

Ayşe Şimşek Çağlar

Introduction

Today around 2.1 million Turkish immigrants live in the Federal Republic of Germany (FRG). They came to Germany after the first bilateral agreement signed between Turkey and Germany in 1961. Although most Turkish migrants were recruited within the guest worker system, designed to serve the labour needs of the host society, and arrived as workers, today they no longer form a homogeneous group as workers. They are not only economically well integrated into German society and its labour market, but are represented at all strata. Initially they came with the expectation that their stay would be a temporary one, but many became settled in Germany to form the largest minority group – 28 percent of all foreigners – in the FRG.

It is well known to students of the subject that Turkish migrants, especially the first generation, who saved rigorously during their stay in the FRG, invest their savings largely in housing in Turkey (Zentrum für Türkeistudien, 1992; Çağlar, 1996). Most German Turks who have been living in Germany for 40 years or more have fully furnished houses and/or flats (sometimes more than one) in Turkey as well as their German one.

The decoration and organisational principles of their flats in Turkey and Germany are strikingly different from one another. The owners of furniture shops in Berlin with mainly Turkish customers say that German Turks furnish their German flats markedly differently from their Turkish ones: items desirable for the former are not found appropriate or attractive for the latter. Moreover, the arrangement of equivalent furniture differs between one and the other.

While choosing furniture for the Istanbul flat of her daughter, Banu (who would be getting married and returning to Turkey to settle), Güllü insisted that the coffee table have a glass top. Banu's father, Mustafa, proposed a tile-top coffee table, like the one in their Berlin apartment, and very popular among German Turks, but Güllü and Banu very firmly objected. Mustafa's argument that they have a tile-top table in their Turkish flat was in vain. Güllü immediately responded that the tile-top table was practical for Germany but inappropriate for Turkey, adding that she would also replace the tile-top table in their Turkish apartment as soon as possible, and that buying it had always been a mistake.

Why does the choice of a simple coffee table initiate such discussions? Why do German Turks' apartment consumption preferences differ in Turkey and Germany? Here, centred around the meanings and functions of a coffee table in the context of German Turks' different domestic interiors in the two countries, I would like to draw attention to how the same group of people use and manipulate the same object to construct their identity and social relations in different ways. In addition to the constitutive role of material culture in the formation of identities and social relations, this chapter also aims to draw attention to the importance of material culture studies for current debates about cultural homogenisation through globalisation.

My ethnographic data focus on the differences between the Turkish and German flats of German Turks, through an examination of the interiors of 20 Turkish immigrants' flats in Berlin. In addition to the interviews conducted with the tenants, the owners of and salespeople in nine Berlin furniture shops that cater to German Turks were interviewed. The domestic interiors of Berlin flats are compared with the interiors of the same tenants' residences in Turkey. As these residences were scattered around different cities in Turkey, only 11 such residences in Istanbul were visited and examined. For the remaining nine such flats, photographs were used. All the living-rooms examined in Berlin were in apartments. For this reason, in Turkey only the apartment residences of the same tenants are taken into consideration. Thirteen of the families owned – in addition to their flats in the cities – houses either in their villages or in holiday resorts (like Çinarcik, Ayvalik and Çanakkale). Although none of the Berlin flats examined were owned by their inhabitants, all the Turkish flats of the same people were their own property. All the families in the sample are 'first-generation migrants' who came to Germany as workers during late 1960s or early 1970s. Turkish flats in the sample are slightly larger (between 80 and 110 square metres) than the German flats (between 65 and 96 square metres).

Consumer goods, images and identities

Goods have a privileged role – especially in a world where images of lifestyles are attached to goods and material objects – more than ever serving as a pivot around which identities are constructed and asserted (Miller, 1987, p.124). Thus the investigation of consumers' manipulation of goods and their meanings, and of the social dynamics of consumption practices, are invaluable in the examination of consumers' identities and social relations.

According to Douglas and Isherwood (1979, p.12), the uses of goods are social, and carry social meanings. For this reason, 'it is possible to read the person's life and personality, and place in society from the goods' (p.59). This ability of objects to communicate is the reason that consumption is seen to be a 'part of an information system operating between rather than within households ...' (p.78). In addition to these symbolic and expressive functions, consumption practices have an important place within the struggles of modern man against the anonymity of city life. Goods acting as markers accomplish both the unity and solidarity of those in the same class, and segregate them from others (Simmel, 1957). In that context, goods associated with a particular lifestyle become a social arena for various groups' struggle for social position. As taste in cultural goods acts as a marker of class, these goods also act as an instrument of distinction between classes or class factions (Bourdieu, 1974).

The conceptualisation of consumption as work (Miller, 1987, p.11) takes these approaches to consumer culture and to the relations between divisions of goods and divisions of people one step further. Here, consumption is conceptualised as a social arena in which identities and social relations are being constituted rather than as one in which prior sets of relations are reflected (Miller, 1988, pp.353–72). Consumption is seen as work, because 'although the object's material form remains constant, as it undergoes the process and practice of consumption, its social nature and meaning are radically altered' (Miller, 1987, p.192).

Thus consumption does not only refer to processes and practices by which the meanings of material objects are manipulated (through distinctive selection, placement and association), but also to practices which are crucial for the constitution of social relations. As objects are firmly integrated in the development of particular social relations and group identity, the analyses of material culture and processes of consumption are crucial for the analysis of the formation and assertion of identities and social relations (p.202). Consumption needs to be approached from within a larger social process. Even if we focus on the ways meanings are attributed to goods rather than on the products of such attribution, we would be unable to grasp this attribution process in acts of exchange and consumption outside the larger social processes in which they are embedded.

Commodities, defined generally as the objects of consumption and exchange, carry not only economic but cultural value, and are thus the locus around which several value-creating processes intersect. As value is not an inherent property of objects, but is something created, an analysis at the level of commodities requires an analysis of how value is created. This, in turn, requires an analysis of the immediate context of transaction, as well as of the macro factors operating on this context. Demand, desire and power all intersect in the creation of economic value, and all these are socially construed (Appadurai, 1986, p.4).

The images of potential life forms are projected via desire onto a demand schedule, and these are the bases for understanding the practice of consumption. They are, essentially, projects of self-definition. However, although they take the form of projects in which subjects invest themselves and their wealth, the source of demand is not within the individual subject, but lies in the definitions negotiated in historically specific social and cultural contexts (Friedman, 1995). For this reason, consumption is part of a larger socially and culturally constituted project, and the understanding of consumption cannot be separated from the question of the way in which consumers are constituted. And the latter question is related to the more general way in which social experience is generated in particular social contexts' (Friedman, 1995, p.22). Although consumption is a social activity often realised by individuals making personal choices, it remains fundamentally collective, and its analysis requires an understanding of the macro projects of commerce, industry and state policy, as well as the cultural images that construe sign-value.

German Turks' 'homes' in Turkey and Germany

Now I turn to the different decoration principles of Turkish migrants' German and Turkish 'homes' to illustrate how the very same group utilises objects in different ways in the two countries to create their own images and relations with the wider societies in question differently, and what kinds of dynamics are involved in their consumption practices.

As stated at the beginning, most German Turks have fully furnished houses and/or apartments in Turkey, mostly in urban middle-class neighbourhoods in the cities in which they initially plan to settle after their return. These apartments are used very briefly during the year, and remain unoccupied for the rest of the year.

Relative to the brief period German Turks spend in their Turkish flats, these residences have an important place in their lives, especially when compared to their Germany apartments. German Turks are willing to invest in these apartments, especially in their furniture, and value and care for them more than their apartments in Germany. The former are fully furnished and meticulously prepared.[1] However, here I do not want to compare and contrast these apartments in terms of their comfort and quality. Instead, I would like to focus on the material culture and the organising principles of the inhabitants' most important room, and its connection to the outside world. This space is selected because it displays the self through the objects in it. I will concentrate principally on a piece of furniture, the coffee table, common to both the German and Turkish homes.

Some explanation of the organising principles of these living-rooms is necessary, because in relation to these principles 'objects receive a new centre which is not located in any of them alone, but which they all manifest through the particular way they are united' (Simmel, 1991, p.69).

The living-room in the German apartment
These living-rooms, usually furnished with items (chairs, sofas, tables etc) bought from second-hand stores and accumulated over time on the basis of value-for-money and need, are quite simple in their decoration. Depending on the income of the household and on the willingness to invest in the German apartment – usually under pressure from children – these different sorts of chairs, armchairs and tables would be replaced by a set of seating furniture and by a coffee table. However, replaced or not, in both cases the seating furniture dominates the room and the decoration of the room is uncluttered. Basically functional furniture combined with a few ornaments give the impression that the space is not filled. Plants (real and/or artificial), family photos, calenders and clocks are basic to their decorations. In some, bric-a-brac and souvenirs are displayed, but these displays are never central to the decoration.[2] In any case, items that are displayed

are items of sentimental rather than high monetary value, and are either associated with Turkey (such as touristic, folkloric souvenir items, like dolls, painted hand-made wooden spoons or hand-made miniature woollen gloves) or are connected to the householders' personal history (such as some present given by a workmate or for a birthday in Turkey, a cheap ceramic plate or a soft toy).[3] The general effect is of a collection of unlinked elements.

In fact, personal relationships and associations with Turkey make up the dominant part of the wall decorations: these are family pictures (wedding photos of children or relatives, of grandchildren etc), calenders or posters with pictures of landscapes or tourist sites in Turkey, or with some Turkish religious and historical themes (heroic or religious poems), wall tapestries and decorations with a religious theme, or some calligraphy.

In terms of quality and nature, living-room furniture and decorations can be categorised into two groups. Items bought to be used in the future, such as tele-visions, stereos and video recorders form the first category. A concern for high quality and durability is apparent in these items (televisions are almost always the largest size, and very good quality). The other category covers furniture or items acquired or bought to serve immediate needs, such as a sofa, armchair, chairs and tables. If the items in this category have not been replaced by a long sofa and a couple of matching armchairs in time, they are usually of bad quality and in bad condition, and rarely match in quality, style or colour. In that sense the furnishings are heterogeneous. If they are replaced by a suite, then a concern for their function and hard-wearing quality is apparent in the choice. In terms of fashion, German Turks follow their own imported style, developed during their Germany experience, rather than following fashions dominant in the home decoration habits of other German social groups.[4]

These living-rooms, with their lack of concern with display and fashion, could be characterised as introverted. They are not conceived as places appropriate to the display of conspicuous wealth. Heterogeneity best defines their style (especially at the initial phase), and biographical references are apparent in the selection of decorative elements. The latter manifests itself in the display of items with strong personal attachments and those strongly associated with Turkey. The references of the decorations, by means of which the environment is rendered non-alien, are to personal pasts or to Turkey. The creation of a non-alien space and of identity are based around this locus.

In short, functionality, introversion and a concern with establishing and displaying biographical continuity, rather than fashion, form the organising principle of German Turks' living-rooms in their German flats.

The living-room in the Turkish apartment

In contrast to their German flats, cohesion (*uyum*, in their own words), which is believed to be established by means of matching furniture sets, dominates German Turks' living-rooms in Turkey. These living-rooms, filled up with orna-ments and items of relatively high monetary value, give the impression of being busy, designed for display. Sofas with matching armchairs and tables, and dining sets with matching glass cabinets reveal a predominant concern with style and fashion. Moreover, a considerable amount of attention is paid to quality and fashion in the choice of furniture, household goods etc. Homogeneity dominates even the items on display. Rather than being acquired or bought second-hand over time, they are new and are bought in sets. The decoration of these living-rooms, which are centred around a display of conspicuous wealth, can be characterised as extrovert. There is an effort to demonstrate that money is willingly invested in their decoration. In fact, these rooms are more parlours than living-rooms.[5]

However, the most significant contrast with Turkish migrants' German apartments is the scarcity of signs referring to the householders' own past. Other than some pictures of close family members, links with personal history are significantly missing. Even references to Germany are very rare. A few souvenirs (for example an engraved plate or a porcelain mug with the emblem of Berlin, or a family member's retirement present) might refer to their life in Germany, but this is not particularly emphasised. Some valuables on display, such as crystal sets or fine china ornaments brought from Germany, stand there like any other imported prestige goods in Turkey, with no apparent relationship to the biographies of the residents. This effort to erode links with their past is also consistent with German Turks' concern with fashion in their decoration of these rooms. In fashion, which conveys a strong feeling of the present, breaking with the past is an important factor (Simmel, 1957, p.547).

In short, the decoration is characterised by homogeneity, through the display of sets of items, an apparent concern with fashion, relatedly a strong interest in the present, and in displaying wealth.[6]

A coffee table in two hands

Now I focus on the contextualisation of a coffee table in these different living-rooms, and its acquisition of a different function and meaning in each. Two factors are crucial to the function and meaning of the coffee table in these different contexts: the presence or absence of a dining table and the nature of the use this coffee table has in the presence of guests. The table in question is a quite common coffee table sold in Germany, and made of wood with a tile-covered top.[7] Here, it is important to note that these tile-top tables are not marketed in Turkey and that they are almost exclusively found in the flats of German Turks in Turkey.

In the living-rooms of the Turkish workers' German apartments, this table is used in the following arrangement: according to the owners of the prominent Turkish furniture shops in Berlin (whose customers are mostly Turks), the most popular furniture among German Turks is a long curved couch with one or two matching chairs and the coffee table.[8] Given that there are no dining tables in these flats (the other table is a small one in the kitchen, used mostly used for breakfast), this table doubles as a dining table, for which the tile-covered top is very practical. This top is indeed a very important factor in its desirability and popularity among German Turks in Germany: it makes tablecloths redundant, and is easy to clean.

   The long curved sofa provides more seats than would chairs around a small table in the kitchen. People eat seated on this long couch and armchair (when crowded, children eat on their knees or seated on low chairs lined along the table's open side). In the presence of guests, meals are consumed in the same eating arrangement. When it is not used as a dining table, but as a proper coffee table, there is usually nothing other than ashtrays and the television remote control on it.

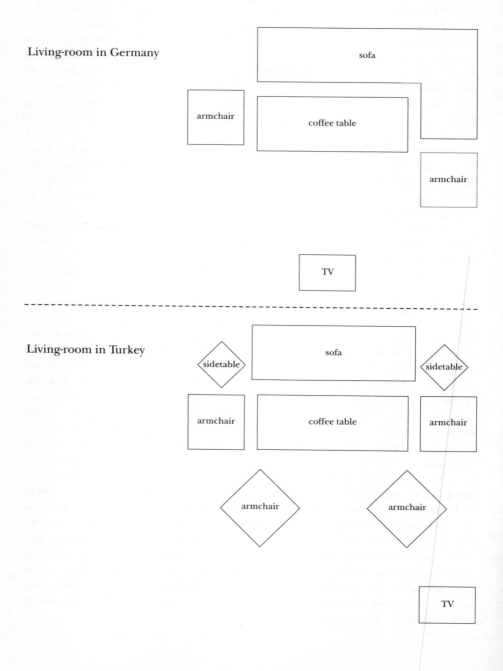

Living-room in Germany

sofa

armchair

coffee table

armchair

TV

Living-room in Turkey

sidetable

sofa

sidetable

armchair

coffee table

armchair

armchair

armchair

TV

In living-rooms in Turkey, however, the same table has a different place and function in seating arrangements. There is always a dining table and chairs, whether or not in use, so the coffee table is not meant to be eaten from. Even if it is used as such when the family is on their own, this use of the table is carefully underplayed. In the presence of guests, utmost attention is paid to dining at the dining table, and the 'proper' functioning of the coffee table is especially emphasised to the outside world. Bric-a-brac and usually a doily on it all underline its sole use. Here it should be noted that the size of the flat does not play a crucial role in the presence or absence of dining table and chairs. Even in Turkish flats with insufficient space, there is still a dining table and chairs, placed sometimes outside the living-room, in the entrance for example. Moreover, second- and third-generation German Turks in Berlin have recently started buying dining tables for their Berlin residences, although they are usually smaller. Thus the constraints of space do not determine the presence or absence of dining table and chairs in either German or Turkish flats.

Ironically, although the coffee table in the German apartment is the most functional element in the living-room, being a place for eating, it is not the locus of the seating arrangement. Seating is not particularly positioned for people's interaction, but rather to follow something together – watching television or videos. Television is the focal point, and the seating is arranged as in a cinema. At this point it is important to underline the fact that watching (mostly Turkish) television is the most important leisure activity of German Turks (Senatsverwaltung für..., 1994, 1997; Zentrum für Türkeistudien, 1995), and the television is always on, whether or not there are guests. People, including guests, are seated together as if they were there for some purpose other than being together.

In the living-rooms of flats in Turkey, although the coffee table loses its function significantly in comparison to its place in the German context, ironically it is the centre of the seating arrangement. The circle is closed, or at least presented as closed, and the coffee table lies at the centre of this circle. It is centred among the people, who are seated face-to-face, ready for interaction. People are seated as if they are there for their own sake. Although television is still present in the room, it is not the focus. The furniture can be, and is, turned around to face the television when the inhabitants are alone, but its place in the room is underplayed.

The doily and the abundant ornaments, the bric-a-brac and the householders' attention to demonstrating that eating is done at the proper dining table all underline the emphasis put on this table's use only as a coffee table. They are keen to demonstrate to others that the coffee table does not double as a dining table. Interestingly, the moment that the table functions only as a coffee table, it becomes replaceable. Moreover, its replacement is particularly desired. Coffee tables with delicate polished surfaces, or with glass tops, are the popular substitutes. Their difference from tile-top tables lies in their high-maintenance material, which makes them impractical and inconvenient for use as dining tables. Thus, the very usefulness of the tile top which makes that kind of coffee table popular in the German living-room is the basis for its undesirability in the Turkish setting. It devalues the table as a proper coffee table.

Why do Turkish migrants insist on replacing these tile-top coffee table in their Turkish apartments? What is the role of this coffee table in their relations with wider society? These questions require first an investigation of Turkish migrants' self-image, 'sense of place' in society, and ideals regarding German and Turkish society.

German Turks' quest for recognition

German Turks' social space can be defined as one that is intertwined, cross-cutting Germany and Turkey. The guest worker programmes were designed to be temporary, and this double-bind situation introduced ambiguities and inconsistencies into Turks' legal, political and social status. German Turks have multiple and multi-local attachments and commitments which cannot be reduced to travelling and simple contacts across nations. They are legally, socially and economically incorporated into both German and Turkish societies. They have business involvements in Turkey and have substantially invested in housing in Turkey. Moreover, the intensive media networks between Germany and Turkey, including daily television broadcasting to Germany from Turkey, contribute to the generation and reproduction of a rhythm of being and living for German Turks that cannot be confined solely to Germany or Turkey, but that incorporates the relationship between these places. German Turks' intertwined social, legal, political and economic presence in both countries shapes and orients their experiences, desires and encounters in a specific way. Its consequence is a complex structure of reference groups, including both places, which shapes their lifestyles (Çağlar, 1995, 1997).

An analysis of German Turks' distribution in social space on the bases of the composition and the overall volume of their economic, cultural and symbolic capital (Bourdieu, 1986) illustrates that their social space in Germany, regardless of their recent internal stratification, is characterised by a severe deficit in symbolic capital. A focus on the social space that German Turks occupy in German society reveals that in terms of economic capital there are no significant differences between German Turks and German workers. Moreover, there is an increasing trend towards stratification among them produced by an upward economic mobility achieved by some German Turks.

Although German Turks have a clear deficit in cultural capital when compared to Germans, their educational qualifications are gradually improving cultural achievement. However, they nonetheless have a real deficiency in their symbolic capital. The distinctive quality of symbolic capital is that 'while the other forms of capital have an independent objectivation, be it as money, titles or behavioural attitudes and dispositions', this form of capital 'only exists in the eyes of the others' (Joppke, 1986, p.60). Thus it is nothing more than economic or cultural capital which is acknowledged and recognised (Bourdieu, 1990, p.135).

Stigmatised as a 'foreign' group with an 'alien' and 'non-European' culture in Germany, German Turks suffer from a lack of social recognition. Moreover, they are aware that this lack of social recognition negates the success they achieve in areas such as business and education. Other types of capital they manage to acquire lose their value because of this deficiency. In short, a deficit in symbolic capital stamps the composition of all German Turks' overall capital in Germany. Volumes of economic and cultural capital vary between the various strata of German Turks, but this deficit in symbolic capital affects them all.

In the eyes of the German Turks, the hostile context disqualifies Germany as a possible place for them to increase their symbolic capital in the near future. At this point, Turkey becomes the most convenient site to anchor their envisioned social mobility, by converting their economic capital into social and symbolic capital.

Despite their worker status in Germany, their self-image in regard to Turkish society is different from that of a worker. Their investments (mostly modest), business involvements in Turkey, and the different value their income and savings in German marks acquire in Turkish lira play an important role in the creation of this self-image.

While their economic capital places most of them parallel with the working class in Germany, with that same amount of capital they see themselves falling close to the middle classes in Turkey. However, their symbolic capital is again insufficient to grant them an acknowledged place among the middle classes in Turkish society. As crystallised in the name they have in Turkish society, *Almancis* ('Germanites'), which is woven into a web of negative connotations, they are not seen as entitled to this social position in Turkey.[9] The middle classes especially show a social disdain towards German Turks and their aspirations to middle-class status in Turkish society. Aware of this resistance by the middle classes in Turkey, German Turks, on the other hand, develop and adopt several strategies (such as providing a good education for their children, and transplanting themselves into a middle-class milieu) to overcome this deficit of symbolic capital and hence to gain access to the middle classes. In their parlours in Turkey, a proper coffee table and the relations it represents in a particular arrangement become an arena in which this social group try to forge relations with the Turkish middle class. Güllü's insistence on a coffee table with a glass top for their returning daughter, and on the replacement of the tile-top table in the parlour of their Turkish apartment, have to be evaluated within the context of the family's efforts to constitute themselves as members of the middle class.

To summarise, as the tile-top coffee table became a part of home furnishing, and attached itself to the lifestyles of the much despised and envied *Almancis*, this group, becoming aware of this representation of the table, tried to detach their living-room furnishing from the negative symbolism of an *Almanci* lifestyle.

Studies on consumer culture demonstrate that different class factions are disposed to engage in different consumption practices, and even if they use the same goods they do so differently, so that the meanings and symbolism of the objects are altered (Featherstone, 1987a, p.37). This difference is usually grounded in the different experiences of these groups.

German Turks' multiple use of a particular table is interesting for the following reasons. First, the different use, value and meaning attributed to the same object by the same group of people, in different contexts, brings the importance of context to the object's meaning and symbolism to the fore. German Turks do not reproduce the same syntax of space in their German and Turkish flats. This challenges the arguments about the strength of the cultural constraints that guide the construction of interior decor. Cultural constraints are usually argued to be stronger than the restrictions of space, stronger than functional and in some aspects stronger than economic restrictions (Chevalier, 1995). By illustrating the presence of multiple syntaxes of space simultaneously among the same group of people, the case of German Turks poses a challenge at least to the convention that there is a stable context independent of syntax of space for a group or collectivity, and that this is grounded in their culture. Transnational collectivities not only have multiple and fluid identities, but also have multiple syntaxes of space which shift according to context. Thus it is misleading to look for a cultural essence or a fixed identity informing their practices. The crucial role of the context may have important implications for discussions of the homogenising effects of cultural flows within the frame of globalisation. Second, the difference in consumption practices and in the consumers' manipulation of an object's symbolism are grounded not only in the consumers' different experiences, but also in their ideals and desires. Such cases draw attention to the fact that we need to focus on the parameters of consumption rather than on the goods themselves. They enable us to situate consumption in a larger social field, in which it can be said to make sense in terms of the social strategies of a particular group.

Conclusion

The force of dislike and the second generation

The notion of generations in reference to German Turks needs to be used cautiously. It is a discursively constituted category. It is one of the crucial topics of the dominant discourse on immigration and on German Turks in particular. The concept of generation used in the literature on immigrants and German Turks is based on a positivistic generation differentiation, and it entails a hidden logic of progress based on a mechanical and quantitatively measurable linear time concept. For a critique of the use of generations in relation to German Turks see Çağlar (1996).

The phenomenon covered here refers to a particular consumer behaviour of the so-called first-generation German Turks. The decoration and principles of organisation of second- and third-generation German Turks' flats – whether in Turkey or Germany – differ considerably. Thus, the immediate relevance of focusing on things past, or becoming past, might be questioned. However, despite the substantial differences between the two, the former has a strong presence in the latter. It is an emotionally loaded partner in a silent dialogue. Ironically, the consumption patterns of the first generation structure the quality- and brand-name-conscious consumer behaviour of second- and third-generation German Turks by creating distaste and aversion. It seems that later generations' dislikes prove to be in many ways more socially diagnostic than their positive desires. Two-thirds of second- and third-generation German Turks, when asked about their preferences in house furniture and about the reasons why they prefer to shop in IKEA, responded by elaborating on the consumption preferences of their parents, and how they did not want to have such items in their apartments. Dislike obviously became a part of their conscious and strategic relationship with goods in their social life.

Although much neglected in the literature on consumption, there is a series of relationships between desire and disgust, or desire and detested objects, and we need to consider dislike or distaste as sources of consumer imagery which are as important as desire (Wilk, 1995). Rather than desiring a lifestyle whose boundaries are well defined, second- and third-generation German Turks relate to the material world through such strong feelings of dislike and aversion. However, taste and distaste do not form simple complementary pairs: taste cannot be seen simply as the inversion, opposite or mirror of distaste in forming social boundaries (Wilk, 1995). The connotation field of the consumption practices of their parents pattern second-generation consumer behaviour. Not buying second-hand furniture for their German flats and not shopping from Turkish furniture shops are desires that come to the fore in shaping their lifestyle. Although they try to constitute a life space different to that of their parents, this generational relationship and a strong desire to differentiate themselves from their parents are more emotionally loaded and forceful because of the stigmatisation of the *Almanci* image in both Turkish and German society.

Moreover, there is a dominant discourse in Germany which formulates German Turks' 'integration' into or 'resignation' from German society, their life prospects, orientations and the question of their belonging around their consumption strategies. Moving away from the consumption patterns of the first generation is taken as an indicator of German Turks' shifting life orientations and future prospects from Turkey to Germany. These patterns become the index of settlement in Germany and a changing belongingness from Turkish into German society (Zentrum für Türkeistudien, 1992, 1995; Senatsverwaltung für..., 1994). German Turks' consumption practices, and particularly their house ownership, are made an index of their belonging to Turkish and German society. Trapped in this discourse, second- and third-generation German Turks forge strategies of consumption to distance themselves from their parents' consumption patterns through distaste, and ironically this becomes part of their consumer behaviour.

Material culture studies and globalisation

Globalisation provides the current framework for the analysis of cultural practices and cultural transformation in the contemporary world. The tensions between cultural homogenisation and cultural heterogenisation set free by the transnational flow of goods, information and images are intrinsic to globalisation processes. In fact, investigation of these tensions forms the axis of discussions of global cultural interaction (Appadurai, 1990)

Those who forecast cultural homogenisation as a major outcome of globalisation underline the impact of commoditised culture on this process. Because the vehicle of universal global culture is consumer culture, the massive flow of consumer culture is argued to erode cultural differences in our interconnected world. At this point, material culture studies have something important to contribute to the homogenisation debate, because these – and especially the studies on consumer culture which demonstrate that 'there is no uniform cultural response to consumer goods and images' (Featherstone, 1987a) – draw attention to the processes of symbolisation and resymbolisation active in the flow of goods and images.

Material culture studies which show that 'goods which are identical at the point of purchase or allocation may be recontextualised by different social groups in an infinite number of ways' (Miller, 1987. p.196) with different meanings and symbolism pose an important challenge to the forecast of world homogenisation. However, the case of the coffee table is significant from a more radical point of view. Here we can see how the meanings, function and significance of a table change in the process not of changing hands, but merely contexts in the same hands.

Notes on Chapter 13

1   Although this attitude is changing over time, the discrepancy of investment and care between their residences is still apparent. Of course, in evaluating this difference it should not be forgotten that they are not tenants in their Turkish flats.

2   In the living-rooms of the second generation there is an increasing interest in display by means of a glass cabinet, but still the seating furniture, not these displays, dominate living-rooms.

3   Presents received from German friends more easily find their way in these displays.

4   For a similar phenomenon regarding a different fashion among German Turkish youth, see Brösekamp (1994).

5   Within the general layout of their apartments in Turkey, these rooms, contrary to those in their Germany apartments, are used to receive their guests, while another room functions as a living-room for the family and close friends.

6   In fact, their concern with keeping up with fashion works against their concern with style and homogeneity. Sets bought according to the fashions of the day result in heterogeneity among sets in time.

7   Although it can be set to a variety of heights, I have never seen this done in Turkish homes.

8   It was not only the apartments I visited during my fieldwork that had this kind of furniture arranged in this way in their living-rooms; representations of Turkish homes in German newspapers, casually revealed during interviews, surveys or in television programmes all reveal this kind of array of seating furniture.

9   The tenor of the negative associations of *Almancı* is, despite the grouping's economically well-to-do position, the lack of all sorts of cultural and social capital.

References

Appadurai, A., (1986), 'Introduction: Commodities and the Politics of Value', in A. Appadurai (ed.), *The Social Life of Things*, Cambridge

– (1990) 'Disjuncture and Difference in the Global Cultural Economy', in M. Featherstone (ed.), *Global Culture: Nationalism, Globalisation and Modernity*, Sage Publications, London

Bourdieu, P. (1974), *Outline of a Theory of Practice*, Cambridge University Press, Cambridge
– (1984), *Distinction: A Social Critique of the Judgement of Taste*, Routledge & Kegan Paul, Melbourne and Henley
– (1985), 'The Social Space and the Genesis of Groups', in *Theory, Culture and Society*, no 14, pp.723–44
– (1986), 'The Forms of Capital', in J.G. Richardson (ed.), *Handbook of Theory and Research for the Sociology of Education*, Greenwood Press, New York and London, pp.241–58
– (1990), *In Other Words: Essays Towards a Reflexive Sociology*, Polity Press, Cambridge
Brösekamp (1994), *Körperliche, Freundheit. Zum Problem der interkulturellen Begegnung im Sport*, Sanht Augustin
Çağlar, A. (1995), 'German Turks in Berlin: Social Exclusion and Strategies of Social Mobility', *New Community*, vol. 21, no 3, pp.309–23
– (1996), 'Consumption, Savings and the Discursive Construction of Generations: The Case of German Turks', paper presented at the 4th EASA Conference, Barcelona, 12–5 July 1996
– (1997), 'Go Go Dog and German Turks' Demand for Pet Dogs', *Journal of Material Culture*, vol. 2, no 1, pp.77–94
Chevalier, S. (1995), 'Learning How to Construct a Meaningful Universe: A Case Study of French and British Interior Decor', paper presented at the 5th Interdisciplinary Conference Research in Consumption, Lund
Douglas, M. and B. Isherwood (1979), *The World of Goods*, Basic Books, New York
Featherstone, M. (1987a), 'Consumer Culture, Symbolic Power and Universalism', in *Mass Culture, Popular Culture and Social Life in the Middle East*, in G. Stauth and S. Zubaida (eds), Campus Verlag, Frankfurt-am-Main
– (1987b), 'Life Style and Consumer Culture', in *Theory Culture and Society*, no 4, pp.55–70
– (1990), 'Global Culture: An Introduction', in *Global Culture: Nationalism, Globalisation and Modernity*, M. Featherstone (ed.), Sage Publications, London
Friedman, J. (1995), *Consumption and Identity*, Harwood Academic Publishers, Switzerland, Australia
Joppke, C. (1986), 'The Cultural Dimensions of Class Formation and Class Struggle: On the Social Theory of Bourdieu', *Berkeley Journal of Sociology*, no 31, pp.53–78
Miller, D. (1987), *Material Culture and Mass Consumption*, Basil Blackwell, Oxford
– (1988), 'Appropriating the State on the Council Estate', *Man*, no 23, pp.353–72.
Senatsverwaltung für Gesundheit und Soziales, Die Ausländerbeauftragte das Senate von Berlin (1994), *Presseerklaerung: Türkische Berliner halten trotz wiedriger Umstaende and der Integration fest*
– (1997), *Berliner Jugendliche türkischer Herkunft*, Pressemitteilung, Berlin
Simmel, G. (1957), 'Fashion', *Journal of Sociology*, vol. 62, no 6, pp.541–58
– (1991), 'The Problem of Style', *Theory, Culture and Society*, no 8, pp.63–71
Wilk, R. (1995), 'Learning Distaste', paper presented at the 5th Interdisciplinary Conference Research in Consumption, Lund
Zentrum für Türkeistudien (1992), *Konsumgewohnheiten und wirtschaftliche Situation der türkischen Bevölkerung in der Bundesrepublik Deutschland*, Essen
– (1995), *Medienkonsum und Medienverhalten der türkischen Wohnbevölkerung in der Bundesrepublik Deutschland*, Essen

14

Negotiating Identities: Media Representations of Different Generations of Turkish Migrants in Germany

Lale Yalçın-Heckmann

Turkish labour migrants are the object, and increasingly the subject, of discussions on identity and also of politics and popular culture in Germany as well as in Turkey (Çağlar, 1998; Karakaşoğlu-Aydın, 1999). That there are different discourses in the media, amongst the German public and across the international borders between Turkey and Germany is a given. This chapter investigates the type of inter-action between these discourses. There is, to begin with, some evidence that not only have the discourses become multi-vocal, so that they have multiple meanings with equal validity and probability, but also that they are being implemented in the struggle for cultural hegemony between different gender, generational, social and ethnic groups. The focus in this chapter is on the contested and negotiated discourses of identity, and especially on media use of hybrid and hyphenated identities for different generations of Turkish migrants. Hybridity and hybridisation refer to plural and fluid identities and identity processes, whereby cultural categories are transcended and subverted (Bhabha, 1994; Werbner, 1997). The questions of who is being portrayed as having a hybrid identity, to whom this hybridity is denied, and what the 'cost' of hybrid identities is will be explored. The first illustration of these negotiations is from a recent film on the multicultural underground world in Germany. In 1998, a young film director, Fatih Akın, who is of Turkish origin and lives in Hamburg, made a film called *Kurz und schmerzlos* (*Short and Painless*) which had great success in Germany. The film is a thriller about a group of three young men in Hamburg and their involvement in the city's criminal world. The three are all of different ethnic origins, one Turkish, one Greek and one Serbian. They form a gang, based on staunch friendship, helping each other in and out of the dangers of the Hamburg underworld. As a back-ground to the story, the family of the Turkish man is depicted, and a background motif is his relationship to his younger sister. Inverting the stereotypes about 'the Turkish family' and the relations within it – which are widespread among the German public – the young man and hero of the film not only supports his sister's relationship with her Greek friend, but also helps her to hide this from the rest of the family. Typical media representations of Turkish families in Germany are dominated by mothers of rural background, wearing headscarves, fathers as typical patriarchs, controlling their daughters and dominating other female family members, and brothers who seem to be interested only in fighting with knives to defend the 'family honour'.[1] The film could therefore be seen as a breakthrough in German images of Turks, especially as it is produced by a second-generation Turk. The story could indeed be seen as a eulogy to the multicultural social reality in Germany. The director and the lead actor, Mehmet Kurtuluş, state in an interview their weariness of stereotypes about Turks in Germany, and claim to represent the reality of the young generation of migrant workers.[2] They express their vision of their role in the German film industry: 'We are brought up in two cultures, we are the new Germans... The mentality of *Gastarbeiter* ['guest worker'] is past, the German film business cannot ignore us anymore'(*Die Zeit-Punkte* 2 (1999), p.86) There are multiple inversions in the film. For instance, the representatives of the second generation of migrant-worker families, whose parents belong to 'traditionally' adversarial social groups (Greeks and Turks, Turks and Serbs) are very close friends as well as in love in the film.[3] Secondly, the Turkish brother and sister, who otherwise would be represented in a tense and hierarchical power relationship, are in this film best friends, supporting one another against the intrusion of conservative family circles. Another – and to my mind one of the most original inversions in the film – is the depiction of the parental generation and the manner of their involvement in the lives of the second generation. This inversion is implied intentionally or unintentionally through the director's fine sense of humour: the parental generation is portrayed as being concerned not with keeping 'law and order' within their families, as in stereotypical presentations, but as occupied with the 'other world', namely religion. The parents of the Turkish hero and his sister are seen mostly praying, either at home or in the mosque. In one scene, when the young man comes home at sunrise after being beaten up brutally by a Mafia gang, the father, who has been praying, seems to take no notice of his son's condition, and asks him to come and pray with him. When the heavily bruised and bleeding son gently but clearly refuses him, the father insists, apparently still ignoring or not seeing his son's state: 'My son, this life, like a film, will come to an end some day, come and pray with me'. The humour in this passage, which is spoken in Turkish, raising associations of kitsch romantic language and parlance in Turkish popular culture, succeeds in inverting the common stereotype of a 'dominating and controlling' parental generation even if – perhaps unintentionally – reproducing another stereotype of the parental generation's Islamic fervour. In all of these depictions, one sees the emergence of a specific attitude, reflecting the perplexity and uncomprehending closeness of the second generation towards the parental one. Until recently, the parental generation was commonly represented as ignorant of the needs and concerns of coming generations; now it is the second generation's turn to look back at the parental one and be equally perplexed and ignorant, albeit with a sensitivity to difference and towards the depictions and representations of the 'other': 'German society'. The parental generation is their 'intimate other',[4] hence a point of departure for them, different to the point(s) available to mainstream German youth, and a social category which could now be re-created from their own eyes, with their own narratives and reclaimed with new subjectivities and meanings.

Further examples of negotiated identities are drawn primarily from a selection of the media and media representations of migrants. This selection entails the agency of the dominant cultural group. Media representations of Turkish migrants in Germany have been multi-vocal, but have also changed significantly since the early 1970s. At the height of labour migration to and family reunion in Germany in the 1960s, before the end of the labour import treaty, there were reports on Turkish migrants, reflecting partly anxiety among the German public of being 'over-run' or invaded by foreigners and Turks. For instance, one of the most widely read weekly journals, *Der Spiegel*, in 1973 had a cover story with the title, 'One million Turks: Turks are coming – every man for himself', which continued with the following short introduction to the title:

> Almost a million Turks are living in the Federal Republic of Germany, 1.2 million are waiting at home to travel here. The pressure from the Boshporus aggravates a crisis, which is already swelling in those densely populated urban centres swamped by foreigners. Cities such as Berlin, Munich or Frankfurt could hardly cope with the invasion. Ghettos are being created and sociologists are already predicting the decay of cities, criminality and social pauperisation, as in Harlem.[5]

In contrast to this dramatising and provocative tone, *Der Spiegel* has produced many recent title stories and pictures representing the situation of migrants in a balanced manner, increasingly quoting the migrants themselves, especially letting members of the second generation speak for themselves, and as spokespeople. In a more recent issue (11 January 1999), for instance, the political debate on dual nationality was taken up with the title 'Who could become German? The operation double pass', and a picture of a young Turkish girl holding two passports, German and Turkish. In the story, this young woman from Berlin is said to be angry with such questions about her identity, whether she is a Kurd or a Turk like her parents, or a German: 'I was born in Germany, I live in Germany, I dream in German ... but I am not so for many people, who would treat me as a Turk'. She is said to wish to be perceived not according to her passport but to what she radiates, namely self-confidence (p.24). As the illustrations show, the self-perception and self-articulation of second-generation migrants (some call them post-migrants – see Baumann and Sunier, 1995) strongly rely on the agency of the media and German public opinion. These self-perceptions, although they have largely adopted the ascriptions of 'others' (such as 'being between cultures', or 'belonging to no one culture fully') and are deeply aware of their own images in the eyes of others, are addressed to the dominant German culture as creative moments of resistance and challenge.[6]

A brief ethnographic and historical contextualisation of this discussion is necessary, however. Turkish labour migrants in Germany, being the largest ethnic minority there, although without any collective status as a minority or ethnic group, form the most significant group of ethnic 'others' in the country. As labour migrants, along with descendants and family members, they live mostly in industrial and post-industrial metropolitan, large or middle-sized urban centres.

They number 2.3 million, accounting for 30 percent of the foreigners in Germany (Germany has approximately 82 million inhabitants, about 9 percent of them foreign). Their migration is relatively recent: the labour import treaty was signed in 1961, and the first wave of Turkish labourers came in the early 1960s. Although many have been residents of Germany for more than 35 years, they possess foreign nationality and are still excluded from all citizenship rights, including voting in local or national elections.[7]

Turkish labour migrants in Germany, due to this specificity and the recent history of their migration, have long been called *Gastarbeiter*. This term contained primarily a legal and political definition of their socioeconomic and political status in Germany. It was, however, a self-identificatory term as well. The Turkish workers have long seen themselves as guest workers, and have believed that they have been called to work in Germany, and that when they have accumulated enough capital they will return to Turkey. The term *Gastarbeiter* could be said to have a derogatory connotation in contemporary usage, and to many its use to describe labour migrants would be considered politically incorrect. In the eyes of the Turks themselves, it is has largely become an unacceptable and undesirable, if not outdated, term. In public and political discourse, they are referred to more often as *ausländische/türkische Mitbürger* ('foreign/Turkish co-citizens'), hence not-quite-real citizens. Depending on the political tendency of the speaker, and on the context of reference, they could also be referred to as 'migrants', 'settlers with a foreign passport', '*Inländer* ['natives'] with a foreign passport', or *Bildungsinländer* (educated within the country). These three terms, for instance, have been systematically used in the last five years or so in the reports of the Federal Commissioner for Foreigners in Germany. Hence they have been adopted within the official language of the governmental authorities, even though the Commissioner had an advisory and politically limited position within the previous Christian democratic and liberal coalition government.

With the social differentiation within the Turkish migrant community, and with increasing debates about the nature of multiculturalism in Germany, there seem to be new trends in public discourse about introducing new identities for migrants. Second-generation Turks in Germany especially are subject to these discussions of identity. For the second generation especially, but also for the first, the term 'German Turk' (*Deutsche-Türken*) is being increasingly used (see Leggewie and Şenocak, 1993; Tan, 1997). Studies of the social differentiation among Turkish labour migrants, such as the work of Çağlar (1995), and texts on Turkish migrant identity and biographical changes through the migration experience by authors like Schiffauer (1991), Pfluger-Schindlbeck (1989), Wolbert (1984 and 1995) and Mıçıyazgan (1986), throw light on the processes of naming, identity discourse and social positioning within the larger society. These studies and my own research on religious socialisation among Turkish families in Germany and on Turkish communities, and their development and internal structures in two small cities in Germany and France provide some of the background to the discussion that follows. Additional material on the tensions experienced by second-generation migrants as they construct their own identities vis-à-vis the first generation has been available all along in the fiction and writing of authors from different ethnic groups of labour migrants in Germany, some of them first- or second-generation migrants themselves. In an essay on the so-called migrant literature in Germany and analysis of the debates on this literature, Fischer and McGowan cite the work of Franco Biondi, who tells the story of a third-generation Italian, Mamo, in Germany:

> Mamo cannot identify with the German society that oppresses him. Yet, born and brought up in Germany, he does not feel an Ausländer. He speaks a teenage working-class argot not specific to immigrants: 'He spoke like the natives. After all he was one'. Much of his bitterness is actually related to his generation and class as a whole, treated as 'broken dolls in a lumber room', trained for useless jobs which will soon be automated ... Mamo scorns the *Pappkoffer* [cardboard suitcase, emblem of the first generation of *Gastarbeiter*] images of immigrants in his well-meaning schoolbooks: 'miserable, moaning figures with cardboard suit-cases ... people choking on their homesickness and their tears'. This is his father's generation ... When the theme of *Gastarbeiter* is discussed at school, he angrily resists the stares of fellow pupils.[8]

Fischer and McGowan's analysis points to the tensions in the process of social positioning and self-identification for the second generation. Their discussion, however, underlines primarily the role of the social environment, of the 'German others' in creating Mamo's consciousness as 'the foreigner' (1996, pp.9–10):

> Gradually ... the experience of prejudice turns him into a *Gastarbeiter* by forcing him to develop a consciousness of his identity as the deviant, disliked Other. It is – like 'Jewishness' in Nazi Germany – an identity created by the oppressor. A fellow pupil taunts him with a *Blutwurst* [blood sausage], which he tells him is a 'Turk's penis', indifferent to Mamo's actual ethnic identity: foreign is foreign. Mamo never felt much in common with Turks, but now begins to feel 'foreign'; he dreams of studying his face in a mirror: that is, he is forced to view his identity as an image of himself as transmitted to him in the gaze of the powerful ...

Neglected in this analysis is the role and structural and symbolic positioning of the first generation, especially how this generation is to be symbolically and socially classified according to the perceptions of the recipient wider society. I suggest that second-generation migrants are involved in more complex processes of identity construction than those suggested in a bipolar relationship between the perceptions of the 'German others' and the second generation. There are third and even fourth interlocutors in this trialogue/quadralogue, namely the parental generation and also the 'other others', as in the case of 'the Turk' for 'the Italian' of Mamo's experience. When one considers the ethnographic material, which helps us to contextualise the processes of naming and self-identification, one is struck by the difficulty felt by Turkish labour migrants and the second generation in finding a single common name for their identity. Some say they are Turks living in Germany, some say they are Turks who happen to live in Germany, some say they are Turks and Berliners and the like, but hardly any say they are Germans, or German Turks for that matter. In fact, in much of the internal discourse among the Turks in Germany the question of locality, that is origins in Turkey, is still relevant. Even the second-generation Turks, born in Germany, when they meet someone perhaps older than themselves, asks 'nerelisiniz?' ('where are you from?') expecting the answer to be some town or region in Turkey. Nicknames with associations of *hemşeri* ('compatriot') and ethnic/regional ties, such as 'Sıvas'lı Ahmet' (Ahmet from Sıvas, a province in Turkey) or 'Laz Mehmet' (Mehmet of the ethnic group of Laz from the Black Sea region of Turkey) are used as frequently among the second generation as among the first.

The usage of media terms like 'new Germans' by the film director and actor already mentioned, or 'German' by the young girl in the recent issue of *Der Spiegel* (February 1999), are almost exceptional, and reflect more the left-liberal political standing of the paper and the journal in which the interviews appeared than the widespread use of the terms among second-generation migrants themselves. They imply a political project of becoming 'new Germans', rather than any acknowledgment or awareness of their own acceptance and incorporation into German society as the new Germans. Other second-generation Turks, deeply aware of this lack of acceptance, express their ambivalent positioning in the media too. In an interview in the same issue of *Der Spiegel* (p.24), for instance, the rapper sisters Sema and Derya Mutlu, who made a name in the German rap scene, express their frustration at being immediately associated with Turkey: apparently because of their names, 'without being able to open their mouths, they would be immediately received with the words, "Rapper? From Turkey? Cool!".'[9] It apparently occurs to very few people that these musicians associate themselves primarily with Germany and Hamburg, even if they rap partly in Turkish and on Turkish themes. The questions here, then, evolve around the processes of naming subjective and objective identities, and processes of differentiation between these. More specifically one could ask why it is difficult for these Turks to call themselves German Turks, even if the ascription German Turk is becoming increasingly common in the media and public. What are the implications for, and positioning of, Turks in Germany with hybrid identities such as German Turk or Turkish German? What is a hybrid identity for Turks? Why are they more inclined to adopt hyphenated identities which combine localism (for instance *Berliner Türke*) with ethnic origins? Are there generational and other differences among the labour migrants in the way they choose to name themselves as hyphenated or as hybrid identities? I have suggested that processes of hybridisation could be seen as a marker of inter-generational difference. In this context, the first-generation migrants can hardly be thought to have possessed hybrid identities at all. One could furthermore ask whether hybridisation pertains only to the younger generations, and only in some contexts like popular culture, music and media representations. In a similar critical evaluation of Bhabha's 'Third Space', Friedman (1997, p.79) questions the limits of the fluidity of identities, which are implied in hybridisation: 'But for whom, one might ask, is such cultural trans-migration a reality?' Friedman goes on to demonstrate that 'the post-colonial border-crossers', as depicted in Bhabha's 'Third Space', celebrate complexity, hybridity and fluidity of identities and attribute 'wholeness and authenticity to the past' (pp.79–80). Similarly, different generations of Turkish migrants are thought to have different and contrasting access to fluid and complex cultural identities: the younger generation has more access to complex cultural identities than the older one, and the older generation is encapsulated in its 'authentic' but 'past' identity.

The theoretical discussions on hybridity and hybridisation point to their symbolic power and capacity to challenge existing social and cultural categories. Those authors who emphasise the symbolic power of hybridisation celebrate these processes especially as a just critique of the culture and spatial boundedness of transnational and migrant identities (Olwig and Hastrup, 1997; Baumann, 1997; Çağlar, 1997). In a powerful critique, Çağlar underlines the insight from consumer-culture studies. She points out that 'A growing number of people define themselves in terms of multiple national attachments and feel at ease with subjectivities that encompass plural and fluid cultural identities' (p.169). She draws attention to the 'unprecedented trans-local flows of capital, labour, people, goods, technology and media images ... [Hence] to confront the resultant pro-liferation of boundary-crossing lifestyles, cultural practices and institutional forms, it is no longer possible to confine our scholarly discourses about legal rights or cultural affiliations to nation-states' (p.169). Çağlar's most forceful objection is to the underlying assumption, which is also found in hybridity theories, about 'one space, one culture'. This point has also been raised by Friedman (1997). Although, she says, 'creolisation and hybridisation are the most celebrated con-cepts used in critiques of cultures as homogeneous, bounded, continuous and incommensurable wholes', they are 'in danger of embracing the very reifications they seek to overcome' (Çağlar, 1997, p.172), because they themselves reify 'one space, one culture' by making them into bounded concepts in trying to show how they are being transgressed.

P. Werbner joins Çağlar in her critical view of the problem of essentialising space and culture in hybridisation, and explores the limits of hybridity herself. She points, however, to issues of the routinisation of hybridity as well as the processes of demarcation of hybridity by hegemonic social forces rather than by ordinary people themselves (1997, p.2). Hence she brings the element of power and the politicisation of culture (Wright, 1998) into the process of hybridisation and cultural essentialisms. Along with Werbner, I argue, as illustrated with various examples above, that hybridisation is very closely associated with the processes of the politicisation of culture, demarcation of 'own' versus 'other/marginal' cultures, and of differential inclusion of different generations of the migrant population.

Çağlar's argument that hyphenated identities, such as German-Turk, British-Pakistani, French-Algerian, European-Muslim 'equate "culture", "nation" and "community"' (1997, p.175), brings up the dilemma of anthropological insight and critique being often diametrically opposed to the culture as practised by the ethnic minorities and multiculturalists. Although the hyphenated identity of the younger generation of migrants essentialises their culture and equates culture with a space and a community, it has nevertheless an emancipatory quality, namely that it is positioned as a political statement against the discursive background of naming the migrants as Turks or foreigners only, as the case of the rapping Mutlu sisters cited above illustrates, or more significantly as being 'torn between'. There were and still are many titles of journalistic and academic writings such as 'Germany in the morning' – taking part in school, work, institutions in German society during the daytime – and 'Turkey in the evening' – family life as a purely Turkish language and social context. The hyphenated identity which is attributed to younger-generation migrants therefore empowers them as belonging to two cultures, encompassing both, not torn between them.

I do not wish, however, to evaluate the usage of hyphenated identity alone and underestimate its ambivalences. Hyphenation challenges the assumed and imagined cultural borders of social unities. Similarly, the hyphenated identities of German Turks are loaded with ambivalence about their social and cultural loyalties to certain spaces and social groups.

Three representations of such younger-generation identities, and one older-generation one in a left-liberal intellectual journal *Die Zeitmagazine*, which devoted this issue (12 December 1997) to Turks in Germany, should help to illustrate my point.

In the first picture, a young German Turk is depicted on the title page, and the text says that she is a 22-year-old law student in Hamburg: 'As her home town she says Izmir although she is born in Hamburg' (pp.1–3). The editors of the journal see an anomaly in this depiction, a split in allegiances and loyalties. In a sense, their perplexity is understandable. How come a young woman born and brought up in a big German city considers another city, which she probably knows only from summer holidays, and perhaps associates with intimate memories of relatives and friends, as her *Heimat*?[10] The editors' misunderstanding seems to lie in their expectation of one single and unhesitating answer. When the young woman's answer is contextualised in our previous discussion of the tactical usage of one cultural space against another (citing Izmir as home town in Germany/to a German audience, but possibly preferring Hamburg as the locality of identification in Turkey/to a Turkish audience). Through such tactical usage and management of identities and meanings, second-generation Turks in Germany try to resist the power of cultural categories of the dominant culture, even if they have to use the same categories of localities, cultures and identities, partly re-essentialising these themselves.

The second picture depicts a young Turkish woman who lives in Munich. The picture is accompanied by an interview with her. The text for the picture says, 'To live in Turkey? Never! Turkish women do not wear mini-skirts and do not go to nightclubs – this is what their parents wish. Ayzit Bostan (in the picture) from Munich lives like a young German. And sometimes she is even ashamed of being a Turk. "Why?" she asks herself.' In the text itself, which reports her own narrative, she says, 'According to my passport, I am Turkish – still. I actually find it a pity that one is defined according to her/his passport; because I feel myself neither Turkish nor German.'

Within this brief narrative, her identity is indexed to her lifestyle, passport, ethnic origin and personal history, and defined by herself and the media with ambivalence and essentialisms: Turkish due to passport, German due to lifestyle, neither German nor Turkish in her feelings; in other words, with all the ambivalences and shades of depiction of hyphenated identities. As discussed above, a salient feature of the hyphenated identity of German Turks is its reference to the parental generation. Even if hyphenation does not necessarily mean a break with the parental generation, it suggests at least a critical positioning for the German Turk. The narrative of the young woman from Munich above is set around the rupture of her bonds with her parents. This rupture is due to her marriage with a German, she claims. Here severing the bond with the parental generation and with everything associated with it seems to be the crucial criterion for hyphenation and hybridisation.

The discourse on hybrid identities of German Turks is richest when it refers to the pop-music industry in Germany and Turkey. Young German Turkish musicians are portrayed as transgressors and subverters of cultural boundaries (Çağlar, 1998). In such media representations, however, the subversion is directed not towards the 'culture' of the dominant majority, but towards the 'culture' of the parents, the minority group.

The third picture shows a young pop singer who became famous in Turkey and among Turks in Germany. The text for the picture says: 'Hip-hop for Atatürk. The *Deutschländer* are the stars of the Turkish pop-music [*Deutschländer* is the German word for the Turkish term *Almancı*, used by Turks in Turkey somewhat derogatorily of Turks in Germany. The usage underlines the relationship of Turks to Germany, that they make a living from the country]. They come from Reinheim or Heidelberg. And they hate the music of their fathers.'[11]

The parental generation is represented in the media with such images as in this fourth picture: an elderly Turkish woman is said to be proudly – as proud as the youngsters are of their graffiti – displaying the cheap kitsch items in her shop. This is her place, the text says. The woman in the picture radiates self-confidence on the one hand, but the 'assumed' authenticity and unambiguity of the parental generation on the other. Her place and identity is in the past and unambiguous, hence clearly juxtaposed with the identities of the younger-generation Turks.

To conclude, although hybridisation and hyphenation of identity processes seem to open up the national polity by allowing Turkish labour migrants and their descendants to claim multiple identities, not all generations are equally affected by this process. The younger generation is depicted as participating in it, but the subversion of the categories is directed primarily towards the 'culture' of parents, subverting through essentialism.

As the rupture with the parental generation seems to be a precondition for the hybrid identities of the younger generation, the predicament of loyalty and of defining the 'community' looms large. Younger Turks, who claim a legitimate space in Germany and the recognition of their identities, either appropriate certain cultural niches as their own, as with break-dance, rapping or Turkish pop music, or, as Çağlar argues, seek recognition through social mobility within Turkey. A third strategy seems to be the appropriation of the images and representations of Turkish migrants in the media. The younger generation tries to provide new images of various generations and hence invert some of the existing stereotypes and perceptions. Here, however, it faces the problem of re-creating its relationship to the 'intimate other' and of being accepted without co-opting into the mainstream images of Turks available in German society. These negotiations with the parental generation, as well as with the wider public, open up new creative and contestable spaces of identity politics for this younger generation of Turks in Germany.

Notes on Chapter 14

1   For such stereotypical yet very popular representations of Turkish families, I cite here two examples: the film *Yasemin* directed by Hark Bohm and produced in 1987–8 had great success and was shown on many television channels. It portrays the love between a Turkish girl and her German boyfriend. In the story, Yasemin is torn between her love for her family and for her boyfriend. Her family shows hardly any support for her feelings, and is basically concerned with defending her reputation as a chaste girl, according to the 'traditions in Anatolia'. The father loves her but cannot resist the pressure of his conservative social background and surroundings; the mother is supportive, in private, but powerless in the face of the father and brother. The brother, again, loves his sister but is not prepared to hear her arguments. In the end, Yasemin is forced to flee from her family, which is determined to send her to Turkey, to protect her from the 'corrupt moral values' of German society. Her German boyfriend rescues her with his motorbike. A teenager version of this story appeared in *Bravo* in 1995, probably the most widely read teen magazine in Germany, under the title 'Aylin – The cry from the heart', a photostory about a Turkish teenager who falls in love with a German boy, gets brutally threatened by her family (father and brothers), is forced to marry an older Turkish man, and is sent to Turkey. She runs away, finds refuge with the German youth social work authorities, and gets support from a circle of German social workers, German friends and of course her boyfriend.

2   See the interview 'Beyond the clichés', carried out with them and other young film-makers of Turkish origin, by Ayhan Bakırdöşen, a journalist of Turkish origin, and published in *Die Zeit Punkte: Türken in Deutschland*, No 2 (1999). In fact, Bakırdöşen describes the story of the film *Kurz und schmerzlos* and the three characters as 'the friendship of three German young men of foreign origin, who get into conflict with the law' (p.86). See below for a discussion of this depiction.

3   Interestingly enough the inversion of 'traditional enmity' among members of various ethnic and national groups is a common theme in various recent films of young directors in Turkey too. There seems to be a wave of films showing stories of love and friendship between Turks and Greeks, Turkish Cypriots and Greek Cypriots, Turks and Kurds. The choice of such themes by young directors seems to be symptomatic of the social conflicts and tensions in contemporary Turkish society.

4   I thank Gül Özyeğin for drawing my attention to this reading of the relationship between different generations of Turkish migrants in Germany.

5   *Der Spiegel*, No 31 (30 July 1973), p.24, cited in Huhnke (1997), p.98. The translation is by the author.

6   How these creative moments are afterwards reshaped to be ordered within the
     hegemonic culture is another story.
7   This will be changing significantly in the near future. The recent amendment to
     the citizenship law prepared by the present Social Democratic/Green coalition
     government, giving extensive citizenship rights to the children of migrants, is
     accepted in parliament, and introduces dual citizenship for the children of a
     large group of migrants born in Germany. They will then have to opt for one
     nationality at the age of 23.
8   Fischer and McGowan (1996), p.9. The citation from Franco Biondi is from his
     Abschied der zerschellten Jahre (*Farewell to the Shattered Years*), Kiel, 1984, pp.24–5,
     40–1, 82.
9   In German: 'Rapper? Aus der Türkei? Geil!'
10   I thank Max Günter Behrendt for drawing my attention to this point.
11   Hip-hop and rap music are popular and encouraged among the younger-
     generation Turks in Germany, and this type of music is seen to reflect primarily
     the taste of the youth as opposed to that of the parental generation. The fact that
     a Turkish-German pop group represented Germany in the Eurovision song contest,
     and incorporated Turkish melodies into their song shows more the 'official'
     recognition of 'multiculturalism' by the media in Germany. Hence the choice
     refers to the cultural negotiations between Turks and Germans. It says, however,
     little about varying tastes and cultural preferences across different generations
     of migrants. I thank Deniz Kandiyoti for drawing my attention to this point,
     although I may have drawn conclusions from this cultural politics different to hers.

References

Baumann, Gerd (1997), 'Dominant and Demotic Discourses of Culture: Their
    Relevance to Multi-Ethnic Alliances', in Pnina Werbner and Tariq Modood
    (eds), *Debating Cultural Hybridity*, Zed, London, pp.209–25
Baumann, Gerd and Thijl Sunier (eds) (1995), *Post-Migration Ethnicity*, Amsterdam
Bhabha, Homi (1994), *The Location of Culture*, Routledge, London
Çağlar, Ayşe (1995), 'German Turks in Berlin: Social Exclusion and Strategies for
    Social Mobility', in *New Community*, vol. 21, no 3, pp.309–23
— (1997), 'Hyphenated Identities and the Limits of "Culture"', in Tariq Modood and
    Pnina Werbner (eds) *The Limits of Multiculturalism in the New Europe* (London,
    Zed) pp.169–85
— (1998), 'Popular Culture, Marginality and Institutional Incorporation: German-
    Turkish Rap and Turkish Pop in Berlin', in *Cultural Dynamics* vol. 10, no 3,
    pp.243–61
Fischer, Sabine and Moray McGowan (1996), 'From "Pappkoffer" to Pluralism: On the
    Development of Migrant Writing in the Federal Republic of Germany', in David
    Horrocks and Eva Kolinsky (eds), *Turkish Culture in German Society Today*,
    Berghahn, Oxford, pp.1–22
Friedman, Jonathan (1997), 'Global Crises, the Struggle for Cultural Identity and
    Intellectual Porkbarrelling: Cosmopolitans versus Locals, Ethnics and Nationals

in an Era of De-hegemonisation', in Pnina Werbner and Tariq Modood (eds) *Debating Cultural Hybridity*, Zed, London, pp.70–89

Huhnke, Brigitta (1997), 'Sprachliche Realisierungen symbolischer Politik in Migrationsdiskursen', in Matthias Jung, Martin Wengeler and Karin Bke (eds), *Die Sprache des Migrationsdiskurses*, Westdeutscher Verlag, pp.89–105

Karakaşoğlu-Aydın, Yasemin (1999), 'Almanya'da Okullarda ve Üniversitelerde Başörtüsü Olayı', in *Toplum ve Bilim*, no 82 (Güz), pp.58–77

Leggewie, Claus and Zafer Şenocak (eds) (1993), *Deutsche Türken: Das Ende der Geduld*, Rowohlt, Hamburg

Mıhçıyazgan, Ursula (1986), *Wir haben uns vergessen: Ein intrakultureller Vergleich türkischer Lebensgeschichten*, ebv-Rissen, Hamburg

Olwig, Karen Fog and Kirsten Hastrup (eds) (1997), *Siting Culture: The Shifting Anthropological Object*, Routledge, London

Pfluger-Schindlbeck, Ingrid (1989), *'Achte die Älteren, liebe die Jüngeren': Sozialisation türkisch-alevitischer Kinder im Heimatland und in der Migration*, Athenäum, Frankfurt-am-Main

Schiffauer, Werner (1991), *Die Migranten aus Subay: Türken in Deutschland, eine Ethnographie*, Klett-Cotta, Stuttgart

Der Spiegel, no 31, 30 July 1973

Der Spiegel, no 2, 11 January 1999

Tan, Dursun (1997), 'Das Ende einer Gastarbeit: Ein Versuch, die Zukunft des deutsch-türkischen Zusammenlebens vorauszusehen', in Hans-Peter Waldhoff, Dursun Tan and Elçin Kürşat-Ahlers (eds), *Brücken zwischen Zivilisationen*, IKO, Frankfurt-am-Main, pp.235–52

Werbner, Pnina (1997), 'Introduction: The Dialectics of Cultural Hybridity', in Pnina Werbner and Tariq Modood (eds) *Debating Cultural Hybridity*, Zed, London, pp.1–26

Wolbert, Barbara (1984), *Migrationsbewältigung*, Herodot, Göttingen

– (1995), *Der getötete Paß: Rückkehr in die Türkei*, Akademie, Berlin

Wright, Susan (1998), 'The Politicisation of "Culture"', in *Anthropology Today*, vol. 14, no 1 (February), pp.7–15

Die Zeitmagazine, no 18 (2 May 1996)

Die Zeitmagazine, no 51 (12 December 1997)

Die Zeit-Punkte: Türken in Deutschland, no 2 (1999)

Afterword:
Recognising the Everyday[1]

Martin Stokes

The Turkish 'everydays' explored in this volume mark a self-conscious, energetic and intellectually buoyant moment in Turkish cultural studies and sociology. It is a moment to celebrate, but also to contemplate, particularly when one considers it as part of a more general movement in Turkish studies (see, for example, Bozdoğan and Kasaba, 1997; Keyder, 1999). Steps forward of this nature should not be taken for granted. How and why has it occurred? Certainly, the dominant alternatives for understanding contemporary Turkey are limited and increasingly unproductive, as Kandiyoti points out in her wide-ranging Introduction. On the one hand lie versions of modernisation theory, in their liberal and Marxian versions, which present national or regional case studies as positions between 'tradition' and 'modernity'. Modernisation theory's inability to account for a 'resurgent' Islam, embracing rather than rejecting modernity, is just one of many failings. On the other hand lie versions of post-colonial theory which do little to account for the specific trajectories and historical experiences of nation-states such as Turkey. This volume might be characterised as an exploration of the limitations of both and a search for alternatives.

However, neither modernisation nor post-colonial theories can exactly be described as being on the wane. Modernisation theory – intellectually discredited but institutionally ubiquitous – is an obvious case in point. Turkey has repeatedly been used by conservative Western scholars as a means of highlighting European historical distinction, and of stigmatising those apparently unable to keep up. The path to modernity was, in this view, unitary, inexorable and inevitable for those that simply had the historical will to break with the past. The image of heroic historical will has underwritten the work of generations of reformers in Turkey, as elsewhere. For those looking on from outside, particularly with commercial and strategic interests at heart, questions of democracy could always be manipulated in the context of the assumption that the imperative of historical will subordinates all else to it. These two sets of interests – that is to say, those of Turkish elites and those of academic Cold Warriors – converged to create a specific way of viewing Turkish modernity whose influence is still hard to shake off. Indeed (viz. Samuel Huntington), this historical wheel keeps getting reinvented for successive generations of policy advisors in the US and Western Europe. Turkey will no doubt continue to be understood in these terms for years to come.

Post-colonial theory is a more complex issue, since one can more plausibly make a case for its validity. It invites, for example, a more global grasp of Turkish particularities, making it more difficult to consider Turkey as 'a case' to be compared and ranked alongside others. There is surely much to be gained from considering Turkish history in the light of those other Southern European nation-states that lost their empires and global pre-eminence over the course of the nineteenth and twentieth centuries. And there is also something to be gained from considering independence and the existence of a large labourforce in Western Europe in terms of the global patterns of dependence with which much post-colonial analysis is concerned. There are certainly problems. Post-colonial theory has produced its own highly normative and institutionally influential ways of reading non-Western modernities. These valorise anti-essentialising forms of hybridity and migrancy, preferably literary, or at least with a recognisable 'high culture' component. Often, as a consequence, they fail to engage fully with the political and economic conditions that shape migrant and post-migrant lives in European and American metropoles. The theoretical problem lies, as with modernisation theory before it, in the fact that Turkey comes to provide little more than an illustrative case study in a history that has, so to speak, already taken place elsewhere. The institutional problem is that this view has simply become a kind of cultural orthodoxy that plays comfortably into the hands of commercial and state interests.

The alternatives are, then, very much alive and kicking. So how can one go about locating the energies that inform this volume? One could turn first to changes in the material and political contexts in which the Turkish intelligentsia have operated over the last two decades, both inside and outside the country. Though the Turkish universities have struggled with the debilitating legacy of YÖK,[2] the press and the printing industry have pressed hard at every emerging crack in the wall of stringent restrictions erected in successive military coups between 1960 and 1980. The energetic translation work of publishers such as İletişim has bought Marxian social theory to a wide and ever-broadening reading public in Turkey, more or less for the first time.[3] The costs of assembling and distributing books and journals dropped significantly in Turkey, as elsewhere. Changes in the material bases of intellectual production have made for a tremendous acceleration in the circulation of ideas. The opportunities provided by travel, the relatively free mobility of intellectual labour, e-mail and desktop publishing enabled fluid but sustained conversations between writers in Turkey, Europe and North America that would previously have required large conference budgets and troublesome logistics. The line which divided, with a few notable exceptions, Turkish scholars publishing in Turkish and non-Turkish scholars publishing in English, French or German seems to have disappeared for good. The somewhat exploitative division of labour between international and 'local' research is in the process of disappearing along with it, and this volume draws on a more equitable two-way traffic in published research.

One should also consider wider transformations. The field of 'the political' has shifted in Turkey, as elsewhere. The politics of class and ethnicity have been

significantly reconfigured by globalisation. Anxieties connected with these dis-
ruptions have been increasingly channelled into new public dramas of gender and
sexuality – the worlds of the *maganda*, the transsexual prostitute, the home-help,
the shop assistant, the veiled political activist, the *flâneuse* discussed so engagingly
in this volume – emergent grass-roots politics that have positively cried out for
critical attention. Finally, the metropolitan nature of modern Turkey has had a
significant impact on the character of social and cultural critique. The figure of
village and villager that once defined the character of Turkish sociology, if only as
a stable and 'known' point of reference, seems to have entirely disappeared. The
escalating violence between the Turkish army and the PKK (Kurdish Workers
Party) throughout the 1990s constituted one reason why 'the rural' seemed to
disappear from the intellectual landscape, partly because the political tensions
bound up with this conflict prohibited constructive public discussion. More
generally, proponents of globalisation have celebrated the emergence of 'global
cities' as a civilising influence, a cosmopolitan space of enlightened consumer
choice that would gradually unravel the narrowness and particularism wrought by
the age of nation-states. Istanbul thus appeared to engulf all, standing for the
whole country and more, bringing people together in unprecedented numbers
and ways, but also – more ambiguously – dividing them out in new kinds of social,
cultural and political isolation. These changing experiences of the city give rise to
the kinds of concerns and anxieties framed by Kandiyoti's opening quotation
from Marshall Berman (1982, p.17):

> as the modern public expands, it shatters into a multitude of fragments, speaking
> incommensurable private languages; the idea of modernity, conceived in numerous
> fragmentary ways ... loses its capacity to organise and give meaning to people's lives.

It would be wrong to define an entire generation of Turkish sociology and cultural
studies scholars exclusively in these terms (that is to say, the changing material and
political circumstances of intellectual production, the changing nature of Turkish
universities, the new mobility of ideas and labour). But they might help us understand why sociologists and cultural theorists working in and on Turkey have turned
so emphatically and energetically to the urban everyday. For globalisation has
significantly transformed an experience of modernity that was previously very much
about looking elsewhere, whether for styles of dress, jobs, books, industrial technologies, musical styles, models of parliamentary democracy, civil administration,
familial sentiment, urban civility and so on. In that context, the Turkish 'here and
now', the stuff of everyday life, was invariably grasped in terms of a locality sub-
mitting to forces of abstraction transcending that locality. It is, however, increasingly
hard to say whose version of modernity provides the model, increasingly difficult
to establish what 'centre' Turkey might now be 'peripheral' to, increasingly difficult
to see the outside world as providing persuasive forms of abstraction and
rationalisation. One has less and less choice but to consider the problematics of
Turkish modernity as being located within the everyday, rather than elsewhere.

But what is 'the everyday'? It is, when one stops to think about it, an evasive
category. For what, after all, is not 'the everyday'? Attempts to define it in common-
sense terms immediately run into meaningless tautologies. There is a general

sense in which one might argue that its value lies precisely in its inclusiveness. The notion of the everyday, for example, opposes tendencies deeply inscribed in many varieties of modernist social and cultural thought to separate public and private, global and local, politics and economics, reality and fantasy, tradition and modernity and so forth. Indeed, one might fashion some sort of definition of 'the everyday' precisely in these terms. But the contributors to this volume also put the concept of the everyday to rather specific tasks, and these might be worth exploring in detail.

One of these might be characterised as using the concept of the everyday to interrogate the legacy of nationalist reformism. The nation-building process in Turkey enshrined specific notions of the vernacular everyday as state policy. In Ziya Gökalp's influential formulation, the categories of 'culture' and 'civilisation' were opposed and, in the Turkish case, deemed to have been mismatched. Eastern/Islamic civilisation was, in this view, an inappropriate historical vehicle for the particularities of Turkish culture. Located elsewhere, it was a distant, cold power that imposed hierarchies and distinctions where there should be none, for example between men and women, and between the classes and estates of Ottoman society. Vernacular language was both signifier and practice of the new forms of intimacy demanded by the nation-state, working its way, self-consciously and deliberately, into the remotest recesses of everyday life. Vernacularisation was thus not only about making the political enshrine the everyday (however fantasised and manipulated by the elites), but also about making everyday life inescapably political.

Two sharply opposed scholarly positions emerged in response. One, characterised by Berkes (1964), for example, stressed the failure of the reformers to create a satisfactorily organic society. What the reforms repressed, then, or set themselves up in opposition to, became the site of a nostalgic complex, a rich fund of affective symbols and practices that could be used either explicitly in opposition to the modernist project, or to fill up the gaps it inevitably left. The other, represented by a number of British social anthropologists (see, for example, Stirling, 1965; Hann, 1990), stressed local-level identification with the state project. On the one hand, as Gellner (1981, p.60) dryly pointed out, the Turkish secularist reformers 'knew their Islam inside-out';[4] whether they intended to do so or not, the reform process was saturated with cultural tropes familiar to both elites and popular classes from their (already quite modernised) religious experience. On the other hand, it was argued, the new citizens of the Turkish state were adept at translating modernist precepts into religious terms and vice versa. Atatürk could be seen as a kind of structural equivalent of the prophet, and the citizens of Eğridir, in Tapper and Tapper's useful analysis (1987), could boast, with little apparent sense of irony, 'thank God we're secular'.[5] Both models could be argued persuasively at different times and places, and both focused attention on the everyday dynamics of the reform process, on ideology in social and cultural action, so to speak.

Both models rely on a certain quality of legibility. One could either reject the reforms (in the first case), or absorb them (in the latter), but only inasmuch as one could read the signs clearly, and position oneself in relation to that reading.

Arguably, it is exactly this quality of legibility – conferred by the then-dominant theoretical paradigms – that has disappeared in recent decades. Indeed, the signifiers of a binarised ideological situation always, one might argue, rested on shaky semiotic terrain, but they had assumed an illusory stability and coherence as a consequence of the converging interests of a broad array of political forces. These no longer necessarily converge, and the old signifiers now give the impression of coming unstuck from something to which they once appeared to be firmly attached. Now, for example, one has to struggle to attach meanings to Atatürkian paraphernalia, and one does so in ways that are marked by a troubled recognition of things that one could once robustly ignore. Political subjectivities are thus increasingly marked not only by their performative qualities, but also by the tensions that they seek, often unsuccessfully and with a great deal of palpable anxiety, to embrace and resolve. The transsexual communities discussed by Kandiyoti are thus understandably absorbed by the opportunities that liberalisation has offered, in terms of their vastly increased ability to connect with the global queer and transsexual worlds that link the sexual demi-monde of Istanbul with that of Bangkok, London and New York. Yet they have also been the victims of heavy-handed state efforts to manufacture a sanitised cosmopolitan everyday for the Habitat II conference in Istanbul in 1996. Understandably, they regard the Islamist liberalism of Istanbul's managers as hypocrisy, and an affront to Atatürkian reformism. Their political subjectivities are thus torn by tensions between libertarian cosmopolitanism and nationalist respectability. Political cultures and the subjectivities they shape are not, then, marked by the kind of legible transparency that seemed to exist before as a consequence of the then dominant theoretical optic (centre/periphery, secularism/religion and so forth) but by ambiguity and tension.

The everyday performative dimensions of the reformist vernacularism are most strongly evoked by Mardin and Öztürkmen in this volume (I will turn to the everyday political performativity of Islamism a little later). Mardin's discussion of the language reforms argues that the ideologically manufactured split between Ottoman and 'pure Turkish' was, and to a point remains, immensely persuasive, but rested on a fiction. Ottoman literature had multiple registers of formality and expressive power, in which vernacular Turkish had always played an important role. Much of the pleasurable complexity of Ottoman poetry lay in its intertextuality, and one of the many impoverishments introduced by nationalist reformism, for Mardin, lay in the way it dismantled this rich web of allusion and intertextuality. Modernity's absolute insistence on vernacular realism, he suggests, seems to diminish the possibilities for linguistic 'gaming' in Turkish society. It is not hard to connect these sentiments with Mardin's influential interpretations of Turkish modernity published elsewhere (see in particular Mardin, 1989). Much hinges, though, on the word 'seems'. His evocation of post-structuralist linguistic theory encourages us to attend to performativity, and with it the notion that meaning is turbulent and unpredictable, and very much entangled with that which is unexpressed, forgotten or repressed. If we attend to the linguistic everyday in modern Turkey in these terms, he suggests, we might come up with a rather different grasp of the process of vernacularisation, and one not limited to the success-story terms the vernacularisation process itself provided. One might also, he hints, consider the possibility that the gaming possibilities inherent in the Turkish language post-reformism are quite possibly enhanced rather than diminished as a consequence of the strictures and tensions that now surround it. Mardin's article has a somewhat post-modern ring to it, but this is tempered by an insistence on understanding the dynamics of the vernacular everyday in historical terms. Without understanding the multiple registers of literary Ottoman over time, he suggests that we can't fully appreciate what the gaming possibilities inherent in the contemporary linguistic everyday might be. For, he suggests, they surely exist.

Öztürkmen's article on the folk dance movement in Turkey is shaped by very much the same set of concerns. If we regard the folk dance movement as, so to speak, the dancing out of an imposed nationalist vernacular, it seems to be a rather simple matter, and certainly rather simple to dismiss in the terms provided by Berkes in Turkey and other critics of 'invented traditions' elsewhere. Tarcan's efforts early in the twentieth century to reformulate the ultra-macho *zeybek* as ballroom dance for couples in tuxedos and ballgowns are, at first glance, entirely off the scale of 'invented tradition' absurdity, but they need to be put in a more sympathetic context. If we regard the folk dance movement as something shaped by the multiple and contradictory forces of nationalism itself, the picture we get is more complex and open-ended than often allowed. Having moved from People's Houses in the early republican period, to the public domain, sponsored by banks, newspapers, universities and private clubs, folk dancing became embedded in a remarkably wide variety of everyday cultural worlds, none of which can simply be 'read off' or assimilated to the state project. The enormous popularity of folk dancing in Turkey is more readily comprehensible when seen in relation to the everyday lives of students and many other young people in Turkish cities over the last couple of decades, as Öztürkmen demonstrates. 'The everyday', for Mardin and Öztürkmen, is, then, one still decisively and actively shaped by the forces of nation-building, but in plural and historically open-ended ways that allow more space for social and cultural creativity than is often allowed.

Büker's discussion of Türkan Şoray raises the question of the relationship between the everyday and the notions of cultural realism put into play by nationalist reformism. Türkan Şoray's homely eroticism, especially when seen in relation to the more exotic appeal of 'the Turkish Greta Garbo', Cahide Sonku, allows Büker to reflect on the cultural gap between elites and popular classes. This was a gap that, if anything, deepened in the early republican period, and, as Büker suggests, evidently came to be seen as such in the 1950s and 1960s. Film, like popular music, was clearly not a matter of great ideological concern to the reformers. Yet they had put into play notions of 'realism' that would constantly return to haunt them. Mass-media culture in Turkey in the decades following independence was either manufactured (such as the reformed folk music of Sarısözen's 'Yurttan Sesler' propagated by the Turkish radio and television from the late 1940s on) or left to largely unregulated market mechanisms (such as the enormously popular translations and versions of American, European and Arab films and popular musical genres). Both, for all their populism, could be considered as ultimately dominated by elite tastes, as 'artifice' remote from Turkish 'realities'.

The populist politics inaugurated by Menderes in 1950 created the ideo-logical conditions in which a counter-culture could flourish in pursuit of that 'real' Turkey vernacularisation had promised but failed to deliver. 'Anadolu rock'[6] is a case in point, though it still awaited favourable material conditions which, arguably, only materialised in the 1990s – hence the apparent 'return' of Cem Karaca, Moğollar, and others on a recent tide of thinking-class nostalgia. The popular culture represented by Türkan Şoray and *arabesk* responded more rapidly to the existence of a new urban proletariat as a consequence of domestic popular cultural mass-production during this period. [7] The 'everyday' of Türkan Şoray and *arabesk* movies was, of course, highly abstract and conventionalised. It might, though, usefully be seen as a response to the cultural worlds produced by political vernacularisation, perceived by many as being remote from 'everyday life'. One might only add, to those inclined to see this counter-realism as 'actually' more 'real' than the state-sponsored vernacular culture it overtly opposed, that the former embodied exactly the same tensions, ambiguities and contradictions, and often worked these out in strikingly similar ways.[8] In both cases we are in a complicated world of fantasies and desires associated with equally imagined everydays.

The chapters by Büker, Mardin, Öztürkmen and Öncü deal with film, dance, cartoons, language, sexuality as relatively clearly marked 'cultural' worlds, marked by commodity form, folkloristic and linguistic fetishisations of grammars, archives, repertories and techniques, and gendered/sexual subculture whose everyday dynamics demand critical attention. Another group of contributors deal with the reverse proposition – that we might comb the unmarked everyday for its formal properties of drama and display. As Durakbaşa and Cindoğlu, Saktanber, Özyeğin and Ayata all indicate, these are predominantly dramas of class identity played out on the stage of conspicuous consumption. Consumption has, with Galleria, Carrefour, Akmerkez, Capitol and the rest, I suspect, never been so con-spicuous in Turkey, at least at a mass level, and in such glittering, theatrical forms. Seen in these terms, this drama of consumption extends deep into the heart of the suburban residential complex, as discussed by Ayata, involving not only relations between middle-class family members themselves but also those who service them as doormen, maids, shop employees and so forth. In the first instance, we are reminded by these essays that hyper-capitalism involves ever-intensifying social relations with others. This is so no matter how much the fetishistic logic of the commodity disavows such social relations, positioning us ideologically in a meta-physical world of things and individual desires. In the first instance, then, this notion of the everyday might be understood as part of a more general critique of consumer capitalism.

To a certain extent, these ever-intensifying relations are marked by older patterns. Hyper-capitalism in Turkish cities has created spaces in which middle-class women, in particular, are able to control their lives in ways that did not exist before. Suburban life enables women to exert more control on household budgets, for example, than men. The vast wealth gap that separates the new middle classes from incoming migrants means that more and more household and childcare work can be done by menials. Malls such as Galleria, Akmerkez and Capitol enable women to window-shop and, as they do so, develop a sense of self as independent agent through a performance of global cosmopolitanism. This is greatly facilitated by the theatrical ways in which the malls are structured. Supporting roles are convincingly played by all involved, from the doormen enlisted to keep out the *esmerler*[9] to the sophisticated, blue-eyed and fair-skinned shop assistants and burger vendors inside. What is new about this situation, though? One could argue, as Durakbaşa and Cindoğlu do, that the *site*, dependence on home-helps, and shopping malls simply underline and popularise trends in middle-class life that have been in existence since late Ottoman times. The new malls, in this view, might be seen as heirs to the late-nineteenth-century arcades of Beyoğlu, and so forth. All of these writers are right to stress historical continuities, where one might be inclined, along with Turkey's liberal elites over the last couple of decades, to stress 'epoch-leaping' rupture and difference.[10] Where modernity is habitually read in terms of the opportunities it offers women, Durakbaşa and Cindoğlu, Saktanber, Özyeğin and Ayata stress continuities in modes of exclusion, alienation and marginalisation too. Middle-class women remove themselves from one space of confinement and control, and relocate themselves in another, less clearly recognised as such. In the second instance, then, this everyday might be understood as a gendered critique of modernist liberal optimism.

We need, emphatically, to put new forms of consumerism in their historical place. We also need to understand how people manage to live with them on an everyday basis, since the commodity form does not, despite appearances, entirely determine the matter on its own terms. Consumer needs are met in a variety of ways, and people develop sophisticated strategies for navigating their way around the new commodity landscape, according to the skills and opportunities they have at their disposal. Complex strategies emerge in the everyday for making sense of the new, for making decisions and choices, and for dealing with novel kinds of social encounter. The Pinter-esque theatre of these worlds is engagingly brought out in Durakbaşa and Cindoğlu's chapter, and Özyeğin's account of the relations between maids, doormen and their middle-class employers. Their portrayal of these everyday dramas, informed by Goffman and others, illuminates the vicissitudes of the performative in public self-management, with all of its manipulation of frames, role reversals and attendant registers of irony, humour and so forth. The maids in Özyeğin's account find themselves, on the one hand, confined to domestic space, dealing with the outside world exclusively through the medium of their husbands, the doormen. On the other hand, their employers depend on them to an extraordinary extent, and this dependence means that maids develop sophisticated skills in the reading of signs of middle-class consumer culture. Many, it seems, become adept at exploiting the situation, skillfully manipulating their knowledge of middle-class consumer codes and the guilt they can elicit from their employers. In the third instance, then, this everyday might be seen in terms of the critical resources that lie within it, resources which provide relatively disadvantaged people with the means of managing the complex and contradictory situations encountered in modern life.

Understandably, this is a process involving a great deal of cultural anxiety for all, but notably the middle classes. The *site* provides space in which men, women and children can 'be themselves'. Armies of home helps and shop assistants provide the necessary support. But what is this 'self'? It is, in the first instance, a middle-class self, but this simply raises the question of what 'the middle class' might now be. In a context of globalisation, as Durakbaşa and Cindoğlu rightly point out, the signs and symbols of middle-classness undergo a thorough re-evaluation and re-contextualisation. On the one hand, globalisation increases opportunities for sections of the mercantile middle classes, whilst restricting them for those involved in the administration, public services, and those commercial sectors (notably agriculture) sheltered by nation-state patronage. The developments in the distribution of goods and services that attend globalisation also mean increased (though invariably unequal) public access to commodities that once efficiently signified difference.

What, then, 'is' the Turkish middle class? This is not simply a theoretical question. The problem haunts the world of advertising and market research wherever the new world order has disrupted economies formerly tightly (dis-)organised by the nation-state. Some kind of comparative ethnography of market research might usefully compare Turkey with India, South Africa, Mexico and Eastern Europe in this regard. In everyday terms, though, for the relatively privileged consumers in Turkey discussed by Ayata, Özyeğin, Durakbaşa and Cindoğlu, this problem means, in the first instance, an ever-increasing dependence on consumption to supply the requisite forms of social difference. With dependence come all of the anxieties that attend the commodity fetish. It also involves complex encounters with others in situations whose signs cannot always easily be 'read', still less controlled. Öncü's discussion of the *maganda* illustrates the point well. Not that long ago, the figures associated with well-entrenched middle-class narratives concerning 'the invasion of Istanbul' by uncultured ruralites signified all too clearly and all too well. For today's *Hürriyet*[11] readers, however, the *maganda*, the latest of these, has become a more shadowy and menacing figure (a point not incompatible with comic-strip humour, of course). A vague yet ubiquitous principle of spatial disruption, he 'means nothing', 'just is', according to the article in *Hürriyet* cited in Öncü's chapter. *Maganda* humour derives much of its power and ambivalence from more general currents of middle-class self-definitional anxiety.

In some senses, the everyday performance of difference and distinction is easier when the clearly marked oppositional identities discussed by White, Navaro-Yashin and Saktanber are involved. Such, at least, seems particularly to be the case amongst the middle-class student Islamists discussed by Saktanber, who can perform resistance – if only in the transitory spaces made available by university life – through the kinds of everyday strategies of commodity re-signification she discusses. This, too, is a world that revolves around consumption, notably of items of dress, such as the headscarf. Navaro-Yashin cautions us against neglecting the economics of material production in the popular cultural world, in which resistance is habitually read in 'cultural' terms. One can get an important critical angle on self-proclaimed cultures of resistance when one looks, in a fairly strict sense, at their economics – how material goods are produced, exchanged and acquire value. In a sense, Saktanber and Navaro-Yashin deal with the opposite sides of the same coin. Saktanber is concerned with strategies through which Islamist youth uses commodity forms (ranging from dress to tastes in popular music) to carve out its own space of sub-cultural values, which are partly concerned with the whole *topos* of modernity, but also with class. Saktanber draws on British sub-cultural theory, Fiske and de Certeau, writers for whom 'the everyday' could be defined precisely in terms of its capacity to supply meanings for the task of resistive identity formation. Navaro-Yashin, on the other hand, addresses the 'parent culture' in which modernity is seen in more instrumental terms, as a tool which can serve Islamist purposes, in the form of Islamist shopping malls (notably the Tekbir shopping centre in Fatih) and so forth. Both Islamist strategies, that is to say both those of subculture and parent culture – if one is to adopt Saktanber's Birmingham school terminology – are inevitably flawed. Consumption-based strategies can never take everything into account. The commodity form is never simply amenable to ideological control. The commodity fetish, as Marx constantly reminded us, leads its own life – it 'thinks us', no matter how much we like to believe we are capable of 'thinking it'.

Navaro-Yashin's 'Islamist everyday' is characterised by this kind of turbulence, generated by the friction between Islamist ideology and the commodity form. It opens up two areas of inquiry. One, somewhat neglected by Turkish secularists, concerns the rather subtle and creative ways in which Turkish Islamists encounter and engage with modernity, rather than rejecting it out of hand. The other concerns the complex dynamics of new Islamist social realities, on the ground, so to speak, that are not easily accounted for either by Islamists or secularists. Islamist fashion shows generate uncertainty as to whether the elegant figures and blue eyes of the fashion models speak to some kind of victory of Islamic form over Western 'content', or subtly acknowledge the reverse possibility. One gets a strong sense reading Saktanber and Navaro-Yashin of a world that self-consciously performs out its own contradictions, that displays them and not only makes them available for, but positively demands, discursive engagement. There is a sense in which the everyday semiotic turbulence she describes is crucial to such events as Islamist fashion shows, its precise purpose being to confront people with contradictions, or gaps between thought and practice which positively demand the formulation of a point of view, a discussion or argument. White suggests something similar of Welfare's political rituals. Political performance here, though, seems to be designed to maximise resonance with as wide a variety of everyday dramas as possible. This is, after all, a populist movement. Welfare's political performance thus blurs, rather than sharpens, issues such as whether or not the movement acknowledges or disavows class as a mobilising factor in Turkish political life, putting them beyond public discussion. It also has the effect of perpetuating fantasies of upward mobility through such notions as 'the new Muslim woman' that, for the most part, are unlikely to be realised under existing economic and political circumstances. The tension between the performative strategies depicted by Saktanber, Navaro-Yashin and White is surely worth stressing. One comes, in the process, to a more complex and interesting sense of the ways in which Turkish Islamism sets out to colonise everyday life than that usually presented by the movement's critics.

Islamist weddings were a conspicuous aspect of the fashioning of an Islamist everyday in Turkey in the 1990s. Erbakan's daughter's wedding, discussed by

White, was a much-debated case of Islamist political ritual writ large, but it drew on widespread 'grass-roots' practice, too. My *kanun* teacher kept himself busy in his retirement as a musician at Islamist weddings in Fatih and Bağlarbaşı, near where he lived. He and the group of friends with whom he performed experimented with various formats in the hope of cracking a lucrative market – not with much success, it has to be said, resulting in frustration and diminishing enthusiasm on their part. The process of patrolling their repertoire and performance style was troublesome. It was difficult to decide, for example, with a given group of guests, whether the classical repertoire (one substantially fashioned by Turkish Christians and Jews) would be acceptable, or whether they would have to string together a performance consisting entirely of *ilahi* hymns.[12] Having made such decisions, it was difficult keeping the performance 'on track'. On one occasion they slid inadvertently into an instrumental rendition of a well-known Beyoğlu drinking song. I remember seeing sweat break out on my teacher's brow. In the event, they made a collective and instantaneous decision to keep going to the end rather than draw attention to their ghastly mistake by stopping. It proved, in the event, to be exactly the right decision. As on most occasions, they were being pointedly ignored by the wedding guests. On another occasion, a particularly fine performance, led by a young singer whose performances of *ilahi* were then being broadcast frequently on one of the Islamist FM radio stations, was met by stony silence. 'Thanks for your warm applause,' he said, tight-lipped, before walking off the stage. That was the last time I saw him perform with the group.

It would be easy to regard these wedding-band experiments as 'emergent', like Islamist fashion displays; the rough edges and contradictions would, in this view, give way to something less rough-edged and contradictory over time, and the gap between 'ideal' and 'reality' narrow. But this would be a misinterpretation. These events enacted a split between an everyday and an Islamist everyday; if intentions could be discerned, they seemed to be more concerned with drawing attention to, rather than deflecting attention away from, the rough edges, contradictions and gaps. Some kind of discursive engagement with the rhetoric that surrounded them was thus rendered inevitable. The musicians were invited, it seemed, precisely in order to sharpen the sense of contrast between what an everyday wedding looked, sounded and felt like, and what the Islamist wedding would ideally be like. Their being ignored, or asked to be silent, was not simply a matter of passivity or indifference on the part of the guests; it was studied, and carefully performed. One went away, as my teacher invariably did, worrying about what had just taken place. There is an important sense in which Turkish Islamists have echoed the vernacularist policies of the nationalist reformers of the 1930s and 1940s, for whom the introduction of a reformed everyday served the purpose of involving everybody in some public form of public presence-affirming discursive engagement, regardless of whether the reforms were being accepted or rejected.

Just as education was crucial in establishing a secular public sphere in early republican Turkey, it has been crucial in establishing a rival Islamist public sphere in recent decades, as Güneş-Ayata and Acar's chapter indicates. There are differences in the ways in which schooling has played a role in the construction of these two public spheres, though. In the first instance, schooling was both a right and duty

conferred by citizenship. In recent decades it has become, at least in part, a matter
of consumer choice, on which political subjectivities and identities hinge. Identities
and subjectivities are not so easily purchased, contrary to rhetoric, as I have already
noted in relation to Saktanber and Navaro-Yashin's chapters above. Commodities
obscure complex and entangled social relations that spread across the entirety of
a social space, even though the process of obfuscation is never total, as Marx
constantly noted. The notion of an Islamist sphere of commodity exchange is
necessarily limited in this regard – a fact that is as true of commoditised education
as it is of anything else. One of the many benefits of Güneş-Ayata and Acar's comparison lies in the fact that it enables us to see just how mutually entangled secular
and religious education cultures are, despite their claims to difference. The ironies
are well noted by the authors. Imam-Hatip lycées appeal to women's desires
(shaped substantially by secularist modernism) for freedom of movement in
public space. They achieve this within the school, but at the expense of a higher
and more general level of subordination, as the authors point out. The secular lycée
in the study institutionalises a familiar elite disposition, in which gender neutrality
is constantly averred, but practice serves to marginalise women in ever more
subtle and effective ways. To compound the irony, it is recognition of precisely this
fact that has impelled many families to seek Islamist education as an alternative.

Finally, the everyday lives of Turkish migrant workers, particularly in
Germany, have come to occupy an important and marked role in discussions of the
Turkish everyday. Some of the complex fantasies associated with the diasporic everyday were made particularly clear by Berlin-based rappers Cartel in the mid-1990s.
On their first appearance in Turkey in 1995, they held out to the intelligentsia the
promise of revived energies in radical popular music-making, which seemed to
have run aground after the brief efflorescence of *özgün* in the mid-1980s and early
1990s.[13] The playful tone with which they deconstructed homely sonic imagery
(using and disrupting samples of TRT-style *saz* and vocal chorus combinations,[14]
for example) indicated that this was music about everyday Turkish experience,
specifically. This produced two different audiences in Turkey, to mutual dismay.
One, well-versed in popularised cultural studies and radicalism, through lively
music journals such as *Çalıntı*, *Müzük*, *Roll* and others, grasped Turkish hip-hop as
a mutually transforming encounter between local and global. It was multilingual,
cosmopolitan and a great step forward for Turkish popular culture. The other
grasped it as an affirmation of a decisively local struggle, borrowing global energies simply to strengthen and validate an already-known and strongly racialised
sense of self. Both conflated Turkish and German-Turkish cultural space, seeing
the latter, by virtue of its location in large European cities, as simply and
inevitably on the sharp edge of modern identity construction. Where German-
Turkish popular culture led, so to speak, Turkish popular culture would inevitably
follow. In fact, as is well known, the great step forward failed to lead anywhere.
Cartel was entirely non-plussed by their warm reception from Turkish fascists on
their Istanbul debut in 1995, and retired, evidently hurt and confused, to Berlin.
One could draw the conclusion from the Cartel episode that Turkey and Germany
are rather further apart in popular cultural terms than they are sometimes
thought to be, but this would, I think, be simplistic.

What it does suggest is the need for a rather more nuanced model of the connections between the two, as both Yalçın-Heckmann and Çağlar's chapters emphasise. The main obstacle to the emergence of such models, both suggest, is the thinking-class fetishisation of hybridity. This has significant institutional dimensions. Notions of hybridity, strongly endorsed by some strains of post-colonial theory, have been enthusiastically adopted by the media intelligentsia in social-democratic Europe, partly because they turn intractable political-economic complexities into something recognisably 'cultural', if not resolutely bookish, and partly because they identify new domains for bohemian distinction-marking. The German media has actively constructed a sense of the German-Turkish everyday not only in terms of desirable kitsch items for German consumers, but also as a way of identifying pleasurable points of reference for urban *flâneurs* – neighbour-hoods to be enjoyed on a Sunday afternoon stroll, and so forth. Hybrid culture, as the critical reception of Fatih Akgün's coolly ironic film *Kurz und Schmerzlos* (discussed by Yalçın-Heckmann) indicates, has become tremendously hip in Germany, as elsewhere.

There are, then, tremendous problems involved in trying to understand German-Turkish households in terms of a stable principle of 'hybrid' identity, despite the fact that the interior decor of many German-Turkish households, the particular combination of TV-set-oriented dining, kitsch artifacts and second-hand furnishing and appliances might suggest precisely such a thing. As Çağlar emphasises, the *uyumsuzluk* ('lack of harmony') one might detect in German-Turkish household decor has to be understood in relation to the abundant and self-conscious *uyum* ('harmony') in the households maintained by the same families in Turkey. Aesthetic strategies, then, have to be grasped in terms that embrace both Germany and Turkey, and indeed wider ideological and commercial worlds. At the same time, one has to look closely at intergenerational differences, and the differing contexts and situations in which Turkish workers and their families in Germany come to construct a variety of hyphenated identities. These negotiate a variety of individual biographical trajectories (Berlin-Turkish, German-Turkish, Hamburg-İzmirli), but also connect in complex and contradictory ways with the forms of classification produced by the German state and media (*Gastarbeiter, ausländische/türkische Mitbürger, Bildungsinländer*, and so forth[15]). In this context, attention to migrant everydays stresses the diversity of hyphenated identities, which have to be grasped critically in relation to the hegemonic constructions of hybrid everydays by significant institutional agencies, both in Germany and Turkey.

If we are to conclude that there are many everydays, and many possibilities for grasping them critically, then Berman's concerns about the fragmented nature of modern experience are real and palpable. Are we left with nothing but fragments? Is there any way of getting at the big picture, or is this merely nostalgic or utopian fantasy, or worse? Berman himself responds to his own concerns in a way that bears reflection at the end of this volume. In response to a critique by Perry Anderson, Berman remarks that the intelligentsia on the left made a disastrous mistake in committing itself to a high-art view on modernity's successes and failures. Modernism promised much, but delivered little, in Anderson's view, once its initial revolutionary energies were exhausted, and the unruly historical energies unleashed by high capitalism were reined back in again by repressive forces contained within it. But the lack of revolutions and masterpieces, Berman responds, is not necessarily indicative of the ways in which modernity's energies might once again be put back on track, or at least the track Marx imagined as a possibility lying latent within advanced capitalism. If we attend to the 'sources of meaning, of freedom, of dignity, beauty, joy, solidarity' in everyday life, he says, 'we might even find some masterpieces or revolutions in the making' (1999, p.168). However, the New Left's arid intellectualism makes this unlikely, he feels.

This failure is not to be taken lightly. It is, he points out, the left that has insisted on treating people as wholes in the context of their everyday lives, and not simply as machines or numbers, and this responsibility should not be passed over lightly. The final paragraph of this essay concludes (p.169):

> Intellectuals can make a special contribution to this ongoing project. If our years of study have taught us anything, we should be able to reach out further, to look and listen more closely, to see and feel beneath surfaces, to make comparisons over a wider range of space and time, to grasp hidden patterns, and forces and connections, in order to show people who look and speak and think and feel differently from each other – who are oblivious to each other, or fearful of each other – that they have more in common than they think. We can contribute visions and ideas that will give people a shock of recognition, recognition of themselves and each other, that will bring their lives together. That is what we can do for solidarity and class-consciousness. But we can't do it ... if we lose contact with what those lives are like. Unless we know how to recognise people, as they look and feel and experience the world, we'll never be able to help them recognise themselves or change the world. Reading *Capital* won't help us if we don't also know how to read the signs in the street.

The intelligentsia has certainly been somewhat slow in learning to read 'the signs in the street', battered as it has been by conservative backlash since the late 1960s, weaker and poorer universities, the diminishing of public arenas for critical discussion, and the policing, overt and covert, of those that remain. It is these very conditions, though, that have released intellectual energies that might yet be put to use in a more broadly shared and participatory political space than has hitherto been the case. The contributors to this volume write about recognisable worlds in a recognisable way for the benefit of a sophisticated reading public in Turkey and elsewhere. Berman's 'shock of recognition' has been registered, processed and put to productive use. This is a significant achievement in its own right.

Secondly, Berman reminds us that whilst critique needs to deconstruct supposedly unitary categories of thought that have had an alarmingly destructive impact on modern life ('nation', 'modernisation' and so forth), it also needs to do exactly the opposite: to see commonalities where they have been suppressed. One must interrogate them constantly, but categories such as class, ethnicity and gender remain vital. It is by virtue of critical attention to these categories that the contributors to this volume are able to point to continuities and commonalities where all is presumed to be fragmentation and incoherence, for identifiable reasons. Where Islamism and secularism are presumed to be absolutely and irreconcilably opposed, it is, for example, vitally significant for people to be able to see that Islamists and secularists share a great deal. This is not to assume that differences will suddenly be overcome in an epiphanic moment in which Selves are suddenly recognised in Others, but that the grasp of disabling binary oppositions will be weakened and new critical options develop. Where assumptions abound that Turkey has, in recent years, 'skipped an epoch' in its development, it is crucially important that the persistence of old problems – indeed the fact that they actually seem to be indispensable to the process of development – be publicly noted and discussed. This kind of public discussion is greatly enhanced by critical scholarship of the kind represented in this volume.

Finally, Berman's conclusion invites us to consider the everyday as an opportunity for a more participatory and dialogic role for the intelligentsia in public life, in which critical rigour and everyday sign-reading skills might be mutually informing and mutually enriching. For these everyday skills are not merely tactical, fragmented and provisional, as many theorists of the everyday have insisted. On the contrary, they always bear the marks of desires and aspirations for the common good and profound critical insights into the ways in which the current situation falls short of the ideal, no matter how much their mode of articulation is often complex, opaque and requiring careful interpretation. The popular political imagination that expresses itself in the everyday contexts discussed in this volume demands serious engagement. In this sense, the fragmentation of Turkish public life over the last couple of decades must be seen not in terms of the incapacity of the Turkish public to 'think big', but exactly the reverse. Whilst this is clearly a difficult and uncertain time for many, the contributors to this volume strongly suggest that it also contains within it the seeds of its own transformation.

Notes on Afterword

1 Thanks to all of the contributors, but particularly Lale Yalçın-Heckmann, Ayşe Saktanber, Yael Navaro-Yashin, Jenny White, Şerif Mardin, Phillipa Brewster and Deniz Kandiyoti for their detailed and thought-provoking responses to the response.

2 The Yüksek Öğretim Kurumu (Higher Education Foundation), established in the wake of the military coup of 12 September 1980, succeeded in depoliticising campus life in Turkish universities, through wide-ranging legislation affecting both students and faculty.

3 Meral Özbek's 1992 *arabesk* study, published by *İletişim*, marked, to the best of my knowledge, the first engagement from within Turkish academia with British New Left thinking in general, and Birmingham school subcultural studies in particular.

4 The first generation of Kemalist revolutionaries, he argues, '...still knew their Islam inside-out, and also had to fight it in their own hearts, and unwittingly fought it in its own style and by its own rules' (1981, p.60).

5 The subtlety of Tapper and Tapper's analysis lies in their insistence that this was never an easy fit. Attention to the differences between women's religious practice and that of men allows them to identify the ways in which in the less obviously

marked public space of women's *mevlut* rituals, religious practice elaborated a metaphysics which could not be so easily 'translated' back and forth between the two domains.

6   Anadolu rock drew on the Turkish circulation of rock-and-roll, European popular genres such as *chanson* and a sentimental radicalism drawing on Turkish folk culture (but which explicitly rejected the regimented voice and *saz* choruses then being shaped by the Turkish Radio and Television Corporation) during the mid-to-late 1960s. Cem Karaca, Barış Manço, Erkin Koray, Okay Temiz and Cahit Berkay are amongst the names associated with the genre in this period. The music largely conformed to the structural conventions of European (rather than American) rock and pop, within which framework Turkish musical elements were quoted. Many musicians associated with the genre left the country or stopped recording after the 1980 coup. For an English-language discussion, see Stokes (forthcoming), which also includes a summary of Turkish-language sources. Anadolu rock never existed on a secure commercial footing in Turkey, despite the exceptional success of singers such as Cem Karaca. Current market conditions, in which CD re-releases and Western rock musical instruments circulate relatively freely amongst those who can afford them, have given the genre a new lease of life.

7   *Arabesk* was able to thrive on cassette production in the 1970s. Unlike Anadolu Rock, it required relatively simple recording facilities, and relatively available technical expertise and material resources (such as musical instruments). Anadolu Rock required a great deal of promotion and sponsorship, for example from Turkish national newspapers during the 1960s, Western European expertise and capital in order to produce recordings, and travel – and great ingenuity – to procure guitars, amplification and so forth.

8   My own account of *arabesk* in the 1980s is sometimes read in these terms. In fact, throughout, I sought to use *arabesk* precisely as a means of deconstructing the centre/periphery divide. When one listens to *arabesk* one can, after all, be struck by similarities between 'official' and 'unofficial' musical worlds, and interpret the huge anxiety of many of those associated with the former in terms of the extensive nature of what they share, aesthetically and materially, if not ideologically (see Stokes, 1992).

9   I draw on Can Kozanoğlu's somewhat polemical discussion of the quasi-racialised idioms in which status difference is often expressed, and in which the *beyazlar* ('whites', or 'Euro-Turks') stand opposed to the *esmerler* ('the dark-skinned ones'). In Galleria, he comments, the presence of the *esmerler* among the whites caused tension; even *lahmacun* (Turkish pizza – proletarian fast-food) tasted better in those places from which the *esmerler* were excluded: 'Galleria'da esmerlerle beyazlar arasında gerilim yaşanıyordu ve lahmacun bile, esmerlerin giremediği yerlerde lezzetliydi' (Kozanoğlu, 1995, p.134). Durakbaşa and Cindoğlu nuance the picture substantially, but confirm the tremendous potency of 'looking European'.

10 Özal once claimed that his liberalisation policies meant that 'we have leaped an epoch' ('çağ atladık'); the phrase seemed to be on the entire country's lips throughout the late 1980s, though the expression was usually uttered, in my presence at least, in tones of heavy irony.

11   *Hürriyet* has generally reflected mercantile interests and the world-view of the conservative urban bourgeoisie. It remains a valuable source of business information and analysis.

12   *Ilahis* are devotional pieces, originating either in popular practice or composed by art music composers. Though relatively simple, sung on their own, they could be strung together artfully in a sequence, and interspersed with instrumental compositions and improvisations.

13   Özgün music continued the aesthetic and political aspirations and orientations of Anadolu rock, though in the context of a music market substantially determined by the production of *arabesk* in the 1980s and 1990s. Prominent names associated with the genre include Ahmet Kaya, Fatih Kısaparmak, Yeni Türkü, Grup Yorum and, somewhat later, Sümer Ezgü. In comparison to Anadolu rock, overt political expression was much muted, with the exception of Grup Yorum. For an English-language discussion, see Stokes (forthcoming), which also reviews Turkish-language sources.

14   See note 5.

15   I am grateful to Jenny White for pointing out that whilst these are concerned with 'in-between' categories of citizenship, they have little to do with cultural 'hybridity' as such.

References

Berkes, Niyazi (1964), *The Development of Secularism in Modern Turkey*, McGill University Press, Montreal

Berman, Marshall (1999), *Adventures in Marxism*, Verso, London

Bozdoğan, Sibel and Reşat Kasaba (1997), *Rethinking Modernity and National Identity in Turkey*, Washington University Press, Seattle, WA

Gellner, Ernest (1981), *Muslim Society*, Cambridge University Press, Cambridge

Hann, Christopher (1990), *Tea and the Domestication of the Turkish State*, Eothen, Huntingdon Littlefield, Lanham

Kozanoğlu, Can (1995), *Pop Çağı Ateşi*, İletişim, Istanbul

Mardin, Şerif (1989), *Religion and Social Change in Modern Turkey: The Case of Bediüzzaman Said Nursi*, State University of New York Press, Albany, NY

Özbek, Meral (1992), *Popüler Kültür ve Orhan Gencebay Arabeski*, İletişim, Istanbul

Stirling, Paul (1965), *Turkish Village*, Weidenfeld & Nicolson, London

Stokes, Martin (1992), *The Arabesk Debate: Music and Musicians in Modern Turkey*, Oxford University Press, Oxford

Stokes, Martin (forthcoming), 'Turkish Rock and Pop', *Garland Encyclopaedia of World Music*, vol. 6, Garland, New York and London

Tapper, Nancy and Richard Tapper (1987), 'The Birth of the Prophet: Ritual and Gender in Turkish Islam', *Man*, NS 22, no 1, pp.69–92

Index